This is the first full-length study of James Joyce to subject his work to both ethical and political analysis. It addresses important issues in contemporary literary and cultural studies surrounding problems of justice, as well as discussions of gender, homosociality, and the colonial condition. Valente uses an original theory and psychology of justice through which to explore both the well-known and the more obscure of Joyce's works. He traces the remarkable formal and stylistic evolution that defined Joyce's career, and his progressive attempt to negotiate the contest of social difference in racial, colonial, class, and sexual terms. By analyzing Joyce's verbal strategies within both the psychobiographical and sociohistorical contexts, Valente unlocks the politics of Joyce's unconscious and reveals the legacy of Western political thought.

JAMES JOYCE AND THE PROBLEM OF JUSTICE

JAMES JOYCE AND THE PROBLEM OF JUSTICE

Negotiating sexual and colonial difference

JOSEPH VALENTE

University of Illinois, Urbana-Champaign

CAMBRIDGE
UNIVERSITY PRESS

Published by the Press Syndicate of the University of Cambridge
The Pitt Building, Trumpington Street, Cambridge, CB2 1RP
40 West 20th Street, New York, NY 10011-4211, USA
10 Stamford Road, Oakleigh, Melbourne 3166, Australia

First published 1995

Printed in Great Britain at the University Press, Cambridge

A catalogue record for this book is available from the British Library

Library of Congress cataloguing in publication data

Valente, Joseph.
James Joyce and the problem of justice: negotiating sexual and colonial difference / Joseph
Valente.
p. cm.
Includes bibliographical references and index.
ISBN 0 521 47369 1 (hardback)
1. Joyce, James, 1882–1941 – Political and social views. 2. Literature and society –
Ireland – History – 20th century. 3. Gender identity in literature. 4. Imperialism in
literature. 5. Sex role in literature. 6. Colonies in literature. 7. Justice in literature.
8. Race in literature. I. Title.
PR609.09V35 1995
823'.912–dc20 94-40293 CIP

ISBN 0 521 47369 1 hardback

To Joanne, with love

Contents

Preface

In the writing of James Joyce, we have an unusually complex and
self-conscious articulation of the problem of justice and its representation as defined under modern or post-Enlightenment conditions of ethical and political practice. My work interprets his formal
and stylistic evolution from *Dubliners* to *Ulysses* as a progressive
attempt to negotiate among the most fiercely contested and structurally significant modes of social difference – racial, colonial, class,
and, especially, sexual – without pretending to a false transcendence.
The interconnectedness of my critical topoi – the problem of justice,
the contextually determined operation of gender, and the historical
position and textual production of Joyce – will be examined from
several angles in order to illuminate three basic areas of theoretical
and literary concern: (1) the nature and value of justice itself,
particularly with respect to the politics of gender; (2) the fundamental mutation in the parameters of justice made possible by the
bourgeois, democratic revolutions and visible by capitalist and
colonialist expansion; (3) most intensively, the manifestation of these
theoretical and material developments in a sexual/textual politics
peculiarly situated to take account of them. I find that Joyce's
struggle to transform the pathos of his own ambivalent subject
position into an ethos of discursive justice reveals both the self-
transformative potential and the profound limitations of that ideal.

Acknowledgments

"Be just before you are generous." *Ulysses*

I cannot possibly do justice to Joanne, for her unwavering confidence and support and her shrewd editorial judgment. I am indebted beyond measure to Vicki Mahaffey, my teacher and friend, who patiently heard, brilliantly answered, and significantly enriched all of my arguments. I am profoundly obliged to Barbara Herrnstein Smith, whose teaching helped to define my theoretical perspective. I cannot thank Geoffrey Harpham enough for intellectual interchanges that have sharpened my ideas and refined my style. Deep appreciation is also due to Jean-Michel Rabate for his encouragement and astute criticism.

I could never, finally, repay my parents for what they have given freely to me.

I am grateful to the *James Joyce Quarterly* for permission to reprint material which originally appeared in that journal.

Abbreviations

Works by James Joyce

AP   *A Portrait of the Artist as a Young Man*, New York: Viking, 1968.

CW   *The Critical Writings of James Joyce*, ed. E. Mason and R. Ellmann, New York: Viking, 1959.

D   *Dubliners*, New York: Viking, 1969.

E   *Exiles*, New York: Viking, 1971.

FW   *Finnegans Wake*, New York: Viking, 1939.

GJ   *Giacomo Joyce*, New York: Viking, 1959.

L II   *Letters of James Joyce*, vol. II, ed. R. Ellmann, New York: Viking, 1966.

SH   *Stephen Hero*, New York: New Directions, 1963.

SL   *Selected Letters of James Joyce*, ed. R. Ellmann, New York: Viking, 1975.

U   *Ulysses*, ed. H. W. Gabler, New York: Random House, 1986.

Other Works

AO   G. Deleuze and F. Guattari, *Anti-Oedipus*, Minneapolis: University of Minnesota Press, 1983.

C   P. B. Shelley, *The Cenci* in *Shelley's Poetry and Prose*, ed. D. Reiman, New York: Norton, 1977.

D   G. Deleuze and C. Parnet, *Dialogues*, New York: Columbia University Press, 1987.

DH   H. Ibsen, *A Doll House*, in *Ibsen: Four Major Plays*, ed. R. Fjelde, New York: Penguin, 1965.

TP   G. Deleuze and F. Guattari, *A Thousand Plateaus*, Minneapolis: University of Minnesota Press, 1987.

Justice unbound

THEORETICAL PRELIMINARIES

The genre of the law is itself subject to what Derrida has termed the law of genre, the principle that the "mark of belonging does not belong" to the corpus so demarcated.[1] This mark of belonging constitutes a point of intrinsic otherness, a double inscription, which "gathers up the corpus and, in the same instant, in the same blink of an eye, keeps it from closing, from identifying itself with itself."[2] The concept of justice can be said to represent the mark of belonging or propriety of the law; to be just is the imperative whose perceived fulfillment translates tyrannical force into legitimate authority. Any system of rule entails, at least implicitly, a canon of justice, some principle of proportional treatment, power, and opportunity among diverse groups, rival claims, and competing perspectives in accordance with relatively fixed criteria for defining and assessing those groups, claims, and perspectives. But at the same time, justice can never simply belong to or be absorbed by that system, for reasons that are themselves strictly *de jure*. The law may indeed wish to enjoy a purely formal, hence integrated existence, as Stanley Fish has proposed, to be a self-monitoring, self-transforming, self-regulating system or autopoesis.[3] But it cannot, either in principle or in fact, so long as it also aspires to the condition of justice. The law of equity is the always imperfect equity of the law.

Let us begin with the law as social agency. Unless the evaluative criteria bear an asymmetrical relation, in some respects, to the various claims, viewpoints, and circumstances that they regulate, an act of judgment, as opposed to random selection, remains impossible. Rules of proportionality work precisely through the disproportionate realities they possess for differently situated entities. There is, accordingly, a basic tension built into juridical conception and practice. The pursuit of justice must proceed according to the rule of law, but the law is by nature universalizing to some degree and so tends to group similar and dissimilar elements together, to decide like and unlike cases by a single standard. The property distinguishing the law from mere capricious violence – its determination to treat all parties "the same," regardless of the individual peculiarities of their condition – carries a capricious violence of its own, scathingly captured in Anatole France's famous epigram: "The law, in its majestic equality, forbids the rich as well the poor to sleep under bridges, to beg in the streets, and to steal bread."[4] The law's sovereign indifference, its impartiality or neutrality, can never be fully severed from the law's in-difference, its systemic failure to account or adjust for the full play of social, cultural, and political difference under its charge. In this respect, justice names the quixotic hope that the law can somehow redeem, rather than simply reducing, the social conflict and heterogeneity in which it lives.[5]

But the law is also a product of social agency. In this dimension, conflict and heterogeneity manifest themselves in the multiple or divergent readings to which any particular series or system of rules is open – as regards its animating purpose, scope, pertinence to specific cases, or importance relative to other social considerations.[6] The respective readings, in turn, answer to different orders of definition and assessment, all of which rest, in the final analysis, upon arbitrary premises and preferences, the zero-degree biases linking logical, moral, and social discrimination. As such, the values these orders substantiate and enforce, on however commensurate a basis, are not without their own incommensurate, not to say invidious implications. The interpretive field upon which the game of justice is played is necessarily uneven, slanted if you will, and the game itself, to the extent that it is about rectifying evident inequity, unfolds in infinite regress through an ongoing reformulation of its own conditions of possibility.

This dynamic becomes especially visible in the more mobile and variegated political culture attending modern capitalism. As Claude Lefort has demonstrated, the real import of the democratic revolutions of the eighteenth and nineteenth centuries lay less in the types of government they immediately established than in their effective evacuation of the ultimate site of social and political authority.[7] The new ideal points of reference, Reason and Nature, were instituted not so much as a court of final appeal but as both the arena and the stake of a continuing process of conflict, negotiation, innovation, and compromise. Geared to the newly dominant discourse of political economy, liberal jurisprudence, in its original contractarian mode, sought to respect and accommodate individual self-interest by mobilizing and synthesizing the partial (i.e. limited and partisan) perspectives of competing social constituencies instead of subordinating them to some *a priori* symbol or incarnation of the whole. To understand the juridical consequences of this event, we must go one step further in our interrogation of the law.

The distinction between the law as social agency and the law as social product is, of course, a purely analytic device and, it turns out, a preliminary one at that. The specific force of the law depends on the fusion of these roles. Because no given body of law is itself possessed of any ultimate grounds of legitimacy, it can only come into being as law, rather than mere contingency or violence, by constituting such grounds retroactively in and through the performative gesture of its own inauguration. As has been prominently noted, the law partakes of a strange, metaleptic temporality: the law posits as a legitimating factor or principle, say the divine right of kings, that which legitimates its own positing capacity in general.[8] The law as authorizing social agency, in other words, can only engender itself as an already authorized social product, its root prejudices retrospectively constructed as received justification. That is to say, the law of genre presides over the institution of the law as such. The supreme authority of the law can neither be simply *a part of* the ethico-juridical edifice, in which case it could not found the law as a whole, nor simply *apart from* this edifice, in which case its pertinence to the law would always remain to be demonstrated, and so remain dependent on yet another authority.

Where the first would be arbitrary because contingent, the second would be arbitrary because groundless. Where justice derives from existing values, the standards of appraisal blur with the objects of appraisal and there is no sure way of picking out the one from the other. Where justice is given by a priori principles, there is no sure way of connecting them up.[9]

Put another way, the condition of authoritative access to the ethico-juridical edifice entails a failure of purchase upon it; the condition of authoritative purchase upon this edifice entails a failure of access. Thus, the authority of the law must somehow "participate in without belonging" to the law, much as the authority of any performative speech-act, be it promise, command, or appeal, is at once inseparable from and yet irreducible to the contextually bound utterance.

Now, it is not that the law in democratic cultures is any more or less performative than the law in earlier political formations. It casts popular sovereignty as a juridically compelling entity even as it bases its own authority to do so upon that sovereignty, a paradox that the archetypal contractarian Jean-Jacques Rousseau fully understood.[10] But this particular inscribed origin or foundation of the law, considered as a legally constituted and juridically effective construct, harbors an unprecedented potential for self-revision. God may have been seen as the unmoved mover, but under the terms of divine-right monarchy His mind only changes once His earthly derivative, the king's law, admits (permits/recognizes) the alteration. As univocal constructs, the divine and earthly *logos* admit of relatively close alignment. The earthly is theoretically subsumed under the divine precisely so that the divine may be practically subsumed under the earthly. By contrast, popular sovereignty, while a formally unified legal fiction, is nonetheless internally differentiated and unevenly empowered; and as such, it bears a recursive force that transforms – through reinterpretation, revision, or simple repeal – the very juridical code upon which its decision-making authority rests. With this secondary motion, the performative gestures of positive law and the popular will alike become profoundly iterative. Each is always repeating itself otherwise, citing its own authority as it has been relayed, justified, and inflected by the other, and, at the same time, anticipating its own authority as it *will have been* similarly mediated, i.e. as the product of a certain *futur antérieur*. The combined intersection and interference of these mutually (self-) legitimating operations renders the presumed coordination of the civil law and the citizens' will structurally undecidable, unpredictable, and unstable. It is through this mechanism that, in Chantal Mouffe's words, "the absence of power embodied in the person of the prince and tied to a transcendental instance preempts the existence of a final degree or source of legitimation."[11]

The Reform Acts in Great Britain, to take one example, altered the very constitution of popular sovereignty, all the while drawing their authority from the popular sovereignty already embodied in the parliamentary representatives. That is to say, the Reform Acts not only reinterpreted the popular will that created them, recasting contention and coalition as consensus, they rendered the expression of that will obsolete even as they legitimated it. They said, in effect, that the process leading to their passage *will have been* truly popular, truly representative, only *after* their passage. At the same time, in laying down the principle of universal democratic participation, this body of law lent its authority to its own future *reinterpretation* as a *precedent* for the further expansion and modification of suffrage. At a certain point, reform law will have "meant" women's suffrage, one person one vote, or even, someday, proportional representation.

In thus decentering the political landscape, the democratic revolutions have not only enabled a political flexibility far exceeding the state apparatus they set in place, they have also generated a corresponding ideal of justice far exceeding their rhetoric about the rights of man: an incontestable and impossible prototype of right that still magnetizes critical jurisprudence today, the achievement of full reciprocity without the exclusion or suppression of difference. Precisely because this *ideal* conception of justice is at once incontestable and impossible, it gives rise to a *working* conception of justice curiously at odds with itself and perpetually in need of further arbitration. In liberal modern cultures, the mark of justice is incommensurably descriptive and prescriptive, positivistic and utopian. On the one hand, justice names the condition of equity *under* law, a respect for the positive codes which assure equality and reciprocity in accordance with certain received criteria: a condition of outright lawlessness would spell injustice in a radical sense. On the other hand, however, justice promises equity *of* the law, a respect for the otherness marginalized by such criteria. Thus, according to the French ethical philosopher Emmanuel Levinas, "[t]o have recourse to the articles of the code, to established institutions, recourse to the letter as that which allows the just to be separated from the unjust – that is unjust."[12] This contradictory imperative cannot be stabilized, because the fulfillment of either form of equity violates and thereby calls forth the other. A perpetual legitimation crisis opens up in which the exclusions and biases constituting each context of judgment can be exposed to challenge, including those which define the challenge itself.

Given the absence of any final sanction, liberal justice cannot be fixed in any determinable state. Yet neither can it subsist in a state of complacent undecidability. Indeed, as a fixed state the undecidable is itself unjust. As Pascal noted, the impotence of justice without force is no better, no less unjust, than the tyranny of force without justice.

So although justice, being undecidable, must always be deferred, justice simultaneously demands that a decision be made – the deferral of justice running hand in hand, as the saying goes, with its denial. The analytic double bind/double bottom of justice, equity under and of the law, carries with it a pragmatic double bind/double drive in which the arbitration of disputes or grievances is at once refused and required. None of this means, however, that the liberal pursuit of justice is arrested in aporia, as Derrida has proposed.[13] On the contrary, the liberal pursuit of justice finds its defining aporia *between* arrest and movement, between the inequities of the status quo and the inequities to be produced in the course of amending it. By way of negotiating this Hobson's Choice, liberal jurisprudence unfolds in a negative dialectic whose immediate goals are always qualified in advance and whose ultimate telos only exists in the manner of Kant's regulative Ideas, unrepresentable except in the experience of finitude that balks it.[14]

The recently controversial policy of affirmative action affords a focused and timely illustration of this dynamic double bind. Equity under law entails the rigorous observation of accepted principles of managing identity and difference in a specified context. An anti-discrimination act, based on the principle of equal opportunity, might be just in this limited sense if job seekers were without exception regarded as identical prospects save in the area of professional status and qualifications, where institutionally approved distinctions would have to be decisive. But justice as equity *of* the law entails the application of these same principles to the structure of presuppositions determining what counts as identity and difference in each instance and for what each form of identity and difference counts. In our greatly simplified example, the principle of equal opportunity would pose a challenge to the positive determinations of identity and difference if it were shown, let us say, that certain variables discounted as nonprofessional and thus irrelevant significantly affected access to the approved means of acquiring professional skills and accreditation. New ways of differentiating the work force might then emerge, ones stressing regional, racial, or sexual factors, and a revision of employment criteria could occur on that basis. Under this arrangement, the same measures that extend the principle of meritocratic parity at the broader social level would infringe this principle within the immediate context of the employment choice itself, raising the claim of reverse discrimination. Whatever new positive determination emerged out of the ensuing debate would necessarily allow or produce still other invidious distinctions and generalizations, which would require further refinements of the underlying legal taxonomy.

In response to this problem, a paradigm shift has recently developed which lends support to my sense of the double inscription of justice. Elizabeth Woolgast, Linda Krieger, and others have helped to fashion a "bivalent" mode of jurisprudence, which divides political right into "equal rights" and "special rights" in order to supplant the abstract, formalist condition of equal treatment with the more substantive, contextually sensitive goal of equal effect.[15] These theorists argue, for instance, that while an equal-rights model may provide for universal access to certain public institutions such as library collections, without "special rights" to specific accommodations like wheelchair ramps the handicapped remain victims of an at least tacit discrimination. They conclude, correctly in my view, that as a departure from simple egalitarianism, "special rights" prove indispensable to the *pursuit* of justice. This "bivalent approach," however, and the special rights it invents do not portend anything like the *achievement* of justice. For if "special rights" are not to annul the "equal rights" they are supposed to accompany, safeguard, and enrich, they must be allowed to redefine those rights. Equal rights concerning public institutions like the library must comprehend not just formal access but a certain reasonable material facility of access. Those who live too far from the building or are too impoverished to afford the trip or those physically disadvantaged in other ways, e.g. the blind, have likewise been victims of passive discrimination, and the introduction of special rights for the disabled that fail to address their specific problems might well amount to an active denial of equity. At the same time, there is no possibility of meeting each and every exigency concerning access. As a result, a decision in favor of special accommodations would unquestionably be indicated, but not as the culmination of a process or even as an advance toward some predesignated ethical *telos*, but rather as a judgment call to be made in the teeth of undecidability. Like affirmative action, special rights create and legitimate new claims, and once again whatever positive determinations arise out of the ensuing debate (what degree of material facility is reasonable, what sort of disadvantages merit relief, what institutions are affected, etc.), they will necessarily allow or produce still other invidious distinctions and generalizations, requiring further refinements in the legal taxonomy.

While these positive determinations are ultimately to be measured against the transcendent standard of heterogeneous collectivity, in which each, as Levinas says, "becomes an other like the others,"[16] the principles informing such a standard can never be completely divorced from the positive juridical context they administer. My own example of equal employment opportunity reflects in its common sense and usage the productivist bias of modern liberal society. This is, one might say, the other side of the law of the genre. If "the mark of belonging does not belong" or "participates without belonging"[17] to the relevant context, the mark of transcendence does not transcend this context, or rather exceeds without transcending its context. As the mark of belonging that does not belong *and* the mark of transcendence that does not transcend, the notion of justice not only legitimates and delegitimates existing law in a single blow but performs each function by way of the other: i.e. a law can only be held just on principles which, operating on another plane of analysis, serve to dispute certain of its implicit assumptions; a law can only be held unjust on principles which, operating on another plane, form part of its rationale. Out of this relation, between restricted economies of justice which nonetheless open toward a theoretical maximum and a Kantian Idea of justice that is still bound to its conditions of formulation, emerges the possibility of what Jean-François Lyotard has theorized under the name *differend*.[18]

In its most significant sense for our purposes, the *differend* may be classified as an unstable state or instance of specifically moral or juridical discourse, wherein a claim, grievance, or point of view that needs to be registered cannot be registered, at least not effectively. "In the *differend*," Lyotard writes, "something asks to be put into phrases, and suffers the wrong of not being able to be put into phrases."[19] Now, the "phrase," in Lyotard's vocabulary, is an instance of practical or effective, not merely verbal discourse, an instance of always multiple linkage, at once constitutive and performative, "where different genres ... enter into conflict over the mode of linking."[20] The "phrase" might be best likened to Nelson Goodman's "ways of world-making," situating addressor, addressee, referent, and sense with regard to one another so as to dismantle the opposition of text and context. In this light, the *differend* would figure as a brake on our moral imagination. Rather than constituting an injustice in the narrow or vulgar sense, the *differend* betokens a conflict whose resolution is inconceivable within the germane legal or ethical context but which nonetheless points, through the feeling of pain produced, to a more nuanced frame of judgment. More than a juridical impasse or problem, the *differend* marks the problematical nature of justice itself, specifically its double status as (1) a restricted value attaching to duly enacted, duly executed rules and (2) a metavalue, the touchstone by which all other ethical and political values are weighed and arbitrated. So while the *differend* remains strictly relevant to concrete juridical situations, as Lyotard's analyses of holocaust revisionism, industrial litigation, and colonial disenfranchisement attest, it is never proper to them, never sufficiently consonant with their prevailing norms and priorities to motivate or endorse specific decisions. Instead, it reveals the impropriety of the contexts themselves, the internal tension between the sense of justice they evoke and the kinds of rules they enforce.

The *differend* may also be understood as a site of latent but radical temporality in the midst of apparently systematic moral discourse. That is because the *differend* stakes the imperfectibility of justice upon the impossibility of "linking" certain contending phrases or idioms on the same plane of operation or within a single logical moment. The Marxist claim of workers' exploitation, for example, cannot be heard or answered within a capitalist labor negotiation, because the recognized vehicle of redress in the latter context, wages, is in the Marxist idiom the form of exploitation itself, the expropriation of surplus value.[21] While there is some point of contact between the managerial "phrase," "offering a raise," and the Marxist phrase, "securing the value produced," they do not, cannot, coincide – either in open conflict or satisfactory agreement. Their linkage is subject to the materiality of time, and justice, accordingly, can only manifest itself in a continuing redefinition of the dispute in question.

Theories of liberal jurisprudence by and large organize themselves around the evasion or the erasure of the *differend* that the actual workings of liberal jurisprudence have helped to produce. They insist upon regarding justice as a synchronic or at least self-contained estate – be it a virtual reality, a contextually delimited good, an eternally revisable ideal, or even a "permanently unresolved question" – instead of seeing it as a self-perpetuating dynamic, continually reopened in the attempt to resolve it.[22]

The dominant metaphor for conceiving this self-contained estate is one of consensus. The forms, projected origins, and underlying motives of this supposed consensus have long provided the focus for the liberal debate on justice – between a model of jurisprudence that is broadly contractarian, procedural, universalist, and rights-based, and a model that is broadly communitarian, teleological, historicist, and goods-based.[23] But *as* such a focus, the idea of consensus simultaneously reveals the common ground of this debate to lie in the tendency of either model to suppress social diversity and stratification in advance and, with them, any disputes that might arise over the first principles and the ultimate aims of the social order. That is to say, through divergent means, the contractarian and communitarian schools have generally contrived to resolve the problem of justice by supposing it to be already resolved at some level, eliminating at the last stage of explanatory regress the very exigencies that make this ethical task so important: difference, discord, dissymmetry. The appositeness of Lyotard's use of the holocaust to illustrate the *differend* haunting Enlightenment discourse becomes evident. What mainstream liberal jurisprudence has attempted, in theoretical terms, is something like an Original Solution.

The contractarian version of this preemptive solution answers and appeals to a normative rationality. Given a shared capacity for choosing and pursuing individual conceptions of personal advantage and the good life and a similarly shared capacity for recognizing and respecting this rational power of self-determination in one another, otherwise discrete human subjects are presumably capable of concurring in the choice of an equitable social arrangement (as in Locke) or at least in the principles of equity that must govern any social arrangement (as in Rawls).[24] At this level of abstraction, the parties to the mythic or implied deliberations remain blissfully unencumbered by the contingent interests, inclinations, and prejudices that presumably motivate their very participation in the confederacy, and so remain undivided by the disparate idioms, perspectives, or value systems that mark their respective social conditions.[25] In effect, contractarianism secretly (de)posits a deep consensus ahead of time only to (re)discover it in the form of the contract itself. Concrete social determination and concrete social activity are elided in the process.

Social contract theories generally come in for criticism on precisely these grounds from the communitarian and organicist school of juridical thought, which gives historically specific and culturally defined ideas of the good strict priority over group and individual rights of self-determination. Communitarians complain that in treating the contracting self as "antecedently individuated," beholden at its core to no social order, contract theories exclude "community in the constitutive sense" and thus maintain the community in a perpetually subordinate role.[26] From this point of view, the social contract turns out to be fundamentally *asocial*. Charles Taylor voices this communitarian objection eloquently:

The basic fault of atomism in all of its forms is that it fails to take account of the degree to which a free individual with his own goals and aspirations, whose just rewards it is trying to protect, is himself only possible within a certain kind of civilization, that it took the long development of certain positions and practices, of the rule of law, the rule of equal respect, the habits of common deliberation, of common association, of cultural development and so on, to produce the modern individual.[27]

For our purposes, however, Taylor's emphasis on liberalism as a monolithic "kind of civilization," and specifically his conflation of common law, common deliberations, and common associations with the whole force of cultural development, is, in structural terms, less antagonistic to than analogous with the contractarian belief in a normative, finally homogeneous rationality. As such, his viewpoint exemplifies the core presupposition that binds the atomistic and organicist positions in conflict: there should be no *differend*. Just as contractarianism tends to consolidate a hypothetical pluralist totality into a single humanistic bloc through an appeal to generalized assumptions about the conditions and operations of rational agency, so the communitarian opposition tends to consolidate real social and historical differences into a unitary tradition or ethos through an appeal to coexistence (in deliberation, in association, in development, in law) *as* commonality.[28] The contractarian strategy separates out the transcendental and the positivistic elements of justice, thus disavowing the *differend* that their entanglement creates, by concentrating the force of legitimacy entirely in the transcendental dimension, in an abstract, *a priori*, and univocal capacity of Mind. The communitarian strategy separates out the transcendental and positivistic elements of justice, likewise disavowing the *differend*, by concentrating the force of legitimacy entirely in the positivistic dimension, in a received body of custom and constraint, an encompassing *doxa* or "form of life." The procedural, contractarian

model embraces the possibility of an equity *of* the law and thus
overlooks the fact that divergent points of view will by definition
construe any compact to which they are a party in divergent ways, so
that further negotiation is perpetually required. The immanent,
communitarian model assumes the possibility of equity *under* law and
thus overlooks the fact that the effective force of law resides in the
disproportionate nature of its impact, which from an ethical point of
view requires a perennial ad-just-ment.[29] In either case, consensus
proves impossible to "phrase" without stipulating it and to some
extent defining it in advance. But to arrest matters in this fashion is
to misrepresent the fundamentally counterfactual progress of liberal
jurisprudence, which cannot entertain and respect social differences,
on its own terms, without continual, increasingly nuanced adjustments in both principle and practice.[30]

The crucial problem confronting a more skeptically oriented
critique, one that seeks to accommodate such counterfactuality, is
how to account for apparently concurrent experiences that justice
can be or has been done. Let us begin with the contractarian model.
If divergent viewpoints will by definition construe any agreement or
contract they strike in divergent ways, how does the dream of moral
consensus or of pluralistic convergence upon a shared political *habitus*
come into being? The answer to this riddle would seem to lie in the
law of appropriation, the dynamic counterpart of Derrida's concept
of iterability or significantly differential repetition.[31] While this law
might be said to govern the behavior of the signifier in general, and
indeed certain brands of deconstruction have been understood as
saying exactly that, its own operation would only come to light – and
so in a very real sense only come to *be* – with the evacuation of the site
of ultimate authority, a development belonging to the epoch of
liberalism.

The law of appropriation entails that the cognitive, affective, and
pragmatic impact of any text or state of affairs will differ irrevocably
and yet not quite irremediably from one perspective to another. Such
perspectives, it is important to remark at the start, should not be
identified with the particularist subjects of classical contract theory.
They must be understood, rather, as pathways of interpretation and
assertion, carved out on verbal lines, and operating at both the intra-
and interpersonal level to mediate among diverse sets of interests and
economies of power. These perspectives are deeply social, which is to
say at once conflictual and symbiotic, constructed as different *from*

one another strictly through their relationship *with* one another. So while their respective takes on a given text or circumstance can never exactly match, they can be reciprocally projected as if they do. In other words, divergent fact–value judgments can be dialogically imputed and understood as essentially the same from one perspective, one social position or temporal frame, to another. The condition of reciprocal appropriation, hence the appearance of consensus, is therefore one with the condition of irreducible difference, hence the inevitability of conflict.

The key to this dynamic is the strange mediating primacy of the mark or the signifier, what we might call its *political* iterability. On the one hand, the mark or signifier serves to represent something outside or prior to itself; on the other, there is no domain beyond its reach, no unmarked space, and so no independent frame of reference against which signification as such can be tested. The signifier always refers to another dimension to guarantee its meaning, and yet the signifier can only be organized and deciphered in terms of other signifiers. As a result, at some point in any dialogue, a coincidence of signifiers comes to *stand in for* that outside dimension which presumably authorizes them. Such a coincidence can thus come to institute or promise, as a performative effect, a convergence of understanding, intention, or investment, a meeting of the minds. In this way, a "shared" reality can be differentially projected. As Lyotard has argued, any presentation of meaning must leave unpresented the meaning of the act of presentation itself, which is to be elucidated only in some further presentation, whose *own* pragmatic force or potential likewise goes unpresented.[32] If this hiatus between the signifying act and the signifying object makes stable, decidable communication impossible, it also fosters the enabling illusion of such communication in the same stroke, opening the space for a mutual, unrecognized accommodation between points of view. Reduced to its simplest dyadic form, perspectives a and b "communicate" insofar as each figuratively identifies the signifiers presented by the other with its own rather differently motivated use and understanding of those signifiers. This interaction, in turn, subtly modifies both the perspectives themselves and the symbolic grounds on which they meet, conditioning the terms on which the next round of reciprocal appropriation can occur. On this basis, some mutual sense of concurrence can arise and some ostensibly shared standard of justice evolve.

Understanding the phenomenology of justice along these lines clarifies the significance of the *differend*. By jamming the circuit of reciprocal appropriation in specific instances, the *differend* threatens to expose the fictive nature of the accords reached under happier circumstances, including that mythic "primal scene" of reciprocal appropriation, the social contract.

Now, to say that the signifier can only be organized and deciphered in terms of other signifiers is to acknowledge that even the most fundamental of social agreements is necessarily forged on the template of some existing cultural code, what Aristotle handed down as the concept of *phronesis*: an immanent body of customs and assumptions, values and constraints, priorities and distinctions, inclusions and exclusions, which cannot but condition the way agreements are joined, who is and is not party to them, how those parties are constituted, and ultimately the substance of those agreements. The guiding hypothesis of social contract theory thus proves theoretically as well as historically untenable: rational deliberations freely conducted and rational decisions freely made cannot, as a matter of logic, be supposed the legitimating grounds of any social regime. Inasmuch as contingent cultural dispositions prejudice the contractual scenario that lends the law its authority, they are necessarily preserved, in some mediated form, in the resulting pact or legislation. What is more, they remain in some measure beyond that law or, more precisely, lodged in inaccessible proximity to it, since they can never be revisited except on terms and by instruments which they themselves have shaped and underwritten. Given this relationship between the openly avowed contract and the obscure, enabling *phronesis*, the sublimation of arbitrary status into contractual rights, by which Henry Main famously defined classical liberalism,[33] must remain forever vitiated; for the arbitrary distinctions to be purged make for an indispensable and informing element of the purgation itself, leaving them permanently alloyed with the "rational" product. To take the most obvious example: the sort of arbitrary and invidious distinctions out of which racial and gender equity laws have generally arisen so disadvantage the populations in question as to induce still other distinctions, whether of readiness, ability, aptitude, assertiveness, etc., which the new laws count as neither invidious nor arbitrary but the stuff of "rational" discrimination. Indeed, the divide I have been exploring between the descriptive and prescriptive aspects of justice – the space of its double inscription – opens precisely because the law remains deeply rooted in the social contingency it seeks to repair.

The dominant alternative form of jurisprudence, communitarianism, begins with a critique of contract theory similar in certain basic respects to the one offered here. But the communitarian agenda goes one fatal step further. It moves beyond using the concept of *phronesis* as a critical lever and locates the only possible legitimating ground of a social regime *directly* in this immanent collective ethos.[34] In so doing, however, communitarianism winds up falling into the same idealist trap as the contract theory it opposes; it reduces the double inscription of justice to a unitary point of origin and goes on to confine the radical temporality of justice within a linear scheme of development.

The communitarian overstep actually comprises two specious inferences from the failure of contract theory. First, because the *phronesis* functions as a necessary condition of any contractual dialogue, it is seen to possess a reality fully prior to and distinct from that dialogue and the reciprocal appropriation that attends it. Second, because no contractual dialogue is conceivable in the absence of prior cultural codes and adherences, these codes and adherences are taken to embody a tacit rapport in which a latent or embryonic model of justice abides. Heterogeneous social connection is identified with achieved social consensus and idealized on that basis. But to accord the *phronesis* an autonomous status and to pronounce it the object of implicit univocal consent is to leave not only unexplained but finally inexplicable any profound social dissension that might subsequently arise on matters of axiomatic import. To replace an originary social pact with an *a priori* social *pax* is both to produce and to beg the basic question of how a truly unified collective could ever manage to engender its own factionalization and disintegration. At this internal limit, the communitarian model remains not only baffled by but essentially blind to the *differend*, which stages a conflict between plausible yet incommensurable claims on the "same" body of assumed principles and thus marks the noncoincidence of the *phronesis* with itself. In the *differend*, heterogeneous connection not only differs from but defeats, even precludes, achieved social consensus.

The complexity of justice thus proves irreducible to a linear narrative, in which presuppositions are taken to exist independently and in advance of whatever presupposes them. The same sort of metalepsis or causal inversion that I traced at the statutory level – where legislative action both presupposes and constitutes the authorizing force of popular sovereignty – operates at the foundational level as well. The *phronesis* is strangely yet inextricably implicated in the scene of contractual dialogue whose unconscious it represents. What I am urging here is the application of the Freudian construct of deferred action to the domain of liberal jurisprudence. Just as no meaningful order or consciousness can emerge except in a belated relation to some other-scene which it proceeds to occult and transfigure, so no other-scene or unconscious can properly be said to exist except in the pressures it exerts and the effects it registers upon that meaningful, occulting order, i.e. as its retrospective condition. The *phronesis* is just such a retrospective condition of the social contract, its *futur antérieur*. What is more, the *phronesis* can only come to inform a social covenant, to orchestrate an agreement where none had existed, insofar as the pressures it exerts and the effects it registers figure differently for the several parties to that agreement. After all, if a *phronesis* were to have an identical force for all the perspectives involved, this very unanimity on matters of ethical and political importance would obviate the need, the motive, for a social accord. It follows that the collective values and constraints that structure the space of contractual dialogue are no more a matter of univocal consent than the text issuing from it. They are themselves subject to reciprocal appropriation in another, less audible tone. Just as parties to a social pact apprehend what is said differently and then veil their differences under the cover of multiply appropriable signifiers, so they respond differently to the pressures of the unsaid, by reason of the varying interests and attachments specific to their social inscription, and then veil their differences under the cover of equally appropriable forms of silence.

Because signifiers and the silences surrounding them are always multiply constructed despite an apparent meeting of minds, the social agreements they render are matters of planned obsolescence, inherently collapsible. Any shift in the context in which the relevant chain of signifiers is taken up or in the purposes they are expected to serve is liable to expose previously unsuspected interpretive and evaluative schisms among the consenting parties. But because this same variability secretly enables whatever meeting of minds exists, the collapse of an agreement carries with it a more or less palpable sense that the meeting was never fully or properly joined in the first place, that a genuine meeting of minds would not have altered when it alteration found. The consensus, that is, does not simply dissolve; it comes to have never really existed. That the breakdown of social agreements, like their formation, should unfold by way of a causal inversion or retroactive impulse testifies to the radical temporality at work in the conduct of moral affairs and to its simultaneously enabling and disabling impact. Viewed in this light, convergence and divergence, assent and dissent, are matters of degree. Appropriation is decisive in either event, but at discrete conceptual levels. If appropriation takes effect at the point of comparison, a working sense of consensus results, overriding any discrepancy as to the substance of the agreement. If appropriation occurs strictly at some prior stage, at the level of *phronesis*, it creates a working sense of mutual orientation without which no conflict could occur.[35] In every discord, then, however stark, there abides a point of projected communality, and in total accord, absolute identification, there abides a point of interference. That is why each may intermittently turn into the other.

The overlap of consensus and conflict in any agreement, no matter how binding, and in any dispute, no matter how fractious, renders the ad-just-ment of the body of law both continually possible and continually necessary. But by the same token, this adjustment cannot move toward restoring some fundamental unanimity, implicit or explicit, which never existed in the first place, but only toward reinventing a rhetorical and pragmatic regime under which effective appropriation can once again play itself out. The issue of any negotiation over particular rules of conduct or categories of being is itself the scene of negotiation by other means. Liberal jurisprudence lives on a boundless *will to treat*, its evacuation of the ultimate site of authority serving to preclude, by design, all utopian outcomes, including hypothetical specimens like Rawls' original position (contractarian) and Habermas' ideal speech situation (communitarian).[36]

As a result, the metaleptic movement of appropriation obtains on the larger historical scale as well. On the one hand, in the absence of any secure overarching authority or frame of reference, collective efforts to shape the social covenant anew must, paradoxically, take their bearings and draw their legitimacy from the broken consensus that they aim to replace. The emerging covenant, accordingly, receives its distinctive stamp by way of its relation to previous understandings, hence to the juridical tradition at large, from which its core normative principles (fairness, openness, consistency, etc.) are bound to derive. On the other, in the absence of a transcendental authority or frame of reference, collective efforts to conceive the social covenant anew are *also* ways of imagining what the previous consensus was and what it meant. The emerging covenant necessarily places its own impress upon the received tradition and its core principles. Each engagement or modification of the social bond is thus doubly articulated in time; it springs forth within a tradition which it simultaneously inflects as a proleptic element of that tradition. Each new appeal to respect the viewpoint of others, each novel reading of what such respect might entail, each institution of procedures to encourage or ensure that respect, simultaneously takes its meaning from and changes the meaning of the tradition in which it operates. The resulting covenant, for its part, cannot but carry forward the hybrid, enfolded character of its origins, reinventing the juridical tradition in its own derivative image while remaining nonetheless derivative for all that. The extension of the franchise to women, for example, neither broke with nor built upon the existing democratic covenant by reversing, as it did, the Victorian assumptions concerning the gendered division of interests, authority, and competence (public versus domestic, marketplace versus home); rather, female suffrage reinvented that covenant, upon which it nonetheless continued to rely. As Laclau and Mouffe have noted, an enlightenment ideology stressing individual sovereignty and egalitarian rights was a necessary precondition of the modern feminist movement,[37] but only insofar as feminism rearticulated these principles in the act of affirming them, an instance of what cultural analysts call performative, as opposed to "pure," repetition. Sustained by this sort of repetition, the core principles of the liberal tradition turn out to be stabilizing and yet themselves unstable, or rather stabilizing by way of their particular mode of instability.

The distinction between this sort of iteration and dialectics, whether Marxist or Hegelian, is crucial to an understanding of liberal jurisprudence, particularly in its relation to literary discourse. However multiple and complex its principles of determination, a dialectic always entails a minimum decidable difference between cause and effect, impulse and outcome, discursive conditions and their conditioned appropriation. But iteration or performative repetition figures a radical foreshortening of this necessary distance, a retroactive construction/alteration of that which enables or

underwrites the retroactive construction/alteration itself. This reversal of cause and effect, anteriority and posteriority, introduces into
every judgment, which is to say, every iteration of consensual values
or principles, an element of indeterminability that greatly complicates the form of its authority. As repetition, each performance of the
guiding value or principle is a derivative and a displacement thereof
and so is substantially de-authorized, marked by its failure to retrieve
intact a fundamental normative imprimatur. As a performance,
however, each repetition is a functional embodiment of that value,
the operative equivalent of the thing itself, and so is substantially self-
authorizing, marked by its effective recreation of a fundamental
normative imprimatur. The self-reflexive particularity that allows
each performative repetition to re-place a given point of supposed
consensus undermines its claim or capacity to re-present that
consensus with any authority.

In this articulation of the continuing force of ethical ideas and
imperatives upon their non-self-coincidence at any discrete moment,
we have in its elementary form the double inscription of justice, its
production as "writing" in the Derridean sense – "writing [that]
both marks and goes back over its mark with an undecidable stroke
[and thus] escapes the pertinence or authority of truth."[38] This
double undecidable stroke of justice is one with what I have been
calling its counterfactual logic: the way its descriptive aspect, the
respect for what is, and its prescriptive aspect, the projection of what
should be, both inform and contaminate one another. In thus
crossing the factual and the imaginary dimension of interpersonal
experience, the imperative to justice exceeds the propositional modes
of discourse within which it is customarily framed – politics, with its
stubborn realism, and ethics, with its equally dogged idealism. By the
same token, the problem of justice finds its proper home in literary
writing, which exceeds the propositional form itself, laying claim to a
"truth" that remains purely fictive. Just as the pursuit of justice
entails the simultaneous application and interrogation of the law, so
the production of literature entails the simultaneous use and
interrogation of language as such, the law or social covenant in its
primordial form. Literature, that is to say, constitutes itself as
destabilizing the authority of its own resources and, in so doing, it
plays out the same sort of double logic as the pursuit of justice, but at
a still more fundamental level. Owing to this shared logic, literary
discourse is in a distinctive position to display and enact the problem

of justice at the same time – to do justice, in the fullest sense, to justice.

HISTORICAL DEVELOPMENTS

By its own lights, the processual model of justice must itself be a processual effect, a product of a convergence of critical perspectives and counterfactual tendencies in both law and politics. No such articulation of adversarial theory and practice has loomed larger in this regard than the discourse of feminism. In her recent book *Feminism without Illusions*, Elizabeth Fox-Genevese obliquely illuminates why this might be so:

If, as Paul Ricoeur says, interpretation is "the intelligence of the double meaning," feminism promises to become interpretation *par excellence*. For feminism has emerged from women's special experience of "two-ness" – the painful living of "objecthood."[39]

Since justice is the ethics of the double inscription, feminism has become, for much the same reason, the jurisprudential moment *par excellence*. In fact, at the heart of its own project, feminism has encountered and identified a double bind strikingly similar to that which haunts the liberal conception of justice detailed so far.

On the one hand, pursuing equal rights for women on the terms given in patriarchal society tends to reinforce the power and legitimacy of those terms. Thus, liberal or first-wave feminism has frequently been criticized for its "assimilationism."[40] The charge operates on at least two levels, a primary and a metalevel. First, in seeking those rights esteemed and enjoined by men, liberal feminism was seen as accepting masculine subjectivity as the norm, acceding to priorities grounded in historically masculine experience at the expense of imperatives biologically or culturally specific to women, in short as petitioning for the right to make women over in agreement with a male standard. The French feminist Hélène Cixous, for example, indicts liberal feminists with wanting "a place in the [patriarchal] system, respect, social legitimation."[41] Second, the discourse of individualism itself, of which the vocabulary of rights is a crucial part, has been seen as reflecting and so continuing to privilege values specific to the male-dominated public sphere of competitive self-interest and rational calculation and as correspondingly alien to and dismissive of the values native to the female-dominated private sphere of domestic affect, nurture, and obligation.

As psychoanalysts like Nancy Chodorow and sociologists like Carol Gilligan have advanced the idea of a distinctively feminine ethics, grounded in mutual connectedness rather than individual rights, a self-consciously feminine/feminist jurisprudence has evolved to translate their insights into the domain of legal interpretation and juridical enactment.[42] I have already taken notice of the key objective of this movement at the primary level, the shift from the equal to the special rights paradigm, from nondiscrimination with respect to some universal norm to the affirmation of normative diversity. At the metalevel, the effort has been to articulate a more communitarian, care-oriented approach to arbitrating gender issues – a strategy more sympathetic to immanent or contextual imperatives than transcendental abstractions, more responsive to intersubjective goals than individual prerogatives, so more in keeping with women's historical experience and the distinctive psychology it has ostensibly inculcated.

On the other side, however, this essentialist or "second-wave" practice of celebrating specifically feminine characteristics tends to reinforce, through a process of semiotic inertia, existing gender stereotypes and the constraints they impose. Ann Jones' comment on the "second-wave" agenda of Hélène Cixous speaks directly to this point. "I myself feel deeply flattered by Cixous's praise for the nurturant perceptions of women, but when she speaks of a drive toward gestation, I begin to hear echoes of the coercive glorification of motherhood that has plagued women for centuries."[43] Essentializing the difference between men and women at the expense of differences among women or of similarities between some men and some women necessarily hardens a broad distinction whose very construction is hierarchical. For this reason, there is, as Ruth Milkman has cautioned, "the real danger that arguments about women's 'difference' or 'women's culture' will be put to uses other than those for which they were originally developed."[44]

One such argument, the special rights paradigm, can produce either a ghettoizing effect, in which the gender-specific criteria justifying needed accommodations for women might reasonably be cited to skirt equitable treatment in other areas, or an internecine effect, in which the needed accommodation might create inequities among the designated beneficiaries. The price of a pregnancy-leave program in a corporation, for example, might well be the production of a rationale for keeping in place a promotional scheme disadvantageous to women. But even taken on its own terms, the institution of pregnancy leave specifically in the name of women's special rights plays into the entrenched patriarchal identification of woman with mother, opening the door for tacit discrimination against female nonmothers. The latter point begins to suggest the kind of complexity that attends political essentialism at the metalevel as well. In assuming the existence of certain more or less distinctive ethical tendencies among women, based on certain more or less common elements of their experience, in particular the experience of a uniquely intimate, sentimentalized form of oppression, feminine/feminist jurisprudence has generated interest in support for a framework of judgment that has been traditionally excluded from consideration under the rubric of the merely private or personal. It does so, however, at the risk of not only embracing general trends as if they were universal truths, but also of actively embracing the sort of "massification" from which cultural minorities have traditionally suffered. With all women grouped under the ethics of care and connectiveness, the intersubjectivity so privileged could be taken for interchangeability, individual women for so many variations on the archetype, or stereotype, Woman. The myth of the Eternal Feminine, whose residual effects might condition such a misinterpretation, would be vindicated in turn by that misinterpretation.

"This debate over equality versus difference," writes Fox-Genovese, "lies at the core of contemporary feminist thought,"[45] and the double bind it manifests is irresolvable in synchronic terms in much the same way as the problem of justice. Read against the grain, Catherine MacKinnon's powerful meditation on this problematic and her attempt to surpass it indicate as much. MacKinnon succinctly enunciates the basic thesis of feminine/feminist jurisprudence in its battle with the liberal model:

Like and unlike, similar and dissimilar, have been the meta-metaphor through which the law has put its systemic norm of equal treatment into effect – like and unlike are "like" equal and unequal ... But why should women have to be "like" men in order to be treated as equal citizens? Why should one have to be the same as a man to get what a man gets simply because he is one? Why does maleness provide an original entitlement?[46]

But to MacKinnon's mind, the second-wave alternative does not really disturb this entitlement either, inasmuch as the feminine difference it emphasizes is implicitly a "difference from" the male standard, which is why "it is... reminiscent of women's exclusion from the public sphere."[47] In effect, she argues, sameness and difference form a single conceptual approach, with a single set of vitiating assumptions:

Concealed [in each] is the substantive way in which man has become the measure of all things. Under the sameness rubric, women are measured according to their correspondence with men, their equality judged by proximity to his measure. Under the difference rubric, women are measured according to their lack of correspondence with men, their womanhood judged by their distance from his measure. Gender neutrality is the male standard. The special protection [rights] rule is the female standard. Masculinity or maleness is the referent for both.[48]

The question to be posed, accordingly, is why do both sides of feminist jurisprudence, the sex equality approach and the sex difference approach, "fail to notice ... that men's differences from women are equal to women's differences from men?"[49]

The answer MacKinnon offers, by way of dismounting this judicial merry-go-round, is that all sexual differences are but the post hoc excuse of sexual domination. That is to say, what codes as sexual difference "are the lines inequality draws, not any kind of basis for it," i.e. whatever supports, legitimizes, or eroticizes female subordination: "sex is inequality and inequality is sex."[50] Justice cannot be pursued on the basis of these differences, since they are themselves the vehicles of inequity; nor can it be achieved, as certain liberal feminists opine, through the effective elimination of these differences, since the idea of gender neutrality is not itself gender neutral but a patriarchal alibi, a tactic for repressing or excluding sexual otherness through an appeal to the light of transcendence. Instead, MacKinnon urges, sexual domination must be attacked directly. After all, "to feminism, equality means the aspiration to eradicate not gender differentiation, but gender hierarchy," and such "equality will require change, not reflection ... a new relation between life and law."[51] Yet for all this MacKinnon's critical program is no less keyed to emphatic gender disjunction than other cases of feminine/feminist jurisprudence. She too counsels the cultivation, through consciousness-raising techniques, of a female epistemology and a female ontology rooted in women's common conditions of sexual inequality and oppression. If anything, she is *unusually* ready to attribute false consciousness to women who experience their condition otherwise – as natural, or fulfilling, or amenable to change – and tends to override variations among women in the name of a totalizing woman's perspective. MacKinnon wants to claim that this more or less monolithic gender difference derives from the institution of a sexual hierarchy and so constitutes a cultural determination of the patriarchy. But because this claim nullifies the very idea of a gender prehistory, disputing that the relevant modes and categories of being can be said to exist before sexual dominion was established, it forecloses the effective distinction between given and created, natural and historically produced gender difference. The contention that sexual difference succeeds sexual domination turns out to be self-refuting, since it destroys on principle the possibility of citing some preceding state and conjecturing upon, let alone explaining, the institution of gender as inequality. This point grows somewhat clearer when viewed from the other side, from the perspective of this unimaginable prior state. Sexual hierarchy is not blind but ordered violence. As such, it cannot even begin to operate blindly, i.e. in the complete absence of intelligible marks and thresholds of selection, exclusion, and discrimination, all the means of circulating power concentrated in the term "difference." This is not to suggest that the postulation of *a priori* gender categories makes for a more coherent account of the basis upon which they have been molded, but rather that the conceptual pairs sameness/difference and dominance/subordination are irreducibly correlative though not coextensive. There is no reason for making (perceiving, constructing, inferring, invoking, etc.) a difference unless it "makes a difference," i.e. draws or draws upon a value discrepancy, a hierarchy of sorts, within a particular context. On the other hand, there is no political discrimination, therefore no political mastery, without perceptual, cognitive, or logical discrimination (difference in sum) *as* its enabling context. In replacing what she calls "the sameness/difference approach" with a dominance–submission approach, MacKinnon does not escape the juridical double bind we have been discussing, but rather takes up another position with respect to it. Just as gender differences can never be justly arbitrated without dismantling the political inequality they instantiate, so inequality can never be tackled except by way of gender differences, which are reinforced even as they are altered in the process, setting the stage for the next counterfactual impulse.

The limits of MacKinnon's work, however, are illuminating, particularly her propensity for taking the hierarchies of power and knowledge that she reviles as gender artifacts and then reproducing them in her denunciation or dismissal of women who fail to express dissatisfaction with their gender condition. These limits suggest that the correspondence I have outlined between the project of feminism and the dynamics of justice marks a deeper structural connection. Because gender hierarchy is instituted at the level of language, the rudimentary social contract, the gender system is the precondition or at least the indispensable countersign of other types of social division, dominance, and exclusion, as well as a particular type with particular exigencies. As we have seen, feminism must take its cause and its subject, hence its definition, from the *doxa* it rejects – the logic of oppositional construction and stratification – and as a result its incremental victories come to participate in the more general hegemony of that *doxa*. At any given point, feminism holds in symbiotic relationship relatively empirical and foundational registers, the concrete facts of historical gender relations and the logical structure of domination as such, whose claims can and do conflict, exacting a perpetual labor of self-adjustment consonant with the juridical sublime. Like the dynamics of justice, feminism comprises not only a double bind but a double bottom. In a sense, the question of gender *is* the question of justice.

The structural convergence of modern feminism and modern jurisprudence manifests itself in a roughly parallel historical development. What we might term the "founding" texts of either movement, Thomas Paine's *The Declaration of the Rights of Man* and Mary Wollstonecraft's *Vindication of the Rights of Woman*, explicitly affirm the idea of abstract equality under the law of reason, but they implicitly accommodate disputes over the nature of that law with respect to which equality is to be determined. While certain contemporary texts such as Mary Shelley's *Frankenstein* actually remark the paradoxical implications of this liberal jurisprudence, the dialogical problematic of (gender) justice, like the philosophical relativism with which it is affiliated, came more fully into evidence with the capitalist–colonialist expansionism of the nineteenth century.

The successive breakdown in the integrity of local, regional, and national economies brought into view a widening variety of ethnic and social differences and a deepening severity of cultural divides. The collision of alien cultures and languages, the construction of new social "others," and the corresponding incorporation of previously small groups in an increasingly stratified hegemonic bloc, the symbolic cross-referencing of different marks of privilege and subordination, the violent internesting of disparate value and belief systems, all these aspects of the colonial encounter contributed not only to a growing sense of ethical and epistemological relativity, but to a doubling and fragmenting of cultural authority and a resulting ambivalence of social identification.[52] In this "liminal uncertain state of being," as Bhaba has it,[53] where mutually exclusive ethico-political orders intersect in the constitution, regulation, and self-reflection of individual subject and group positions, the prospect of justice can be seen to open up between or outside the authoritative closures within which judgment necessarily occurs.

A good deal of interplay between gender and colonial politics in the West served to compound the effects either one had upon the functioning of justice as both a value and a *metavalue*, i.e. a concept naming both the satisfactory arbitration of various claims under law and the satisfactory arbitration of various constructions of the law or systems of law.

On one side, the colonial experience occasioned a challenge to patriarchy's self-privileging claim to being the original and universal basis of human governance, by way of a new mode of political theory called comparative jurisprudence. In 1861, Sir Henry Maine published *Ancient Law*, an attempt to consolidate the fifty-year ascendancy of the patriarchal theory of the social bond.[54] The outflow of texts contesting his study in the name of the "mother-right" theory indicated that a paradigm crisis was at hand, created, as Rosalind Coward notes, by "the expansion of the colonizing movement" and "the impact of the expansion" on colonizer and colonized alike.[55] To compare the mother-right and patriarchal theory of the time is to hear uncanny echoes of entrenched gender stereotypes and of their transposition in contemporary feminine/feminist jurisprudence. According to Bachofen, its leading exponent, mother-right constituted a universal phase preexisting the patri-archal system by which it was viciously suppressed. He holds the principles of mother-right to involve a connectedness expressive of the mother's material relation to the child: "It is accessible to sense perception and always remains a material truth." At the same time, mother-right is religiously oriented, concerned with the miraculous, the supernatural, and the irrational, and universalistic in scope, partaking of "the undifferentiated unity of the mass."[56] The patriarchal system that replaced it, conversely, expresses the inferential or deductive relation of father and child and so represents an advance in reasoning capacity and a liberation of the intellect from the material–sensual realm. Joyce's own framing of paternity as a "legal fiction" in *Ulysses* reflects his interest in and awareness of this recent debate.

With respect to feminist politics and the cause of gender justice, this outgrowth of colonial expansionism yields bittersweet fruit. As Coward observes, mother-right theory was by no means intended to challenge orthodox Victorian intersexual relations, and Bachofen's particular elaboration does much to reinforce them. Not only does his argument rely heavily on the standard stereotypical doubling of femininity – women as material/miraculous, natural/supernatural, immediate/enigmatic, bodily/religious – but it contrives to marginalize women conjointly with non-Western people as backward, preintellectual, and insufficiently emergent from the material dimension. But the very positing of a distinct mother-right formation, its presumed inferiority notwithstanding, introduces at least the hypothetical possibility of a transvaluation of all values on a specifically gendered basis, where the female-identified categories of being would no longer function as stereotypes in the service of the violent rationality that suppressed their reign, but as the ontological levers of an organic social community modeled upon the idealized domestic sphere of nineteenth-century bourgeois life. Such an opening could not but nourish the essentialist feminist currents that had run just under the surface of liberal feminism from the outset and then rose to prominence over the course of the century as the cult of domesticity and the maternal mystique combined with the activity surrounding the Contagious Disease Act and the temperance movement to produce the popular conviction of women's "natural superiority" as moral agents and forces of social cohesion.[57] As Coward makes clear, "the meaning of mother-right was by no means only interesting for the study of societies for its own sake. Political philosophy, sociology, Marxism, psychoanalysis and sex psychology were all involved in these debates."[58] Not least among the contributions was that of a budding socialist–feminist alliance, exemplified by the Saint-Simonians, "which threw its weight behind the hypothesis of radical transformation in familial organization."[59] Its rhetoric counterposed a "democratic 'maternal' communism" to an "individualistic patriarchal capitalism," a strategy which may be seen as prefiguring the suffragette movement's "reanimation of the militant allegorical female figures of justice and liberty ... for feminist purposes. ''[60]

Since the real-world origins of the mother-right thus promoted were certain familial–social formations invaded and colonized by the Western powers, this antipatriarchal brief carries an implicit anti-imperialistic thrust as well. The critique of orthodox gender assumptions and the patriarchal division of sexual labor passes almost imperceptibly into a critique of racial and cultural assumptions and the geopolitical division of labor, thus testifying to the historical concurrence of these problematics in occasioning the possibility of a truly radical jurisprudence.

On the other side, the imperialist enterprise of the West was, for purposes of ideological justification, filtered through normative tropologies of gender disjunction, exclusion, and stratification. In figuring the conquerors as exponents of a principle coded and valorized as masculine and the conquered as the embodiment of a principle stereotyped and depreciated as feminine, imperialist discourse traced a vicious symbolic circle in which sexual and socioeconomic dominance mirrored and authorized one another. Colonial rule was naturalized as the latest historical signifier of an inherently gendered cosmos; gender hierarchy was naturalized as the ultimate reference of the colonial mission. This dynamic has been lucidly critiqued with respect to European incursions in Asia and North Africa under the rubric of Orientalism. Edward Said has famously demonstrated how Western anthropologists, ethnographers, explorers, poets, and politicians of the nineteenth century constructed the Oriental as irrational, available, supine, and enigmatic as opposed to the lucid, accurate, energetic, and decisive Westerner. And as we shall see, in short order, many of these same Manichean disjunctions were taken to inform the relationship between the "manly" Anglo-Saxons of England and their "essentially feminine" wards in Ireland.[61]

With respect to the politics of colonial resistance, the gendered allegory of racial and cultural supremacism likewise bears an ambivalent import, exaggerating the "hybrid" status of the colonial subject and the colonial polity. Taking India as his object of analysis, Ashis Nandy has shown how this imperialist rhetorical strategy could induce the colonial elite to develop the especially macho, what he calls "hypermasculine," potentialities of their own institutions, to try and reverse the political and military success of their colonial governors by mapping onto the ideology that informed it.[62] In this form of ideological mimesis, the colonial elite tend to underwrite vigorously the *positive law*, the patriarchal code, of gender hierarchy the better to contest its imperialistic translation into the register of ethno-cultural difference. The practice typically involves educing the virility of the native warrior tradition as a way of collectively cultivating a more militant or martial ethos in the present day, while elaborating or renovating an ideal of woman that could at once subserve and authorize the emergent hypermasculine code as its negative polarity. In Ireland, the political propagandism and literary writings of people like Padraic Pearse, Maud Gonne, Lennox Robinson, D. P. Moran, and, occasionally, W. B. Yeats exemplified this defensive reflex. But since any society tends, in the first instance, to ascribe value in line with its own developed strengths, this sort of agonistic "identification with the aggressor" served to enhance the existing advantages of the colonizing powers – in industrial capacity, technological advancement, military organization, etc. – and the dislocating impact such an identification must have on native social arrangements and cultural standards could only leave them more vulnerable to the manifold pressures of the colonial order. Nandy remarked that colonialism "creates a culture in which the ruled are constantly tempted to fight their rulers within the psychological limits set by the latter,"[63] and in this instance the colonized were far less able to certify their cultural manhood on the terms given than they were liable to tighten the imperialist stranglehold in the attempt.

Still, this dynamic turns out to be rife with paradoxes. Precisely by extending the positive law of gender beyond its established range of application, the imperialist allegory incurs the risk of severing gender norms and assumptions from their biological grounds of justification and removing sexual differences from their secure bodily inscriptions, from which the cultural dictates of gender were suspended. By grafting gender categories upon racial, regional, and even cultural taxonomies, the imperialist allegory runs the risk of denaturalizing these categories altogether – of exposing gender as an ideological construct rather than an innate reality, a purely figural and relational status rather than a substantial self-identity, a performative effect rather than a permanent fixture, and an ethico-political rather than ontological matter. Furthermore, precisely because the affirmation of the positive law of gender in colonial hypermasculinity has such self-destructive implications for certain elements within the colonized society and for the society at large, it facilitates a recognition in certain quarters of the gender instability and ad-just-ability disclosed in the imperialist allegory. Nandy analyzes Mahatma Gandhi's intervention in the Indian nationalist movement as constituting just such an enlightened departure from the hypermasculine attitude then prevalent and detects in Oscar Wilde's literary subversion of substantialist notions of gender and sexuality a critique aimed at the underlying structure of British imperialism.[64]

Thus, colonial hypermasculinity comes to serve ultimately as both a recipe for reproducing the colonizers' ethos within the colonized society and a transitional stage toward focusing sexual and imperial oppression as a common enemy; on one side, a redoubling and reinforcement of the positive law, on the other, an entering of the positive law into a dialogue with itself which produces an opening to justice. Nor need these alternatives be taken as mutually exclusive. The hybrid construction of subject positions crossed and recrossed by significant social differences and the explicit political articulation of these differences enables an amphibolous ethico-political stance toward the forms of authority and resistance alike, a posture especially attuned to the double inscription of justice. James Joyce, I contend, enjoyed or suffered such a fate.

As the native of a metropolitan colony, that most liminal of political formations, Joyce derived an acute sense of the double inscription of justice from his own borderline or, as Deleuze and Guattari would say, his "minor" social position.[65] He experienced the double inscription most obviously, of course, in the splitting of his (British) legal status and his (Irish) national origin or of his (British) national origin and his (Irish) ethnic status – the borders themselves in this case are doubled and undecidable, making each division an overlap as well. However one defines this articulated rift in personal origin, it translates practically into an articulated rift between the two main principles of political legitimation: positive or fundamental law, here embodied in the quintessentially positivistic legal scheme, the British common law, and popular right, here embodied in the Irish tradition of constitutional and physical force resistance. Indeed, this complicated split was overtly re-marked again and again within the Irish nationalist movement itself, in ways and in locales likely to have made an impression on Joyce.

The institution of this rift in the discourse of Irish patriotism extends back at least as far as the days of Swift, whose famous screed against Wood's halfpence turned on a distinction between the power of legal precedence, the government's historical authority to manage currency, and the principle of natural rights, humankind's inherent exemption from the imposition of tyranny.[66] But since Swift's appeal to the latter on behalf of Irishmen was at least theoretically inclusive of the unrecognized Catholic majority, his piece was only politically viable if interpreted within the framework of the positive law of Protestant exclusivism, i.e. as a strictly limited departure from the legal precedent he questions.[67] The founding document of Irish literary nationalism was thus breached by the double inscription of justice.

The divide of law and right was marked more dramatically but sustained no more absolutely in the carnivalesque juridical practices of the whiteboys. Predominantly Catholic if officially nonsectarian, the whiteboys represented the peasant perspective of the late eighteenth century. They wished to restore the "moral economy" of landlord–tenant rights and obligations recently eroded by the modern British doctrine of property rights. That is to say, they counterposed an ideal rule of equity, what I have called the equity *of* law, to the existing rule of equity, equity *under* British law. To achieve their ends, they established alternative legal codes, alternative means of enforcement, and even alternative judicial rituals. R. F. Foster's description of their program denotes its relevance for our discussion:

They were part of an underground that had learned not only to separate the formal laws from popular notions of legitimacy, but also how to impose an alternative discipline through intimidation. Their proclamations parodied the legal documents of the day; sometimes an enemy's horse or cow were symbolically tried, found guilty and executed.[68]

The whiteboys actually conceptualized their activity as supplying a "superior justice" in the service of the community and on that authority appropriated to themselves the exclusive prerogative to insurrectionist activity. In their political philosophy, they prefigured a vitally important notion in nineteenth-century Irish irredentism: the idea of the virtual Irish nation already established free and whole in men's hearts and defined by a commitment to justice under a specifically communalistic or communitarian ideal. At the same time, however, the profoundly parodic nature of their enterprise, the mimetic coloration of its every facet, could not but mark the dependency of their idea of superior justice on the positive law they would transcend. On the other side, even the element of communalism which they took to sanctify their extralegal escapades derived not from some moral empyrean but from another positive code, the ancient Irish law of Brehon. For this reason, Oliver MacDonagh contends that the Ireland of the time "was a multilegal society rather than a lawless one," as is generally believed.[69] I would say rather that *because* Ireland was a multilegal society, it was lawless from the official ruling perspective and that this is precisely the condition in which a dialogical conception of justice can emerge, the crossing of the totalizing and the particularistic.[70]

Joyce's great-grandfather, "the Ur-James Joyce," as Ellmann calls him,[71] was a whiteboy; and to judge from *A Portrait*, Joyce's father must have adverted to this stage of his career frequently. During the famous Christmas dinner scene, Simon Dedalus appeals to the fictive version of this progenitor as an authority on the perfidiousness of the Catholic hierarchy to an irredentist cause undertaken in the name of the Catholic community:

He pointed to the portrait of his grandfather on the wall to his right.
—Do you see that old chap up there, John? he said. He was a good Irishman when there was no money in the job. He was condemned to death as a whiteboy. But he had a saying about our clerical friends, that he would never let one of them put his two feet under his mahogany. (*AP* 38)

It is likely, then, that Joyce himself was familiar with the lore of these early hillside men, and familiar with it specifically in the context of the doubly inscribed laws and divided loyalties shaping Irish culture and Irish subjectivity. In fact, the "Festy King" episode of *Finnegans Wake*, in which the accused proves to be a prize pig, seems modeled in part after the symbolic animal trials of the whiteboys; and it centers precisely on the tendency of the Irish law itself to lapse into internecine conflict: "[t]he litigants [were] local congsmen and donalds, kings of the arans and the dalkeys, kings of mud and tory, even the goat king of Killorglin" (*FW* 87).

Joyce's people also claimed relation with the pacifist heir to the whiteboys' alternative jurisprudence, Daniel O'Connell, who became the leader of Catholic Ireland by way of his activist legal practice. His Repeal [of the Union] Association "tried to furnish," in Oliver MacDonagh's words, "a supplementary law and order." "Arbitration courts determined disputes over land rights and duties," reinstating the moral economy in a quasi-legalistic form.[72]

In addition, O'Connell projected a council of three hundred, a surrogate house of commons, and an autonomous Irish police force. Once again, the purpose of these indigenous substantive legal organs was to supplant British law in the name of a higher justice, what O'Connell himself called "full justice," which, in keeping with his own training in liberal jurisprudence, turned out to be an infinitely elastic category.[73]

This variable split of fundamental law with the finality of justice received further impetus from the catastrophic potato famine. In 1850, a priest in County Clare succinctly summarized what had now become the prevailing attitude in the Irish Catholic countryside: "My advice to you is to throw over altogether the legal rights of the landlords and seek for your just rights and not your legal rights. I would not give anything for the landlords' legal rights but to tell you to throw them over altogether."[74] Having set "the legal rights of the landlord" over against the audience's "just rights," the priest slips in the phrase "and not your legal rights," the awkward redundancy of which, in the context, betrays some sense of the way his entire formulation tortures the idea of Right. Right cannot be reduced to law on one side and justice on the other, for the term "Right" refers to law and justice simultaneously, marking the inseparability of the two in their very difference from one another.

The lapse here is not incidental but exemplary of a jurisprudential knot, a species of *differend*, that the colonial condition foregrounds. For Right to be right, it must *exceed* the law, in this case the British law of property, warranting whatever is in effect from some unimpeachable vantage; it must constitute a transcendental ethical causality in the Kantian sense.[75] But for Right to be right, it must also *be* the law, in this case the working law of property; it must be *in effect* itself. And these twin imperatives can never be fully reconciled. They can only converge in a conceptual slippage or lapse. All the more so when the subjects of the existing law are, like the Irish, neither full nor willing members of the community of this law, but are rather undecidably within and outside the polity in question. That is why Lyotard actually chooses the colonial estate to illustrate the *differend*:

A Martinican is a French citizen; he or she can bring a complaint against whatever impinges upon his or her right as a French citizen. But the wrong he or she deems to suffer from the fact of being a French citizen is not a matter for litigation under French law. It might be under private or public international law, but for that to be the case it would be necessary that the

Martinican were no longer a French citizen. But he or she is. Consequently, the assertion according to which he or she suffers a wrong on account of his or her citizenship is not verifiable by explicit and effective procedures.[76]

The alternative Irish legislative and judicial institutions that we have cited were defined precisely to establish a site where the metropolitan–colonial *differend* could be litigated, where the silenced wrong of the British/non-British community could become an adjudicated grievance, where "explicit and effective procedures" could verify the assertion that expressed the injuries of the colonized.

The elaboration of this alternative machinery continued well into Joyce's time, with the Land League courts and the projected shadow government of Sinn Fein. But insofar as these supplementary legal strategies proved increasingly efficacious, they did so by progressively taking upon themselves the positive force of law within a given context, and as such they resolved the *differend* at hand – allowing a colonial wrong to be heard – at the cost of still other *differends*. On this score as well, Lyotard's analysis is relevant to the Irish situation. He notes that the resolution of a *differend* produces a discursive hominess through an exclusion or repression of other potential disturbances:

It's in the *pagus* that the *pax* and the pact are made and unmade. The *vicus*, the home, the *Heim*, is a zone in which the differend between genres of discourse is suspended. An "internal" peace is bought at the price of perpetual differends from the outskirts. (The same arrangement goes for the ego, that of self identification.)[77]

The self-styled juridical structures of the whiteboys, the Repeal Association, the Land League, and the tellingly named Sinn Fein (Ourselves Alone) aimed at securing a home not only in the sense of a self-determining Irish nation but in the sense of a stable, cohesive, more or less monolithic community organized around a single value and belief system: the moral economy in the eighteenth century, a Catholic Irish-Ireland in the nineteenth. Not just an Ireland free of the invader, then, but an Ireland purged of internal dissonance, not to say difference, as well. While this exclusionary tendency is the legacy of the internal ethnic and sectarian strife produced by colonial plantation, its reach extended from questions of racial and religious status to philosophies, lifestyles, and secondary characteristics with racial and religious overtones, and from there to any stirring that did not conform with the stipulated communal norm. The whiteboys' opposition, the underground activities of other groups, the Repeal

Association's vexation with the Young Ireland movement, Sinn Fein's provocation against the national theatre and the Anglo-Irish Literary Revival, in each case the speaking of a certain metropolitan–colonial *differend* turned into the silencing of another under the aegis of the one "true" community. Even as these extrajuridical institutions re-marked the fundamental hybridity of the colonial condition, they tried to refute or eradicate that hybridity, to secure an "internal" peace, only to reproduce that hybridity once more "at the outskirts."

This paradox was replicated in turn in Joyce's own experience. While the nationalist tradition I have traced taught Joyce something of the double inscription of justice attending colonial life in general, its modern avatars brought home the irreducibility of that double inscription by revealing to Joyce his own liminality to the nationalist movement and ethos. That is to say, Joyce experienced this double inscription most intimately and most profoundly as an insistent ambivalence concerning his own cultural identity and allegiance. He occupied a border zone between a minority, irredentist society he called his own, whose cause, dignity, and cultural warrant he repeatedly avowed, and an imperialistic civilization, in whose language he conceived and framed such avowals, upon whose liberal ideology he paradoxically based them, and from whose literature he drew many of the standards to which they refer. The object and resources of his cultural legitimation thus remained at different levels unalterably opposed and irreducibly connected.

Nowhere does this dilemma of ideological hybridity manifest itself more plainly than on the question of what is axiomatic to justice itself. A votary of the anarchist philosopher Benjamin Tucker,[78] Joyce espoused an individualism linked in the Irish popular imagination with the detested British-Protestant influence, and he grounded his nationalism on a principle of self-determination closely linked in his own mind with individual choice and ethical and aesthetic freedom. His collegiate essay "Drama and Life" explicitly assimilates the goal of Irish cultural autonomy with the values of a radical Enlightenment dramaturgy:

Drama will be for the future at war with convention, if it is to realize itself truly … drama of so wholehearted and admirable a nature cannot but draw all hearts from the spectacular and the theatrical, its note being truth and freedom in every aspect. It may be asked what we are to do, in the words of Tolstoi. First, clear our mind of cant and alter the falsehoods to which we have lent our support. Let us criticize in the manner of a free people, as a free race, wrecking little of ferula and formula. The Folk is, I believe, able to do so much. (*CW* 42)

Joyce here tries to coopt the most powerful contemporary nationalist myths, the chauvinistic cult of the Irish peasantry, to the cause of intellectual liberation. To the same end, he cleverly conflates the idea of a "free people," a collection of individuals, with a "free race," an individuated collectivity. Nevertheless he was well aware that the Irish masses were by and large coming to express the right of self-determination in terms antipathetic to his own and, further, that he would have to resist the Catholic ideal of a parochial, self-sufficient, and morally unanimous nation-state in order to save his own soul, or rather, the own-ness of his soul.

The ambivalence of social identification this position cost him focuses the fictive representations of this period of his life in both *Stephen Hero* and *A Portrait*. What Stephen's discussions with Madden (*SH*)/Davin (*AP*) in particular reveal is how a self-privileging Gaelic collectivism, articulated as a superior justice of and for Ireland, functions as arbitrarily as any positive law in enforcing limits upon "serious" or credible political discourse, limits which repress the hybridity, the ambivalence, that is the very hallmark of the colonial condition. In *Stephen Hero*, Stephen's concession to the obvious, that he is "an Irishman after all and not one of the red garrison" (*SH* 51), is immediately converted into an injunction to support the language movement and a racially defined national autonomy. In *A Portrait*, the terms are reversed, with Stephen's deviation from the Sinn Fein party line serving to cast doubt upon the authenticity of his Irishness. When Stephen notes a contradiction between the Irish support for universal peace and the physical force option, Davin dismisses the point solely on the grounds of its being inconsistent with nationalist fervor and therefore, he infers, non- or anti-Irish:

—That's a different question, said Davin. I'm an Irish nationalist, first and foremost. But that's you all out. You're a born sneerer, Stevie ... I can't understand you ... One time I hear you talk against English literature [*sic*]. Now you talk against the Irish informers. What with your name and your ideas ... are you Irish at all? ... Then be one of us. (*AP* 202)

Stephen tries to enunciate briefly a libertarian nationalism along the lines Joyce set out in "Drama and Life," interfusing belonging and independence: "This race and this country and this life produced me

... I shall try to express myself as I am" (*AP* 203). But Davin's response treats Irish patriotism as a confessional ideology not fully distinguishable from Catholicism and equally demanding of absolute submission and self-sacrifice: "Try to be one of us ... In your heart you are an Irishman, but your pride is too powerful" (*AP* 203). Stephen's final "non serviam" has political as well as religious meaning precisely because Irish nationalism has constituted itself as a religion.

Much has been made of Stephen's rejection of Ireland and the Irish cause, but it would perhaps be truer to speak of a mutual polarization, in which the nationalist refusal to tolerate analysis or ambivalence, let alone opposition, helps to push Stephen toward a stance of elitist apostasy. Davin insists, "a man's country comes first. Ireland first, Stevie. You can be a poet or mystic after" (*AP* 203); only then does Stephen slander Ireland as "the old sow that eats her farrow" (*AP* 203), a formulation which has rather more direct relevance to the present conversation with Davin than has been generally recognized. Stephen has portrayed himself as the product, the child, if you will, of the Irish situation, striving to express his particular refraction of and reflections on that situation. Davin responds by insisting upon the incorporation of Stephen's vision into the nationalist mythos of Ireland. That mythos, however, most frequently saw Ireland personified as a maternal figure calling her sons to the ultimate sacrifice (witness Yeats' *Cathleen Ni Houlihan*, the definitive nationalist redaction of Gaelic myth).[79] So it is actually Davin who figures his country, at least implicitly, as a mother rapacious of her young, devouring the very sort of hero-martyr he would have Stephen become. What Stephen does is register his alienating ambivalence and the colonial hybridity that generates it. He gives a simultaneous translation of Davin's nationalist myth into its ancient Irish root term, the desirable and devouring Celtic sow-goddesses, and into the contemporary English stereotypes of the Irish as pigs and as an essentially feminine race.[80] He thereby marks the ideological complicity of Irish exclusivism with British imperialism, for he shows how the pursuit of an essential racial and national identity, whether retrieved or constructed anew, is always already compromised by the colonizers' stereotypes, ingredients of which have invaded and occupied that identity. The old sow eating her farrow is an emblem of self-defeat at the level of the word as well as the deed.

With this line, however, Stephen casts himself likewise as an Irish "incorruptible," an aesthetic intelligence averse to any compromise or rapprochement with his community of origin. In striking this posture, he allows the Sinn Fein resolution/repression of the colonial *differend* to dictate an adversarial resolution/repression of *his* ambivalence. By contrast, Joyce himself contrived to remain *in* the *differend*. By conducting a lifelong self-exile from Ireland as a perpetual literary return, Joyce enacted the ambivalence of his minor or borderline social status as an ontological double inscription.

The ambivalence of colonial minority is fixed, exacerbated, and infinitely complicated by its implicit and explicit correlation with the sex/gender system.[81] As I argued above, being the most entrenched, the most ubiquitous, the most effectively naturalized social distinction, and yet for all that a *social* and therefore *constructed* distinction, gender offers problems of definition and assessment fundamentally consonant with the problem of justice. Moreover, the asymmetrical binarism of gender construction and association bears a manifest structural relation to the colonizer/colonized binarism. Indeed, the junior branches of these pairings have historically been prey to homologous forms of double inscription:

(1) What Bhaba calls, from a racial perspective, the not quite/not white phenomenon.[82] As I shall examine more closely in Chapter 3, women and the colonized alike have been treated as virtual subjectivities, capable of being brought up to speed (not quite), and as absolute nonsubjectivities (not white).

(2) In the latter mode, they are either idealized or fetishized, in a manner that is either implicitly or explicitly condescending; or they are demeaned, disdained, or ridiculed, in a manner either implicitly or explicitly vicious.

It is precisely this parallel construction of sexual and socioeconomic dominance that enables the imperialist gender allegory explicated above, the identification of the colonizer and the colonized with the masculine and feminine principles respectively. But the deployment of this allegory, in turn, complicates the structural parallels tremendously, particularly in the case of Ireland.

The sexual inflection of colonial hegemony and subordination was unusually explicit in the case of Ireland. First of all, its hybrid status as a metropolitan colony left it especially susceptible of familial metaphors. Long nicknamed the Sister Isle, Ireland was increasingly imaged in wifely terms as the nineteenth century wore on, the implied connubial connection with England serving to naturalize that long-standing bone of contention, the Union. Oliver MacDonagh writes,

The sexual image was in constant use in nineteenth and early twentieth century England to express the dominator's concept of the relationship between the two islands – with perhaps Gates' Acts dimly perceived as a sort of counterpart to the Married Woman's Property Acts and the British retention of the power of political decisions subconsciously validated by similar psychological mixtures of assertion and insecurity.[83]

As MacDonagh's reference to the Married Woman's Property Acts indicates, the analogy also served to express a gendered sense of the geopolitical spheres of activity occupied by England and Ireland. A major political power, England moved in the geopolitical equivalent of the male public sphere as a citizen of the world. As a domestic colony, literally, Ireland represented the imperialist equivalent of home ties, John Bull's ball and chain, the most troublesome and yet the least dispensable of his possessions.

Switching the symbolic focus from the Irish nation to the Irish race, early ethno-anthropological discourses reinforced this gender-izing dynamic by depicting the Irish as spiritually or psychologically feminine and so attuned to the private sphere of Great Britain's colonial life. The virile efficiency of the Teutonic races was contrasted with what Matthew Arnold called the "nervous exaltation and feminine idiosyncrasy of the Celts,"[84] which made them aesthetically apt but unreliable in practical affairs. Working from the same assumptions, another writer found the Irish "a people of acute sensibilities and lively passion, more quick in feeling wrongs than rational in explaining or temperate in addressing them."[85] Such discourses played on and played into the modern, radically gendered schism of mind and body, thought and sentiment, reason and fancy, in order to suggest that the Irish, like women, were constitutionally ill-suited to the dispassionate pursuit of state and social policy and were for that reason properly dispossessed of any real historical agency. Indeed, as a feminine race, the Irish were assumed to be historically passive or inert. The Celts are among those races, Lord Acton writes, "which supply the materials rather than the impulse of history, and are either stationary or retrogressive ... They are a negative element in the world."[86] In short, the Irish were, to paraphrase Luce Irigaray, "a race which is not one."

   The gender system acted as a uniquely serviceable frame of
reference for discriminating the English from the Irish in a hierarchical manner in order to rationalize the English appropriation
of Irish land and liberty, while at the same time acknowledging the
profound cultural intimacy of the two peoples. By the end of the
century, in fact, the men of middle-class Britain had begun to
categorize the Irish with their wives and daughters as cultural minors
and wards.[87] At the same time, the feminist struggle of the nineteenth
century was achieving critical mass in an increasingly radicalized
suffragette movement and the more general social, economic, and
literary impulse toward female emancipation collectively known as
the New Woman. As these developments were arousing anxiety and
antagonism in the sovereign male population, the assignment of
feminine traits to a minority group like the Irish effectively
discredited their claims to self-determination.[88] The phrase "home
rule," on which Joyce puns in *Ulysses*, had acquired a highly charged
double valence. At the same time, those supposedly female qualities
that rendered the Celt incapable of self-government – undependability, instability, "nervous exaltation" – remained linked to a
masculinized predilection for violent action, so that the periodic
agrarian and IRB outrages were seen *not* as part of a rational if
desperate revolutionary program, but as auguries of the anarchism
dwelling in the female soul of the Irish.

   Viewed from the Irish perspective, these same outrages were *not
only* part of a rational if desperate revolutionary program but *also* a
reaction, at least subconsciously, against their feminization by the
British. In order to put an incontestable distance between themselves
and the very idea of a metropolitan marriage, the militant Irish
leadership mounted a virile display of political and paramilitary as
well as cultural resistance. They answered British paternalism by
tapping into the history and mythic lore of Ireland to valorize the
codes and institutions of a native patriarchy. The consequences of
this classic instance of colonial hypermasculinity on internal gender
relations and representations, in turn, were dramatic.

   Elizabeth Cullingford has correctly argued that the hypermasculine ideal of the manly man depends upon a marked sense of
gender disjunction and so requires as its ideological anchor the
counterideal of the womanly woman, an exaggerated version of
normative wife–mother stereotypes.[89] But in the case of Catholic
Irish-Irish nationalism, the fetishism of pure, denatured yet maternal

woman was complicated and intensified by an identification with
her. The womanly woman was not only an ideological anchor and
countersign of "the cause" but its ideological telos as well. Some
variant or other of the pure and passive woman had served as the
national personification throughout the colonial occupation. This
figure was then adapted as a symbol of the quest for home rule:

Even the Hibernophiles…might explain themselves in terms of arch-
femininity. Harold Bigbie, the Daily Chronicle journalist, introduced his
Home Rule Tract of 1912 with Ireland a young and capable matron seated
at her fireside, who raises her gray eyes to the visitor and says, with a
whimsical and ingratiating play of laughter on her lips, "I wish to do my
own housekeeping."[90]

With the resurgence of the sovereignty myths of the Caillac Beare and
Cathleen Ni Houlihan, the renewal of this feminine ideal had come
to allegorize the "virtual Irish nation," already free and whole.
There was, moreover, an underlying coherence to this symbolism. As
we have seen, this "nation" was to be governed on values and
principles historically identified with the private domestic sphere of
women and currently inculcated by Mother Church: the communalistic orientation, the premium to be put on moral conformity
at the expense of individual liberty, the premium to be put on
sentimental togetherness at the expense of rational self-interest,
spiritual purity at the expense of material prosperity and worldly
strength, and stability at the expense of progress. As a result of this
gender allegory and identification, any deviation from the idealized
conceit of Irish womanhood, whether in the actual conduct of Irish
women or in the aesthetic representation thereof, carried the stigma
of being unpatriotic, while remaining nonetheless consistent with the
patriarchal expectation of female treachery. The subconscious logic
runs: if women fail to vindicate Ireland as a female paragon, fulfilling
the nationalist gender allegory, then Ireland turns out to be a
feminized possession after all, vindicating the imperialist gender
allegory.

The complex dialectic of imperial and colonial hypermasculinity
helps to explain the outraged protests of Yeats' play *The Countess
Cathleen*, the outright riot over Synge's *Playboy*, even the embattled
dismissiveness of Joyce's classmates toward modern drama in general
and his beloved Ibsen in particular. Since the figure of woman was so
identified with Ireland, the dignity of the country itself seemed to
require that actual women be unswervingly recognized in the moral

eminence that male desire had conferred upon them and then continually held to the repressive standards that desire enjoined. The same symbolic logic helps to explain, in reverse fashion, why someone like the Citizen, Joyce's satirical specimen of Irish hypermasculinity, would trace his country's political disenfranchisement to the sexual lapse of a woman. Since Ireland is so identified with the figure of woman, the country's manifest indignities might seem to derive from the failure of actual women to live up to the moral expectations foisted upon them by male desire and thus to avert the contempt that is always the flip side of such idealization. On the other side, this dialectic helps to explain why, despite the hypermasculine ethos of late Victorian Ireland, the Irish women's movement was able to garner so much male support, at least initially, even from otherwise misogynistic characters like Padraic Pearse, by pressing the analogy between gender and racial oppression, and why that same national-istically influenced movement was so distinctively lacking in any element, any discourse, any contingent, openly concerned with sexual as opposed to gender liberation.

Joyce found himself simultaneously attracted to and alienated from each of the interanimating currents in the colonial gender dialectic I have described. Opposing British imperialism on principle rather than on specifically racial grounds, he was not beyond adopting an imperialistic posture toward his own people, one with a decided gender component. The missionary aesthetic Stephen espouses in *A Portrait* does not depart substantially from Joyce's attitude during the represented period:

How could he hit their conscience or how cast his shadow over the imaginations of their daughters, before the squires begat upon them, that they might breed a race less ignoble than their own. (*AP* 238)

I go ... to forge in the smithy of my soul the uncreated conscience of my race. (*AP* 252)

Even as he was composing *A Portrait*, in fact, Joyce continued to see his art in much the same light as the British saw their colonial enterprise, as a racially inflected form of "soul-making." To Nora he wrote, "I am one of the writers who are perhaps creating at last a conscience in the soul of this wretched race" (*SL* 204). On the other side, in narratives such as "Ivy Day in the Committee Room" and the "Cyclops" episode of *Ulysses*, Joyce skewers the venal hypocrisy of Irish politics as usual by implicating its exponents in a kind of vicarious complicity with the rakish escapades of King Edward. He thereby links sexual, material, and imperial conquest as allied forms of phallic aggrandizement, suggesting that he who supports one collaborates in the others, even when he also happens to be their victim. Joyce's strategy here further indicates that while he feared and loathed the communitarian dogma of Irish Catholic nationalism as repressive of individual difference and freedom, he was no less ready to condemn the masculinized and English identified pursuit of individual self-interest, when it came at the expense of a common resistance to colonial aggression – what he would see as a type of simony. It is a measure of Joyce's bilateralism in this regard that he could enthuse over the anarchism of a Tucker or a Bakunin while conditionally supporting certain aspects of Arthur Griffith's highly communalistic Sinn Fein idea.[91]

Once again, Joyce's creation of the Citizen in *Ulysses* reflects his disgust with colonial hypermasculinity as regards the bigoted exclusivism and repressiveness of its ends and the violence of its means. But Stephen's refusal to sign the peace resolution, combined with his calling Davin "my tame little goose" (*AP* 202) for agreeing to do so, suggests that Joyce was not so dislocated from or ambiguously determined in his primary gender position as to escape anxiety over colonial feminization and the loss of male entitlement it implied. What is more, while Joyce flatly rejected the hypermasculine ideal of the pure and passive womanly woman, he clearly drew the Citizen's related sexual attitude, his preoccupation with female treachery, out of the "long pocket" (*U* 9.742) of his own energetic jealousies, his simultaneous fear of and fascination with sexual betrayal.

As the last phrase suggests, however, the structure of Joyce's erotic desire was similarly doubled, comprising both a demand for absolute possession, amounting almost to incorporation, of the body and soul of the beloved – a remnant, as we shall see, of his maternal abjection – and an equally powerful investment in the independence, the autonomous self-will, of the beloved, a dual insistence reflected in his predilection for limning formidable, sexually accessible women. The former, traditionally masculinist ingredient accentuates the inequity implicit in the construction of gender difference by mapping it onto the subject–object split. The latter, protofeminist ingredient enshrines the admittedly vexed ideal of subject–subject symmetry. Joyce's seemingly contradictory sentiments toward the Irish women's movement arose in large part out of this ambivalence. For his sympathy with the general aims of sexual equality and a respect for sexual difference were not always strong enough to overcome his dissatisfaction with the movement for promoting, in collaboration with Irish Catholic nationalism, severe limitations on women's sexual freedom (hence on his own opportunities for sexual pleasure) which he could correctly if not impartially criticize as limitations on individual freedom. In *Stephen Hero*, Stephen's conversation with MacCann, the fictional Skeffington, about his feminist convictions illustrates this tendency, which was no doubt exaggerated by the fact that Joyce knew and socialized with members of the movement's avant-garde (*SH* 49–52).

The cumulative effect of these binocular or bilateral investments on Joyce's part was a certain purchase on gender as a pervasive yet variable tissue of power rather than as a natural and permanent state of being. The investments themselves arose out of the same contradictory social inscription that fostered Joyce's dialogical sense of justice, prompting him to find in the question of gender its most fully answerable focus. Not only did Joyce occupy a rich nexus of socially calibrated differences, where the double valence of gender in relation to the others could best be appreciated, he also lived and wrote in a highly ambiguous relation to the hegemony that these distinctions articulated and enforced. His semicolonial station endowed him with impulses and identifications resonant of both an authorized, normative subjectivity and a subordinated, pathologized other. As an Irish Catholic intellectual and *paterfamilias*, he was a patriarch who had known feminization and felt the pressure of hypermasculinity, a self-proclaimed Aryan who had known racial denigration, a Christian who had known religious intolerance.

Joyce was also the son of a man who flaunted his coat of arms and complained that his wife's common name stunk in his nostrils.[92] Joyce attended baronial Clongowes Woods with the Catholic elite and continued at similarly distinguished Belvedere. Yet his family descended from comfort to beggary, from plenty to hunger, and from the suburbs to the slums, largely on the strength of his father's all too common indolence and drunkenness. Joyce was in socioeconomic terms *petit bourgeois* verging on *lumpenproletariat*. Yet culturally he was and felt himself a near aristocrat. In *Stephen Hero*, the religious fathers of Dublin life woo a renegade Stephen precisely on the basis of his "aristocratic intelligence," his desire to be "of a patrician order," and his dread of having to pander to "spiritual slovens" (*SH* 205–6). In *A Portrait*, conversely, Stephen's growing physical and domestic squalor curtails his eligibility as a suitor to the daughters of middle-class Dublin and hence his ability to reproduce the social status of his own youth.[93] From Joyce's childhood, when his parents' sexual difference was troped as class difference as well, to young adulthood, when his social dignity was upheld by the religious patriarchy and slighted in contact with the same young women who founded modern Irish feminism, Joyce's class identifications and class resentments were distinctively mediated through gender roles and positions.

From this thumbnail portrait of the artist, it is evident that Joyce was both the beneficiary and the victim of warring species of patriarchal imperialism – familial, religious, economic, racial, geopolitical – and as such he had a powerful stake in seeing the general form both maintained and dissolved and a powerful motive for defending and deconstructing its fundamental law, sexual division. As we have seen, he operated between the hedges of authority at any given point, a subject in many ways like but never at one with the socially delimited others of his experience.

The trajectory of Joyce's fiction describes the struggle to transform this pathos into ethos, an ambivalence suffered into justice achieved. But the idea of struggle must be emphasized. If, on the one hand, his own double inscription came to render those stakes of centrality and marginality extraordinarily negotiable and interdependent for Joyce, facilitating a virtually deconstructive insight into exclusionary gender and racial arrangements, there are also moments when biased attitudes and invidious assumptions or ideals emerge as weapons to cut the Gordian knot of his agonistic interpellations and clarify his claims to social privilege. His literary method of working through these conflicts consists in an oscillation of internal and external perspectives, analogous in principle to the formal counterbalancing of lyrical and dramatic epiphanies or the tonal shifting from sympathetic identification to ironic distance in *A Portrait*. In this case, the interactive components are dramatic representations that problematize the issue of justice and self-referential gestures that problematize the justice of Joyce's representational medium, motives, and propensities.

From the beginning of his career, Joyce saw the artist as properly engaged, even in his most lyrical moments, with questions of social organization. In *Stephen Hero*, for example, he has Daedalus dis-

tinguish himself from "cynical romanticists," like Cranly, who refuse
to acknowledge that "civic life affect[s] individual experience"
(*SH* 174); and Stephen's mature brand of historicism, summarized in
the quotable remark, "[h]istory is a nightmare from which I am
trying to awake" (*U* 2.377), would seem to develop out of this basic
animadversion. Throughout his career, moreover, Joyce repeatedly
addressed these issues of social organization and "civic life,"
especially as they pertain to gender and ethnic difference, in
specifically juridical terms. In this respect, Joyce was more attuned
than his nationalist critics to the ways of ancient Irish culture, in
which "every *file* or poet was also a brehon or judge."[94]

While he was composing *Dubliners* and *A Portrait*, Joyce was also
writing numerous newspaper articles in which he set out to represent
"the Home Rule question" to a European audience from the
perspective of "an Irishman" and to do so "sincerely and objectively." He subsequently planned to collect these essays in a book
to be called *Ireland at the Bar*. The title positions Joyce himself as a
certain kind of advocate, a legalist rather than a propagandist, and
thus expresses his belief that colonial problems could only be resolved
in a juridical register, by an appeal for justice, rather than by a
reliance on power or an appeal to blind racial solidarity. The book
itself never materialized, but Joyce used the title for an essay which
makes explicit what the book's terms of address were to be. "Ireland
at the Bar" (*CW* 197–200) works an analogy between the plight of a
Gaelic tribal patriarch, Myles Joyce, on trial in a British court of law
and the place of Ireland itself making its case for nationhood in the
court of European public opinion. The emphasis on justice in this
essay is particularly significant because, unlike other rhetorical
dominants he might have selected, it allows Joyce to explore not only
the patent abuses of English law in the Myles Joyce trial, but also the
hidden complicities of the Irish themselves in the affair. And an
examination of the remainder of Joyce's *Piccolo della Sera* articles
indicates that the book *Ireland at the Bar* would have carried a
similarly double-edged valence. That is to say, the appeal to justice
was the rhetorical mode or vehicle whereby Joyce could take sides in
the colonial conflict while simultaneously problematizing its oppositional construction.

The trial scenario consistently appears in Joyce's fictional texts as
well, where it likewise reflects his understanding of justice as a
regulative Idea in the conduct of political struggle. A crucial

peripeteia in *A Portrait*, the pandying incident, concludes with the schoolboys' impromptu arraignment of Father Dolan, a quasi-juridical proceeding in which generational resentments are staged and assuaged. The climax of *Ulysses*, the *Walpurgisnacht* of "Circe," centers on the double trial of Leopold Bloom, during which he undergoes a gender translation that has provided a focus for the varying critical assessments of the novel's sexual politics. *Finnegans Wake* offers a parodistic version of the Maamtrasna trial of Myles Joyce, the so-called "Festy King" episode, in which manifold switchings and doublings of sexual identity are accompanied by a complex permutation and overdetermination of racial genealogies and of clashes between and within racially defined groups. The strategic effect is to show how gender and colonial distinctions may subvert as well as support one another, reconfiguring the context in which they operate. Lastly, *Finnegans Wake* features the court case of Anita and Honophurious, in which both the aims and modalities of sexual desire proliferate and conflict endlessly. Each of these trials forms a site of transformation and masquerade, involving the most salient categories of social identity and cultural affiliation. Like Joyce's journalistic efforts, his fiction testifies to his preoccupation with justice as the supreme ethical and political value, but it also points to the arbitrariness and instability of those grids of social definition that underpin any body of positive law – whence the purely counterfactual status of that supreme value.

In my closing chapter, I shall return to all of these trial scenarios, fictive and non-fictive, and examine them in greater detail. But Joyce's treatment of justice in the narrow sense, his depiction of juridical proceedings and his use of particular juridical theories, is not the focus of this book, just evidence that the book's focus is indeed relevant to Joyce's overall project. This book is not, finally, about the representation of justice *in* Joyce, except insofar as that topic participates, as it surely does, in a more comprehensive problematic: how the liberal imperative to justice, theorized and contextualized above, acts as a shaping force in Joyce's representational and counterrepresentational strategies.

In charting this larger problematic, I shall have occasion to take up some of Joyce's less canonical works, such as "A Mother," *Giacomo Joyce*, and *Exiles*, and to analyze them as keys to the remarkable evolution which produced the major novels. "A Mother," for example, will be seen both as crystallizing the gendered division of authority that informs the narrative structure of *Dubliners* and as looking beyond the "scrupulous meanness" of the book's style. *Giacomo Joyce* and the experience it documents will be shown to have helped alter Joyce's political attitude in ways crucial to the development of *Ulysses* as we know it. *Exiles* will be seen to reveal the fundamental incompatibility between these altered political attitudes and representational writing and thus to prepare for some of the more radical stylistic experiments of Joyce's later career. All of this is to say that employing the idea of justice as an interpretive key affords not just a relatively new angle on Joyce but a relatively new Joyce – not an undiscovered Joyce to be sure, but an *underdiscovered* Joyce, a corpus that has yet to receive the extensive scrutiny to which his more standard works have been subject. Integrating these minor works into the Joycean canon on both thematic and theoretical grounds will, I hope, prove to be a significant if corollary benefit of my approach.

CHAPTER 2

Joyce's sexual "differend": an example from "Dubliners"

To live in a metropolitan colony such as turn-of-the-century Ireland was to experience acutely the always double inscription of justice. Joyce's awareness of the condition of *differend* manifests itself near the outset of his career, in an undergraduate essay on the poet James Clarence Mangan, the very type for many modern Irish literati of a colonized creativity. Writing of the deeply ambivalent attitudes held by Celtic revivalists toward a considerable, recognizably Irish poet who was "so little of a patriot," Joyce declares, "Certainly he is wiser who accuses no man of acting unjustly ... seeing that what is called injustice is never so but as an aspect of justice" (*CW* 76). In context, Joyce's statement points up how the idea of justice participates in the doubleness inherent in the sociopolitical circumstance of Ireland in general and particularly of its eastern pale. So too does Stephen Dedalus' theory that the domestic politics of colonial Ireland operate according to a "compensative system" in which would-be patriots manage to extract a measure of economic "justice" for themselves from an imperial regime whose injustice they otherwise deplore (*SH* 64).

A more general or sweeping instance of the *differend* informs the divisions haunting modern Ireland, what has since come to be known as phallocentrism. Because the gender system at large is organized with reference to norms and values that privilege masculinity, the binary syntax in which issues of sexual identity and difference can be raised at all tends to appropriate and subordinate the figure of woman to a phallic standard. As a result, claims and grievances made on behalf of women, appeals to justice made in their name, suffer a certain unphraseability, being betrayed, compromised, or diverted in their very emergence by the moral and metaphysical discourse in which they must be translated. In other words, injustice is regularized precisely "as an aspect of [a] justice" always already conceived on a

49

sexual bias.[1] Since, as we have seen, this gender system served as something of a symbolic blueprint for modern colonial relations, yet persisted, in sometimes aggravated forms, within the colonized societies themselves, the grievances attendant to each regime were at once competitive and indissociable, greatly complicating the efforts of differently interested parties to ignore, suppress, or resolve them.

I would like to focus here on a narrative wherein the colonial *differend*, toward which the author himself bore the status of disenfranchised other, intersects with a sexual or gender *differend*, regarding which he occupied a position of relative privilege. In this way, I hope to unchain the multiple contortions of the question of justice at the level of both the action represented and the act of representation. The text to be considered is "A Mother," in which a Nationalistic Recital is the scene for the airing of a gender complaint which cannot be "phrased" or sustained.

In her fine article "Rediscovering Mrs. Kearney," Sherril Grace counters the derogatory and dismissive attitude generally leveled at the protagonist by pointing out that she is denied her rights, dealt with unjustly, and so wins the sympathy of a resisting reader.[2] While sharing Grace's view of the previous criticism and appreciating the value of her counterinterpretation, I would suggest that she leaps rather too quickly from the rules actually governing the ethical and social situation portrayed to a body of civil law that has no apparent force but whose citation ensures the "feeling" Lyotard calls the *differend*.

The positive rules in question involve the rigorous topographical and stylistic division of gendered authority that Joyce delineates in *Dubliners*. As indicated by the agonistic triangle of Father Flynn, old Cotter, and the boy narrator in "The Sisters" – and the analogous triad of Father Butler, the old josser, and the narrator in "An Encounter" – male authority is exercised and reproduced in public and institutional space under conditions of conflict and resistance that animate this space;[3] and it focuses on questions of knowledge, that variety of human expression most clearly shaped in terms of public testability and institutional accreditation. In the initial woman-centered tale, by contrast, the dutiful lineage of Mother Mary Alacoque, Mrs. Hill and her daughter (the Eve-line behind Eveline) indicates that female authority is exercised and reproduced in private, domestic space through the direct transmission of notions of affective obligation and personal propriety, which likewise give this space its social definition.⁴ Thus, further along in the volume, Little Chandler contests in the public house Gallaher's savvy, cosmopolitan authority, which he respects and envies, and submits at home to Annie's maternal dictums, which he has come to resent. Mrs. Mooney exerts an immediate, wordless authority over her daughter, Polly, in private and relies on a panoply of agonistic male forces – the priests, the Great Catholic wine merchants, her brutal son, Jack – to facilitate her more public schemes. Finally, Gabriel Conroy presides as master of ceremonies over his aunt's annual party, a semi-public affair, and true to the distribution of authority noted, he successfully rebuffs, belittles, or discounts all female points of view any way contrary to his own. The power shifts dramatically, however, once the Conroys depart. On the carriage ride to the hotel, Gretta takes control of their tête-à-tête precisely by withdrawing into her private memories. And in the end, Gabriel finds his magisterial composure shattered and his world transfigured by the moral authority of his wife's intimate, sentimental secret, which she discloses, appropriately, in the half-light of their hotel room.

What I am speaking of here is in fact a system of justice, a system, that is, of symmetry, reciprocity, and proportionality, of mutual ad-just-ment in accordance with a certain frame of reference. It is not, to be sure, a *just system* by our lights (or Joyce's), but that is a matter of the infinite re-marking of legitimacy. For the reasons adduced, any closed system of social relations fails of justice in the transcendental sense, necessitating forms of exclusion and stratification which its own principles of right, taken to their logical conclusion, must find illicit. So to understand this traditional disposition of sexual authority as a localized system of right is by no means to ignore its role, its *strictly correlative* role, as a system of power and domination.⁵ It is rather to begin to explain the source of its insidious control over its subjects, the stake that both victims and beneficiaries have in its continued operation, which is precisely what Joyce dramatizes in "A Mother."

Mrs. Kearney assumes her own sort of control over the upcoming concerts during her drawing-room meetings with Mr. Holohan, at which time she secures a contract for her daughter's performance. But her authority and that of her contract are from the first confined by and within the domestic site. The progression of the narrative reflects as much:

She brought him into the drawing-room, made him sit down and brought out the decanter and the silver biscuit-barrel. She entered heart and soul into the details of the enterprise, advised and dissuaded; and finally a contract was drawn up by which Kathleen was to receive eight guineas for her services as accompanist at the four grand concerts.

As Mr. Holohan was a novice in such delicate matters as the wordings of bills ... Mrs. Kearney helped him. She had tact ... Mr. Holohan called to see her every day to have her advice on some point. She was invariably friendly and advising. Homely in fact. She pushed the decanter towards him, saying:

—Now, help yourself Mr. Holohan! (*D* 138)

Mrs. Kearney's talent as an impresario, while not suppressed, is filtered through a precious sentimental idiom so as to reflect the pressure of a gender system which allocates business expertise to men and social sensibilities to women. The slight dissonance which results between the tones of the drawing room – "she entered heart and soul," "delicate matters" – and the terminology of the office – "the details of the enterprise," "the wording of the bills" – prefigures the more substantial discord between Mrs. Kearney and the Committee. As always in Joyce, human conflict is at some level a problem of style. As for the contract itself, mention of the formal legal document here is completely enveloped in an account of personal hospitality and charm. The passage preceding the contract's appearance indicates that Mrs. Kearney has garnered her influence through a display of social graces or "tact," whose material embodiment is the decanter and silver biscuit-barrel. The paragraph following the legal agreement indicates that it is the tactfulness of her approach, the charm of her influence, that registers with Mr. Holohan, and not the commercial ends they furthered. This is made particularly clear with the sudden shift out of third-person oblique into Holohan's mind with the phrase, "Homely in fact," the remembered impression. From the moment of signing, the contract has already been privatized and so in a sense delegitimated.

Two related matters factor into the vitiation of the contract. First, unless performers were famous, "theatrical and musical contracts of this quasi-amateur sort were regarded ... as more promissory than binding," contingent on the financial success of the event.[6] There is, accordingly, an undecidable idiomatic nuance surrounding the term "contract" that is relevant to this general type of situation; it not only makes Mrs. Kearney's grievances impossible to "phrase" or sustain but also hides this impossibility from her. This theatrical tradition itself, however, arises from the identification of aesthetic activity with the feminine as opposed to the masculine business of business – a sexual division of labor doubling and thus reinforcing the sexual division of authority. The workings of justice are thus confirmed within the positive context as the experience of *differend* is exaggerated.

The second factor involves an entanglement of the sexual and the colonial *differend*. Since the concert was sponsored and arranged by Eire Abu, its primary impetus is presumably a love of Irish culture and the desire to propagate it, rather than a view to material profit. Mrs. Kearney deviously acts to capitalize on that love by presenting her daughter as an aptly named revivalist, so it is not unreasonable that the organizers should assume Kathleen's love of things Irish and her attendant willingness, under straitened circumstances, to accept the role of amateur (from the Latin *amator*, a lover of something). Their working assumption is that a common devotion to the cause will, in a pinch, soften and even suspend all putatively legal obligations. It is for this reason, at least in part, that Mr. Holohan ultimately exclaims, "I am surprised at your Mrs. Kearney... I never thought you would treat us that way" (*D* 148). So while Mrs. Kearney's countercomplaint "that the Committee had treated her scandalously... [and] would never have dared to treat her that way if she had been a man" is undeniably veracious, it does not tell the whole story or point to any definitive new dispensation for arbitrating the dispute. To be sure, in refusing to respect Mrs. Kearney fully as a business associate or her contract as fully binding, the organizers are responding to the gender stereotype which confines women to intimate and domestic matters; yet when it suits their purposes, they turn around and expect her to violate or transcend that same gender role by placing ethnic and political imperatives before the interests of her daughter. But this argument cuts both ways. Mrs. Kearney wants to participate in the public, "masculine" domain without broadening or reordering her received priorities ... meaning, in this case, that she wishes to participate commercially and culturally without making political sacrifices, even though what is being commercialized is nationalist culture. Since the nationalist movement is not without its own phallic assumptions and values, a clean confrontation between these racial and sexual prerogatives cannot emerge. They remain suspended in irresoluble conflict centered appropriately enough on the question of how to "treat" and be "treated" (148.6,

11, 30, 31). If a *differend* is only phraseable with reference to some model of justice unavailable in the immediate ethico-political context, this sort of contest of *differends* cannot appeal to any standard of right short of the utopian idea of radical reciprocity with radical difference.

When Mrs. Kearney finally complains to Mr. Holohan about being shortchanged, he said that it wasn't his business. "Why isn't it your business?" she responds; "Didn't you yourself bring her the contract?" (*D* 144) But, as we have seen, Mr. Holohan's visits with Mrs. Kearney, as defined by both place and manner, were more social than business calls; and in fact all of the players here, following their intuitive sense of the social rules, initially conspire to keep their squabble out of public view. Mrs. Kearney first accosts Mr. Holohan outside of the dressing room (140); she then pigeonholes Mr. Fitzpatrick away from his screen (141); she later adjourns with Mr. Holohan "down to a discreet part of the corridor" (144). Through his careful blocking of the action, Joyce transforms the geography of the Antient Concert Rooms into a metaphor for the gendered differentiation of discourse. In the process, he begins to turn the positive context of the law against itself, training its own avowed principles of proportion or symmetry on the biased assumptions underpinning them. Since the opposition of public and private is always implicitly hierarchical, it can only be reduplicated *within the public sphere itself* in oppositional terms such as main versus marginal, the broad versus the narrow, the hall versus the screen, the dressing room versus the corridor.[7] The practical effects of this transposition are decisive. Exercising the female prerogative of personal suasion turns out to be an act of self-enclosure, a concession to the tendentiously drawn and unevenly permeable limits on discourse. Mrs. Kearney must appeal to the male organizers in a private forum, which, by definition, issues no hard evidence of the deliberations, no mutually affirmed, officially recognized story or interpretation. The male organizers in turn appeal from this situation to a public bureaucratic form, the Committee, from which Mrs. Kearney finds herself excluded and in which, accordingly, their construction of the affair will prevail uncontested. So when Mrs. Kearney acidly wonders, "And who is the *Commetty* pray," but suppresses the question because "she knew that it would not be lady-like" (*D* 141) to ask, she simultaneously testifies

(a) to the extent of her subjacency. She does not even know in whom the power adjudicating her complaint resides;

(b) to her forced participation in that subjacency. For fear of losing her status as a lady and so whatever authority she does command, Mrs. Kearney cannot challenge that mysterious power or inquire too deeply into its workings.

Mrs. Kearney's first response to the closeting of her objections is to bring along her husband, whose image in her own mind is an unmistakable index of his textual function: "She respected her husband in the same way as she respected the General Post Office, as something large, secure and fixed... she appreciated his abstract value as a male" (*D* 141). The reference to the Dublin Post Office, with its Greco-Roman architecture, the carefully placed pun on "male," anticipating Shaun's role in *Finnegans Wake*, and the insistence on "abstract value" all clearly establish Mr. Kearney as the phallic signifier conceived in terms of the classical ideal of public discourse, the letter of the (specifically civil) law. It is therefore significant that his one meaningful action is to try and keep the dispute as private as possible by asking his wife to lower her voice. Although he takes her side until the end, tacitly affirming the rightness of her cause, he intervenes only to safeguard the law of discourse, actively affirming the justice of its divisions.

Even Mrs. Kearney's ultimately disruptive means of forcing the issue pays a certain lateral respect to this same law. In silently imparting to her daughter a felt obligation to strike the concert, in despite of her own interests, the mother relies on the normative mode of female authority in *Dubliners* and reproduces the traditional mother–daughter relationship exemplified by Eveline and Mrs. Hill, Polly and Mrs. Mooney.

Once Mrs. Kearney's complaint explodes into the public arena, the barriers to phrasing shift from the spatial to the stylistic or idiomatic, to differences between what Lyotard calls "genres of discourse." Much has been made of Holohan's use of the word "lady" as a rhetorical means of discrediting Mrs. Kearney, and I won't dwell on it here, except to note that it answers perfectly the formal requirements of Lyotard's notion of *differend*. If Mrs. Kearney were a lady, she would not voice her charges in public and so could be taken to have no serious grievance; if Mrs. Kearney voices her charges in public, then she is not a lady and so her grievance need not

be taken seriously. This sort of "differend between two parties,"
Lyotard points out, "takes place when the regulation of the conflict
that opposes them is done in the idiom of one of the parties while the
wrong suffered by the other is not signified in that idiom."[8] In this
instance, the male organizers insist on responding to Mrs. Kearney in
the idiom of drawing-room propriety rather than in the vocabulary
of civil law, as her wrong requires. She exclaims "My daughter has
her contract." Holohan's reply, "I never thought you would *treat* us
this way," resonates faintly of her erstwhile hospitality. "I'm asking
for my *rights*," she declares. "You might have some sense of *decency*,"
he retorts. Mrs. Kearney is more trenchant than she realizes in her
ensuing complaint, "I can't get a *civil* answer" (*D* 148–9, my italics).
For her, a civil, meaning decorous or polite, response would be one
couched in terms of (civil) law or, at least, one respecting contractual
rights and obligations. For the organizers, the register of civility or
decorum excludes such civil claims or legal instruments. In effect, the
differend at issue marks the unavailability to the parties involved of a
completely civil answer, which would consist in a formula that might
compass for all concerned a satisfactory relation between public and
private, law and manners.

The phrase "civil answer" makes for a sort of climax to this
idiomatic duel, because in its ambiguity it adduces that the *differend*
arises not from the rigorous semantic purity or isolation of the
dissenting genres of discourse but precisely in and through their
mutual contamination at the level of the phrase, a competitive
inmixing that can be neither separated out nor resolved into unity.
The dissenting genres are bound alike, and so bound together, by the
same abstract conditions of sense and reference: that signs are always
repeatable and yet disparately appropriable from one phrase or
context to another and that signs bear meaning in relation to other
signs as they have been repeated and appropriated from one phrase
or context to another. Indeed, the apparent heterogeneity of these
genres as interpretive systems, i.e. modes of linking phrases together,
actually presupposes their differential contact in the activity of
interpretive linkage itself. It is this contact, in turn, that defines and
redefines their respective borders, which, in this case, are finally
indistinguishable from their internal structure. As Geoff Bennington
has remarked, "[i]f there were no such communication between
genres (and that communication can be thought of as warfare) then
there would be no genres, no establishment of generic proprieties,

which are thus never properly proper."[9] On the other side, the phrase itself only exists in and as an idiomatic tension, so that any cooperation (communication/combat) in the activity of interpretive linkage simultaneously presupposes a heterogeneity of discursive genres. Lyotard summarizes the matter succinctly: "The phrase which links and which is to be linked is always a *pagus*, a border zone where genres of discourse enter into conflict over the mode of linking. War and commerce. It's in the *pagus* that the *pax* and the pact are made and unmade."[10] In other words, the unenforceability of Mrs. Kearney's contract, while closely tied to historically specific social and symbolic arrangements, points to a more fundamental aporia, touching upon the (im)possibility of contracting itself. That is to say, the social contract, of which Mrs. Kearney's is an emblem, is ineluctably or rather constitutively broken.

The economy of discourse proceeds by way of segments demanding linkage and linkages that resegment. No phrase carries its own message or effect. Each subjects preceding phrases to the retroactive power of its interpretive articulation and is subject to retroactive qualification in turn. For this reason, special significance attaches to the so-called "last word," a phrase which cannot of course mark or constitute a closure in and of itself, but which is linked onto (whether by socially encoded forms of silence or affirmation, gestures of boredom or changes of topic, etc.) as provisionally concluding and so retroactively delimiting a particular exchange. It is therefore material for our reading that the terminal use of the drawing-room style occurs after the rout of the Kearneys, when the linkages can be assured of affirming rather than contesting its ideological power.

—You did the *proper* thing, Holohan, said Mr. O'Madden Burke, poised upon his umbrella in approval. (*D* 149, my italics)

With his phallic umbrella,[11] finely balanced, and his previously mentioned "moral umbrella," a "magniloquent Western name," veiling his economic impotency, Burke ironically represents the paternal lawgiver as the figure of justice. Accordingly, his resumption and appropriation of the counterlegal idiom is telling. If the private, feminine world reduplicated in the public space becomes marginal, occupying a corridor or passage way and confessing its own subordination, the formal masculine world reduplicated in the Other's language is centralized, able to mediate between and dispose of alternative idioms. Here again the remarking of the symmetries reveals their underlying bias, on the basis of which Burke's pronouncement can acquire the metaleptic performativity characteristic of the law as such, i.e. the juridical force and standing to determine what has or, in Mrs. Kearney's case, does not have juridical force or standing. Whereas Mrs. Kearney is compelled to resort to prescriptive discourse, posing values and rules for group attention and challenge, Burke can afford to employ normative discourse, citing values and rules as concrete, objective facts – "the proper thing" – and thereby legitimating them. What is at stake finally in this gendered pragmatics, which is also the pragmatics of gender, is access to and control of an ethico-political metalanguage, that dimension of discourse which, in Lyotard's words, subjects all "phrases, whatever their heterogeneity might be, to a single set of stakes, justice,"[12] but whose capacity to do so is rooted in and to some degree routed by the social circumstances out of which the disputes emerge in the first place. Thus, the closure of the positive context of judgment, punctuated by Mr. Burke's ferule, opens the gap of *differend* and points to the necessity of a new articulation.

What "A Mother" offers in the way of rearticulation is a sort of poetic justice based on an allegorical subtext connected with the colonial *differend*. The immediate cause of the Kearneys' rout is the defection of Miss Healy to the camp of the organizers and artistes. Following hard upon "Ivy Day in the Committee Room," this tiny vignette of Irish betrayal is designed to recall, by way of the patronymic "Healy," the most notorious betrayal in modern Irish political history, the desertion of Parnell by a group of his disciples led by Tim Healy. Nor does the parallel stop here. Neither Mrs. Kearney's defeat nor that of Parnell actually bears on the matter of their fight. Mrs. Kearney is "condemned on all hands" for not being a lady, just as Parnell lost his place for not acting like a gentleman. Mrs. Kearney's downfall involved a transgression in and of the public–institutional space, the site of male authority, while Parnell's involved a transgression in and of the private–domestic space, the site of female authority. Finally, they occupy chiasmic positions with respect to the gendered division of discourse itself.

Mrs. Kearney assumes the partition between the spheres to be permeable even as she plays upon the governing distinction, insinuating herself the more effectively into the business of concert arrangement and promotion by adopting an ingratiatingly domestic air. When Mr. Holohan cries, "I thought you were a lady" (*D* 149), he is seizing precisely upon her apparent amenability to the unspoken rules of social behavior. He is saying, in effect, "I thought you understood and worked within the gender divisions, taking those advantages reserved to you and accepting with grace the (greater) constraints placed upon you." In other words, Mrs. Kearney stands accused, however implicitly, of wanting it both ways, of acceding to the system of (gender) justice and so the justice of the system when it serves her ends and rejecting them when it does not. Her situation reveals, if you will, the other side of the *differend* and exemplifies the hegemonic force of positive juridical codes. Because such a code necessarily combines at different levels a symmetrical distribution of rights, considerations, and obligations with their asymmetrical design, and vice versa, it offers relatively excluded or disempowered groups and individuals a real incentive for cooperating in their own subordination, i.e. forestalling the possibility of outright oppression. Relative disempowerment is, after all, another name for limited franchise. But occasional complicity with the system of equity can be held hostage against future criticism thereof. The contextual shifting between assent and dissent, however vital to the aspirations of those excluded, is likely to strike more privileged eyes and to be framed in more influential discourse as cynical opportunism, a mode of behavior whose self-interested inconsistency violates not only the rule of law in dispute but the higher standards of justice to which the excluded groups themselves implicitly or explicitly appeal.

Parnell, conversely, assumed the partition between the public and the private spheres to be impermeable, even as he repeatedly broke the wall by his own actions.[13] Confident that the boys' club rules of political engagement prohibited his enemies from turning personal scandal to partisan advantage, he used his British mistress as an intermediary with Gladstone, and, more seriously, purchased the silence of her husband by twice supporting him in parliamentary elections, against the stated principles and best interests of the nationalist cause – the second time running him against a fervid nationalist in Galway, despite Captain O'Shea's unwillingness to take the party pledge.[14] Because Parnell's nationalist colleagues, including Tim Healy, rallied around their leader almost instinctively in the first blush of the divorce scandal, their subsequent decision to jettison him could not be set forth or defended solely on the basis of sexual morality. They framed a supplementary argument for doing so around Parnell's *active* infringement of the segregation of private and public life, thereby ratifying his own *stated* assumptions. Healy specifically complained that in the Galway election Parnell "was prostituting a seat in Parliament to the interests of his own private intrigue."[15] It will be noted that Healy reverses the customary direction of the metaphor of prostitution: instead of the corruption of personal affects and carnal desires by their subjection to public interest and exchange, the traditionally feminine application, Healy speaks to the corruption of public interest and exchange by its subjection to personal affects and carnal desires. Ideologically (if not logically) congruent with this line of attack was the alternative gambit of sparing Parnell direct criticism by focusing the umbrage and vitriol of Irish popular opinion upon his paramour, Katherine O'Shea. By installing her as "the werewolf woman of Irish Politics,"[16] the nationalist press made her the symbol of the more generalized threat that the feminine realm of "private intrigue" and affiliation was taken to pose for the settled oppositions of the masculine political order: us versus them, British versus Irish, negotiation versus compromise, liberal versus nationalist, individual versus common ends, and so forth. Paradoxically, however, these assaults on Mrs. O'Shea, far from taking some pressure off Parnell, combined with Healy's more direct approach to discredit the chief even further by *feminizing* him. They implied a view of Parnell as henpecked, uxorious, even emasculated, unable to control the private affective side of himself, as evidenced by his destructive passion for Mrs. O'Shea, and unable likewise to contain the private, affective side of his life, as evidenced by his supposed susceptibility to her political views and machinations.

A certain symmetry and reciprocity specific to these patriarchal criteria of definition and assessment thus reasserts itself. But it does not do so to the ultimate benefit of the patriarchs of Dublin. On the contrary, with the loss of someone like Parnell to the home rule fight, or the efficient, knowledgeable Mrs. Kearney to its cultural equivalent, the masculinist division of sexual labor and legitimacy could only serve to prolong the subordinate and, as Shari Benstock has noted, the feminized status of the Irishman vis-à-vis his British rulers.[17] In other words, patriarchal law in a colonial context militates at some point *against* the colonized patriarchy, which is always *also* in the position of the feminine. As we have seen, this gender inflection of colonial relations was more than usually explicit and more than usually entrenched in the case of Ireland. Under these circumstances, positive gender justice can give rise to its *own differend*. That is to say, the disposition of claims will be based on criteria of definition and assessment that have already been exposed to the colonizer's re-mark (of male as female, head as heart, culture as nature, public as private, disinterested ends as irrational whims, universal perspective as local preference, etc., distinctions/ displacements unexceptionably germane to the English portrayal of Ireland). As such, the strictest proportionality the colonized patriarchy can here produce will necessarily be disfigured, even on its own terms.

The spiral of imposition is that much more involved when one considers that the modern, intensively gendered, economically oriented public/private schism addressed herein is not itself of native Irish growth, but is rather a concomitant of an increasingly claustrophobic nuclear family structure which responded, at least in part, to the threat posed to patriarchal hegemony by class divisions and employment patterns specific, in the first instance, to British industrial capitalism. This schism, accordingly, sustains the ascendancy of Mr. Holohan and his kind only by way of its implication in a competitive, materialistic value system antithetical to their stated beliefs and personal interests, exploitative of their collective energies, and inimical to their nationalist aspirations. The control they ultimately wield on the local stage reflects in its manner and reinforces in its effects their impotence in the larger context. The emblem of this castration is Mr. Holohan's limp, which makes for the "devious courses" of his proceedings (*D* 144). In this instance, the genre of law is not merely subject to but actually approaches the law of genre: it is itself doubly inscribed.

Is this double scene an enabling condition of Joyce's *écriture* "femaline" in *Finnegans Wake*, a writing beyond patriarchy? It may be. But it may also be the occasion of ever more subtle reinscriptions of the patriarchy in response to an even more pressing anxiety over gender distinctions. Indeed, it would be theoretically naive to expect the disruption of the logic of identity in one sphere of rhetoric or social practice to have a homologous effect upon another, even if that effect were to be the disruption of homology itself. Internally divided by definition, the movement of (self-) difference, or *différance*, fixes hierarchical oppositions, seals taxonomic categories, delimits integral entities, even as it destabilizes, relativizes, and compromises them. Recentering is thus a constitutive moment, an *essential* possibility, in the decentered economy of social and semiotic relations. Joyce's position as a colonized male intellectual, subject as it was to a certain inflection or re-mark of sexual otherness, did help to facilitate an assault upon traditional representations of masculinity and, by inference, the masculinist system of representation, but because it failed to encourage an equally profound assault upon traditional conceptions of femininity, it also helped to facilitate a certain recentering of the masculine as the element capable of absorbing and synthesizing opposed gender associations.

The political allegory of "A Mother" affords a telling instance of these coherently contradictory tendencies in Joyce's writing. Miss Healy's decision to forsake Miss Kearney is the symbolic trigger connecting a squalid affair of sexual bias and recrimination with what Joyce saw as the great national tragedy of modern Ireland and implicating, in the process, the existing code of gender justice as a whole. The incident thus constitutes the linchpin of the story's self-conscious sexual politics, which fall within the penumbra of feminism and anticipate in the realistic dimension Joyce's later subversion of phallocentric literary forms.

But the incident also conveys certain antifeminist connotations. It sunders one of the very few female friendships actually depicted in *Dubliners*. And in thus closing this story's cycle of events, the incident lends retrospective significance to the failure of female camaraderie at the outset, where the sniping of Mrs. Kearney's girlhood friends, which precipitates her rather soulless marriage, is repaid by her similarly vindictive accounts of its material comforts:

However, when she drew near the limit and her friends began to loosen their tongues about her she silenced them by marrying Mr. Kearney, who was a bootmaker on Ormond Quay. (*D* 137)

Every year in the month of July Mrs. Kearney found occasion to say to some friend: – My good man is packing us off to Skerries for a few weeks. (*D* 137)

The undercurrent of antagonism among women in this story, beyond complicating and perhaps diluting the case for gender injustice, calls to mind how rare female and cross-gender friendships are in Joyce, pointing up his own perpetuation of a sexual stereotype with particular relevance to the gendered allocation of authority that he dissects.

Incorporating friendly feelings toward romantically cathected women is something of a rite of passage for Joycean alter egos, an advance in emotional development portending a decisive change in their life experience. After Gretta Conroy's climactic revelation, "a strange friendly pit for her entered Gabriel's soul" (*D* 222), preparing him for his ambiguous "journey westward." As Stephen Dedalus makes ready for his own voyage outward in *A Portrait*, his tortured, self-reflexive feelings about E— C— resolve themselves into a novel sensation of fellowship.

Now I call that friendly, don't you?
Yes, I liked her today. A little or much? Don't know. I liked her and it seems a new feeling to me. (*AP* 252)

On neither occasion, however, is the woman shown to have a corresponding propensity or aptitude for this type of agape.

As for women's friendships, Bloom punningly opines that they are stand-ins for their erotic attachments to men and are duly extinguished by them.

Be sure now and write to me. And I'll write to you. Now won't you? Molly and Josie Powell. Till Mr. Right comes along then meet once in a blue moon. Tableau ... Picking holes in each other's appearance. You're looking splendid. Sister souls. Showing their teeth at one another. How many have you left? Wouldn't lend each other a pinch of salt. (*U* 13.813–20)

Joyce not only supplies proleptic evidence for this view in the mean-spirited rivalry of Cissy, Edy, and Gerty for Bloom's good opinion, but subsequently has Molly confirm Bloom's account of her relationship with Josie Powell and then universalize, from her domestic isolation, the unsociability of the female sex:

you're always in great humour she said yes because it grigged her because she knew what it meant because I used to tell her a good bit of what went on between us not all but just enough to make her mouth water but that wasn't my fault she didn't darken the door much after we were married I wonder what she's got like now after living with that dotty husband of hers she had her face beginning to look drawn and run down the last time I saw her. (*U* 18.213–19)

they have friends they can talk to we've none either he wants what he won't get or it's some woman ready to stick her knife in you I hate that in women no wonder they treat us the way they do we are a dreadful lot of bitches I suppose it's all the troubles we have makes us so snappy. (*U* 18.1456–60)

The conclusion to this interlude suggests a fractiousness born of oppression; the politically charged word "troubles," in particular, links the ill will among women and the similarly internecine enmity of the Irish. But the narrative situation and discursive sentiments represented in *Ulysses*, as in *Dubliners*, conspire to leave the impression that friendship among women is a woefully uncultivated art, if not a contradiction in terms.

Jacques Derrida has pointed out that "all the great ethico-politico-philosophical discourses on friendship maintain a double exclusion" of friendship between women and between men and women. "These exclusions of the feminine," Derrida writes, "would have some relation to the movement that has always politicized the model of friendship at the very moment one tries to remove the model from an integral politicization."[18] This movement involves precisely the division of sexual authority we have been examining. Whereas love has been seen to annul the distance between people and so is associated with the internal or domestic space assigned to women, and politics has been seen to separate people under the sign of self-interest and is associated with the masculine public space, friendship has been represented as maintaining a distance, hence an individual autonomy and dignity, within interpersonal union. Friendship thus represents an emotional state that mediates and in a sense compre-hends the private ties that bind and the public alliances that serve, and the tendency of "ethico-politico-philosophical discourses" to reserve the capacity for true friendship to men is clearly a powerful patriarchal strategy. By conflating the gendered division of social authority and labor in a single term and identifying that term exclusively with man, these discourses maintain sexual difference on a bias, installing the masculine as both center and circumference and the feminine as the masculine *manqué*. Insofar as Joyce implicitly underwrites that tradition, he not only deconstructs but reconstructs the gendered division of social space and discourse, and to that extent, he is identifiable not only with ALP, releasing the poly-semantic, polysexual potential of language, but also with O'Madden Burke, controlling and adjudicating still gendered idioms.

GNOMON

Joyce's handling of the Parnell allegory in "A Mother" crystallizes a double-sided sexual politics that is at work in the stylistic organization of *Dubliners* as a whole. As I have argued in another context, the polyphonic mobility of the narrative voice in *Dubliners* marks and marks itself off from the strict ideological rigidities of the characters portrayed. The individual Dubliners are shown to be confined and controlled by competing yet complicit species of patriarchal discourse – a church-ridden feudalism and a state-engineered commercialism – of which their own distinctive voices are so many strains or variations. The implied narrator, by contrast, displays no such circumscribed idiom. His style might best be characterized as a capable negativity, a privileged movement of difference; even as it mimes the assorted voices of Dublin, it sets them off as deviations from an invisible norm.[19] In thus refusing the system of limits that a signature style entails, the Joycean narrator, it could be argued, offers symbolic resistance to the paired patriarchal orders constraining Irish subjectivity, beginning with the cell from which both grow, the institution of stratified sexual division. Moving in and out of discrete and decidably gendered accents, idioms, mind sets, and evaluative stances, classifying and criticizing each by way of the others, the narrative presence comes to embody polyphony as freedom from particular sociosexual inscription. But as Joyce himself indicates in "A Mother," such triumphant neutrality is the hinge upon which patriarchal gender relations turn and, as such, is always already both masculine and masculinist. Indeed, in its demiurgical self-effacement, its simultaneous immanence in and withdrawal from the viewpoints represented, the narrative voice of *Dubliners* can be equally seen to express Joyce's lingering attachment to the aesthetics of transcendence he affected "as a young man." It can be seen, that is, to instantiate Stephen Dedalus' Flaubertian idea of the properly aesthetic mode of enunciation: "The artist like the god of creation remains within or behind or beyond or above his handiwork, invisible, refined out of existence, indifferent, paring his fingernails" (*AP* 215). Such a creative approach necessarily retails the founding principles of the gender system: separation, subordination, objectification, mastery. Blind to the depth and complexity of his investment in patriarchal structures, Joyce deploys in the telling a juridical syntax that he discredits in the tale, representing gender claims from a position ostensibly beyond gendered motives, prejudices, and limitations. *Dubliners* thus enacts a performative contradiction that simultaneously enables and impedes what we might term Joyce's emergent feminism by allowing, on the one hand, for the deconstruction of a specifically Irish brand of phallogocentrism with its own tools and, on the other, for a reconstruction or perpetuation of that order, the effective existence of which consists precisely *in those tools*, in oppositional structures and hierarchical practices, whether they be enrolled under the law or in its critique.

In the next chapter, we shall see Joyce begin a movement away from the aesthetics of transcendence and toward a resolution, always necessarily imperfect, of the performative contradiction it entails, a movement toward the sovereign surrender of the authorial ethos of mastery.

CHAPTER 3

Dread desire: imperialist abjection in "Giacomo Joyce"

I

Unpublished in the author's lifetime, *Giacomo Joyce*[1] was probably unintended for publication at any time, not only because it is so fragmentary, a mere sketchbook of the artist,[2] or because it is so intimate, a lover's diary wherein Joyce confesses in a less than foreign language, but because it is so ideologically uncensored, constituting, as Vicki Mahaffey has amply demonstrated, a gallery of invidious portraitures (of women, Jews, Near Eastern peoples, Italians, etc.) which Joyce would dramatically revise and rework in his later writing,[3] thanks in large part to the ethico-political understanding he achieved in living this interlude and composing this artifact. The one provision Joyce did make for the audience of history was to go back to this self-indulgent production and enclose, by way of the wry title and a single, profoundly leavening interpolation, the beginnings of a critical reassessment. The technical innovations that Joyce introduced as a function of this effort simultaneously define *Giacomo Joyce* as a transitional stage in his development as an artist and a somewhat tortured reaction to a moment of political as well as emotional delirium, an attempt to expose and situate his dalliance with some of the deadliest impulses of modern European culture. Thus, the often facile equation between the formal/stylistic experimentation of (post-)Modernist writing and its presumed political engagement or radicalism – epitomized in the phrase "the Revolution of the Word" – is to a degree borne out in Joyce's case by the creative history of this largely overlooked interstitial document. To adapt Roland Barthes's terminology, Joyce translated *Giacomo Joyce* from a rudely formed work to a willfully multivalent text for a specifically ethico-political reason, the desire to do justice.[4]

In this respect, *Giacomo Joyce* encapsulates the trajectory of Joyce's

career from the minimalist realism of the early epiphanies to the
carnivalesque pyrotechnics of *Finnegans Wake*. And if the last and
most involved of Joyce's productions attempts to explore the ethico-
political workings of the dream state, a dream coterminous with
Joyce's own unconscious, *Giacomo Joyce* might well lay claim to being
what Freud called "the navel of the dream," a super-dense yet
supposedly unimportant textual site whose very opacity and marginality are a paradoxical testament to its profound connection with
everything else in the life of the subject.[5] The navel of the dream is the
often disregarded or discounted nexus of the dream text that plunges
into the entire chain of significant, unconscious associations in which
the psyche itself consists. Accordingly, if *Giacomo Joyce* seems a rather
slender document upon which to hang the analysis to come, or a
rather obscure document (in every sense) to occupy a central place in
this study, I would urge readers to consider, first, the slender threads
upon which psychoanalysis hangs – rat fantasies, wolf dreams, Irma's
throat, etc. – and second, how the end game paradigms of justice
critiqued above come to grief upon unassimilable, distinctively
minoritarian, apparently trivial differences whose very exclusion
transforms them into the defining moments of the paradigm itself.
Whether undertaken across a body of national literature or within
the œuvre of an individual author, the process of canonization aspires
to this static condition of justice, erecting monuments of literary
value, distinction, and regularity upon forgotten, nearly illegible
remainders. *Giacomo Joyce* is *the* remainder in Joyce studies, the
"literature" we Biddy Dorans have only recently begun to "look at"
and scarcely begun to appreciate.

Appended at some indeterminable point, in an anonymous hand,
the title *Giacomo Joyce* shifts the referential burden of the sketchbook
from the model rendered, the unidentified Amalia Popper, to the
rendering mind.[6] It asks the reader to consider the source, if you will,
of these aesthetic images and ethico-political judgments – James
Joyce, to be sure, with all of the literary weight that name carries, but
James Joyce as an imaginary or would-be Casanova.[7] His early
method of characterization, fashioning fictive protagonists out of
diminished and diluted versions of himself, is here recalled and
reversed. Joyce casts a recognizably factual image of himself in a
fictive or at least fantastical light as a way of ironizing his own
sentiments and perceptions without pretending to contemplate them
altogether objectively and without renouncing his connection with or

responsibility for them. With this title, he thus executes a double ethical design, retracting and yet standing to account for his feeling and convictions, bringing himself *to* justice even as he brings himself to *do* justice. In so doing, Joyce enacts his own conversion from the aesthetic of transcendence announced by Stephen in *A Portrait*, a vision of the artist dwelling both within and beyond his work, to the aesthetics of finitude intimated by Stephen in *Ulysses*, a vision of the artist materially inscribed in his work, unable to master fully "the wisdom he has written or ... the laws he has revealed" (*U* 9.477–8).

Even more significant, for our purposes, is Joyce's addition of the long scene in "the narrow Parisian room" (*GJ* 45) after the fair copy of the sketchbook was completed and probably over six years later.[8] The factual and phantasmatic material Joyce contrived to squeeze into the only available space in the manuscript reflects his subsequent change of attitude and is associated, as he explicitly notes, with his great antihierarchical epic, *Ulysses*. It would seem that Joyce retrospectively incorporates his distanced, ironical perspective on the experience *Giacomo* represents as a part of that experience, interrupting the chronological sequence of recorded impressions shortly before the resolution in order to disclose another, unsuspected teleology. In this move, we see foreshadowed the recursive narrative method of *Finnegans Wake*, in which the competing interpretations surrounding the dream letter (the *Wake* itself) recirculate as effects or variations of the letter itself and so disrupt that unitary progression of events upon which all authoritative world views finally rest.

More specifically, this belated and anachronistic interpolation links a reappraisal of Joyce's relationship with Amalia to an analogous questioning of his relationship with Ireland, especially his quixotic role as the spiritual–intellectual savior of his people:

It is the other. She. Gogarty came yesterday to be introduced. *Ulysses* is the reason. Symbol of the intellectual conscience ... Ireland then? And the husband? ... Why are we left here? ... Intellectual symbol of my race. Listen! ... She speaks ... Voice of wisdom ... voice I never heard. (*GJ* 45)

Furthermore, by staging these twinned reappraisals as an indirect response to the fanfare surrounding *Ulysses*, Joyce highlights and transvaluates the numerous sentiments expressed in *Giacomo Joyce* which are retailed, modified, decisively ironized, and even defeated in his later work. He sets up a metaleptic reversal of present and future contexts, the surrounding discourse of *Giacomo* being transformed into an allusive field by the name "Ulysses," which it everywhere anticipates. The overall impact of this prospective re-vision, this pre-post-erous gesture, is a sort of double textuality: the poisonous writing of Joyce's narcissistic desire for Amalia Popper is supplemented by his antidotal re-reading, which takes some account of her positive otherness, acknowledges, however obscurely, her separate perspective, agency, and value, and, in the process, alters the internal design of the work so as to bring out the systematic stifling and gradual emergence of her voice. The rhetorical violence of *Giacomo Joyce* is by no means effaced in this manner, but it is theatricalized by reference to a future in which Joyce wrote in deliberate opposition to this sort of sexual, racial, and cultural imperialism. The text thus settles down rather uncomfortably between the contradictory postures it adopts and the more complete political evolution it predicts.

The double valence of *Giacomo Joyce* bears the imprint of Joyce's borderline cultural status, his occupation of a no man's land between a majority, aggressively imperialistic culture, whose language he spoke, literature he read, and liberal individualistic ethos he affected, and a minority, aggressively irredentist culture he called his own, and also between positions of relative empowerment and disempower-ment with regard to European culture in general, as defined by a complex of gender and class determinations. If, as Homi Bhaba has written, the enunciative position of the colonial estate is one of "hybridity,"[9] where the positions of authority are themselves part of a process of ambivalent identification, then the enunciative condition of a metropolitan colonialism such as Joyce's might be termed radically hybrid, i.e. neither marginal nor normative as ordinarily conceived, but on the margin between the margin and the main-stream. This *radically* marginal status animated Joyce with impulses and identifications associated with both an authorized, normative subjectivity and a subordinated, pathologized other, allowing the prejudicial attitudes cited above to act as an instrument for sorting out his warring identifications and clarifying his claims to social entitlement. But this dual experience also came to render those states of centrality and marginality peculiarly negotiable, permeable, and symbiotic for Joyce, conditioning his critical insight into the hierarchical and discriminatory arrangement of modern socio-cultural practice. That is to say, paradoxically, that Joyce's initial susceptibility to the prevailing strains of modernist bigotry (sexism, racism, Orientalism, intellectual elitism, etc.) was part of a larger economy of experience that produced his eventual challenge to the underlying structures of such discourse.[10]

At perhaps no other point in his life, however, was Joyce so liable to lapse into the discourse of patriarchal imperialism as in his relationship with his Triestine student, Amalia Popper. The comparative social authority he enjoyed as a mature, Gentile, Western, pseudo-Aryan, northern European pedagogue confronting a young, Jewish, Orientalized, southern European female student was further reinforced by his role as a *de facto* agent of the strongest empire on earth, toward which he nonetheless remained, ethnically and confessionally, a subaltern. As a newly minted *"maestro inglese"* (*GJ* 13), subjective and objective genitive, Joyce found himself suddenly deputized to advance the sprawling hegemony of British culture to an already colonized people whom he characterizes, without apparent irony, as "a multitude of prostrate bugs [that] await a national deliverance" (*GJ* 22). The latter phrase effects a double objectification that labors to render Joyce's own subdominant ethnicity less obviously relevant. Embracing both Italians and Jews in its implicit field of reference, the phrase takes the act of stereotyping, the elision or disregard of individual differences, to a supra-racial level, yielding a new and still more indiscriminate other. Inasmuch as discourse is no less performative than descriptive, the phrase simultaneously illustrates Joyce's double empowerment as an officially recognized "subject who knows." Deemed a *"maestro inglese"* by Amalia's father, in a classic patriarchal transfer of power, Joyce is in a position to define as well as instruct his charge, to define her in the course of his instruction and to instruct her on the basis of his definition. In this overdetermined political context, even Amalia's evident superiority in class or economic terms does not act as a simple counterforce in her relationship with Joyce, at least not directly, but combines with his own acute professional frustration at this point in time to challenge his rather ambiguously sanctioned *amour propre* and, in so doing, to intensify his will to possess her – intellectually, emotionally, aesthetically, and sexually.[11]

The key to the unreconstructed modernism of the main body of *Giacomo Joyce* is a highly politicized, characteristically liberal species of abjection which I take to form the common bond between Orientalist/colonial and sexist/patriarchal discourse. While my formulation of abjection does not conform precisely to its well-known source, Kristeva's psychoanalytic construct, it does designate a condition that derives from and recalls the primordial emergence of subjectivity that she delineates – a secondary abjection, if you like.

Before proceeding with my reading of the text, then, I should like to set forth this ethico-political extension of the theory of abjection. This task cannot be done in haste since it involves nothing less than an articulation of desire in its psychoanalytic dimension with the question or problem of justice.

II

In *Powers of Horror*, Kristeva defines the experience of the abject as that which "preserves what existed in the archaism of the pre-objectal relationships, in the immemorial violence with which the body becomes separated from [an-other, a-mother] body in order to be."[12] In other words, abjection sustains a remnant of the "pre-objectal" in the form of a radical ambivalence lived by the emergent subject as s/he passes from the Imaginary state of mother–child union into the Symbolic order of sexual difference and social interaction.[13] Driven by a sense of lack or doubt regarding its own state of satisfaction, the emergent subject repels the maternal body in order to clear a fully differentiated space for itself and to secure a certain measure of self-sufficiency. Such doubt, by the way, is indistinguishable from the nascent subject's perception of the mother's lack or desire, which in turn allows the paternal function to be valorized, the law of castration internalized, and a gender identity assumed.

Thereafter, everything that speaks of the infant's originary attachment to the phallic mother, which is to say the very materiality of its existence, resonates at some level of an immemorial loss of individuation and hence the threat of death.[14] Precisely because it is irreducible, however, this immersion of the infant in the maternal realm can be neither denied nor dissolved; it is rather to be disguised through the imaginary construction of a body conformable with the requirement of stable, coherent self-identity, a body that has been abstracted, purified, distanced from its material embarrassment, what Kristeva calls the "clean body."[15] Accordingly, the infant begins to consolidate its subjectivity by expelling from its perimeter or body ego those physical realities that mark its palpable interchange or confusion with the outside:

The objects generating abjection – food, feces, urine, vomit, tears, spit – inscribe the body in those surfaces, hollows, crevices, orifices, which will later become erotogenic zones... [on] the space between two corporeal surfaces. These corporeal sites provide a boundary or threshold between what is inside the body, and thus a part of the subject, and what is outside the body and thus an object for the subject.[16]

This expulsion occurs through a denigration of the bodily processes – as odious, disgusting, or somehow beneath the self – and indeed of the body-as-process, the body as unsublimated, intractable flux. On the other hand, the maternal body remains a primary if imperfect repository of pleasure for the emerging subject and, as such, the object of a nostalgia no less powerful than the repulsion it attends. Accordingly, everything that speaks of the subject's irreducible attachment to the maternal–material dimension also resonates, at some level, of the extinction of difference and the pain it entails, and hence of the promise of paradise.[17] In the presence of borderline stimuli, then, disgust and desire at once reinforce and dissimulate one another, blending into the play of abjection. For this reason, "the unconscious contents remain excluded but in a strange fashion; not radically enough to allow for a secure differentiation between subject and object, yet clearly enough for a defensive position to be established – one that implies a refusal but also a sublimating elaboration."[18]

Once the infant is channeled into the Symbolic order, the dynamic of abjection does not dissipate altogether, but unfolds in reverse order. The psyche is no longer primarily engaged in the production of identity through (self-) fission, though of course this dynamic is never really finalized. Its more pressing task at this stage is to maintain the integrity, consistency, agency, and self-referential capacity of selfhood against an always possible subversion, dissolution, or fragmentation. As Kristeva notes, the child's originary separation "represents a violent, clumsy breaking away with a constant risk of falling back under the sway of a power as secure as it is shifting."[19] Under this threat, the subject no longer abjects that which seems stifling in its intimacy but rather that which seems threatening in its alterity. Put another way, secondary abjection does not react to/against the zone of permeability or indifference preceding the abjected relationship, but to/against certain sets of distinctions (gender, race, class, etc.) that work to reproduce that relationship in the broader social context.

Even this formulation, however, is insufficiently precise. For the fundamental tension between self-identity and self-division is not reduced or clarified in the move from original to secondary abjection, but is simultaneously diffused and complicated through a distribution of the ambivalence across different layers of (un)consciousness. Secondary abjection in fact consists in a *conscious* reaction to/against a socially determined set of subject–object distinctions and grows out of an *unconscious* recognition that such diacritical markers are structurally unstable, i.e. susceptible, as a condition of their existence, of collapsing once again into a zone of indifference or interchangeability.

As a result, while the experience of abjection alters from the primary to the secondary phase, owing to a change in subject position and thus perspective, there is a good deal of overlap in the sites and catalysts of the experience. The same borderline phenomena abjected for their intimate otherness to the subject-in-formation will be abjected for their estranged proximity to the subject-in-crisis. But because secondary abjection operates within the Symbolic order of meaningful distinctions, the range of phenomena occasioning the experience and the ideological currents giving it specific dimension do draw upon a much more extensive and ramified social economy. Broader political and cultural attitudes and affiliations are brought to bear in determining what Kristeva calls "those stifled aspirations toward the other as prohibited as it [*sic*] is desired."[20] Nevertheless, to abject this broader secondary material, such as gender or racial differences, is precisely to identify them with the originally abjected somatic stratum, to repeat the archaic experience in the new.

How are this socially instantiated multiplicity and this psychodynamic tendency to repeat interrelated? Or, to put it another way, how do we account for the abject in its endless variety and its monotonous regularity? An effective method, in my view, involves reading the relationship between the psychic process of abjection and the social problem of justice. More specifically, abjection might be taken up as the affective condition under which justice becomes both *necessary* as a critical lever or metavalue and *impossible* as a definitive principle or achieved finality.

Abjection is, first of all, the crucible of privilege. Inasmuch as authority and subordination are inescapable facts of social life, abjection constitutes a universal yet variable bottleneck of personal growth. Everyone must pass through it in order to participate, in the fashion and to the extent that they are enabled to do so, in a social schema predicated upon the myth of individuation, the sovereign self-equivalence of the subject. That is, the ordeal through which the sense of self-possession is attained reflects the disparate modes and degrees of autonomy, agency, etc. that different societies prescribe or proscribe, penalize and reward, for differently marked and positioned subjects. As such, the process will be molded by the same socially encoded contingencies, such as racial, sexual, and ethnic distinctions, which become, in the secondary phase of abjection, the text of the experience. Indeed, in one of those pre-post-erous reversals to which postmodern philosophy has so sensitized us, primary abjection turns out to be always already mediated by secondary abjection: in the first place, the fundamental ambivalence of the child takes its shape and direction from the more complexly politicized ambivalence of his/her authority figures and role models; in the second place, the originary ambivalence of the child only imprints upon later life through the vehicle of unconscious "screen memories," whose relative construction/displacement of the past likewise takes its shape and direction from the more complexly politicized ambivalence of the adult world. Primary and secondary ambivalence thus form a recursive loop; they vary with differences in the social locations of the subject and mold, through a kind of deferred action, the subject's estimation of those differences.

So construed, abjection represents the enabling underside of the double bind/double bottom of liberal jurisprudence. As my earlier discussion indicates, democratic ideology embraces at least a theoretical commitment to the potential reversibility of all social and political determinations. Under this regime, individual subjects are placed within the Symbolic order as so many possible sites and angles for its ongoing interrogation, reappropriation and, thus, revision. The positive law of this order – the assigned values organizing the social ties – remains at once the agency and the object of legitimation. Abjection, for its part, sets an affective limit to the interpretability of the law, at least in the first instance, and so to its variability as well. Through the recursive movement of first- and second-stage ambivalence, an economy of desire primordial to subjectivity itself invests and stabilizes the specific articulation of assigned values and cultural constraints in force at any given point. Marinated in both the memory and the threat of abjection, the prevailing marks of positive and negative distinction, mastery and subordination, belonging and exclusion all secrete a significance far in excess of any practical realities they might otherwise advance or reflect. They hold the psychic equivalent of the power of life and death, the affective charge attendant upon the anticipated emergence or engulfment of the ego. It is perfectly coherent with this logic that Stephen Dedalus' dunking in the square ditch should have precipitated his fantasies of imminent demise. A social reduction to the status of abject materiality is always a question of life and death for the signifying subject.

But the signifying subject only subsists insofar as it is always already a signified subject, the bearer of a more or less individuated and hierarchized sociosymbolic position, i.e. a more or less privileged ensemble of differently, often contradictorally, ranked and identified attributes, attachments, associations, and, most importantly, idioms or modes of enunciation, all of which serve to determine the specific qualities and degrees of autonomy and self-possession each subject is prepared to enjoy. These established social distinctions are likewise routed through the prospect of abjection. In their joint role as social determinants and social rankings, the assigned values and dis- criminating marks of which I have spoken render more or less accessible varying opportunities for and ranges of personal sov- ereignty, historical agency, cultural initiative, and interpersonal mastery, so that the social identities thus formed are by definition unequal in their command of the acknowledged evidence or stuff of subjectivity, unequal therefore not just as already constituted subjects but in the kind of constitutive, which is to say socially approved, claims to subjectivity that they have been entitled to make; and so unequal finally in their relation to that Imaginary zone shadowing and embarrassing ego formation, the abject. Because disparate cultural preferences and idioms, for example, have taken on social meaning in terms of their supposed association with or dissociation from the material or somatic stratum, they have tended to mark not just differently ranked subject positions, but different potentials for the achievement of subject positionality itself. Thus, the justification of discrimination and brutality against certain groups on the grounds that they are not really human is not a casual rationalization, but a systematic rationalization, i.e. a rationalization consistent with the logic of social difference in modern liberal societies.

It is for this reason that a *differend* is never simply a neutral proposition, an affair of mutual incomprehension, but rather designates a dispute that must be conducted exclusively in the idiom of one of the parties because the other's standing in and purchase on the Symbolic order is insufficient to make itself heard, to "phrase" its claim or grievance. It is also for this reason, however, that differently placed subjects, while bound alike to accede to the prevailing Symbolic order as the price of whatever subject-function they possess, have significantly disparate stakes in reproducing or contesting that order, reproducing or contesting not just the specific means or marks of social distinction but the logic or machinery of distinction itself. The power and purchase to be forfeited by the subject upon any radical break with this law are fractionally withheld in various respects from properly enrolled subjects, generating a profound sense of alienation that is the precondition of any full-blown cultural resistance. The foreclosure of language known as psychosis, for instance, constitutes a refusal to enlist in the prevailing Symbolic order and typically denies the individual in question the opportunity to occupy or achieve positions of authority and privilege; but these same opportunities are fractionally and sometimes substantially denied properly enrolled subjects, owing to the ostensible variance of their accent, diction, phraseology, idiolect, etc. from some imaginary norm or ideal, owing, that is, to the *particular mode* of their inscription in the Symbolic. That is to say, their proper enrollment in the Symbolic order counts against them, remains in its very propriety improper, a circumstance of radical dislocation.

The potentially revolutionary force of such dislocation has important theoretical as well as practical implications. Even as the liberal ideal of justice remains tethered to the body of law it would exceed, taking its definition at any given point from the principles implicit therein, the abject, its enabling other, is the site of a certain slippage in the positive symbolic law that it would stabilize and enforce, a point of self-subversion. The *differend* that marks the impossibility of ultimately achieving justice always produces an indefinable "feeling" of wrong, and the reason this "feeling" remains indefinable is that the *impropriety* to which it responds, the nullification of the grieving subject's "phrase" or idiom, is an effect of that subject's *proper* or mandated position within the Symbolic order. As such, this mute "feeling" is nothing other than the displaced voice of abjection, which exerts a steady counterpressure on the status quo. That is to say, the "feeling" produced by the *differend* may be indefinable within the juridical phrase regimen, but by bringing psychoanalytic discourse to bear, we can understand this feeling in

terms of the abject, which Kristeva characterizes as "an effect and
not yet a sign."[21]

At certain points then, the profoundly conservative dynamic of
secondary abjection can be seen to feed into the counterfactual
dynamic of liberal jurisprudence and so to further the alteration of
the very law that it otherwise enforces. Not surprisingly, this entire
interplay transpires along the psychic border that joins and divides
the signifying subject and the signified subject, the first moving to
transcend his place in the social order by asserting control over its
language, the second remaining immanent to the social order in
being marked by its language.

The law of subject formation in post-Enlightenment political
culture calls for consolidating a transcendent core of autonomous self-
referential identity by expelling from its boundaries material–
corporeal process and particularity, upon which the subject nonetheless continues to draw, regarding them as its property. The subject
is at once severed from its (maternal) cause and set above its own
(material) condition and is thereby outfitted to attain to a free and
equal status under law. In a parallel movement to a contradictory
destination, social hierarchies take hold through the stronger or
weaker associations of different social groups and their telltale traits
or signifiers with the consolidated or expelled aspects of the self
respectively: transcendent reason and its effects on one side, corporeal
immanence and its affects on the other. Thus, the stereotyped social
image of subaltern constituencies figures an immediate connection
with the material–body stratum rather than or *in addition to* an
achieved separation from it and so confesses a differential continuity
between the thinking self and its bodily alterity that normative myths
of subjectivity are specifically designed to repress. Furthermore, since
these liberal myths define subjectivity in strictly monological terms,
as that which is self-actuating, self-contained, and self-coincident, the
perceived hybridity of the subaltern, its either–and intimacy with the
corporeal realm, counts ideologically as a total immersion therein, a
profound lapse into the heteronomous conditions of materiality.
Symbolically overembodied, Other-people pass imperceptibly into
other than people.

The ironic corollary, then, of the democratic injunction against
stratifying subjects as subjects is the persistence of social hierarchy
through a relegation of certain groups and individuals to the domain
of pre- or para- or nonsubjectivity. If the liberal metavalues of

equality and freedom, unhinged from any moral or metaphysical finality, can serve the disempowered as an ever-present court of appeal against discriminatory practices, the liberal humanist category of subjectivity can serve the hegemonic social formation as a device, a sort of sluice gate, for controlling access to these same metavalues and thereby denying or deferring in particular cases entitlements that continue to be promulgated generally. Couched in the terms of our juridical model, this is an instance where the double bottom of justice, which permits ever more radical challenges upon the biases implicit in the positive law, encounters the double bind of justice, which is that the positive law ultimately demarcates the condition of each challenge. Here, the radical potential that liberal ideology fosters for contesting the status quo, the extension of innate political rights to all persons, calls forth and coincides with the selective extenuation of the status of personhood.

The discourses of modernity, ranging from the nascent human sciences of anthropology, sexology, and ethnography to the pervasive bourgeois ideal of social respectability to the neo-Kantian aesthetics embraced at different points by Pound, Eliot, Lewis, T. E. Hulme, and Joyce himself, collaborate in enshrining a neutral, transparent, disembodied rationality as the essence of humanity itself, hence the preferred instrument and arbiter of our cognitive and pragmatic norms.[22] And they join in devaluing and marginalizing whatever smacks of somatic passion, attachment, or obscurity: intuitive sense, instinctual response, sentimental adherence, libidinal impulse, excretory abandon, etc. At the same time, these and related discourses implicitly and explicitly identified such normalizing mastery with a quite exclusive population, defined in familiar gender, ethic, class, and cultural terms. The ostensible capacity of this elite for restraining or commanding the presubjective in themselves, the irrationality of desire or affect as such, licensed their domination of the presubjective-as-others, those subalterns supposedly given over to bodily sensation or emotional effusion. Such licensed domination, in turn, allowed this social elite to ventilate as well as repress its own irrational affects, to indulge its forbidden desires in displaced forms under the guise of advancing Enlightenment ideals.

In the administration of the British empire in Ireland, for example, the ascendancy of the Anglo-Saxon male found its legitimating principle in his presumed ability to conform his conduct to the rational and transcendent *logos* instantiated in certain repressive codes of deferred gratification (sexual restraint, the work ethic, prudential investment and calculation, social and professional duty, codes of honor, etc.) and the corresponding incapacity of the native population to overcome their fleshly and/or affective immanence to do likewise. But the rule itself required and sanctioned a whole set of desublimating attitudes and practices whereby the denied irrationality of the normative Anglo-Saxon subject could be expressed and released: rituals of gratuitous self-congratulation and equally gratuitous cruelty and contempt toward the colonial other, rituals which were themselves legitimated by the supposition of a self-mastery that should have rendered them unnecessary.

As the last point suggests, the positive relationship between a repressive self-identity and a materialized other is inherently reversible and, in some sense, already reversed. The symbolic surplus embodiment of the subaltern functions as the negative value upon which, after all, the entire ideological system hangs. On one side, the stereotyping association of various subaltern groups with the abject not only acts as a social sanction on the groups themselves, devaluing their bodily and behavioral styles, but acts additionally as a social threat to other, more privileged groups, discouraging them from approximating too closely those styles of being. In this role, the stereotyping associations enforce the kind of repression that creates and sustains social norms. On the other side, these associations turn the same bodily styles and forms of behavior into a kind of taboo or fetish and, in this role, they facilitate a certain return of the repressed.

The anatomy of the process described becomes clearer in the light of Judith Butler's celebrated antifoundationalist account of subjectivity. In *Gender Trouble*, Butler argues that sex–gender (and we might add race–ethnic) identities do not constitute fixed and essential ontological states, but are phantasmatic norms or ideals at once produced and displaced, inscribed differently, if you will, by each socially conditioned endeavor to imitate and, ultimately, appropriate them. As such, these identities are the effects of the performative repetition/alteration of certain salient bodily and behavioral ensembles taken to constitute a given sex–gender norm or ideal; and *no less importantly*, they are the effects of the repeated performative refusal of those bodily and behavioral ensembles taken to vitiate that norm or ideal.[23] The subject, on this view, cannot simply embody or come to occupy a given social category, but can only enact a rendition thereof; and because its effective reality resides in its specific difference from other such enactments, this rendition paradoxically both solidifies and subtly reconfigures the social category in question and those related to it. An elite, normative identification, accordingly, does not achieve the required repression of corporeal immanence on its own or in a self-referential manner, but by way of an aggressive dissociation from certain subaltern-identified traits and stereotypes. Yet its elite status is thereby mortgaged, in its otherwise unsecured state, to those same traits and stereotypes for a kind of negative assurance, on which basis they become as secretly desirable as they are openly denigrated. In this profound relativity of elite and subaltern states to one another, and the profound anxiety it arouses for anyone with an investment in their continued disjunction, lies the recipe for a new round, a more fully interpersonal and overtly political round of abjection. It is this abjection that figures so prominently in *Giacomo Joyce*.

III

The relatively empowered and therefore normative subject is susceptible of a truly violent ambivalence toward his culturally demarcated other.[24] Even while disdaining them, he desires attributes of the other for their socially charged difference, the appropriation of which by the subject, whether as knowledge, pleasure, or enrichment, consolidates his own privileged mode of self-identity and the assumed inferiority of his other. Owing to the reciprocal constitution of the respective positions, however, the subject fears, dreads, or shrinks from the contact with the other that such appropriation entails, finding in the significant difference to be possessed a source of potential contamination, inundation, castration. The subject's dread of contamination and castration feeds the desire to subsume the other outright, which desire works to contain the dread in a dream of absolute mental and physical possession, the self finally completed and reintegrated by the other. Conversely, the subject's desire to take hold of the other feeds the dread of being contaminated thereby, which acts in turn to check the desire by insisting on the alternative ideal of rational self-possession, the self finally completed *over against* the other. Each of these forms of sovereignty is purchased with some portion of the other that sustains it. The transcendence of self-possession entails a certain withdrawal of social power, a loss of reach; the enjoyment of other-appropriation entails a certain self-abandon, a loss of grip. What drives imperialist activity, in the broad sense of the term, is precisely its internally corrosive structure. The power of the authorized subject is not only supported by but alienated in the powerlessness of the other, and it is owing to the paradoxical structure of this interchange that the former is so frequently cast in patriarchal/imperialist literature as a potentially tragic figure, weak in his very greatness, while the latter comes off as an enigma, dangerous in her vulnerability.[25]

The focus of Joyce's dread and desire of Amalia Popper is not her body as such but his own aesthetic embodiment of her, an indication of the self-mirroring quality of the colonizing impulse. She is first introduced in fact as a social abstract, a cipher bearing the telltale marks and attributes of her station:

Who? A pale face surrounded by heavy odorous furs … she uses quizzing glasses. (*GJ* 1)

Cobweb writing, traced long and fine with quiet disdain and resignation: a young person of quality. (*GJ* 2)

High heels clack hollow on the resonant stone stairs. Wintry air in the castle … Tapping, clacking heels, a high and hollow noise. (*GJ* 4)

These hollow or surface trappings of social prestige are contrasted with Joyce's condescending display of intellectual substance:

I launch forth on an easy wave of tepid speech: Swedenborg, the pseudo-Areopagite, Miguel De Molinos, Joachim Abbas … Her classmate, re-twisting her twisted body, purrs in boneless Viennese Italian *Che coltura!* (*GJ* 2)

If there is what Abdul JanMohamed calls a "manichean allegory" taking shape here – i.e. "a field of diverse oppositions between … good and evil, superiority and inferiority, intelligence and emotion, rationality and sensuality, self and other, subject and object"[26] – then as yet its basic terms are *lire* versus *logos*, class versus culture. That is to say, not the classic supremacist antinomy of spirit/matter, but spiritualism/materialism, an opposition which in addition to carrying more distinctly anti-Jewish overtones moves to discount in advance Amalia's economic ascendancy. Later in the piece, Joyce not only extends this conventional anti-Semitic caricature to

Amalia's family, but identifies their supposed venality with the practice of simony, in which just a hint of displaced sexuality can be detected –"The sellers offer on their altars the first fruits: green-fleck lemons, jewelled cherries, shameful peaches with torn leaves. The carriage passes through the lane of canvas stalls, its wheel spokes spinning in the glare. Make way! Her father and two sons sit in the carriage. They have owls eyes and owls wisdom" (*GJ* 23). In keeping with this rhetorical tenor, the intonations of sexual desire remain sublimated early on, one gaze penetrating another: "The long eyelids beat and lift: a burning needle prick stings and quivers in the velvet iris" (*GJ* 3). But these intonations remain nonetheless profound. If, as Lacan has proposed, the exercise of the gaze can figure the possession of the phallus by returning the (male) spectator to a sense of imaginary, pre-oedipal wholeness, the eye as I, then the answering gaze on the part of the other, her resistance to being consigned to the role of appropriable artifact, can both figure and trigger the anxiety of castration, a state of affairs mythologized in the power of Medusa.[27] Instead of ignoring or eliding this scopic self-assertion on the part of Amalia, Joyce's representation here makes a great show of taking it into account and subduing it in an expression of phallic mastery that is all the more confident and forcible for accommodating the illusion of a certain reciprocity.

The equation changes demonstrably once Joyce's erotic Oriental fantasy begins to surface with the first of several harem images, this one representing concubinage not as an institution of or within Amalia's racial sect, but as the very form of that sect's existence, a metaphor for the condition of the Jews in modern Europe: "Rounded and ripened: rounded by the lathe of intermarriage and ripened in the forcing-house of the seclusion of her race" (*GJ* 6). Relying on what were, or were becoming, fairly stereotypical associations of Jewishness – secretness, exclusiveness, dark sensuality, passivity, erotic mystery and danger – Joyce sets up an implicit ratio, that Jewish culture is to the larger European society as the harem culture is to the larger (Near) Eastern society whence the Jews themselves originally came. In one stroke the analogy sexualizes and contextualizes the group isolation of the Jews in terms of their genesis in and exile from an exotic "other" world. What is more, because the leading motifs of both male supremacism and Orientalism are distilled in the idea of the harem, Joyce's emblematic use of this motif here and throughout the sketchbook have the effect of situating the

Jew along the common border of these discourses as their joint creation. Amalia Popper is not just a Jewish woman in *Giacomo Joyce*. Compact of the sexual mystique of racial sequestration, she represents the Jew as woman and the woman as Orientalized: i.e. as the tacit, supine element inviting Western/male incursion, as the mystery demanding Western/male solution, as the treasure tempting Western/male seizure, as the secret provoking Western/male curiosity, as the fertility tempting Western/male potency, as the instinctive other seducing Western/male consciousness. In so doing, Amalia no less importantly facilitates Joyce's disavowal of those feminine or feminized associations that attached to Irishness over the latter half of the nineteenth century.[28] Joyce was, of course, familiar with Otto Weininger's notorious racial–sexual taxonomy, *Sex and Character* (1906), identifying all Jews with women; and the frequent recourse he had to this schema in conversation, particularly the manner in which he rallied Ottocaro Weiss for his racially "feminine" characteristics, suggests that his interest in Weininger's model was in good part defensive, at least initially.[29]

From precisely this juncture in the sketchbook through its pivotal event, Amalia's operation and recovery, Giacomo personifies the life of the mind, percipient agency, and Amalia the fascination of the flesh, perceptual and aesthetic effect, the corpus. Even as his libidinal investments grow more insistent and perverse, they continue to emanate from a disembodied voice and gaze (a transcendent eye/I) located at some indeterminable aesthetic distance, which Joyce remarks by the high cultural allusions in which he swaddles Amalia's image: Beatrice Cenci, Beatrice Portinari, Hester Prynne, Hedda Gabler, Ophelia, etc. Amalia, for her part, is reduced to a state of mute animality. Her voice, like her gaze, is essentially preempted and she is represented as capable of little more than parroting other people's ideas or "sighing" and "twittering" like a bird. In fact she utters not a single articulate thought of her own until after the pivotal crisis of the narrative, her surgery. Until then, the reader would never guess that in point of historical fact Amalia Popper was one of Joyce's finest students.

At this stage, Joyce indulges the full narcissistic potentiality of the sketchbook format. By aestheticizing his erotic attraction for Amalia on one side and eroticizing his aesthetic objectification of her on the other, he fully assuages neither his desire nor his dread but contrives to give an indivisible and indemnifying expression to these conflicting impulses. He appropriates her at arm's, or I should say at art's, length; and in that subtle remove lies sheltered his presumed sovereignty and dignity as a creative subject. The ideology of aesthetic transcendence which sets the limits of Joyce's vision of gender justice in *Dubliners* allows him to perpetrate, at least initially, the most flagrant representational injustice upon Amalia as a means of fortifying his own authoritative position. From the high Modernist vantage to which Joyce as yet clung, the gaze of the artist finds legitimacy in its own genial power, its projection of a uniquely creative sensibility. Thus, Joyce's spectatorship not only consolidates his self-concept by opposition to the feminine spectacle that it dominates, but works to privilege, even apotheosize, that self-concept as well. Secured behind the veil of his fetishizing viewpoint, disavowing the castration that Amalia is taken to display, Joyce is able, in this period of professional desperation, to affirm his aesthetic mastery as a displaced mode of sexual virility.[30] For that very reason, however, the sense of his erotic will to power cannot but pervade his representation of Amalia, and in its effects the aesthetic and the voyeuristic are confounded once more. *Giacomo Joyce* becomes the whirlpool in which commingle Joyce's fabled command of and enthrallment to the images of his own devising.

Joyce's fantasy of preparing Amalia for an evening out not only instantiates, but can be seen to allegorize, this compromise formation:

She *raises* her *arms* in an effort to *hook* at the nape of her neck a *gown* of *black veiling*. She cannot: no, she cannot. She *moves* backwards towards me mutely. I *raise* my *arms* to help her: her arms *fall*. I hold the websoft edges of her *gown* and drawing them out to *hook* them I see through the opening of the *black veil* her *lithe* body sheathed in an orange shift. It *slips* its ribbons of moorings at her shoulders and *falls slowly*: a *lithe* smooth naked body shimmering with silvery scales. It *slips slowly over* the slender buttocks of *smooth* polished silver and over their furrow, a tarnished *silver shadow* ... Fingers cold and calm and moving ... A touch, a touch. (*GJ* 19, my italics)

Inasmuch as evening dress, in particular, involves preparing a distanced, harmonized, relatively sublimated view of one's self and one's body for a projected audience or community, it makes for a compelling allegory of aesthetic representation. It is therefore significant that Joyce's efforts to aid Amalia in this endeavor should occasion his single most intrusive, concupiscent, and prurient image of her person. Indeed, I have quoted the frame in toto because its rhetorical design no less than the matter narrated underscores the duality of the episode, the symbiosis of its aesthetic and pornographic energies. The action traverses a set of binary oppositions whose symbolic charge or value is strictly pertinent to these respective forms of discourse: it progresses from the top to the bottom ("nape of neck" to "slender buttocks"), from covering to exposure, mediation to invasion (from attaching the black veiling to peering through the black veil), from visual to tactile impression ("a touch, a touch"), and from the cultural sublimation of the evening gown to the sexuality of her "smooth naked body" and the animality of its "shimmering ... silvery scales."

The verbal repetitions that punctuate the passage, however, serve to bind these polarities together *in both directions*, showing them to be but different spirals of the same winding thread. The first series of repetitions, comprising the terms "raise ... arms," "hook," "gown," and "black veil," identify the movement to conceal and adorn the body with that which uncovers and in a sense violates it. Joyce's intent to secure the veil, to finish the creation, as they say in *haute couture*, dovetails with his willingness to exploit the "opening" in that veil, to unwrap his "soft merchandise," as they say in the *demimonde*. Conversely, the second series of repetitions, comprising the terms "lithe," "smooth," "slip," "slowly," and "silver," correlate the exposure and the reinvestiture of Amalia's bottom as mutually imperative moments in the voyeuristic experience. Reference to her "silvery scales" and "tarnished furrow" suggests a certain discomfort if not dread in Joyce's contemplation of her nakedness, the disavowal of which, always an essential element of such fetishism, requires an undoing, whether by way of mediation, inhibition, or interruption. Whereas the allegorical tendency of the first repetitive series is to demystify the aesthetic project, conjuring forth its libidinal, appropriative source of energy, the second series touches upon the ambivalence of this erotic motive, silently reaffirming the psychic and political basis for aesthetic mystification. This double move, in turn, corresponds to the *mise-en-scène* of the frame itself, which advances even as it remarks the conflict of dread and desire informing the work as a whole.

This sort of compromise formation is typical of Orientalist and sexist discourse alike, which is doubtless one of the reasons each is so committed to the genre of fantasy, whether in the form of adventure tales, romances, or pornography. No doubling sense of ambivalence attaches to these textual manifestations for their consumers, however, because it is always already transferred, within the representation itself, onto the figure of the other, as a part of her ontological make-up. For this reason, objectification is a crucially imprecise metaphor for the imperialist (racist/sexist) construction and treatment of the subaltern. Such textual forms, and *Giacomo Joyce* is no exception in this regard, frame the other as neither subject nor object nor even as an objectified or reified mode of subjectivity, but as incompletely or insufficiently emergent from the material stratum of existence.

All of this is to say that imperialist rhetoric typically casts its other(s) as

(a) virtual subjects, so that they seem to solicit supervision and control, if only for the purpose of realizing their imputed potential, specifically the potential of the Other to be the Same, to be just like the colonizing subject and so accountable to his rules of measure.[31] Here we can place the empire's self-appointed civilizing mission in which Joyce undeniably implicated himself with the writing of *Giacomo*, his "sentimental education of a dark lady," to paraphrase Ellmann's unwittingly biting *précis*.[32] Here too we can place the patriarchy's gender-biased educational practices in which Joyce was likewise enlisted, specifically the cultivation of women as diminished, distorted, or otherwise defective mirror images of a (male) subjectivity that they secure through their own imputed shortcomings. Difference, the imperialist hope runs, can always be settled or annulled on terms dictated by the authorized subject in the name or interest of the ventriloquized other. Any resistance to such assigned norms can be dismissed in advance as either insufficiently representative ("they don't really mean no") or representative of a certain insufficiency ("they don't really know");

(b) virtual objects, and so irreducibly inferior, yet pointing to a state of ecstasy, a *jouissance*, which can only be achieved through self-abandon, self-escape, self-extinction. Here we can place the stultifying fetishism of the other's distinctive attributes, i.e. the debasing projection upon those attributes of the wishes, anxieties, and distastes of the authorized observer. In Joyce's case, this symptom threatened his competence as a professional educator; and in certain colonial contexts, it regularly led to a more dramatic social and professional default popularly called "going native." Difference, the imperialist fear goes, might always be settled at the expense of the normative subject (his coherence, integrity, or self-awareness) on the other's terms or terms identified with the other. As I suggested earlier, this sort of imperialist abjection bears an inverse relation to the liberal ideal of justice, turning the now familiar double bind of equality and difference inside out, so that it expresses not the dream of their mutual resolution, or even the possibility of their negotiation, but an unconscious desire for their mutual cancellation. In the frame under discussion, Joyce finds himself prompted by Amalia's virtual reality qua subject, her notional equality in the eyes of God and man, to take control of her acculturation, asserting his superiority over her; while at the same time he finds himself drawn by her materiality qua object, her difference from the phallic and racial norm, to his own dissipation, an impulse that somehow redounds to her degradation rather than his.

The characteristics marking the supposed insufficient emergence of the other vary from one imperial situation to another, but the descriptive categories covering them are relatively consistent, in keeping with the Manichean allegory outlined above: sensuality, sentimentality, irrepressible sexuality, promiscuity, changeability, unpredictability, childishness, bestiality, herd mentality, inter-changeability, an unreadiness for self-discipline or self-restraint, hence for personal or political freedom[33] – all framed as a lack or failure of the positive aptitude for making or embodying, conserving or enacting the "hard" abstract discriminations proper to a mature rationality. As we have already begun to see, *Giacomo Joyce* assembles an entire array of such motifs of equivocality or indeterminacy in its representation of Amalia Popper, toward whom Joyce himself displays a corresponding ambivalence.

Directly following the harem image that initiates Joyce's erotic fantasy comes the first verbal incarnation of his dream girl. There is a physical murkiness or mushiness about Amalia:

A rice field near Vercelli under creamy summer haze. The wings of her drooping hat shadow her false smile. Shadows streak her falsely smiling face, smitten by the hot creamy light, grey wheyhued shadows under the jawbones, streaks of egg yolk yellow on the moistened brow, rancid yellow humour lurking within the softened pulp of the eyes. (*GJ* 7)

The frame offers a quite literal illustration of an incomplete emergence from the material stratum of existence, a state of *pre-*

composition. Most obviously, Amalia's features lack any solidity; they appear ready at any moment to melt back into a primordial ooze. More subtly, by once again turning verbal repetition to rhetorical effect – creamy, false(ly), streak(s), shadow(s), yellow – Joyce moves the impressionistic catalogue seamlessly from elements of the external environment to facial features emblematic of Amalia's character. In this manner, he evokes a confusion of subjective and objective space, implying the lack, in her case, of any decidable hiatus between them and thus a failure of that rudimentary transcendence proper to a fully human mode of being. The Amalia given us initially, then, is the very picture of *primary*-stage abjection.

By the end of *Giacomo*, in keeping with the metaphorics of nineteenth-century ethnography and caricature, Amalia's physical sedimentation is taken to be homologous with a viscous quality of mind that promises to benefit from and threatens to engulf the rigor of Joyce's own thought: "My words in her mind: cold polished stones sinking through a quagmire" (*GJ* 37). A few frames later, however, the fear of engulfment by Amalia passes into and is swallowed up by the dream of a radical appropriation of her, dread transposed and mastered in the key of desire, all under the banner of Oriental sensuality:

She leans back against the pillowed wall: odalisque-featured in the luxurious obscurity. Her eyes have drunk my thoughts: and into the warm moist yielding welcoming darkness of her womanhood my soul, itself dissolving, has streamed and poured and flooded a liquid and abundant seed ... Take her now who will! (*GJ* 42)

If the psychospiritual stakes in this passage (my thoughts, my soul) disguise the phallic content of Joyce's desire, however flimsily, they positively expose the displacement of castration anxiety that the desire entails. The sexual relation imagined here guards against the very loss of ego-function that it figures. Even as Amalia receives his *logos*, she remains all vessel, all body, the symbolic equivalent of generative matter: humid, opaque, recumbent, inchoate. Even as Joyce releases his spirit into the morass of her being, he somehow regains his coign of transcendence, his purchase on the alterity in which he is engrossed. Indeed, the act itself purports to assure an eternalized proprietorship over her. His parting shot claims that now he has (or has "had") her no matter what, or who, the sequel. At the same time, by employing a psychospiritual vocabulary, Joyce continues to trope and so legitimate his desire for phallic mastery as a civilizing–edifying mission.

Drawing once again upon nineteenth-century Orientalist discourse, the harem motif here reinforces the displacement of dread in desire by connecting the stereotype of Oriental sensuality with that of Oriental despotism. Giacomo's own sense of erotic enslavement, caught in the compulsive cycle of a racially tinctured attraction and repulsion, is transferred to Amalia as the legacy of that guilty racial condition. By casting her father as "the Grand Turk [of the] harem" (*GJ* 11), Joyce can portray himself as not only a free agent but a potential liberator. He implicitly appeals to a classic topos of European imperialism, a defense of forays into non-Western communities on the grounds that they supplant archaic patriarchal regimes with more enlightened modes of governance. Gayatri Spivak's capsule summary of this justification, "white men are saving brown women from brown men," elegantly captures its fusion of racial and sexual energies.[34] (Joyce's invocation, after meeting Mr. Popper, of Loyola, the founder of an aggressive missionary order, seems ironically apposite in this regard.) There is, I would argue, an essential link between imperialist dread and its heroic conceits. One solution to the disorienting ambivalence of the dread/desire for the other is a metonymic displacement of the dread onto an obstacle or rival standing in the way of the desire. Since the project of cultivating the still virtual subjectivity of the other already ennobles that desire, overcoming such displaced dread and the object to which it attaches automatically feels heroic.

The inverse cycle, desire feeding the dread that controls it, marks Amalia's body as an effect of the artist's gaze. Joyce takes an affective ambivalence that goes to his own self-division, the abjection of the Orientalist/patriarchal Imaginary, and naturalizes it as a racial and gendered property of his model, a function of her incomplete transcendence of the material realm. Take the voyeuristic encounter anatomized earlier. By picturing Amalia's body as "shimmering with silvery scales," Joyce lends her the appearance, or at least the metonymic value, of a mermaid, a mythic archetype of precisely this halfway estate, split between the human and the animal, air and water, the surface and the depths, and so, symbolically, between subject and object worlds – reason and instinct, mind and body, consciousness and unconsciousness. This incident is exemplary in that Joyce's erotic meditations upon Amalia's manipulated image repeatedly give way to similitudes of her to various forms of animal life. In a single move, each such delineation of Amalia not only asserts her racial inferiority, the nature of that inferiority, and the menace it accordingly poses to his dignity, but expresses the dread that prospect arouses as distaste or even revulsion. One more frame in particular underlines this point, linking Amalia's imperfect purchase on her own bodily reality to both Joyce's voyeuristic indulgence and her own bestial status – "A skirt caught back by her sudden moving knee; a white lace edging of an underskirt lifted unduly; a leg-stretched web of stocking. *Si pol?*" (*GJ* 26)

Taken en masse, these representations tend to consolidate Joyce's self-image by opposition to the mercurial Amalia, who traverses a veritable bestiary in just sixteen pages. She is likened, in whole or in part, to a filly foal, mollusks, a mermaid, a sparrow, a pampered fowl, an antelope, a bird, a pullet, a basilisk, and a night snake. In what amounts to a romantic variation on the "Proteus" episode, Joyce situates himself as the "subject who knows," a stable independent mentality holding to the underlying secret of material flux epitomized in the slippery figure of Amalia.[35] For her part, the changeability of Amalia's physical presence is transcribed in the moral register as feminine faithlessness and Jewish treachery, much as the murkiness of her physiognomy (anchored, incidentally, by a "false smile") is later troped as a murkiness of thought. Through this analogical structure, Joyce enlists his cherished motif of betrayal in the labor of a Freudian projection: he translates a crisis of self-division born of his own sexual and racial attitudes into a wrong inflicted upon him by Amalia in keeping with her gendered and racially marked failings.

In an extended mytheme, Joyce portrays himself as a crucified Christ figure regarding whom Amalia initially indulges her stereotyped proclivity for the sentimental:

In the raw veiled spring morning [mourning] Paris ... as I cross the Pont Saint Michel the steel-blue waking waters chill my heart ... Tawny gloom in the vast gargoyled church. It is cold as on that morning: *quia frigus erat.* Upon the steps of the far high altar, naked as the body of the Lord, the ministers lie prostrate in weak prayer ... She stands beside me, pale and chill, clothed with the shadows of the sin-dark nave, her thin elbow at my arm. Her flesh recalls the thrill of that raw mist-veil morning, hurrying torches, cruel eyes. Her soul is sorrowful, trembles and would weep. Weep not for me, O daughter of Jerusalem! (*GJ* 28)

But like the sentimentalist of George Meredith and Stephen Dedalus, she proves unwilling, in Joyce's eyes, to take responsibility for the thing done or felt.[36] Her sympathy is withdrawn in deference to the Jewish mob, the weakness of sentimentality passing easily into the weakness of social conformity:

They spread under my feet carpets for the Son of Man. They await my passing. She stands in the yellow shadow of the hall … and as I halt and wonder and look about me she greets me wintrily and passes up the staircase darting at me for an instant out of her sluggish sidelong eyes a jet of liquorish venom. (*GJ* 44)

The weeping "daughter of Jerusalem" plays once more the "virgin most prudent," at least that is the way Joyce chooses to interpret Amalia's decision to marry Michele Risolo.[37] In the last installment of this mytheme, not just Amalia's opinion but her point of view, indeed her very presence, have been absorbed into a mass decree: "*Non hunc sed Barabbam!*" (*GJ* 48). At this moment, racial and sexual markers, which have cooperated throughout *Giacomo Joyce* in the construction of Amalia as the abject, simply collapse together, effacing all sense of a separate identity. Abjection approaches annihilation, and it is worth noting that in the two remaining frames of the notebook Amalia appears strictly as a reified absence.

IV

There is a lot more going on here than meets the eye, however. Amalia's image is consigned to the nether reaches of abjection in this particular narrative sequence because this is the symbolic juncture at which Joyce encountered his own powerful sense of abjection. The first installment, frame 28, refers not only to the day of Christ's death but to the Good Friday service which Joyce attended the day he was notified of his mother's impending demise. Taken in this light, the messianic Joyce can be seen as doubly crucified by an imperfectly resolved grief for his mother, herself a Christ figure, and by his imperfectly requited desire for his student; and we can see Amalia as being fixed in a correspondingly double posture of consolation: a Madonna grieving for her son's affliction and a daughter lamenting the plight of her champion. This profound imbrication of the remembered and the imagined event, of past bereavement and present lack, mother love and other longing, uncovers a subterranean layer, a more intimate set of stakes, to Joyce's psychic investment in Amalia. It has its unconscious roots and derives its obsessive vitality from the finally irreconcilable break between Joyce and his mother over his spiritual direction during the period of her fatal illness. We must, accordingly, pause to examine that crucial episode in Joyce's life.

When in *Ulysses* Joyce compresses the twilight agon that he and his mother waged over his soul[38] into a single deathbed confrontation, centered on Stephen's refusal to kneel and pray, he displays an acute appreciation of the mythic character of the episode, its ability to tap and crystallize a certain primal energy. The incident possesses this virtue, I would argue, because it raises the problematic of abjection to the eternal dimension. It replays and at some unconscious level revives the painfully contradictory dynamic of individuation in circumstances where the issue is no longer just a psychic disjunction from the (m)other, but her irrevocable disappearance, her literal death, i.e. in circumstances in which primary abjection directly implicates its terminal counterpart, crucifixion.

Joyce clinches the symbolic overlap of abjection and crucifixion in the reversible mirror of the "Circe" episode, a textual register that precisely encapsulates the contest and confusion of identity which the mythical deathbed episode involves. The *de*composition of Stephen's mother's face eerily recalls the *pre*-composition of Amalia Popper's countenance, each betokening a submergence of personality in material process. His mother's "worn and noseless" face, her "scant and lank" hair, "her bluecircled hollow eye sockets" (*U* 15.4159–60), parodying Lucrece's "bluecircled ivory globes" (*U* 9.474–5), and the "green rill of bile trickling from a side of her mouth" (*U* 15.4189) all combine to form a graphic image of Stephen's sense of primary abjection.[39] But the words of this overembodied wraith are of still greater significance:

THE MOTHER: I pray for you in my other world. Get Dilly to make you that boiled rice every night after your brainwork. *Years and years I loved you oh, my son, my firstborn, when you lay in my womb.*　　　(*U* 15.4201–3)

THE MOTHER (*in the agony of her death rattle*): Have mercy on Stephen, Lord, for my sake! Inexpressible was my *anguish when expiring with love, grief and agony on Mount Calvary.*　　　(*U* 15.4238–40, my italics)

Note that the voice articulating abjection with crucifixion does not belong to Stephen, or to Mrs. Daedelus, but to Stephen's hallucinatory projection of/visitation by "The Mother," i.e. to both and to neither indeterminably. Keeping in mind this complex mode of enunciation, the first profession of *amor matris* above contemplates a filial immersion that exceeds the threshold of birth, a filial dependency that exceeds the limits of childhood, and a reciprocal fixation that exceeds the strictures of death – in other words, the perpetuation of a mirror-stage narcissism in which the psychic boundaries of self and (an)other remain fluctuating and permeable. The second profession of *amor matris* above contemplates Stephen's active expression of autonomy, his detachment from the maternal sphere, as a transgression on his part invoking a crucifixion on hers. These alternatives, in turn, correspond exactly to the options Joyce himself confronted in dealing with his mother's death.

For Joyce to embrace Mother('s) Church at the close of her life would have meant attaining a symbolic form of permanent unity with her, at the cost of renouncing not just certain principles and convictions but a deeply cherished and fiercely held way of intellectual being. The repressive vigilance needed to sustain this hard-won atonement, moreover, could only have whetted his self-defining inclination to criticism, skepticism, and apostasy, generating further conflict, demanding still more exhaustive self-censorship, and precipitating an arrested state of abjection.

On the other side, for Joyce to resist, as he did, his mother's desire at this juncture meant asserting once and for all his independence, but only by way of incurring a spiritual form of eternal separation from her. His decision (from the Latin *decidere*, to cut off) can be seen as reenacting the arduous process of severing the psychic umbilicus, all the more so since Joyce's difficult sojourn in Paris had brought him particularly close to his mother at this time and, to judge from his letters, had revived a certain incestuous charge between them.[40] Still, it is the intervention of death in this case which makes all the difference, precisely because it absolutizes the difference already at issue.

Theoretically speaking, the violent ambivalence of primary abjection is relegated to the unconscious by a paternal interdiction which broaches sexual difference, springing libido from its absorption in the mother's body, and enforces the Symbolic order, diffusing libidinal energy among substitute objects in a circuit of distinction and exchange. As a practical matter, however, resolution of this affective crux depends upon a controlled, calibrated distancing of mother and child intimacy – closely related to the transitional space of object relations theory – in which the nascent subject's warring demands for attachment and separation can be satisfied together, but in reciprocally limited and compromised forms, so that all the positive and negative emotions specific to each (anxiety, expectation, rage, aggression, *jouissance*, fear) are set in moderating interplay. Indeed, it does not seem too far fetched to see this infantile negotiation between the maternal and paternal imagoes, with their associated valences, or between desire and the law in all of their agonistic inseparability, as the psychological matrix of the imperative to justice. This paradigm would help to explain, in developmental terms, why gender furnishes the exemplary object of this imperative and abjection its enabling underside. The need for just this sort of regulated distance, with the accompanying diffusion of libidinal tension, was renewed for Joyce by his mother's appeal and then utterly frustrated by her death. Valid without expiration, his final rebuff to her fundamental beliefs was in some sense immeasurable, and any bridge over the fissure thus opened between them was bound to remain in some degree disappointed. The *lex eterna* which stayed about the decision had the effect of polarizing the choices, exaggerating the implications of each, and so sharpening their mutually exclusive quality. Joyce could not avoid submerging his spiritual being in his mother's without inducing a profoundly distressing schism between them and, further, transmitting to this dying woman a reflected version of his own ambivalence. (The latter consequence is likewise denoted in "Circe," where the specter of Mrs. Dedalus vacillates between lavishing affection upon Stephen and admonishing him for his infidel-ity.) Put another way, Joyce could not refrain from betraying the law of his being without betraying his mother instead; he could not settle accounts with himself except by defaulting on the immense debt that was due her for countless, vital exertions on his behalf. After her "crossed" life, her certain death represented to Joyce's mind a species of crucifixion for which his own otherwise defensible course of conduct bore part of the blame. In a letter to Nora, for instance, written during Joyce's period of mourning, he includes his own "cynical frankness of conduct" among the causes of his mother's death (*L* II, 48). Accordingly, the repressed ambivalence activated in him by the episode at large would be neither diminished nor essentially transformed by the outcome, but preserved, as it were, in translation, entering his consciousness in the displaced form of a contest between guilt and self-justification, remorse and relief, paralyzing grief and the determination to forge ahead.

In the time surrounding his mother's death, the repressed traces of Joyce's abjection became newly available to cognition, but in an inverted form, as though held up to a mirror. What operated subliminally as radical ambivalence – a contention of interdependent drives delimiting and de-limiting Joyce's personality – was consciously experienced as an internal conflict, a struggle of distinctly opposed sentiments subsumed by the personality in torment. The "self" which continued to have an unconscious existence as an open-ended nexus, suspended between attachment and detachment, could only emerge in the Symbolic as a riven and embattled enclosure. Through a sort of figure–ground shift, the constitutive forces underlying Joyce's personality became intelligible as its warring aspects or effects.

Initially, this shift occasioned a bout of dysfunctional behavior on Joyce's part. Two of his self-destructive actions in particular attest to an unconscious reaction against the loss he was suffering and the spiritual break he was precipitating respectively and evidence a corresponding wish to restore the primordial mother–child dyad. Joyce's sudden descent from steadfast temperance to dangerous alcoholic excess evinces a veiled, thanatotic desire to rejoin his fate with his mother's in the only manner possible. His concurrent repudiation of an aesthetic calling which he himself conceived in decidedly egoistic terms shows a veiled desire to expiate what he was unwilling to alter: the self-assertion implicit in both his apostasy and his refusal to compromise with even the direst circumstances in maintaining it. That he should have justified the drinking and the creative inactivity to Stanislaus with the words, "I just want to live" confirms the turbulent extremity of his delusion at the time.[41]

By the same token however, the figure–ground shift allowed Joyce to interpret the turbulence as his own, his effect, not in the sense of being immediately at his disposal or under his control but of being at least formally subordinate to him. This may have been his motive in telling Nora, of all people, that his mother died of his "cynical frankness of conduct." However specious or paltry this sort of self-appropriation might seem, it is the first step toward bringing meaningful experience out of inchoate excitement and is, therefore, an absolute pre-condition for fostering the stronger enabling illusion of agency and autonomy. Indeed, the aesthetic of self-objectification, which informs Joyce's fiction from *Stephen Hero* through *Finnegans Wake*, can be seen as serving precisely this end. By putting the psychosocial forces that worked him onstage, Joyce could submit them in turn to the dictates of his creative will and, in yet another twist of the dialectical screw of self-consciousness, he could simultaneously inscribe the process of doing so in symbolic form. In *Giacomo Joyce*, this last self-reflexive tactic has the added benefit of bringing forth an incipient awareness of the intimacy that continues to exist, beyond any repression or disavowal, between the consolidated authorial ego and its abjected other, here embodied in Amalia. And, as a result, the problem of representational justice can begin to emerge, however unsteadily, from the practice of representational violence.

The crucifixion fantasy is central in this regard. "Pale and chill," "clothed in shadows," her elbow "thin," "at his arm," Amalia's body plainly calls to Joyce's mind the wasting flesh of his mother, even as her touch communicates the jagged "thrill" associated with the day Joyce learned of his mother's doom. But Amalia's sorrowful soul suggests that matters are being put to rights, that the emotional alignment binding Joyce to his mother in guilt and regret is or seems to be undergoing something of a reversal. Amalia stands in for the mother not as immolated victim, her dominant image in Joyce's recollection, but as specifically unburdened of those sacrificial afflictions, nurturing a son whose own suffering can appear, for that very reason, redemptive. The editorial principle determining the pattern of Joyce's allusion to the Biblical *figura* is designed in large part to underscore its empowering potential. First, the frame dwells upon the "chill" of each relevant Good Friday morning, suggesting a like atmosphere of rigor for the naked Christ and his ministers and the emotionally naked Joyce, whose heart is chilled in reaction. Second, the frame downplays the new messiah's tribulation in favor of the grief he elicits from the maternal Amalia. Third, the frame closes with Joyce's grand gesture toward alleviating that sorrow: his admonition "weep not for me" is his only citation of Christ's actual speech, a telling choice in contrast with, say, "why hast thou forsaken me?". With each of these decisions, Joyce declines the pathos of the abnegatory gesture he has made, opting instead for a more heroic, self-actuating gloss on his ordeal. Concordantly, Amalia is represented as expressing not only pity and solace for Joyce's suffering but also an appreciation of his sublimity, a sorrow for her loss as well as his pain. In this fashion, Amalia's spectatorial part in the Golgotha scenario contributes to its function as a vehicle of Joyce's continuing struggle to firm and defend the shifting borders of selfhood, even as the maternal complexion of her role facilitates his more regressive fantasies of death as a return to the charmed pre-oedipal dyad, a dying into the womb.[42] Joyce thus contrived to finesse in some measure the experience of abjection, forestalling its dangers while anticipating its attendant pleasures.

At the same time, however, this frame sees Joyce assuming a role reversal with his mother which signals in turn a still deeper level of transference and, with it, a still deeper threat of abjection. By adopting the position of the sacrificial parent figure and externalizing that of the bereaved child, Joyce evinces his strong continued identification with his mother while casting Amalia as his own surrogate or stand-in. Notice how the previously cited crucifixion passage pivots upon the double syntax of Amalia's corporeal memory: "She stands beside me, pale and chill, clothed with the shadows of the sin-dark nave, her thin elbow at my arm. Her flesh recalls the thrill of that raw mist-veiled morning, hurrying torches, cruel eyes. Her soul is sorrowful, trembles and would weep" (*GJ* 28). If Amalia's flesh "recalls" that fateful day to Joyce's mind, simulating in its chill pallor the wasting body of his mother, Amalia's flesh also "recalls" that day itself, harboring the memory as Joyce's experiential double. That is to say, the complex gender and generational valences infusing this episode converge upon the verb "recalls," so that Amalia's Madonna-like bereavement doubles as filial commiseration, and her position in Joyce's family romance becomes to that extent reversible with Joyce's own. Now, there is clearly an element of wish fulfillment in this aspect of the fantasy as well. Amalia does not just relive, in her mourning of Joyce–Christ, Joyce's mourning of his mother; rather, she registers as his proxy a depth of sentiment that he felt and yet found inhibiting.[43] She thus gives an idealized rendition of Joyce in mourning. Just as Amalia figures Joyce's mother relieved of her pain in his imaginary sacrifice, so she symbolically "channels" his expression of the grief, affection, and regret motivating that sacrifice. Joyce's fractured reconciliation with his deceased mother is thereby completed, as it were, from the other side. Given the contradictory logic of abjection, however, it is precisely in fulfilling Joyce's wish that the crucifixion fantasy confirms his fears, and in completing Joyce's reconciliation with his mother that the fantasy counteracts it, specifically by imperiling the fragile psychic margin necessary to maintain the sense of distinct, self-identical subjectivity.

This psychodrama of separation and reconciliation plays itself out in accordance with a gendered division of symbolic labor from which it derives its specifically ethico-political dimension. In her renowned study *The Reproduction of Mothering*, Nancy Chodorow analyzes how the childrearing arrangements typical of the patriarchal, bourgeois family have impelled post-oedipal boys to sever their identities more quickly and more completely from the maternal imago than post-oedipal girls and to consolidate and defend experienced ego boundaries more emphatically.[44] Moreover, gender would seem to be the crucial factor not just analytically but phenomenologically, i.e. from the perspective of the developing child. Her disciple, Coppelia Kahn, explains:

For though she follows the same sequence of symbiotic union, separation and individuation, identification and object love, as the boy, her femininity arises in relation to a person of the *same* sex, while his masculinity arises in relation to a person of the *opposite* sex. Her femininity is reinforced by her original symbiotic union with her mother and by her identification with her that must precede identity, while his masculinity is threatened by the same union and the same identification.[45]

Under these circumstances, different forms of gender-specific treatment and different sets of gender-specific expectations, all grounded in profound ideological infrastructures like the incest taboo and the heterosexual contract, have tended to instill in male children a comparatively high likelihood and degree of detachment, initiative, competitiveness, will to mastery, rational self-directedness, independence, etc. Within bourgeois liberalism, of course, these same qualities have counted as the distinctive ingredients, the transcendental markings, of humanity itself, in which regard they have served to legitimate male dominion. The effectiveness of this modern reproduction of the patriarchy, in turn, depended in part upon the conceptual disguise given its operation, a naturalizing inversion of cause and effect. In a wide variety of cultural, political, and scientific discourses, the attributes listed were taken to inhere in the male of the species, to be essentially masculine in and of themselves, while their opposed attributes, having been to some degree encouraged in female children, were interpreted as manifestations of a supposedly feminine principle: e.g. personal connectedness, social conformity, emotional responsiveness and dependency, passivity, other-directedness, submissiveness, etc. Accordingly, as Seyla Benhabib has argued, "the rational and autonomous subject of the Enlightenment, the quintessential Modernist, is a male."[46] Put another way, masculine privilege has been instituted at so fundamental a level as to belie or defeat the putatively neutral taxonomy of gender. In a still more radical ideological inversion, a particular determination of subjectivity, the masculine, has all but subsumed the genus, while the feminine has been reified as the other of both simultaneously. Hence, the bearers and beneficiaries of patriarchal authority, like Joyce, almost reflexively confused their continued existence *as subjects* with their hierarchical standing *as men*, at least in the first instance, and so their abjection of women proceeded as a matter of course.

v

In Joyce's crucifixion fantasy, he not only takes over from his mother the role symbolically associated with division and separation, he converts this role into something of a *parade virile* or manly display, superseding her more or less passive victimage with a voluntary and heroic ideal. His part in the fantasy, in other words, is to make amends even as he achieves separation. The emotional component of the reconciliation, on the other hand, that element which raises the promise and the threat of Kahn's "symbiotic union," is supplied in his place by Amalia. Her trembling, her weeping enable Joyce's approach to this primordial affective condition precisely by preserving him at a certain remove from it, a *distance* troped as gender *difference*. That is to say, in this crucifixion fantasy, Joyce not only externalizes the role of the bereaved, he converts the role into something of a *parade feminine* or womanly display, substituting for the defensive reticence of his own regret a daughter's more demonstrative grief.

Stephen's Shakespeare theory, which Joyce actually espoused, testifies to just this psychodynamic, establishing the girl child ("Marina ... Miranda ... Perdita" (*U* 9.421)) as the consummate agency of reconciliation for the exiled or alienated hero:

What softens the heart of a man, shipwrecked in storms dire, Tried, like another Ulysses, Pericles, prince of Tyre? ...
—A child, a girl placed in his arms, Marina. (*U* 9.402–6)

What is lost was given back to him: his daughter's child. *My dearest wife,*
Pericles says, *was like this maid.* Will any man love the daughter if he has not
loved the mother? (*U* 9.422–4)

Stephen, of course, postulates a creative analogy between
Shakespeare's drama and the drama of Shakespeare's life. Here,
Pericles' response to the discovery of his daughter, his sense of
renewal after the "loss" of his wife, supposedly bodies forth in
displaced form Shakespeare's own experience upon the birth of his
granddaughter, his sense of reconciliation both to Anne's supposed
infidelity and to his youthful "undoing" at her hands. But a like
analogy can be drawn between Stephen's biographical theory and
his own turbulent biography.[47] The sexual trauma and betrayal
dividing Shakespeare's husbands and wives, the sense of reconciliation binding his fathers and daughters, these are legible displacements of Stephen's powerful obsession with sexual trauma, betrayal,
and reconciliation centering upon his mother. (More subtle is the
proleptic intimation of this displacement: Stephen's substitution of
the fox's buried grandmother for his mother in the "Nestor"
riddle anticipates Shakespeare's supposed substitution of Pericles'
daughter for his own granddaughter.) Behind both the Shakespeare
theory and its role in the narrative of Stephen's desire stands James
Joyce himself, in whom the displaced and the displacement coincide.
The tertiary analogy of both the theory and the narrative to Joyce's
life experience emerges quietly in the ambiguity surrounding the use
of the terms "daughter" and "mother" in the last-cited passage.
Stephen's use of the nonpossessive article "the" allows the sentence
to be read, "Will any man love the [his] daughter if he has not loved
the [his] mother?," so that the father–daughter tie can be seen as
redressing in some way the mother–son schism, a possibility which, in
this biographically saturated context, must be referred to the psychic
topology of the author. The "spirit of reconciliation" that Stephen
uncovers in Shakespeare's later works indirectly expresses the sense of
reconciliation Joyce himself achieved by way of a partial identification with daughter figures like Amalia, or the subjective position
of daughterhood itself, where the indulgence in grief or the longing
for mother love need not signal emasculation.

It is in these terms, perhaps, that we can understand why Joyce
identified so much more closely with his daughter, Lucia, than with
his son and first-born, Giorgio, and from there assess the impact
Lucia had upon his textual construction of Amalia. Prevailing

opinion has pegged Joyce's identification with Lucia as an empathetic response to her worsening derangement, and there is no doubt that Joyce came to regard her mental condition as a skewed correlative of his own.[48] So powerfully did Joyce come to identify with Lucia that his friend Paul Leon determined, "Mr. Joyce trusts one person alone, and that person is Lucia. Anything she says or writes is the thing by which he is guided."[49] For his part, Carl Jung thought Joyce's "own Anima, i.e. his unconscious psyche, was so solidly identified with her, that to have her certified would have been as much as an admission that he himself had a latent psychosis."[50] Joyce's wavering opinions tended to corroborate Jung's diagnosis. When Joyce could bring himself to acknowledge the severity of Lucia's disturbance, he would see it as a metonymic effect of his genius: "Whatever spark of gift I possess has been translated to Lucia and has kindled a fire in her brain."[51] When he could not bear to acknowledge its severity, he would see her mental being in metaphorical likeness to his own. He insisted, "she is no madder than her father," and ascribed her breakdown to factors more properly associated with his brand of creative endeavor: "The poor child is not a raving lunatic, just a poor child who tried to do too much, to understand too much. Her dependence on me is now absolute."[52] But in the chiasmic interplay of his absolute dependence on her ("trusts one person alone") and her "dependence ... absolute on [him]," we can discern a reprise and a reversal of the dynamic of maternal abjection, a pattern fundamental indeed to Joyce's "Anima [or] unconscious psyche" and clearly anterior to the onset of Lucia's symptoms. *Joyce did not identify with Lucia on account of her illness; rather he could identify so readily with her illness partly on account of his long-standing sense of mystic participation with her*, a fellowship he had already insinuated into the relationship of Leopold and Milly Bloom.[53] I want to suggest that Joyce's identification with Lucia originally attached to the *structure* of the father–daughter relationship insofar as it transposes the gender and generational terms of the mother–son relationship. This is the point at which one might locate the oft-remarked narcissism of Joyce's love for Lucia;[54] but it is not *just* the narcissism of endless self-elaboration and self-engrossment, which seeks to aggrandize the psychic enclosure by colonizing the other, it is also a primary or mirror-stage narcissism in which the ego models itself *after* the other in order to get its bearings *from* the other, to reinforce or reestablish the psychic enclosure itself.

Of primary significance in this regard, as in most things with Joyce, is the question of the name. Joyce had the name Lucia in mind during Nora's first pregnancy; but when the child turned out a boy, Joyce decided to name him after his deceased brother, a gesture aimed at symbolically reconstituting a secondary object relation. Joyce then decided to name his daughter after the patron saint of vision, after light itself in effect, properties which Joyce had been surrendering progressively from early childhood and stood in danger of losing permanently.[55] His naming of Lucia, accordingly, was an attempt to restore or secure by way of the signifier a lost attribute of the self. As such, the naming can be seen to replicate, metaphorically speaking, the constitutive gesture of subjectivity, the attempt to re-place or re-present in the symbolic chain the imaginary, *pre-objectal* plenitude of the mother–child dyad, what comes to be figured retrospectively as the lost (m)other portion of the self. In other words, Joyce not only gave his daughter the name of his desire, as Phillip Kuberski argues,[56] he gave her his name for desire *as such*, the light whose withdrawal defines subjectivity in terms of lack, the empyreal side of maternal abjection. The overriding importance of Lucia's gender status to this particular psychodynamic cannot be overstated. It helps to explain why Joyce put not only the name Lucia but the traditional prerogative of patronymic identification on hold for two years,[57] and why he invested his daughter, rather than his son, with the Name of the Father in its more complete form. For Joyce – and here we may be close to the psychoanalytic key of his entire career – the Name of the Father, the fundamental law of language and desire, functions primarily as a vehicle for reopening negotiations with the trace of the Mother, the interfold of personal identity and difference, connectedness and separation, in which the exigency of justice begins to make itself felt.[58]

This cross-gender imperative takes a still more developed form with respect to Joyce's fictive elaboration of his self-identity. By Ellmann's account, Joyce's decision to rewrite his autobiographical novel, *Stephen Hero*, as a "gestation of the soul" in *A Portrait* occurred *only* and *immediately* after Lucia's birth,[59] even though the earlier version was well underway and clearly in need of formal correction by the time Giorgio was conceived. Now, for Joyce to pattern the development of his alter ego after the embryonic growth of his newborn daughter represents an extraordinary act of identification, not with a person or even an image, but with a certain locus in the intersubjective network of the family, a "feminine" signifier or shadow-term under whose aegis the narrative confrontations with the maternal–filial nexus could unfold. For Joyce to author himself in accordance with the metaphor of gestation, to mother himself, so to speak, it was necessary for him to project himself into the subject position of a girl child, to daughter himself. It is the purely structural nature of Joyce's identification with Lucia, his identification with the daughter position *as such* that allowed Amalia Popper to fit so easily into the role of surrogate child *as* surrogate for Joyce himself.

Joyce earmarks Amalia as a daughter figure early on in *Giacomo* by transforming her seemingly chance encounter with Lucia (in her *only* appearance) into a moment of symbolic communion, a ritual interchange of identity: "A flower given by her to my daughter. Frail gift, frail giver, frail blue-veined child" (*GJ* 8). What is most striking about this transaction, however, is that Joyce does not pose a performative, functional, or imagistic equivalence between Amalia and Lucia so much as he aligns them in a structural analogy mediated by "a flower," the emphatic alliterative and syntactic priority of which makes it the defining rhetorical figure (or "flower") of their interrelation: "flower given ... Frail gift, frail giver, frail ... child." The flower, of course, is the ancient emblem of femininity and, more specifically, of the female genitalia. Accordingly, the "frail" quality of the flower, of Lucia, and of Amalia cannot but recall Hamlet's famous declaration, "Frailty, thy name is woman." Congruent with this sense of irresistible change, the flower itself marks an imminent stage of fecundity (the falling of the bloom heralding the appearance of the fruit) and so serves to symbolize a nearly mature or incompletely ripe stage of female sexuality. In both of its dominant significations, then, the flower token conjoins Amalia and Lucia as incestuously regarded daughters. As the officially designated "giver" of the token, however, Amalia simultaneously performs the maternal function of symbolically bequeathing her femininity and her incipient sexuality to Lucia, passing them on, as it were, through the act of being *literally* de-flowered. That is to say, a scene evidently designed to amalgamate Amalia with Joyce's child finds her slipping back into the maternal position, or rather shimmering back and forth between the two. From this, a couple of crucial inferences may be drawn.

(1) The underlying stakes of Joyce's identification with Lucia do in fact lie in its reconfiguration of the mother–son tie. The gender/

generational double-cross allowed Joyce to exercise his compulsion to repeat the experience of maternal abjection in the hope of mastering it (the daughter standing in for the mother), while at the same time allowing him to refuse ultimate separation by denying the necessity of gender differentiation (the daughter standing in for the self).

(2) Joyce's adulterous interest in Amalia may well have arisen *both* from a need to displace this dynamic *and* with an eye to enacting it in all of its complexity. Amalia was capable of halving the generational distance between mother and child in Joyce's imagination – unlike Lucia, still strictly a child, or Nora, who, having graduated to the place of mother, seems to have forfeited her childlike aura in Joyce's eyes. Specially situated to afford a combined site of identification and abjection, Amalia is constructed as the displaced figure of Joyce's own liminal femininity and feminized liminality. It is by virtue of this marginal location in the Joycean imaginary, engaging his self-image in a mirror play of absolute difference and possible equivalence, that she becomes an ethico-juridical as well as sexual object in the notebook. Whereas Stephen Dedalus represents Joyce's alter ego, a fictionalized version of authorial consciousness, another self, Amalia proves to be Joyce's sub-alter(n) ego, a fictionalized variant of authorial unconsciousness, an other-self.

The idea of the sub-alter(n) ego is, in my view, crucial to understanding how the imperative to justice makes itself felt in *Giacomo Joyce* and, by extension, Joyce's later works. What abjection is to the problem of desire, the rhetorical formation of the sub-alter(n) ego is to the later-phase, higher-order problem of psychic identification. But this shift in the plane of operation alters the dynamic itself. Because abjection forms a recursive cycle, detailed above, in which secondary ambivalence informs the primary ambivalence whence it nonetheless continues to derive, abjection can in effect turn (over) on itself when raised to the level of self-reflection, which is what the sub-alter(n) ego entails. So while abjection antedates and in some sense survives the teasing apart of attraction and repulsion through which the personality itself takes shape, the sub-alter(n) ego addresses and productively complicates the *effects* of this lingering unconscious ambivalence, specifically the dichotomizing of intimately related terms into points of absolute affiliation and disaffiliation: the avowed and the disowned self-image, the idealized and the denigrated other. The sub-alter(n) ego represents a fictive externalization of what Jane Gallop has called "the other within,"[60] a point of rhetorical access to the differential constitution of the subject in its innermost properties.

As such, the sub-alter(n) ego does not consist in a simple projection outward of some censored affect or aspect of the self upon some more or less fictionalized other. This rhetorical move tends to moralize the socially coded differences between the dominant subject and its designated other as a means of fetishizing or vilifying that other and thus ensuring the normativity of the dominant subject, i.e. his capacity both to dictate and to embody the cultural norm. The designated other comes to define the upper and nether limits of the human condition which the dominant subject alone exemplifies. Nor does the sub-alter(n) ego consist in a simple appropriation of the other to the self or the specularization of the self in the other. This rhetorical move assumes the ideal homogeneity of self and other as a means of preempting the other outright and thus extending the dominance of the normative subject across the entire social field. The other comes to be defined entirely by the lights of the normative subject, as his double or extension. Instead, the sub-alter(n) ego combines these colonizing tendencies in such a way as to expose their underlying interdependence, thereby allowing each to counteract and transvalue the other.

In a context governed by the subject's projection of censored material upon the subaltern, a countervailing movement in which the subject regards the subaltern as his double or extension has the virtue of safeguarding the formal possibility of a certain psychic identification with her, however reflexive it might be, and so of a certain limited will to reciprocity as well. On the other side, in a context governed by the subject's appropriation of the other as his enlarging mirror, the projection of censored material upon her serves to mark, however fetishistically, her difference from the self, and thus has the virtue of safeguarding an otherwise imperiled awareness of the independence of her perspective, the heterogeneity of her world. By bodying forth the profound entanglement of these colonizing tendencies, the way they both feed and constrict one another, the sub-alter(n) ego opens up a prospective recognition that the other is necessarily both inseparable from and irreducible to the self, a recognition, that is, both of the subjectivity of the other and the alterity of the self and of the correlation between them, the mutuality of being distinct and being decentered. In this recognition, one might say, resides the injunction to interpersonal justice, the demand for an equitable representation of the other. And yet, paradoxically, the practice of representation itself is necessarily animated by the continuing operation of those colonizing tendencies, the positive law of desire, which precludes the finality of justice.[61]

The juridical implications of the sub-alter(n) ego can be usefully fleshed out by recourse to the heuristic of Lacanian psychoanalysis, which has become so prevalent of late in Joyce studies. In these terms, the sub-alter(n) ego figures an inversion of the ambivalence attendant to what Lacan calls the mirror stage of consciousness, in which the emerging subject assumes a totalized body image as a way of replacing the lost plenitude of the mother–child dyad. To this end, Lacan proposes, the ego fashions itself after another and then struggles to incorporate that other's image or position as his own exclusive property. That is to say, the ego proper enters into being through a drama of imitation-cum-rivalry. The sub-alter(n) ego, conversely, comprises a drama of rivalry-cum-recognition, in which the subject defines himself over against the image of the other he seeks to dominate, only to find its alterity inwrought with his own make-up. With the sub-alter(n) ego, the effort to attain or maintain an illusory sense of wholeness by assuming control of another, an effort characteristic of Giacomo's gaze to this point in the text, issues in the inverse perception of both a primordial lack and a primordial interconnection. Needing a certain socially coded and ranked difference from the other to be himself, the dominant subject can, under certain circumstances, grow conscious of that difference, that otherness, as constitutive of his own identity and yet beyond it.

Such a perception is, of course, actively discouraged within the prevailing psychological and ideological framework of modern, patriarchal society. The splitting of the ego that occurs during the mirror stage carries over into the Symbolic order by way of its patriarchal mainstay, the law of the phallus. That is why the feminist critic Margaret Whitford views the Symbolic as a hegemonic variant of the masculine Imaginary.[62] Never completely detachable from its biological namesake, the phallus (Law of the Father) represents a unitary gauge or measure to which everyone is to be assimilated, thus ensuring specular commutability, and by which everyone is to be judged and ranked, thus ensuring moralized differences. And just as the patriarchal Symbolic complies to some degree with the Imaginary dimension that it supersedes, so the specifically ethico-juridical register of the Symbolic, its most fully socialized aspect, has tended to

reproduce even as it seeks to refine this violent Law. In fact,
previously elucidated impasses such as the liberal–communitarian
divide, founded upon the incompatibility of right-based and good-
based notions of justice, or the equal rights–special rights dispute,
rooted in the differential articulation of equity under and equity of
the law, or even the basic equality versus difference bind, these may
all be seen as nuanced elaborations upon the Imaginary antagonism
at the heart of the phallic order. The psychic formation that stages a
reversal of this antagonism, accordingly, points the way toward a
new ethical dispensation based upon the contradictory implication of
all socially encoded differences in one another and hence the need for
some measure of "agonistic respect"[63] amongst them. Whereas the
primordial ambivalence of abjection energizes the institution of the
fundamental break opposing sameness and difference, upon which
all hierarchical modes of organization rely, the hybrid aftereffect of
this ambivalence, the sub-alter(n) ego, complicates or compromises
this break; and it thereby facilitates a metonymic form of psychic
identification, in which the fundamental differences of ego and other
can be seen to rest upon their equally fundamental articulation – an
identification in otherness. This sort of double syntax poses tremendous resistance not just to a given body of social and cultural
regulation, but to the binary logic through which such regulation
might be *either* affirmed *or* disputed. Accordingly, the interests it
promotes, the energies it expresses, and the forces it serves are
themselves *radically marginal* in the sense outlined above, a sense
largely conformable with Joyce's personal and sociocultural situation.

VI

We can begin to unpack the significance of the Joycean sub-alter(n)
ego by tracking the textual reverberations of the Good Friday
fantasy. Taken as a screed on the perfidy of the grieving figure, the
latter installments of this crucifixion mytheme (frames 44 and 48)
would seem to project onto Amalia the author's mistrust of his own
motive in sentimentalizing someone whose domestic martyrdom may
well have been embittered if not hastened by his faithlessness – both
to her and to her allegorical extension, Mother Church. The portrait
of Stephen in *Ulysses* does tend to corroborate Joyce's anxiety over
who or what killed his mother, while the parodic rendering of Simon
Dedalus' ostentatious grief at his abused wife's grave in the "Hades"

episode attests to Joyce's shrewd indignation at guilty displays of mawkishness. In allegorizing Amalia's supposed treachery in Biblical terms, however, and pegging it to her gender and, ultimately, her racial status – "*Non hunc sed Barabbam*" (48) – Joyce effectively establishes a certain psychic distance from his own affect. He thus exemplifies the classic abjection response, to inscribe differences-of (those which disturb or subvert self-identity) as differences-from (those which consolidate it). To borrow from Stephen Tifft's definition of trauma, Joyce manages "to convert a betrayal (exposure) of his conflicted desires to a betrayal by the other."[64]

At the same time, because this conversion or displacement proceeds by way of an exchange of roles, wherein Amalia figures as Joyce's double or surrogate, the very act of establishing a psychic distance from her releases an immediate and equally powerful identificatory impulse, with which his perception of her otherness is to remain interfused. This movement displays the workings of the sub-alter(n) ego, where the proximity of the alien and the estrangement of the selfsame can come into play and intersect, forming the psychic condition for a pursuit of justice. This countervailing trend to the abjection of Amalia likewise proceeds, shadowed and shadowing in turn, to the end of the sketchbook. Its effect on the narrative progression, or perhaps it would be truer to say syncopation, of *Giacomo Joyce* commences with the passages immediately following the Good Friday scenario, the interlude surrounding the central "event" of *Giacomo*: Amalia's ailment, operation, and recovery.

The first of these frames (29) specifically remarks the confusion of parental features with those of the erotic object: "Hamlet ... is rude only to Polonius. Perhaps an embittered idealist, he can see in the parents of his beloved only grotesque attempts on the part of nature to produce her image ... Marked you that?" (*GJ* 29) The elements distinguishing this sentiment from its like expression in Stephen's Shakespeare theory in *Ulysses* – that it is the aspect of the beloved rather than the self that is menaced by family resemblances – undeniably reflects the incestuous pressures of the Good Friday fantasy. And if Joyce represses any mention, or for that matter any awareness, of the involvement of his own mother's image in this erotic confusion, the passage immediately following prepares for her symbolic return.

In frame 30, Joyce identifies Amalia with the superimposed figures of the two Italian Beatrices: Portinari, whose unbending sanctity in

Vita Nuova is the object of Dante's sexualized adoration, and Cenci, whose indomitable innocence in Shelley's drama is the object of "an incestuous passion, aggravated by every circumstance of cruelty and violence" (*C*, Preface), leading ultimately to her execution in the name and in the defense of a corrupt legal and religious authority:

She walks before me along the corridor and as she walks a dark coil of her hair slowly uncoils and falls. Slowly uncoiling, falling hair. She does not know and walks before me, simple and proud. So did she walk by Dante in simple pride and so, stainless of blood and violation, the daughter of Cenci, Beatrice, to her death... *Tie / My girdle for me and bind up this hair / In any simple knot.* (*GJ* 30)

The combined force of these associations places Amalia, for the very first time, in the role of the Crucified, with all of the resonance that such martyrdom carries in the Joyce family romance. The closing, italicized phrase, in fact, is a direct quotation from Beatrice Cenci's death speech. But what is of overriding importance here is that in conflating these figures, Joyce registers an understanding of the intimate relation that exists between his idealization and his desecration of Amalia. He presents them as two phases of the same fetishistic cycle. He even seems to suggest that his obsessive regard of and for Amalia sentences her to a kind of death, death by reification, appropriating her properly discrete being ("simple and proud") to the ambivalent structure of his erotic delirium, with neither her explicit consent ("she does not know") nor her tacit encouragement ("stainless of blood and violation"). It is not *just* that Joyce has found himself espousing the sexual ethics of Dante Aligheri and Francesco Cenci concurrently, but rather that he has discovered in his Dantean worship the vital pith of Cencian injustice, the imposition of one's desire upon another. Just as phallic sexuality cannot, as Shelley's *Cenci* demonstrates, be fully dissociated from the problem of incest, such imposition cannot be fully divorced from the dynamic of abjection, and for much the same reason. Insofar as Joyce continues to apprehend Amalia as an instance of The Woman,[65] a fantasy figure consolidating man in the economy of his desire, she must remain decidedly other yet not quite distinct, harboring her specific socially defined difference *strictly* in relation to him. That Joyce here seizes upon the murderous implications of this arrangement signals an incipient reversal of the way sameness and difference have been articulated heretofore, a direct consequence of his access to and use of a sub-alter(n) ego. In addition to constructing Amalia as *his* other, a rhetorical tendency in which he undeniably persists, Joyce seems prepared to identify with Amalia in *her* separateness. In addition to constructing Amalia's socially relevant differences as something to be mastered, possessed, and disdained by turns, Joyce is just beginning to construct these differences as defining a mutually held no man's land that problematizes any claim to mastery whatever, including self-mastery.

Joyce further encodes his developing insight by aligning his voyeuristic persona in the sketchbook with the character in *The Cenci* who most clearly incarnates the complicity between veneration and violence, self-regard and other-obsession, the double-dealing Orsino. Vicki Mahaffey has proposed that a salient property uniting Amalia's disparate literary correspondences in *Giacomo* is that all are worshiped and/or pursued more or less secretively, just as Amalia is by Joyce.[66] When it comes to Beatrice Cenci, Mahaffey points out, Orsino is the covert suitor, and he characterizes his amorous fantasies in specularizing terms that Joyce could not but apply to his own: "I clasp the phantom of unfelt delights/Till weak imagination half possesses/The self-created shadow" (*C*ii:2, lines 141–3). In addition, Orsino, like Joyce to this point in the notebook, manifests some anxiety at the vivisective power of his beloved's return look: "Yet I fear / Her subtle mind, her awe-inspiring gaze, / Whose beams anatomize me nerve by nerve / And lay me bare, and make me blush to see / My hidden thoughts" (*C*i:3, lines 83–7). As the last clause indicates, Beatrice's scopic challenge accomplishes more than the Medusa's, more, that is, than simply interrupting the imaginary plenitude of the phallic I / eye.[67] In answering his specularizing gaze in kind, she reveals to him his image in her eye, as it were, provoking him to reflect upon the predatory nature of his desire: "Beatrice unveiled me to myself, / And made me shrink from what I could not shun" (*C*ii:2, lines 115–16). Orsino's muted elusive presence in *Giacomo* is itself a testament to the effect Amalia had begun to have in stimulating Joyce to similarly self-accusatory reflection.

Indeed, the true relevance of Orsino's character as a model or a metaphor for Giacomo resides in the treacherousness of his amorous passion, a truly radical treacherousness which does not just belie the homage he pays to Beatrice but also exposes the ideological assumption that his homage mystifies: the equation of value, particularly feminine value, with (male) property. Without forswearing or even seeming to contravene his esteem for Beatrice, Orsino schemes to acquire her dowry, considers Beatrice the "profit" to be drawn from his machinations, and, once these machinations come a cropper, sacrifices her to the exigencies of self-interest: "a name and country new and a new life, fashioned on the old desires" (*Cī*:5, lines 89–90). The phrase "a new life" translates in Orsino's native tongue as *vita nuova* and thus sets this lover of Beatrice and the other one, Dante, in an ironic juxtaposition, which Joyce then internalizes and reworks, using it specifically to note the element of betrayal he detects in his own passion for Amalia. There is in the first instance, of course, the betrayal of Amalia herself, which like all betrayals in Joyce takes the form of a crucifixion analogue or fantasy. But there is also a betrayal of the integrity of his own avowed feelings and perceptions, bad faith if you like, the internal corrosiveness intrinsic to unconscious ambivalence. In this regard, it is worth noting that the other primary victim of Orsino's treachery in *The Cenci* is a namesake of the Joycean persona here: Beatrice's brother, Giacomo. Through this citational web, Joyce contrives to criticize quietly the representational violence he has done Amalia, and to do so from his recently adopted standpoint of psychic identification with her, here expressed in terms of sibling fellowship. This mode of affiliation actually emphasizes and so takes responsibility for the incestuous abjection out of which Joyce's new desire to be fair has emanated, especially inasmuch as the sibling tie can be read as a way of figuring his conflation of Amalia as surrogate child with Amalia as surrogate self.

At the same time, it is hardly fortuitous that Joyce immediately follows this frame with an impressionistic rendering of Amalia's actual or presumed brush with death during this period. The concurrence is especially telling since certain metonymic connections between Amalia's malady, calling for an emergency appendectomy, and Mrs. Joyce's liver cancer might well have been of sufficient strength and proximity to trigger Joyce's latent anxiety over both his mother's death and the crucifixion fantasy just rehearsed. On this score, we should not overlook the anatomical proximity of Amalia's area of complaint to that of May Joyce. Nor should we overlook Joyce's conflation of that area of complaint with the maternal womb – "The surgeon's knife has probed in her entrails and withdrawn, leaving the raw jagged gash of its passage on her belly ... O cruel wound! Libidinous God!" (*GJ* 32) Joyce's closing imprecation of a desiring if divine father clearly positions Amalia at the maternal vertex of an oedipal triangle, where her troubles represent a threat of separation analogous to that posed by his mother's terminal illness. Once again, Amalia's ability to split the distance between the status of mother and daughter, to shimmer along both sides of the parental–filial divide, proves crucial to her ethico-juridical function in *Giacomo Joyce*.

Viewed by itself, Joyce's initial thought at the prospect of Amalia's passing seems utterly conventional. He worries that she has departed from him "in a moment, without a word, without a look" (*GJ* 31), a romantic cliché which takes the lover's dispossession at the time of death as a synecdoche for the timeless separation that death institutes. Viewed in context, however, this initial reaction proves rather more intriguing. As I have stated more than once, Giacomo's erotic imperialism, in its alternate modes of Pygmalionesque aestheticism and domineering lust, founds and naturalizes itself by denying (that) Amalia (possesses) her own voice and perspective, i.e. treating her as still immanent to the bodily–material stratum of life. That Joyce should now find himself longing for her distinctive address and thus her distinctive purchase on the world not only tends to oppugn his past treatment of her, crediting her with a degree of transcendence he has hitherto denied, but lends an ironic credence to his recent fantastic apprehension that his attraction for Amalia has been in certain respects fatal, that she too was his victim.

Visiting the convalescent Amalia, Joyce takes the measure of the "look" he feared he would never see again. At first blush, his representation of her gaze signals no change in his attitude, but recalls and renews his earlier practice of mastering Amalia's presence and, with it, his own sense of lack, by reducing her to a condition of mute and passive animality whose meaningfulness and value are entirely at his disposal ("I see her full, dark, suffering eyes, beautiful as the eyes of an antelope" (*GJ* 32)). Amalia's gaze suffers Joyce's gaze much as the bird girl suffers Stephen's in *A Portrait*. But this silent exchange also contains a crucial allusion to *The Cenci* which provides a subtext linking this passage to the progress of the preceding frames and riveting the connection between the figurative doom of Amalia–Beatrice in frame 30 and Amalia's literal collapse in frame 31.

Hard upon his analysis of Beatrice's "awe-inspiring gaze," whose "beams anatomize [him] nerve by nerve / And lay [him] bare,"

Orsino disavows (denies/concedes) its critical potency and the castration anxiety it arouses by likening himself to "a Panther... panic-stricken by the Antelope's eye" (*C*1:3, lines 89–90). Now, given the citational pattern already in place, Joyce's use of the phrase, "the eyes of an antelope" in this context would seem to signify his implicit recognition (awareness and respect) of the potential incisiveness of a gaze which nonetheless continues to strike him as vulnerable, tractable, and quiescent. Joyce thus remarks his own tendency to disavow Amalia's moral agency, and in the very act of doing so, he begins to slough the tendency as well, bringing forth from the desire for Imaginary plenitude an acceptance of primordial lack and primordial interconnection. Instead of seeking to master Amalia's gaze through an act of mental and spiritual penetration, as he does at the outset of *Giacomo Joyce* (*GJ* 3), Joyce sufficiently masters his own castration anxiety, for the moment anyway, to admit (concede and receive) the analogous moral penetration of her gaze. In the same elusive motion, he also discloses his persistent reluctance to do so, thus confessing to his own share of vulnerability. The binocularity of his symbolic identification with Amalia affiliates it that much more closely with the construct I call the sub-alter(n) ego. For it is along that psychic margin, where the mutuality of being distinct and being decentered insists, that Joyce's still tacit recognition of the sovereign subjectivity of Amalia can awaken a sense of his otherness to himself and to his own designs.

As the abbreviated closing movement of *Giacomo Joyce* unfolds, the rehabilitation of Amalia's point of view comes to serve as an increasingly decisive counterforce to her continued abjection. Over the same span, and correlatively, cracks begin to appear in the imperialist stronghold of Giacomo's Imaginary: his faith in and will to self-possession and self-enclosure, aesthetic mastery and transcendence, and ethno-sexual superiority and domination are all progressively if haltingly eroded. Joyce did not come to grips with the underlying conditions and implications of this development until some years later, however, and the interpolated passage I discussed at the outset of this chapter was his means of inscribing not only his revised aesthetic and political judgment in the text but his related understanding of how they came about. A textual supplement in the Derridean sense, the interpolated passage (45) supplies a retrospective gloss on the entire notebook that directly alters the text itself and so must be taken into account *ahead of time*. In its staggered composition, *Giacomo Joyce* actually stages the strange temporality of justice, interpretive and otherwise, the *futur antérieur*. Giacomo's attitude toward Amalia unfolds under the sign of the "will have been" and demands a kind of double reading on that basis. At the same time, the interpolated passage serves both Joyce and his readers as a vehicle for placing the more intimate stakes of his desire for Amalia, his renewed struggle with maternal abjection, back into the historical and specifically colonial context that gave this ambivalence its distinctive shape.

VII

The leavening influence of this textual revision is in fact so profound and so manifold that to avoid oversaturation the frame must be subdivided and the irradiating effects of the respective passages treated in sequence. The frame begins:

A soft crumpled peagreen cover drapes the lounge. A narrow Parisian room. The hairdresser lay here but now. I kissed her stocking and the hem of her rustblack dusty skirt. It is the other. She. Gogarty came yesterday to be introduced. *Ulysses* is the reason. Symbol of the intellectual conscience... Ireland then? And the husband? [Michele Risolo]... Why are we left here? ... Intellectual symbol of my race. (*GJ* 45)

This dream interlude is momentous in connecting an implied reassessment of Joyce's colonizing aggression toward Amalia to an analogous reassessment of his intellectual stance toward Ireland, specifically that internally imperialistic mission of soul-making summarized in the phrase, "to forge the uncreated conscience of my race" (*AP* 252), which is unmistakably recalled here. In the dream context, the hairdresser blends into Amalia, who in turns stands forth as Joyce's symbol of the Irish intellectual conscience. The casting could not be more precisely and devastatingly ironic. For the kind of Manichean allegory that keys Giacomo's representation of Amalia was immediately familiar to Joyce because it corresponded in such great detail with the British iconography of the Irish during the mid and late Victorian period. As I have shown in previous chapters, the comparatively raw, politically motivated ethno-anthropological discourses of the nineteenth century produced several sexual taxonomies of the races in which the Celts, like the Jews, were classified as essentially feminine and grouped with the Oriental races on that basis. In fact, Otto Weininger's pseudoscientific feminizing of the Jews, which so intrigued Joyce,[68] picked up on an ideological tradition popularized by Ernest Renan's pseudoscientific feminizing of the Celts.[69] No less august an expert than the historian Lord Acton likened the Irish to the "Hindoos" in their passivity, their indolence, their luxuriousness, and their absence of real historical agency, all stereotypically feminine attributes associated with the material–bodily stratum;[70] while Matthew Arnold located the femininity of the Celts in their supposed sentimentality, their emotional instability, and their undependability.[71] Finally, in the heated atmosphere of the Land War and the Plan of Campaign, the London newspaper and penny weeklies, many of which made their way to the Sister Isle, regularly depicted the Irish as ignorant, bestial, and inherently treacherous. (Madden makes explicit reference to these caricatures in one such publication, *Punch*, during his argument with Stephen over patriotism in *Stephen Hero* (65).)[72] So by identifying Amalia with the Irish race, after having assigned her each of the above traits at one point or another in the text, Joyce figures his previous indulgence in sexist/anti-Semitic rhetoric as a mediated betrayal of the sub-dominant position and minority heritage of his own people.

This sort of negative identification in otherness with Amalia seems to have been helped along by Joyce's feeling that they shared, in their different ways, the condition of exile. Ellmann reports that during this period Joyce gradually "began to recognize his place in Europe to be as ambiguous as theirs [the Jews']."[73] Manganiello confirms that while on the continent Joyce gradually came to see the similarity of his position to that of the Jews primarily as regards the state of exile.[74] Exile had, of course, long been a part of Joyce's self-definition, and as the play *Exiles* suggests, the idea was taking on richer and more poignant shadings at this juncture, as Ireland seemed to be moving toward home rule. A more decisive sense of banishment may well have seized Joyce at this point, which would explain why he became keen on the analogy to the plight of European Jewry. On the other hand, Joyce fixes on the term "exile" in good part to differentiate the course he had adopted from the mass Irish emigration of the nineteenth century, a phenomenon whose parallel with the Jewish diaspora had been a familiar topos since the days of the potato famine. This is important in understanding the passage in question, for by situating Amalia between past abuse and present redress, literal Jewishness and symbolic Irishness, Joyce suggests that the elitism or supremacism he had entertained is the flip side of colonial self-disgust: either sensibility manifests his internalization of the phobic bodily antinomies that ground sovereign subjectivity (the clean versus the defiled body, the whole versus the castrated body, the sublime versus the submerged body, etc.) as they have been filtered through the symbolic grid of European and specifically British imperialism. Joyce unmasks this very form of colonial mimesis in the more virulent strains of Irish jingoism, rejecting, in his words, "the old pap of racial hatred" (*SL* 110–11), a trope which expressly places the racist impulse, what we might call body hate, as a transferential form of maternal abjection. But in *Giacomo*, Joyce discovers (displays and witnesses) his susceptibility to a subtler variant of the same pathological mimesis. Because his Manichean construction of Amalia resonates so distinctively of the English depiction of the Irish, Joyce is not only given new insight into the purely performative status of the criteria distinguishing different classes of normative and subaltern subjectivity, he was also given to understand how vital a stake he continued to have in hegemonic performances from which he otherwise suffered, how deeply his sense of sovereignty was implicated in them, and so how responsible for and complicit in these practices he remained, his own victimization notwithstanding. Indeed, the structure of the interpolated passage implicitly acknowledges that in treating Amalia in an Orientalizing and misogynist manner, he had basically "identified with the aggressor" in the unconscious desire to exorcise the Orientalized and feminized associations of his own Irishness.[75] Once detected, this purpose reflects rather badly on Joyce's doggedly adversarial disposition toward his homeland. What he had believed a noble, even heroic, effort to save Irish culture by criticizing it he could now see as tainted by a certain "West Britonish" collaboration. Under these circumstances, for Joyce to identify with Amalia is a step toward resisting his interpellation to metropolitan subjectivity, toward renouncing the master's values and the values of mastery, and toward reasserting the marginality of his specific social inscription.

By introducing these doubts about his past micro and macro political practice as an indirect response to the fanfare surrounding *Ulysses*, Joyce simultaneously underlines and transcribes all of those sentiments expressed in *Giacomo Joyce* which are to be subsequently retailed, recontextualized, and decisively ironized in the later work. Two examples of this technique seem especially pertinent to our argument. Joyce's previously cited use of the phrase "prostrate bugs" (*GJ* 22) to describe the Triestine Jews is subject to a highly mediated qualification by this reference to *Ulysses* which brings into the textual play an analogous association of Jews and bugs made by the reprehensibly chauvinistic "Citizen" of the "Cyclops" episode: "Those are nice things," says the Citizen, "coming over here to Ireland filling the country with bugs" (*U* 12.1141–2). Since the violently anti-Semitic Citizen is both an ostentatious Irish nationalist and a secret traitor to the cause, the implication here would seem to be that the exclusionary sensibility that Joyce forswears in alluding to this satirical butt signifies a sham or perfidious commitment to colonial liberation. The second example reinforces this perception. In frame 24, Joyce makes the snide remark, "They [the Triestine Jews] love their country when they are quite sure which country it is" (*GJ* 24), the substance of which he later attributes to J. J. O'Molloy in reference to Bloom during the same anti-Semitic interlude in "Cyclops." O'Molloy imagines that he is standing up for a natural conception of Irishness, but he more generally exemplifies what Joyce took to be the singularly Irish proclivity for duplicitous charade. Attempting to trade hard-luck tales for handouts from cronies employed by the Castle, whose patriotism, therefore, is likewise spurious, O'Molloy can properly be characterized as a parasite's parasite. Once again, promoting exclusionary identity–politics in the name of colonial integrity correlates with a certain undermining of that integrity. This connection is ratified, finally, by the presence in this frame of Oliver St. John Gogarty. His persona in *Ulysses*, Buck Mulligan, adopts a strongly anti-Semitic posture, implying a substantialist view of race and racial mores. All the while he himself indulges in such self-serving forms of mummery that he earns the semi-official designation, Ireland's "gay betrayer" (*U* 1.405). His practice thus shows how naturalizing distinctions among races of people are themselves a peculiarly malicious factor in the perpetual masquerade which they feign to refute. With this cluster of citations, Joyce simultaneously announces, displays, and renounces the sort of unadmitted, unholy alliance he has joined in abjecting the culturally defined subaltern(s) and, by inference, his own colonial origins. He thereby enacts in the (inter)text of the interpolated passage a shift in orientation from ego, conceived as the primary structure of selfhood, to sub-alter(n) ego conceived as the zone of primordial (self-) difference or relationality.

The result of Joyce's more intensely self-conscious shift in subject position is a more intensively self-conscious identification in otherness with Amalia and the correspondingly overt accommodation of her viewpoint. The interpolated frame continues

Listen! The plunging gloom has fallen. Listen!
—I am not convinced that such activities of the mind or body can be called unhealthy – She speaks. A weak voice from beyond the cold stars. Say on! Oh, say again, making me wise. This voice I never heard. (*GJ* 45)

The wisdom that "this voice" – the voice "of the other ... she" – has to impart would seem to consist in the objection it raises to the phobic and pathologizing take on nonetheless fetishized "activities" which characterizes so much of *Giacomo Joyce* and contributes so much to the silencing of Amalia's voice. The passage thus intimates a fundamental reversal in the pedagogical relationship of the protagonists.[76] But what is even more important is the way that it maps onto and throws in relief the play of voice(s) that gives the notebook its comprehensive ethico-political structure: the counterpoint of Joyce's suppressive monologue before Amalia's operation (frames 1 through 30) with the emergent dialogue between them thereafter (31 through 50). Having deprived Amalia of her voice through the long first movement, Joyce here makes a concentrated effort to discern it: "listen! ... Listen! ... She speaks ... Say on! Oh, say again." In recalling a similar attempt during that past – "bend and hear" (20) – this effort indicates that the problem of silence lay not with the speaker but with the auditor, who at first could only pick up the "thin breath of a sparrow" (*GJ* 20) and even now only hears her as a "weak voice from beyond the ... stars" (45). At the same time, given their prescriptive form, these phrases can be taken as commanding the reader, Joyce himself, or anyone else to rehear the case of Giacomo with an ear to discovering the voice of Amalia. In a sense, it is this very mandate, directing the author/reader back into the text in a certain way, that renders this politically charged play of voice(s) apprehensible in the first place and so might be seen as realizing or inducing it as such. Joyce certainly insinuates as much when, standing virtually at the end of the dialogical second movement, he declares, "This voice I never heard" (45).

Undertaking the retrospective search prescribed in the text, one learns that Amalia's voice first finds representation during the postconvalescent period, which is to say directly after Joyce shows some awareness of the autonomous moral force of her gaze. It is as though Amalia's flirtation with becoming a corpse, the ultimate site of abjection, awakens Joyce to the abjectifying effects of his erotic and aesthetic agenda. Dread shifts from the object of desire to the loss of that object, the permanent stilling of Amalia, and produces a greater if still largely preconscious responsiveness to her voice. Vicki Mahaffey has isolated Amalia's surgery as a narrative turning point for another reason: thereafter images of death progressively intrude upon Giacomo's interaction with Amalia.[77] These two trends, I would submit, are not unrelated. Amalia's brush with death creates the emotional climate compelling Joyce to attend to her voice and gaze, which, in making him the object of *her* desire, threaten him with a kind of death necessary to any metonymic identification, a puncturing of the illusion of properly authorial subjectivity – whole, autonomous, and self-imaging.

As one might expect, given the constitutive nature of the fantasy at issue, the ethical adjustments Joyce makes in response to this crisis, while decisive, are by no means simple or absolute. His initial impression of a recuperated and giddily relieved Amalia is for our purposes nearly indistinguishable from his past caricatures. He represents her as, well, a birdbrain ("Once more in her chair by the window, happy words on her tongue, happy laughter. A bird twittering after storm, happy that its foolish life has fluttered out of reach of an epileptic lord and giver of life, twittering happily, twittering and chirping happily" (*GJ* 33)). Joyce moves from silencing Amalia outright to granting her the faculty of speech only to deny her, at least implicitly, the power of genuine articulation and, quite explicitly, the aptitude to say something weighty or even sensible. But then he turns around in the very next frame and negates this impression by recording her observation on being recruited as a reader of his autobiographical fiction, " *The Portrait of the Artist*" [*sic*]. Now, just by sounding Amalia out on his work, Joyce necessarily induces some nascent respect for her taste, intellect, or critical acumen, albeit a respect deeply bound up with his own need to be admired both as a man and as an artist. But the comment with which he credits her indicates just how fraught his gesture really is: "She says that, had *The Portrait of the Artist* been frank only for frankness' sake, she would have asked why I had given it to her to read" (*GJ* 34). Amalia astutely taps into the eroticized self-exposure Joyce's offering effects. Since the text in question is not only autobiographical but intimate and, for the time, scandalous, Joyce can be seen as engineering a complex, asymmetrical, but nonetheless dramatic reversal of scopic roles: he adopts the position of aesthetic *exhibitionist* in addition to that of voyeuristic author; Amalia *inherits* the role of voyeuristic reader and critic while remaining an involuntary aesthetic *exhibition*. That Joyce should engineer an interchange of this type evinces what I have called his metonymic identification with Amalia, the specularizing element of which depends upon and combines with an element of genuine recognition. He enlists her as his symbolic double and ideal reader, an enlarging mirror for his ego, precisely by submitting his image to the already acknowledged difference of her desire and her judgment.

Joyce's attitude in the aftermath of his offering (gift/tutorial assignment) corroborates its fundamental duplicity. On the one hand he contemplates his words entering and occupying Amalia's brain, rather in the manner of a colonizing force. Indeed, it is at this stage that he introduces the previously cited frame beginning "My words in her mind" (*GJ* 37). At the same time, he senses having transferred to her a recursive if not exactly reciprocal power in the bargain. He finds his self-representation alienated in her gaze as she was in his, subject to her curiosity, inspection, intrusion, and interpretive recreation as she was to his. "Those quiet cold fingers," he writes, "have touched the pages, foul and fair, on which my shame should glow" (*GJ* 38). Even the hazard of sexual contamination seems to be running in the other direction at this point. But what makes this experience so astringent for Joyce is his increasingly *radical* sense of her difference, i.e. his positive incertitude as to the exact parameters of that difference or even whether there are exact parameters.[78] Witness his stereotypical and yet self-conscious marmorealizing and aestheticizing of Amalia's hands: "quiet and cold and pure fingers. Have they never erred?" (*GJ* 38) By figuring Amalia as a marble or alabaster statue and then questioning the moralized gender assumptions on which his own metonymy is based, Joyce registers an understanding of (sexual) difference as an open-ended iteration of cultural codes rather than a brute instantiation of biological law. Such an understanding is the condition of possibility for any identification in otherness to occur.

Likewise, and for much the same reason, Amalia's specifically aesthetic scrutiny and judgment pique Joyce in both senses of the term. They irk him, provoking resentment, and they arouse and stimulate him, provoking respect. His retort to her observation is snidely sexist, turning gender difference into an occasion for dismissing an insight he finds embarrassing: "oh you would, would you? A lady of letters" (*GJ* 34). But it is also tinctured with faint surprise and teacherly pride in her literary perspicacity. If "*lady* of letters" exposes a gynephobic condescension, "lady of *letters*" conveys professional regard.

That there might also be a personal, cross-gender identification at work in the phrase "lady of letters" was corroborated retroactively by Joyce's dogged scheme to install Lucia as his lady of letters or *lettrines* further along in his career. Joyce encouraged his daughter to devise filagreed inaugural letters, *lettrines*, for use in a collection whose eponymous title, *The Joyce Book*,[79] allowed father and daughter to be subsumed together under the name of the Father. Having deemed her work "exquisite," he subsequently commissioned her *lettrines* for a manuscript version of *Pomes Penyeach*, which he had deposited in the Bibliothèque Nationale and the British Museum.[80] Ultimately, he used her *lettrines* in manuscripts of two episodes of *Finnegans Wake*: "The Mime, Mick, Nick and the Maggies" and "Storiella as She is Syung."[81] Given the central narrative and thematic significance of letters in the *Wake*, both as characters and as missives, in particular the letters of the schizoid daughter, Issy, and given further the prominent role of elaborate calligraphy in underscoring this significance (e.g. *The Book of Kells*), a textualist reading attentive to the bibliographical codes of the *Wake* can trace a *literal* convergence of father and daughter on its pages and in its authorial function.[82] In this regard, it might be worth mentioning that the signifier, *lettrine*, occupies a middle ground between "letter" and "latrine" and so provides a paranomasic link between Issy's urinary self-exposure, which provokes Earwicker's fall, and Issy's epistolary exposure of the fall itself. Extending matters only slightly, the *lettrine* serves as a metaphor for the link between Lucia's impact upon Joyce's creativity, which he everywhere associates with transgression or lapse, and Lucia's own graphic role in marking that impact. Indeed, Joyce's belief in the correlation between Lucia's progression on her *lettrines* and his progression on the *Wake* provides direct biographical support for such a reading.[83] All of this suggests that Joyce's paternal cross-gender identification contributed to his developing sense of justice and his literary ethics in general by helping to militate against the aesthetic economy of splendid, elitist isolation he had prescribed for himself in his youthful manifesto, "The Day of the Rabblement" (*CW* 69).

In just this respect, Amalia's comment about the possibility of gratuitous frankness in the *Portrait* is really quite germane with respect to the trajectory of Joyce's artistic evolution. In the preceding chapter, I contended that by representing and adjudicating incommensurable gender claims from a vantage ostensibly beyond the fray, the mobile polyphonic voice of *Dubliners* heralds a lingering attachment to the aesthetics of transcendence, the underlying principles of which – separation, objectification, subordination – recapitulate the axiomatic tendency of the patriarchal sex/gender system. The key to such an aesthetic program is maintaining the illusion of a "whole" or "clean" authorial self, unembedded in the material text he has produced. The stylistic design of *A Portrait*, with its famous equipoise or oscillation between sympathy and irony, aspires to an even more rarefied level of aesthetic transcendence: the deliverance of the authorial ego from the contamination and castration, the loss of wholeness and control, accompanying the consignment of his self-image to the play of textuality. The doubtful artist, Stephen, subject to the oscillation of stylistic perspective, is split off from the assured prototype, Joyce, who manipulates him. Amalia's point about frankness does more in this instance than question whether Joyce's text achieved this sort of critical purchase on its own dynamic. By making reference to the specific site of this aesthetic transaction, she uncovers some valuable lessons about the structure of aesthetic exchange in general. To wit, the artist's life and limitations leave their trace in his or her productions; the act of aesthetic revelation, therefore, always involves a degree of self-exposure as well; so, in the end, the literary work does not constitute an object or an anonymous circuit of meaning but an intensely personal if highly mediated and displaced mode of communication. These ideas, in turn, comport with the aesthetic model Joyce enacts in *Ulysses* and *Finnegans Wake*, where he counters the dominant T. E. Hulme–T. S. Eliot axis of detached or "cold" modernism by abandoning at last his own neo-Kantian roots.

In the spirit of this midcourse correction, we must attend closely to the complex, specialized ethical and political conditions of this transaction with Amalia, rather than focusing exclusively on the seemingly universalizable aesthetic truths it yields. The imperialistic (racist/sexist) thrust of Joyce's gaze on this occasion shapes the defensiveness of his reaction to this further reversal of pedagogic roles and leaves him vulnerable to feeling annulled by Amalia's probing, readerly scrutiny. Homi Bhaba has analyzed this phenomenon under the category of colonial mimicry.[84] The colonizer justifies his appropriation of the other in terms of realizing her as a virtual subject, educating or edifying her as Joyce does Amalia. But because she only remains appropriable insofar as she is *also* a virtual object, irredeemably inferior, her adaptation or capture of the colonizer's belief and value structure, her appreciation of his tastes and interests, her facility with his language, her mastery of his criteria of judgment, all with a subtle yet profound inflection, call into question both their elite status and their universal validity and thus challenge both the superiority and the coherence of his social identity. Abjection as dread *desire*, the will to impose the self on the other, leads the colonizer to a perception of his own underlying hybridity, which abjection as *dread* desire, the will to secure the self over against the other, aims to avert.

But as a metropolitan colonial, a racially feminized male, an impoverished and declassed intellectual, a *"maestro inglese"* (*GJ* 13) who was underling to both the *inglese* and, in some sense, to his own protégé, Joyce inhabited a much more complex affective and political situation than the one Bhaba explicates. His relation to the normative subject position *itself* is deeply compromised in *Giacomo*, so that at a certain point maintaining the coherence of his social identity comes into conflict with the whole matrix of hierarchical distinctions and sign values that undergirds his equally self-defining pretension to elite status. For Joyce to defend the peculiar conformation of his social identity, inscribed as it is along and athwart the colonizer/colonized, dominant/subaltern divide, would seem impossible in much the same way as achieving an ultimate state of justice is impossible. For he was simultaneously required to reject the elite standards and received logic of value in order to avoid allying himself with imperialist oppression and to continue relying on those standards and that logic in order to mark himself off from some more purely subaltern status. It is this aggravated condition of colonial hybridity, a double or multiple syntax, that Joyce's imperialist abjection of Amalia has to this point served to disguise or deny, by emphasizing the socially entitled elements of his own profile. So as Joyce begins to take stock of and responsibility for this abjection, he loses not only the security of assumed privilege, but the privilege of assumed security.

He has to confront the ethico-political undecidability that attaches to his subject position as a result of its incompatibility with more recognizably hegemonic and subaltern stations.

As one might expect, the effects of this lived dislocation are immediately evident in Joyce's reaction to the emergence of Amalia's perspective. On the one hand, while he allows her previously stifled voice a hearing, he does not perform this liberation joyfully or even dispassionately, but as though he were unleashing an irresistible menace to his authorial identity. Having moved so far toward identification with Amalia, Joyce appears to encounter the limits of this odyssey, beyond which he will lose the moorings of subjectivity altogether. On the other hand, even as he represents the emergence of Amalia's voice as undoing his own self-conception, he insists upon exposing himself to it and effecting its release in the text, and the duress involved only underscores the depths of his investment in the performance. This contorted attitude reflects the radical marginality of Joyce's social inscription – between the margins and the mainstream – and the warring allegiances that it elicits. At once a dominant and a subdominant subject, Joyce is torn between his attachment to and his reaction against the racial and sexual ideologies of his time and the conflicting profiles these interconnected regimes offered of his own character and his own standing in the world. In his dealings with Amalia, Joyce structures this conflict in terms of means and ends. He undertakes the *act* of liberating the voice of Amalia while he shrinks from the *fact* of its liberation. He perversely finds proof of his rhetorical authority and validation of his elite artistic identity in summoning forth the subaltern voice that challenges or at least qualifies that authority and threatens to dislodge that identity. In this light, Joyce's messianic self-imagings in *Giacomo* and elsewhere seem less an indulgence or a delusion of grandeur than a strategic compulsion, a way of valorizing a contradiction he could not dispel: that the affirmation of his subject position was inextricably bound up with his dissolution.

Joyce figures the dissolution of his identity in the concluding frame of *Giacomo* as a *petite mort*. Just as his suppression of Amalia's voice culminates in her dalliance with death, his liberation of her voice precipitates a series of apparently lethal transmissions from different points on her person. First, her hair and dress are seen to mirror "the hue of the illusion of the vegetable glass of nature and of lush grass, the hair of graves" (*GJ* 36). Next, in a typically Joycean series of puns, her face appears "gray and grave" surmounted by "dank matted hair" (41). Then, her kiss communicates the "vapor of death" in a "sighing breath" (41). Finally, as her fatal charm concentrates itself in her gaze, the transmission takes on a phallic quality, signifying a turnabout in the gender masquerade. Joyce ascribes a baneful potency to her "black basilisk eyes ... *e col suo vedere attosca l'uomo quando lo vede*" (43), and in a convergence of this narrative sequence and the crucifixion theme, Amalia turns an ejaculating gaze upon the messianic Joyce, "darting ... out of her sluggish sidelong eyes a jet of liquorish venom" (44). At this point, Joyce's intent to realize Amalia's potential to be like him comes to an ironic fruition in the desubstantialization and destabilization of gender norms.

Capping and crystallizing this sequence is the interpolated passage, the concluding segment of which reads as follows:

> She coils toward me along the crumpled lounge. I cannot move or speak. Coiling approach of starborn flesh. Adultery of wisdom. No. I will go. I will. —Jim, love! —Soft sucking lips kiss my left armpit: a coiling kiss on myriad veins. I burn! I crumple like a burning leaf. From my right armpit a fang of flame leaps out. A starry snake has kissed me: a cold nightsnake. I am lost! —Nora — (*GJ* 45)

The reversals we have seen in scopic power, pedagogical authority and sexual roles here pass directly into a reversal in vocal or representational prerogative. Joyce is silenced ("I cannot ... speak") before Amalia's "adultery of wisdom," which has already been metonymically linked with her faculty of speech: "voice of wisdom, say on! O, say again making me wise. This voice I never heard" (45). In this oneiric mixture of memory and imagination, Joyce incurs the sort of aesthetic and sexual objectification he had inflicted, testing it, so to speak, on his own body. What Amalia actually says, "Jim, love!" connects this voice transplant with the most sweeping of the reversals mounted in *Giacomo Joyce*, a reversal in sexual and amorous agency. In keeping with the recovery of her voice, Amalia becomes an aggressive, pleasure-seeking subject; in keeping with the loss of his, Joyce becomes the passive, suffering, and embodied object ("I cannot move").

Joyce gives this reversal of erotic energy a markedly gendered figuration. Amalia's action unfolds throughout the scene in terms of patently phallic imagery – "She coils toward me ... Coiling approach of starborn flesh ... A coiling kiss ... a fang of flame ... A starry snake has kissed me" (45). Her erogenous target, Joyce's armpit, is notable for being a relatively gynemorphic part of the anatomy, bearing the rounded, hollow, recessive shape associated with the female body in general and the womb in particular. Joyce figures the armpit as a penetrable part of the anatomy as well – her "fang of flame" goes in one and out the other. By pegging normative masculine and feminine sexual attributes to the possession and privation of voice respectively and then reversing them on that basis, Joyce supplants an essentialist with a constructivist mode of gender dimorphism and, more than that, he treats sexual difference as primarily grounded in power relations, as inextricable from sexual dominance. It is precisely on this view that gender appears less a simple law than a thorny problem of justice: how, to paraphrase Irigaray, can "women be ... equal to men" without being "like men, therefore not women," and how can women "accrue value" to themselves as women when that which is held to define women as such, the cluster of attributes called femininity, is "a role, an image, a value imposed on them by a male system of representation"?[85]

At the same time, however, Joyce's picture of Amalia at this moment finds something unnatural, even monstrous, in her new stature, betraying his continued investment in that "male system of representation" that he has been willing to violate. The reptilian aspect in which he envisions Amalia combines with the sinister thrust of her own imagined gaze to evoke the figure of the Medusa, the mythic archetype of the phallic woman as castrating bitch, and Amalia's searingly painful method of seduction works to confirm and carry forward the allusion. Under these circumstances, Joyce's appeal to Nora as a protectress can be seen as counterposing the fantasy of the phallic mother, the ultimate guarantor of male satisfaction, to the phallic woman, the expropriator of male privilege, in an almost instinctive recurrence to the old gender typologies. Thus, it becomes clear that while Joyce's powerful ambivalence toward Amalia has been relieved and enriched over the course of the notebook, it has not dwindled away so much as changed dimension. Instead of a conflict between his dread of and desire for his racial and sexual fantasy of a luxurious, enigmatic, and compliant Amalia, Joyce is torn between the persistence of this fantasy and his daunting recognition of her effective autonomy, agency, and acuity, all of which he has difficulty conceiving without a decidedly masculinized inflection. The resulting conflict concentrates itself in the portrayal of Amalia as a grotesque,

properly defined as an aesthetic representation which, being constituted in contradiction, defies the effective categories of intelligibility.[86]

Bella/Bello in *Ulysses* is another such grotesque, and her/his
connection to Amalia is more than casual. What we have in *Giacomo*
is a kind of (non)dress rehearsal for Bloom's masochistic, cross-
generational, transsexual encounter in "Circe." Like his Odyssean
protagonist, Joyce experiences the interchange of sexual positionality
as an imminent threat of personal extinction. Indeed, the whole
litany of mortal images I have been reciting is neatly condensed in
this gender-reversal passage: the words "starborn" and "starry"
recall Amalia's weakened voice from "beyond the cold stars," the
"coiling kiss" recalls Amalia's "sighing" kiss and its "vapor" of
death, and the "starry snake" with its "fang of flame" recalls
Amalia's "basilisk eyes" with their "jet of liquorish venom." Joyce
supplements this chain of associations at the end with the simple
pronouncement, "I am lost," the contextual nuances of which
interrelate the dislocation of identity with outright annihilation.

The affirmation of Joyce's specific social identity enters in precisely
with the insistent reiteration of this *petite mort*. He declares himself in
all of his radical marginality through a Nietzschean willingness to
undergo repeatedly the imagined touch of death in order to encounter
finally and authentically the alien voice of Amalia, an effort
motivated by his gathering sense of the mutually implicated otherness
of their racial and colonial status. The end game of *Giacomo* sees the
author exposing himself to the profound difference of Amalia's being,
not with the aim of mastering her otherness in order to consolidate his
sense of self-identity (a classic abjection pattern), but rather as a way
of expressing the distinctive centrality of such difference, such
otherness, to his own subject position, as a way of expressing, in short,
his solidarity with the abjected. The sexual reversal in the interpolated passage not only dramatizes this solidarity, but associates it
with the possession of vatic percipience and, by extension, with
Joyce's aesthetic *métier*. Joyce confronts the *deprivation* of his I / eye
("I am lost"), i.e. castration/death, in order to be at-oned with the
sociosexual other against whom he has been defining himself, "the
voice I never heard." But the ordeal actually winds up *enriching* him
with the indispensable gift of wisdom ("making me wise"). Loss, we
might say, is Joyce's gain, which is doubtless why he felt it was
Shakespeare's as well (*U* 9.476); and in this transaction, where the

pain of solidarity brings the gain of wisdom, the specifically ethical and aesthetic stakes of Joyce's own much-discussed masochism begin to emerge.

In her book *Joyce and the Law of the Father*, Frances Restuccia identifies Amalia Popper as a prototype of the dominatrices of Joyce's fiction, his first Venus in furs.[87] Relying upon the groundbreaking work of Gilles Deleuze, Restuccia goes on to describe the male masochist as conferring the phallic function of final judgment and ultimate authority upon the figure of a woman in order to expiate his native complicity in the patriarchal order or, as Deleuze puts it, "his resemblance to the father and the father's resemblance to him."[88] Restuccia concludes that the masochist's construction of the punishing female phallus "serves as a protest of the ideal against the real."[89] I would append one qualification: the pain the masochist needs to incur *en route* to his liberating pleasure testifies to the continued effect of the "real" as both a constraint on and a condition of the "ideal protest" against it, or, in our vocabulary, his pain testifies to the effect of the positive law as both a constraint on and a condition of any ethico-juridical move to transcend it. In this light, masochism might be seen to constitute a sensationalizing and eroticizing of the aporia of sexual justice, for it achieves its transgressive ideal and the attendant *frisson* by continually acknowledging, even reinscribing, the law to be exceeded, the (positive) Law of the Father.

In the frames immediately following this interpolation, Joyce proceeds to underscore the intercourse between writing, as he conceives the practice, and his prospective extinction before the eye and voice of the other. Reflecting upon the end of the flirtation, Joyce tells himself, "It will never be. You know that well. What then? Write it, damn you, write it! What else are you good for?" (*GJ* 46) What Joyce goes on to write points up how far the reversal of scopic and vocative privilege has gone in this relationship and how important such voluntary forfeiture or transfer of authority is coming to be in Joyce's creative scheme. If the affair itself reflects Joyce's scopic interest, its ending reflects Amalia's:

"Why [did it end]? Must you marry?"
"Because otherwise I could not see you." (*GJ* 47)

In Joyce's impressionistic rendition of this ending of the affair, his very prose swoons into a silence that awaits the emergence of Amalia's word: "Sliding – space – ages – foliage of stars – and

waning heaven – stillness – and stillness deeper – stillness of annihilation – and her voice" (*GJ* 47). Joyce selects what is perhaps the
most personal and idiosyncratic of stylistic approaches, free association, and then trains it to the self-effacing purpose of maximum
receptivity, a maneuver which epitomizes the trend of the notebook
as a whole. He is in the process of redefining his writing as a highly
specialized and individualized mode of audition, not so much blank
recording as simultaneous translation, in which the irreducible
distance from and the inexpiable obligation to the other command
joint recognition. In this merger of style and focus, mode and object
of reference, Joyce marks the need to take on and yet to respect the
différend. *Giacomo* thus enacts a critical development in Joyce's literary
project: the move from justice as the subject of writing to writing as
a subject of justice.

ENVOY

In this light, Joyce's final representation of Amalia by way of her
personal effects can still be read as an objectifying strategy consonant
with the sexist and racist tenor of much of the notebook, but it can
also be seen as a strategy of authorial self-effacement consonant with
the newfound desire to allow Amalia to speak for herself. Because in
a literal as well as a symbolic sense, the independence of Amalia's
voice coincides with her independence from Joyce, a heraldic rebus of
her family name[90] is left to stand, dreamlike, for genuine utterance on
her part:

A long black piano: coffin of music. Poised on its edge a woman's hat, red-
flowered, and umbrella, furled. Her arms: a casque, gules, and blunt spear
on a field, sable. (*GJ* 49)

Arranged one way, the hat and the umbrella can be seen to form an
"a," as Vicki Mahaffey has argued, but arranged differently, they
can also be taken to form a "p." In keeping with Joyce's tendency to
embrace both poles of any either/or proposition, the coat of arms
here would seem to form a composite or "cubist" portrait of Amalia's
name, emphasizing her comparative autonomy at this point in the
notebook.

Joyce's last image of Amalia, her umbrella, deliberately identified
with her person, provides additional ammunition for this interpretation – "Envoy: love me, love my umbrella" (*GJ* 50). As we
witnessed at the end of "A Mother," the umbrella, as a kind of

modern-day augur-stick, has interchangeably phallic and judicial resonances for Joyce. In that case it marked the phallocentric structure of judgment itself, the arbitration of any formal symmetry, beginning with gender, on terms set by, expressive of, or favorable to one side of the equation. The visual, phallic symbolism surrounding Burke's closed, "poised," "finally balanced moral umbrella" obscures and preempts the feminine, gynemorphic associations of the umbrella, particularly when opened, the "elle" of the umbrella if you will. Joyce's envoy seems designed to undo this preemption and restore the decision-making authority symbolized by the umbrella to the representative female figure, Amalia. To love her, the envoy suggests, is to love the irreducible distinctness and the effective force of her judgment, even when her judgment is to leave.

But why, it might legitimately be asked, does the umbrella remain furled, that is, in the phallomorphic position, and why is it cast heraldically as a "blunt spear"? To go back a step, why did the allegorical instantiation of Amalia's voice, the rebus formed by her personal effects, actually encode her patronymic, the sign of her emplacement in the patriarchal order? Or further still, why does Amalia turn into a snake woman upon the transfer of authority and agency to her? These textual moments amount to local but exemplary indices of the internal limitations on the performance of justice, the way in which the mutual undercutting of projection and specularization inevitably leaves a remainder. Joyce's envoy is about remainders, a left umbrella, a residual feeling; and in the ethico-juridical dimension what remains is the positive law of gender, the positive law of genre, which conditions in some degree any attempt to go beyond it in the pursuit of justice. In this case, the law of gender imposes a positive impasse between according sovereignty, initiative, and individuality to the sexual other in her otherness and according her these same qualities already transformed in the image of her specific difference, i.e. without their masculinized baggage (the phallic umbrella) or inflection (furled). The former attempt, which Joyce makes, not only differs profoundly from but actually *precludes* the latter, so that his liberation of Amalia's perspective or voice carries with it a certain preemption as well, a diversion through the pro-portions of masculinity.[91] This is not a matter of specularization in the ordinary sense, i.e. the treating of another as a mere extension of the self; it is a matter of living in the mirror of language, which begins and ends with an always gendered name.

CHAPTER 4

Between/beyond men: male feminism and homosociality in "Exiles"

THE "GIACOMO JOYCE" CONNECTION: RICHARD AND BEATRICE

Joyce composed his one play, *Exiles*, after finishing the main body of the *Giacomo Joyce* notebook, but well before appending that frame, 45, which, as we have seen, has the retroactive effect of leavening and to a certain extent salvaging the whole. The chronological placement of the drama between the layers or variants of the palimpsestic sketchbook accords with what I take to be one of its more intriguing designs: refocusing, extending, and externalizing the situation secretly recorded in *Giacomo Joyce* and doing so from a vantage point attained in large part through that interlude. Joyce harvests individual motifs and even lines of dialogue from *Giacomo* in a methodical enough fashion that a reader conversant with the prior document and its context in Joyce's life can discern in *Exiles* a public translation of the hitherto private experience.

The crucial figure in marking the transition out of *Giacomo*, Beatrice Justice, is also the first to appear in *Exiles*. A host of affinities drawn throughout the play establish her as a dramatic avatar of Joyce's Triestine student, Amalia Popper:[1] her "dark" coloration, on account of which Bertha explicitly identifies her with the women of Italy; her spectacles, which recall Amalia's quizzing glasses; her mandarin social status, which prompts Bertha to call her "her ladyship" (*E* 94) as Joyce did Amalia (*GJ* 4); her literary service as both muse and subject of Richard Rowan's latest book, which he himself likens to "a painter['s]... book of sketches" (*E* 16) in an unmistakable allusion to *Giacomo*; her near fatal illness, which seems bound up with her relationship to Richard much as Amalia's appendicitis took on significance through her relationship with Giacomo; her use of the phrase "otherwise I could not see you"

(*E* 18), which performs the same kind of reversal in the erotic dynamic with Richard that Amalia's usage did with Joyce; her given name, which redoubles Amalia's dual identification with the heroines of *Vita Nuova* and *The Cenci* respectively; and her surname, which brings the ethical problematic around which this dual identification turned to the surface of the new work.

In light of the correlation of Beatrice with Amalia, which my catalogue by no means exhausts, the protagonist of the piece, Richard Rowan, appears not only as a Joycean alter ego as he would in any case, but as a dramatic projection of Giacomo Joyce, more specifically Giacomo at the end of the sketchbook, a disenchanted version of Giacomo, whose avowed amorous objective is the freedom rather than the possession of a woman. The skeptical object of this new liberating spirit, which we saw beginning to develop in the latter movement of *Giacomo Joyce*, is not Beatrice but Bertha, a surrogate for the author's wife, as Joyce's notes to the play make evident. Indeed, his perception, in one of these notes, that "since the publication of the lost pages of *Madame Bovary* the center of sympathy appears to have been aesthetically shifted from the … fancy man to the husband or cuckold" (*E* 150) may be taken as a displaced signal of the reversion of his own interest from the prospective mistress to the faithful wife. In keeping with this change of focus, Bertha also dominates the attention of Richard's friend, *doppelgänger*, and fraternal rival in the play, Robert Hand, another Joycean alter ego and a proponent of the idealizing and ruthlessly appropriative mode of eroticism that *Giacomo Joyce* indulges and ultimately undercuts. Since Robert was the first lover of Beatrice Justice and since he traces his philosophy of passion to the inspiriting ideas of Richard's youthful rebellion and self-exile, it seems not unreasonable to regard him as in this respect a dramatic revenant of the *early* Giacomo. Between them, Robert and Richard, the early and late Giacomo, do in fact amalgamate Joyce's own erotic nature, at least as represented by his friend Frank Budgen: "the Joycean conception of sexual love (at any rate on the male side) is an irreconcilable conflict between a passion for absolute possession and a categorical imperative [i.e. a law to be applied *universally*] of absolute freedom."[2]

None of this is to claim that a strict characterological equivalence obtains between the *dramatis personae* of *Exiles* and their respective antitypes in *Giacomo Joyce*. What these characters do share, however, is a set of structural correspondences vis-à-vis the core ethical and political concerns enacted in either text, positional analogies not fundamentally dissimilar from those which constitute the famous mythic method of Joyce's novels. The importance of these correspondences for the reading of *Exiles* is particularly compelling in view of Joyce's express opinion that drama, more than literature in general, properly operates at the level of deep-structural relationships:

Human society is the embodiment of changeless laws which the whimsicalities and circumstances of men and women involve and overwrap. The realm of literature is the realm of these accidental manners and humors ... Drama has to do with the underlying laws first, in all their nakedness and divine severity, and only secondarily with the motley agencies who bear them out. When so much is recognized an advance has been made to a more rational and true appreciation of dramatic art. (*CW* 40)

Now, recognizing the distinction between fixed underlying laws and motley changing surfaces can only transpire through a process of iteration guided by various correspondences drawn between past and present experience, literary or otherwise. In this case, an awareness of the filiation of *Exiles* upon *Giacomo* not only shifts our attention from the distinctive psychologies of the major characters to their exemplary enmeshment in the patriarchal order, as Joyce's own theoretical pronouncements recommend, it illuminates the structural relationships at work within the play itself and so helps to clarify the precise dimensions of its ethical and political problematic.

Read in the light of *Giacomo Joyce*, *Exiles* has as its governing topos neither ideal love (Dumerowski), free love and open marriage (Brown), individual freedom (Kershner), or creative desire (Henke), but gender justice.[3] Read in the light of *Giacomo Joyce*, further, the good-faith pursuit of such justice on the part of its self-appointed agent, Richard Rowan, should neither be assumed (Maher, Brown) nor dismissed as merely "ostensible" (Henke) or as an "egregious exercise of patriarchal power" (Kershner) but rather understood as deeply problematic in its relationship *to* patriarchal power.[4] Read in the light of *Giacomo Joyce*, finally, the failures attending Rowan's ethical project should not be ascribed exclusively or even primarily to his individual moral defects, such as his arrogance (Henke),[5] but rather to the double bind implicit in his specific moral situation: the desires motivating his pursuit of justice and the conception of justice orienting that pursuit both remain mortgaged at some point to the positive law of patriarchal domination that the effort itself must resist. This strange logic, which channels the narrative trajectory of the play, is precisely encapsulated in the titular metaphor, *Exiles*. Still animated by the law he at some point transcends, Rowan finds himself in a condition of double exile, both from the law itself and from his own ethical endeavor and self-image, outside and yet enthralled to either one. At the same time, since he and Bertha are differently affected by that law, are eccentric to and confined by the patriarchy in different ways, they continue, despite their best efforts, to be exiles to one another.[6]

To begin, then, the core action of *Exiles*, Richard Rowan's attempt to open for his wife a room of her own, beyond the reach of his culturally instituted authority over and construction of her, plainly grows out of Joyce's own developing project in *Giacomo*, the cultivation of a receptivity and respect for the independent voice of his culturally defined other. There is in fact a quite deliberate re-marking of the transition of one to the other in the initial scene of *Exiles*, a conversation between Richard and Beatrice which also stands as a kind of emblematic microcosm of the play's ethical structure, as her surname intimates. Joyce uses this encounter to establish both the earnestness of Richard's will to justice and its already compromised nature. The interview begins with Richard expressing some anxiety over any wrong he might have done Beatrice in his writing, either by using her as a subject without her approval or by his "sometimes cruel" (*E* 17) treatment of her. He first asks Beatrice, "do you blame me?" (*E* 16) and rather than complacently accept her negative response, he presses the rather more pointed question, "Do you think I have acted towards you – badly?" (*E* 16) and then pumps her once again for the answer she seems shy of giving. Richard's last attempt to extenuate if not excuse his suspect conduct supplies the most overt link to the *Giacomo Joyce* experience and so constitutes Joyce's own confession in a foreign tongue: "If I were a painter and told you I had a book of sketches of you you would not think it so strange, would you?" (*E* 16) Beatrice's retort, "It is not quite the same case, is it?" (*E* 17) disallows Richard's claim of aesthetic license and, with it, any refuge he, or before him Joyce, might have taken in the distance of the gaze. But what is more significant, from our point of view, is the alacrity with which Richard yields to her objection and takes it as a catalyst for a still more intensive inquisition of his literary and emotional obligations to her.

I use the term "inquisition" advisedly, for the most remarkable feature of this interview is its marked inversion of the judicial, as well as the jesuitical, strain. It plays as an aggressive cross-examination in which Richard does double duty as both the prosecuting attorney and the accused, a format which concretizes the ascetic mode of interpersonal justice wherein the ethical subject is responsible to hold himself hostage to the demands of the other.[7] At the very least, Richard's insistence on treating Beatrice's sentiments and judgments as determinative of his guilt or innocence should be taken to reflect the scrupulousness of his ethical commitment.

The subtext of Richard's renewed interrogation involves a question as to whether some personal or emotional injury he had inflicted upon Beatrice contributed to her recent illness or present "convalescent" state (*E* 21). The association of physical breakdown with imaginative or affective violence is once again a clear carryover from *Giacomo Joyce* that is remarked as such in the text, with Beatrice revealing the nature of her feelings for Richard in a phrase pilfered directly from Amalia Popper. Whereas he holds the relationship to be a marriage of true but independent minds, Beatrice points to its concealed aspect of erotic attachment and emotional dependency:

RICHARD: Perhaps you feel that some new thing is gathering in my brain; perhaps you feel that you should know it. Is that the reason [you come here]?
BEATRICE: No...Otherwise I could not see you.   (*E* 18)

In this exchange, she deftly trumps his claim of scopic distance with a declaration of scopic investment. What is more, Beatrice declines to allow the division of psychic labor that Richard presumes to exist between the affective/erotic and professional/aesthetic sides of their relationship. When Richard, working from the marketplace assumption of reciprocal autonomy, suggests that he has repaid the intellectual debt owed her by giving voice to her point of view, to feelings that she lacked the courage to express, she cryptically reminds him of the high emotional cost she has incurred in the transaction. Joyce seems to be using the more fully socialized quality of the dramatic mode to call into question or at least to acknowledge the limitation of the central ethical achievement of *Giacomo*:

RICHARD: Tell me, Miss Justice, did you feel that what you had read was written for your eyes? Or that you inspired me?

BEATRICE: I need not answer that question...

RICHARD: (with some vehemence) Then that I expressed in those chapters and letters, and in my character and life as well, something in your soul which you could not – pride or scorn?...

RICHARD: And so you have followed me with pride and scorn also in your heart?

BEATRICE: And loneliness. (*E* 19)

This loneliness is the subjective correlative, so to speak, of Beatrice's permanent convalescence, the very condition for which Richard suspects he is in part responsible. Yet he cannot come to grips with his incrimination as it is presented here. His sense of having "acted badly" is contractual, involving a possible violation of the conditions of the relationship in which he and Beatrice have engaged as free, autonomous agents or of her individual dignity as such an agent; but Beatrice's injury persists in precisely these conditions, in Richard's insistence on viewing their relationship as just such a "pact of withdrawn selves."[8] The conflict therefore cannot be regulated except on terms already set or presupposed by one of the contending parties, the basic condition of the *differend*. What is more, neither party has access to the investments and expectations of the other, the seedbed of their sense of injury or responsibility, except by way of a representation of the other regulated by those same presupposed terms of engagement. Joyce registers this representational impasse dramatically through the blocking of the characters and the parsing of the action. By way of expressing their mutual alienation, a stricken Beatrice averts her head and Richard walks away from her to pause, "for some moments," by the window, thus introducing a significant caesura into the interview (*E* 19).

Since to be a human subject is to be sexed, there can be no metagender position in discourse, no superintending perspective on the question of gender and its associated baggage. That is the burden of Joyce's fictional argument in "A Mother," if not the implication of the stylistic format of *Dubliners* as a whole. What Joyce begins to adumbrate here is a salient ethical consequence of this state of affairs: ideals of gender justice are themselves gender inflected, which is to say at some point gender biased. Accordingly they constitute sites of maximum ethical and political tension, for they must remain objects of appropriation even as they present themselves as the goal to be achieved. To take any ideal of gender justice on its own terms, i.e. as *the* ideal, is to allow it to eclipse or silence other such ideals and thus to degenerate immediately into mere law, to lose its distinguishing claim to justice altogether.

The specific form in which Joyce casts this dilemma anticipates the efforts of the most prominent exponents of second-wave feminism to formulate the principles whereby sexual difference translates as ethical difference: psychoanalysts Nancy Chodorow and Dorothy Dinnerstein, sociologists Carol Gilligan and Elizabeth Fox-Genovese, juridical scholars like Robin West, Suzanna Sherry, and others.[9] Although the psychoanalysts ascribe the phenomenon to the effect of gender difference on maternal separation and primary subject formation, the sociologists to the effects of conventional gender roles and expectations on the socialization of children and adolescents, and the juridical scholars to the division between the competitive male-dominated public sphere and the sentimental female-identified domestic sphere in liberal society, they join in contending that while "masculine" ethics tends to be atomistic and agonistic, giving priority to individual rights and freedoms, "feminine" ethics tends to be intersubjective in orientation, giving primacy to communal goals and contextual imperatives. Whereas masculine ethics, the argument runs, is about aggressively defending the personal boundaries and valuing the distinct conceptions of the good life that they entail, feminine ethics is about preserving personal connectedness and valuing cooperative efforts to attain communally defined versions of the good. Whereas the former seeks to assure the reciprocal independence of fundamentally discrete subjects, the latter seeks to foster the mutually beneficial interdependence of fundamentally social beings. Whereas one is centrifugal and competitive, the other is centripetal and nurturing. One, accordingly, sees justice in terms of an abstract equality of status or opportunity with respect to a relatively fixed set of principles; the other sees justice as responding to the particular exigencies of concrete situations in ways that take the welfare of each member of the group into account. These gendered models of justice, however, do not exist in simple opposition to one another, which would imply some metalevel or supplementary dimension upon which they might collide. Rather each one represents the other in denial. The competitive or agonistic tendency of the masculine mode constitutes a preservation in denial of inter-subjectivity, while the nurturant element of the feminine mode, since it must accord some people priority over others, represents a preservation in denial of the idea of individual self-worth. Instead of an opposition, then, the two paradigms together form a *differend*, an impasse of the inseparable from/irreducible to.

The respective ethical mind sets of Richard and Beatrice substantially conform with the schematic gender division I have recounted and with one explanation in particular of its social genesis. Richard's libertarian or anarchistic ideology of radical personal autonomy, individual rights, free and equal exchange, etc. not only affords a conventionally masculine take on their collegial friendship, it also serves to recreate a liaison situated along the border between the professional and the personal spheres in terms proper to the former domain alone. In an obverse manner, Beatrice's repose in what she takes to be the affective content of the relationship not only represents a conventionally feminine posture, it pushes the affair off the categorical fence and into her culturally assigned zone of authority. In either case, ethical tendency shades into political tendentiousness, a subtly exerted will to secure his or her own position.

That Beatrice's tack is less efficacious in this regard speaks first to the underlying bias on which apparent gender symmetries are invariably constructed and, second, to the danger this implies for the essentialist or second-wave feminist. Rejecting single-standard paradigms of gender justice in the interest of celebrating distinctively feminine powers or faculties may wind up assisting in the retrenchment of the old stereotypes and the constraints they inscribe. Beatrice's privileging of sentiment over abstract principle, her belief in "happiness" as "the best, the highest, of aims" (*E* 22), her respect for domestic values, evidenced in her dismay at Richard's continuing rancor toward his deceased mother, all enjoin Beatrice to weigh how her intimacy with Richard, pressed to a certain degree, would trespass on his common law marriage and against Bertha, his wife. Her dialogue with Bertha at the outset of the last act belies the pressure of that consideration:

BEATRICE: I spoke to my cousin about Mr. Rowan when he was away and, to a certain extent, it was I…
BERTHA: I see. And that is on your conscience. Only that?
BEATRICE: I think so.
BERTHA: (almost cheerfully) It looks as if it was you, Miss Justice, who brought my husband back to Ireland.
BEATRICE: I Mrs. Rowan?
BERTHA: Yes you. By your letters to him and by speaking to your cousin…
BEATRICE: (blushing suddenly) No. I could not think that. (*E* 124)

As it was for Mrs. Kearney, though for different reasons, the authority of the private sphere proves self-limiting for Beatrice, confining her snugly enough within the stock Victorian image of virtuous femininity that a surprising number of readers have mistakenly understood a repressed or attenuated sexuality to be her dominant characteristic. Richard's ethical position, on the other hand, allows him to define his dealings with Beatrice as basically irrelevant to his marriage, provided only that he does not exploit the traditional double standard to deny Bertha prerogatives, rights, and freedoms commensurate with his own.

Far from resolving matters on the homefront, Richard's zealous adherence to just this philosophy renders his *differend* with Beatrice a prelude to his *differend* with Bertha, which drives the main action of the play. In fact, Joyce draws some careful parallels between the attitudes of Beatrice and Bertha toward Richard's anarchism of everyday life. Bertha no more credits the professional, artistic basis of Richard's relationship with Beatrice than Beatrice herself does: "All those things you sit up at night to write about [pointing to the study] in there – about her. You call that friendship?... What else is between you but love?" (*E* 66–7) Further along, she asserts, "I understood more than you think about that business" (*E* 68), where the word "business" trembles between its formal, professional reference and a slang sexual one. (Later, in a more pointed double entendre, she demonstrates to Beatrice how that study also served as Richard's bedroom, *E* 125). Richard's response to Bertha's jealousy on the first occasion consists, predictably, in an appeal to the ideal of personal autonomy and his own possession thereof: "You are trying to put that idea [his love for Beatrice] into my head but I warn you that I don't take my ideas from other people" (*E* 67). Like Beatrice, however, Bertha refuses to place abstract individual rights before cultivating the possibility of shared human happiness and, on these grounds, spurns her husband's guiding principles – "what you call complete liberty" (*E* 66) – a point to which I shall return. Thus Bertha's seeming conventionality, which a union with Robert could only have exacerbated (see Joyce's projected sketch of Mrs. Hand, *E* 150), grows out of her somewhat greater sensitivity to the intersubjective production of experience. She responds to Richard's declaration of intellectual independence and reaffirms her own jealous suspicions in terms calculated to accentuate their marital *differend*:

BERTHA: I am right. (following him a few steps) What would anyone say?

RICHARD: ... Do you think I care?

BERTHA: But I care.

(*E* 67)

In the performance, the physical action of Bertha following Richard takes on an important dramatic value, communicating a sense of the adhesive intimacy she wishes to foster and opening a space in which her cutting insight into his need for distance or separation can be staged. Finally, Bertha, like Beatrice, assumes the priority of domestic life and amity to more abstract concerns – "ideas and ideas," she sniffs – and, to that effect, she follows Beatrice in voicing chagrin at Richard's animosity toward his mother: "A mother is always a mother, no matter what. I never heard of any human being that did not love the mother that brought him into the world except you" (*E* 64, 65). These repetitions not only show Bertha redoubling Beatrice's ethical tendencies in a more concentrated form, they serve notice that, for the purposes of the drama, the tendencies in question are gender aligned rather than an individual growth. The deportment of the two women toward one another at the outset of Act 3 clinches the point. They not only embark upon a friendship, a fact significant in itself given the previously noted dearth of female friendships in Joyce, but both attest to a long-standing wish for just such a consummation, despite their mutual suspicion (*E* 130–1). Now, such assurances might well be taken for white lies except that Bertha had previously scolded Richard, "I feel for her more than you can *because I am a woman.* I do, sincerely" (*E* 68, my italics). The ethical implications of this homosocial dynamic are telling, particularly when juxtaposed with the play's specimen of male homosociality. Whereas Richard and Robert express their fellowship in a relentlessly competitive mode, organizing their fondness for one another along loosely contractual lines, Beatrice and Bertha deal with their palpable hostility by cultivating sympathy and a sense of obligation, organizing their very competitiveness on a sentimental intersubjective basis.

In accordance with his characteristically masculine scale of values, Richard adjudges Beatrice and Bertha's respectively passive and open resistance to his ethico-political agenda as importing a want of courage or at least daring. But as Vicki Mahaffey has incisively noted, *Exiles* conducts an extensive anatomy of the precise relation between expectation and resistance,[10] and in our case Richard's differing preconceptions of the two women lead him to differing gender-based accounts of their behavior, and his conclusions, in turn, combine to illustrate an emphatic double bind at the heart of his sexual egalitarianism.

Richard has perceived Beatrice as his intellectual correspondent in every sense of that word – philosophical, epistolary, and legal. She is his elected double precisely to the extent that she seems to be her own person, roughly the position Joyce develops for Amalia Popper by the end of *Giacomo*. Nor is Richard alone in supposing her an uncommonly detached, self-reliant person, particularly as measured by contemporary gender-specific standards. Bertha's comment on her ungenerous nature suggests as much, albeit with a pejorative twist, as does Robert's observation about her "queer" and "characteristic way" of "getting about [town] alone" (*E* 27). Presented with the unmistakable if undecided link between her physical breakdown and her emotional attachment to him, Richard is moved to revise his assessment of her *modus vivendi* and what it signifies about her character, ultimately hinting at a fault in her femininity, an inability to fulfill the gender norm to which she as a woman evidently still responds.

This process begins immediately after the break in the interview, at which point both the tone and the topic change. During this pass, Richard's solicitation of Beatrice's viewpoint takes on a faintly combative edge, and his ironic questions dwell upon rather meticulous distinctions of etiquette and social custom. There is, in short, a sense in which the caesura marks not only an impasse in Richard's pursuit of personal justice but its degeneration, for the moment, into a legalistic exercise. This is appropriate in that Richard's line of questioning builds toward a verdict enforcing the patriarchal law of gender. Motivationally speaking, one could say that being unable to puzzle out his lived sense of guilt for Beatrice's condition, Richard adduces her earlier and likewise abortive relationship with Robert Hand as a way of definitively exculpating himself. His initial strategy is to assert that her engagement to Robert had always distanced him from her anyway: "Yet that separated me from you. I was a third person I felt. Your names were always spoken together ... as long as I can remember" (*E* 20). His ensuing cross-examination is devoted to establishing just how serious and advanced that relationship was by the time of his expatriation. Beatrice, however, takes the opportunity to declare that at the time "I saw in him a pale reflection of you" (*E* 21) and thereby introduces the play's *doppelgänger* motif, a crucial element in the symbolic dimension of *Exiles*, wherein the individual culpabilities of the "motley agents" (*CW* 40) are subsumed under the structural inequities of the sex/gender system. As I will flesh out further along, Robert functions as both the exponent and the personification of the positive law of this system – what he calls the "natural law" of male appropriation – and in this light Richard's symbolic fraternity with him, their triangulation upon Beatrice and then upon Bertha, can be seen to figure the complicitous aspect of Richard's will to justice. Richard's supplementary strategy of self-acquittal supports this view. Drawing a parallel between the lapse of Beatrice's engagement to Robert and the lapse of her friendship with himself, Richard traces her present infirmity to her failure, rather than her unwillingness or refusal, to live out the self-sacrificial ideal of Victorian womanhood: "You cannot give yourself freely and wholly ... You were drawn to him as your mind was drawn towards mine. You held back from him. From me too in a different way. You cannot give yourself freely and wholly" (*E* 22). Beatrice does not dispute this contention ("It is a terribly hard thing to do ... to give oneself freely and wholly – and be happy" (*E* 22)), but what concerns us here is the implications of his tacit indictment of Beatrice for his own ethico-political stance. While giving himself out as an agent of sexual enlightenment and gender justice, Richard clings to the existing gender norms, as heuristic devices if nothing else. Here he unconsciously echoes William Stead's notorious "womanly woman" critique of the *Diary of Marie-Bashkirtfeff* (which Shaw called "the literary sensation of the day") to the effect that "a natural woman with a heart to love, and a soul ... finds its supreme satisfaction in sacrifice for lover or for child" – a critique retailed and ridiculed in Shaw's *The Quintessence of Ibsenism*, which Joyce owned, read, and found congenial.[11] Richard thus seems to be seizing upon Beatrice's convalescence as the occasion for at least entertaining the double standard pervasive in the gender politics of modern liberal society, i.e. the subordination of the values of individual sovereignty and mutual equality to the naturalized prerogatives of masculinity and the naturalized restrictions on femininity.

In the context of *Exiles* as a whole, the attitude Richard strikes at this point is particularly arresting and more than a little curious. For the play's main event consists of Richard trying to reverse his wife's long-settled practice of giving herself "freely and wholly" to him and to incite her to think for herself and act on her own counsel in defiance of the bonds of social convention, personal obligation, or "even of love" (*E* 146). The difficulty he experiences in convincing Bertha points not to a defect *in* her femininity, as he sees it, but to a weakness *of* femininity as constructed in the traditional monogamous heterosexual marriage. In a play known to be riddled with contradictions, this may well be the most glaring and the most pivotal. There are many ways of resolving the knot according to the generic specifications of realistic psychodrama, for instance by debunking Richard's ethical project as a self-deluded, self-aggrand-izing program of emotional manipulation. His flatly inconsistent charges to Bertha and Beatrice, directing each to adopt something resembling the other's mode of being, appears to derive less from his professed dedication to anarchistic principle than from his un-acknowledged attachment to the paternalistic authority he would jettison. But I believe the myriad contradictions that mark the play's surface are designed in part to balk a facile recuperation of the dramatic spectacle, which Joyce elsewhere likened to consuming medicine in a darkened theater,[12] and to compel the audience to look for those "underlying laws" (*CW* 40) that a character might be taken to figure. The oscillation of Richard's perspective as he moves back and forth from Bertha to Beatrice provides a temporalized image of the aporia haunting the institutions of gender justice as a material or historical reality. On the one hand, the effective if performative and provisional norms that anchor the gender terms (M/F) to be equilibrated – norms of interest, competence, attitude, occupation – harbor their own invidious and exclusionary force and so cannot be simply respected as such in the pursuit of justice. On the other hand, the lived experience and historical pressures of these evolving norms have produced gender differences, nonetheless effective for being provisional and performative, which must be respected in the pursuit of justice but which remain inextricably if unevenly implicated with those same invidious norms.

Given the development of the suffrage and female emancipation movements, with their demand for equal rights and opportunities, and given the concurrent and countervailing rise of the theory of sexual dimorphism, with its emphasis on inherent and dramatic differences between the sexes, this aporia was just becoming urgent and recognizable in the cultural conjuncture of early Modernism. Joyce himself had connections in both camps: school chums like Francis Sheehy-Skeffington (whose sexual politics Stephen pillories in *Stephen Hero* by reference to just this aporia), Hanna Sheehy-Skeffington, James and Margaret Cousins were all driving forces in the Irish women's movement, while avant-garde intellectuals on the continent, like Joyce's recent contact, Ezra Pound, were much taken with theories of sexual dimorphism.[13] In addition, Joyce read and drew upon a fairly popular book, Charles Albert's *L'Amour libre*, the Afterword of which, "On the Woman Question," tried to reconcile these lines of argument, albeit in a fairly traditional manner.[14] Joyce himself, characteristically, evolves an inclusive, binocular, and therefore equivocal posture in *Exiles*. Richard's pendular prescriptions denote both the practical difficulties this aporia entails and the danger of failing to negotiate it somehow, the danger that the pursuit of justice itself will turn into an arbitrary imposition of will. These difficulties and dangers, in turn, become the subject of Joyce's more extensive treatment of the marital crisis of Richard and Bertha.

THE IBSEN CONNECTION: RICHARD AND BERTHA

That difficulties and dangers attend and perhaps thwart Richard's ethical endeavor does not vitiate the endeavor entirely, even though these are not extrinsic pitfalls but organic laws that bespeak or at least lend themselves to a significant degree of corruption or bad faith. Joyce is interested, I would submit, in exploring certain intrinsic limits to what might be loosely called male feminism, a task which requires him to make it clear that his represented specimen, Richard Rowan, is worth anatomizing. To this end, Joyce systematically articulates the programmatic effort of Richard, the authorial double and onstage manager, to liberate his wife, Bertha, the real Nora's imaginary alter ego, with the programmatic effort of the great Norwegian playwright/stage manager, Ibsen, to effect the literary emancipation of his own Nora (Helmer), whom he often imagined to be a real person.[15] Joyce is known to have concurred in the widespread opinion of Ibsen as a great feminist writer. He informed Arthur Power that he admired Ibsen's plays for their deliberate attempt to reformulate the interaction between men and women on a more equitable basis:

you do not understand him. You ignore the spirit which animated him. The purpose of *A Doll House*, for instance, was the emancipation of women, which has caused the greatest revolution in our times in the most important relationship there is – that between men and women; the revolt of women against the idea that they are the mere instruments of men.[16]

Even allowing for the hyperbole that can creep into disputes over aesthetic tastes, his endorsement constitutes a pretty clear invitation to read a play like *Exiles*, which most agree is Ibsenite in technique and which clearly focuses on gender politics, by way of *A Doll House* – even more than such other likely candidates as *When We Dead Awaken*, *Lady from the Sea*, and *Rosmersholm*.

Yet there is not even a consensus that the feminist leanings that Joyce attributes to and approves in *A Doll House* are entertained and engaged, let alone promoted, in *Exiles*. One passage in Joyce's working notes for the play accounts for some legitimate resistance and uncertainty and must be dealt with before proceeding:

Richard must not appear as a champion of woman's rights. His language at times must be nearer to that of Schopenhauer against women and he must show at times a deep contempt for the long-haired, short-legged sex. He is in fact fighting for his own hand, for his own emotional dignity and liberation in which Bertha, no less and no more than Beatrice or any other woman is coinvolved. (*E* 154)

R. B. Kershner adduces this passage to propose that "Joyce's first gesture is to distance his work from that of Ibsen and other feminist ideologues";[17] and even Richard Brown, who sees Joyce's work tracking Ibsen's political footsteps quite closely, approaches this note as something of an obstacle to be sidestepped.[18] For my part, I do not understand on what grounds the identity of Richard's sexual politics with Joyce's sexual politics may be assumed, why, that is, the author's self-instruction not to overplay his protagonist's feminist leanings should be taken to dissociate the text at large from (Ibsen's) feminism. Beyond that, I would observe that Joyce's repeated use of the phrase "at times" here points precisely to the sort of oscillation we remarked in Richard's perspective, which works to defamiliarize and problematize but certainly not foreclose upon his ethics of gender justice. Finally, I would call attention to the strange interplay in this passage between questions of appearance and fact. If Richard is "in fact fighting for his own hand," to which the fates of Beatrice, Bertha, "or any other woman" are ancillary, a non- or antifeminist position, it is hard to conceive why Joyce would have had to worry about

Richard appearing to be women's champion. But if the fate of "*any* other woman," meaning all women, is "coinvolved" with Richard's "emotional dignity and liberation," where "coinvolved" has the connotation of irreducibly bound up and thus in some sense essential, then his position does "in fact" have a distinctly feminist strain more or less in spite of itself. The semblance of straightforward advocacy on Richard's part would then have to be carefully avoided indeed if the play is to fulfill its aim of investigating male feminism as a political compromise formation, the principled effect of a nonetheless duplicitous economy of desire. Taken in this vein, the passage, far from distancing Joyce's work from Ibsen's feminist ideology, connects it in an interesting way with the history of Ibsen's feminism, vis-à-vis *A Doll House*, a history with which Joyce would have been generally familiar through the work of Ibsen's friend and exponent Georg Brandes.

In sketching out *A Doll House*, Ibsen wrote his own working notes to the play, the metaphorics of which intimate that what was initially and almost universally received as his feminism could be as properly described as an interest in gender justice:

A woman cannot be herself in the society of today, which is exclusively a masculine society, with *laws* written by men, and with *accusers* and *judges* who *judge* feminine conduct from the masculine standpoint. (my italics)[19]

A Doll House itself retains this judicial rhetoric, broaching a gendered conflict between the positivity and the possibility of the law which closely resembles contradictions I noted earlier between the imperative to equity *under* law and the imperative to equity *of* law. When the previously disgraced Krogstad informs Nora Helmer that her recent misrepresentations were no less criminal than his own had been, she replies

NORA: You? Do you expect me to believe that you ever acted bravely to save your wife's life?
KROGSTAD: Laws don't inquire into motives.
NORA: Then they must be very poor laws.
KROGSTAD: Poor or not ... you'll be judged according to law.
NORA: This I refuse to believe. A daughter hasn't the right to protect her dying father from anxiety and care? A wife hasn't the right to save her husband's life? I don't know much about laws, but I'm sure that somewhere in the books these things are allowed.   (*DH* 67)

Discovering her surety misplaced, she later complains, "I found out

... that the law's not at all what I'd thought – but I can't get it through my head that the law is fair" (*DH* 111). The play does not simply recommend Nora's point of view to the audience; Krogstad's initial question, "But didn't you even consider that this was a fraud against me?" (*DH* 66), hangs in the air without receiving an ethically satisfying answer from Nora: "You were no concern of mine" (*DH* 66).[20] Instead, anticipating Carol Gilligan's results with the same ethical conundrum,[21] Ibsen proposes that there have come to exist incommensurable modalities of the just – an abstract contractual model favored by men and a common-sense situational model favored by women – and that preferring without any possible warrant the one over the other, as the positive law currently does, cannot itself be called "fair" or "just."

This thematic, whose resonance in *Exiles* I have already begun to document, put Ibsen, like Joyce, in the position of assailing the patriarchy on its arbitrary institution of a metalanguage as well as on the female subordination, infantilization, and objectification that have been its practical effects. That is to say, the specifically juridical impetus of Ibsen's feminism gave it a more theoretical edge and a more comprehensive scope than the women's movement at that time was generally understood to possess, and like Joyce he was concerned to protect his purchase on a general as well as a restricted economy of sexual politics. So with the feminist spirit of his most famous play openly avowed in the note cited above, Ibsen nonetheless made the following statement before the Norwegian Women's Rights League at a birthday dinner given in his honor, on May 26, 1898: "I thank you for the toast, but must disclaim the honor of having consciously worked for the women's rights movement... True enough, it is desirable to solve the woman problem, along with all the others; but that has not been the whole purpose. My task has been the description of humanity."[22] In its play between acknowledging and disclaiming the honor of being a feminist champion, in its uncertain articulation of the woman problem and "all the others," Ibsen's demurral could and indeed might have supplied the germ of Joyce's textual note. And as if to confirm the analogy, his speech's effect, like that of Joyce's note, was to call into dispute the author's support for the cause of female emancipation.[23] Many have used this quotation to dismiss the so-called woman question as too one-sided for Ibsen's universalizing interest, instead of knitting the woman question into the whole fabric of his writing to reveal his universalizing interest therein. For his part, Joyce threw in his lot with thinkers like Havelock Ellis, who regarded Ibsen as an unmitigated force of liberation, and Georg Brandes, who felt Ibsen was enthusiastic about the women's movement as "one of the great rallying points of human progress."[24] Moreover, Joyce seems to have seen Ibsen's advocacy as deriving from some ingrained capacity for cross-gender identification based upon a feminine admixture to his own personality, an aptitude not entirely alien to Joyce's own social inscription – "Indeed, if one may say so of an eminently virile man, there is a curious admixture of the woman in his nature. His marvelous accuracy, his faint traces of femininity, his delicacy of swift touch, are perhaps attributable to this admixture" (*CW* 64).

Even when it came to drama, however, Joyce was not a mere epigone of Ibsen. In 1907, he wrote a letter to his brother, Stanislaus, proclaiming Ibsen's dramatic methodology "too simple" for the coming age and taking particular issue with Ibsen's penchant for easy heroics.[25] In *Exiles*, Joyce extends his critique to the ideological soil of those heroics: what Joyce elsewhere termed Ibsen's "anarchist" individualism, with which Joyce himself still intermittently identifies but which he ironizes here in the figure of Richard Rowan, his markedly Ibsenite alter ego. The latter gambit is itself the effective onset of the critique. Stephen Dedalus' famous theoretical dictum that in the dramatic mode the artist properly "remains within or beyond or above his handiwork, invisible, refined out of existence, indifferent, paring his fingernails" (*AP* 215) derives at least in part from Ibsen's actual dramatic practice of effacing his creative personality behind the text or production. This aesthetic philosophy, stylistically enacted in *Dubliners* and *A Portrait*, coheres with the political philosophy of anarchism in its faith in the possibility of individual transcendence, an unconditional mode of agency or critical purchase leading in the one case to a perfectly self-contained object of beauty and in the other to a political utopia. But in the area of sexual politics, this belief repeats even as it rejects the fundamental gesture of patriarchal hegemony, the laying down of a metalanguage, i.e. a canon or perspective that assumes superintendence over and exemption from the play of systematic forces, aesthetic or political, in which it remains nonetheless enmeshed. By installing his own persona as a problematic agency of justice in *Exiles* – and not a past persona like Stephen but a currently recognizable version of himself – Joyce insists, contra Ibsen, that any aesthetic or political representation of a given predicament necessarily bears the mark of the author's energetic immersion in circumstances in some way related to that predicament – in short, the mark of his or her desire. And since the author cannot by definition comprehend this immersion, his or her blindness to such a mark paradoxically constitutes one of the hidden and most prevalent reminders of its existence. Whether as aesthetic or political methodology, Joyce intimates, simple heroism signals contradictory investments.

Accordingly, instead of emulating Ibsen's liberationist project in *A Doll House*, with its defiant heroic conclusion, *Exiles* uses Rowan to frame the project itself and make it the central dramatic topos, as a way of taking stock of its immense perplexity and its less than straightforward nature. Richard Rowan proposes to disinherit himself of his gender patrimony, his priority and privilege as a male and a husband, in order to institute an entirely new noncoercive intersexual order in his marriage, symbolized by his openness to Bertha's prospective alliance with Robert. His attempt is allusively counterpointed with Torvald Helmer's endeavors to retain his gender patrimony and maintain the old, androcentric, fundamentally coercive order in his marriage. As we shall see, Richard is deliberately staged as an anti-Torvald. But on a polemical reading of *A Doll House*, particularly one that punctures the realistic illusion, the original anti-Torvald is none other than Ibsen himself. That is to say, Ibsen stands forth as his protagonist's chief detractor and rival, orchestrating the deliverance of Nora Helmer, whom according to friends and biographers Ibsen "admired, even adored."[26] Now since he represents Joyce's alter ego as stage manager, Richard's systematic critique and inversion of Torvald's paternalistic design and practices place him in a role analogous to that of Ibsen. He directs the action to the same emancipatory end. But of course this end never comes in *Exiles*. Precisely because of his faith in his own transcendence, his failure to respect the positive law of circumstantial constraint,[27] Richard's program issues instead in a marital crack-up that at a certain crucial point even mimics the climactic confrontation of Nora and Torvald in *A Doll House*. Joyce thereby registers a still more sweeping critique of the patriarchal form of life, one that encompasses not just brazenly phallocratic resistance to female emancipation but cryptically phallocentric support for it, not just would-be agents of the retrenchment like Torvald, but would-be heroes of the revolution like Richard, not just a Stead but an Ibsen.

For our purposes, Richard's performance is counterposed to Torvald's most broadly in the verbal style that defines them. In keeping with his objective of consolidating his control over family and business, over the emotional and moral life of his charges, and above all over every aspect of his wife's existence, Torvald consistently employs or is associated with the rhetoric of closure. As the play opens, Torvald is celebrating his new job at the bank and inviting Nora to do likewise, precisely because it is "a safe, secure job" (*DH* 47), more so, presumably, than his former post as an attorney. Torvald expresses a similarly prudential and covetous bent in his amorous regard for Nora. When she resists his advances after the tarantella he asks, "Can't I look at my richest treasure? At all that beauty that is mine, mine alone – completely and utterly" (*DH* 100). There is a repetitiveness, an excessiveness, an insistence to this verbal formulation that carries it beyond the conventional endearment and touches upon the phantasmatic, where the focus, significantly enough, is not on Nora's worth but on the certainty and exclusivity of his possession. As his next ploy in the same seduction, he confesses to her a recurrent and completely formed sexual fantasy which displays again, in a repetitive insistent language, an almost cloistral possessiveness, an erotics of the closet:

I'm imagining then that you're my *secret* darling, my *secret* young bride to be, and that *no one suspects* there's anything between us ... then I pretend ... that for the first time I'm bringing you home to *my* house – that for the first time I'm alone with you – completely alone with you, your young trembling beauty. (*DH* 100, my italics)

Torvald even seems to relish the prospect of Dr. Rank's demise because then he and Nora would be "thrown back upon each other completely" (*DH* 104).

As this last desire of Torvald suggests, his eroticization of the cloistral is bound up with his keen sense of his role as Nora's protector. This role has a moral component which emerges when he is apprised of her forgery. He figures himself as a strong domicile fortifying her against a "flimsy" ethical constitution inherited from her father and "swept down" in turn by the tide of her irresponsibility (*DH* 105, 106). After the storm, however, the element of moral protection is incorporated in an image of middle-class domestic contentment and asylum, eroticized through a resumption of the animal similitudes Torvald applies to his wife throughout the play.

Notice, in particular, the way the phrase "your poor shuddering heart" picks up on the "young trembling beauty" of his secret young bride:

You can rest easy now; I've got wide wings to shelter you with ... how snug and nice our home is, Nora. You're safe here; I'll treat you like a hunted dove I've rescued out of the hawk's claws. I'll bring peace to your poor shuddering heart ... Don't be afraid of anything Nora ... I'll be conscience and will to us both. (*DH* 107, 108)

It is precisely this idea of marriage as refuge, of course, as it is enacted in their everyday life, against which Nora reacts so violently. Taking up the rhetoric of closure, she translates Torvald's blissful enclosure as imprisonment in a doll house and translates the "sacred vows" with which he tries to bind her as secondary, even diversionary obligations. Further, she suggests that his preoccupation with moral and domestic closure has not produced any real closeness: "I was exactly the same, your little lark, your doll, that you have to handle with double care now that I'd turned out so brittle and frail ... Torvald – in that instant it dawned on me that for eight years I've been living here with a stranger" (*DH* 113). Ultimately, Nora demands her release by trading in the ultimate symbol of marital enclosure: "Don't feel yourself bound, anymore than I will. There has to be absolute freedom for us both. Here, take your ring back. Give me mine" (*DH* 113). Her famous door slam, then, confirms and seals off the narrow confines of Torvald's marital vision even as it announces her liberation.

Exiles operates something of a cross-gender pastiche of *A Doll House*. In Joyce's play, it is the *paterfamilias*, Richard, who calls for absolute freedom for both himself and his wife under the repeated phrase, "complete liberty." Torvald's rhetoric of closure is replaced with a rhetoric of aperture, a substitution in which the titular metaphor of the play cooperates. Instead of a protected, let's pretend enclosure, a doll house, we have a dangerous, extra-territorial condition, exile. This is significant because if Torvald is defined as a character by his obsession with controlling a stable secure state, Richard is defined as a character by his willingness to expose himself to what lies beyond the confines, friendly or insidious, soothing or stultifying, of ordinary *petit bourgeois* existence. He may not long, as Robert says of him, "to be delivered ... from every law ... from every bond" (*E* 112), but he does long to permit himself and others that option. He has dwelt outside the borders of his national community and the reigning communitarian values thereof, legal wedlock and the primary restrictions thereof, conventional adultery and the compulsive dishonesty thereof, and the ordinary limits of friendship. (Even his sedentary occupation turns into an open-air affair, taking him into the night to confront the insubstantial voices of those who "love" him.)

Regarding his relationship with Bertha, the natural sexual freedom Richard recommends is based on a broader principle of openness, both in the sense of liberality and in the sense of candor or exposure. Thus, in their first dialogue, Richard specifically links his openness to her having an affair with Robert to his insistence that everything be totally above board:

RICHARD: (controlling himself) You forget that I have allowed you complete liberty and allow you it still.
BERTHA: (scornfully) Liberty.
RICHARD: Yes, complete. But he must know that I know… It is not jealousy. You have complete liberty to do as you wish – you and he. But not in this way… You don't wish to deceive me – or to pretend to deceive me – with him, do you? (*E* 65–6)

His subsequent intrusion to inform Robert of his knowledge is entirely consistent with his libertarian position that true freedom cannot operate in the dark. In this regard, it is significant that Joyce is so emphatic about making Richard's fraternal nemesis, who is the apostle of erotic appropriation, a devotee of stealth, secrecy, and darkness. Richard asks Robert why he wishes "to keep secret [his] wooing" (*E* 75), admonishes him for proceeding "like thieves – at night" (*E* 71), and is answered, indirectly, when Robert tells Bertha "secrets can be very sweet" (*E* 103). For his part, Richard felt compelled in Italy to confess his affairs to Bertha, knowing that they "pierced her heart" (*E* 84), so that she would know him as he was. In Ireland he feels compelled to tell Robert as well, though it amounts to giving his friend added license. Indeed, the two results are structurally related; for in telling Bertha of his affairs, in keeping with the imperative to candor or exposure, he effectively announces her right to do likewise, in keeping with the imperative to reciprocal autonomy central to his sense of gender justice: "I will reproach myself then for having taken all for myself because I would not suffer to give to another what was hers and not mine to give, because I

accepted from her her loyalty and made her life poorer in love"
(*E* 87). Staying in character, Robert cannot understand why Richard
is driven to tell his wife in the first place.

A number of critics have asserted that Richard does not really give
Bertha freedom at all in that he chooses to intervene with Robert
ahead of time and thereby make known to Bertha his residual
jealousy, albeit in a disavowed form. Kershner speaks of this
maneuver as placing an "infinity of constraints" on the freedom
Richard allots.[28] As we shall see further on, Richard's emergent
jealousy does indeed figure importantly in the structural manipulation of Bertha, evoking constraints for her that Richard does not
fully grasp, let alone intend. But since he does not actively prevent
her assignation with Robert, or openly discourage it except as to
manner, the argument that he grants her no real freedom is slightly
reductive in its haste, a bottom line without the calculations that
make the bottom line telling. It does, however, begin to address the
vital point that the kind of openness Richard is promoting allows him
to command a significant degree of stage managerial control. There
is in his observation of Robert and Bertha's tryst a strong element of
scopic mastery, which he wants to believe targets only the interloper,
Robert –

ROBERT: You were watching us the whole time?
RICHARD: I was watching you.
ROBERT: I mean, watching me.   (*E* 75)

– but it is clearly complemented by his inquisitional mastery over
Bertha. She can do whatever she wants but she must, apparently,
uncover everything that she does. In that sense, Richard denies
Bertha a truly *independent* experience after all, an effect likewise
implicit in his decision to tell her of *his* sexual encounters. Far from
being adventitious to the problematic of gender justice, this paradox
illustrates the historically masculine complexion of the paradigm of
formal equality and reciprocal autonomy. Insofar as this paradigm
sees any circle of social relations as at once organized and atomized
by the centrifugal force of agonistic self-interest, it positively requires
the vigilant surveillance of individual behavior to preserve the circle
intact and so is scopophilic in its very construction, the ethical
equivalent of the male gaze. This is particularly true in a case like
Exiles, where freedom is defined in almost exclusively *sexual* terms.
Since this mode of freedom is instituted, moreover, not in the ideal

philosophical space of a hypothetical community but upon the ground of an existing relationship of material dependency, Richard's monition becomes the means for retaining at least some of the mastery that his commitment to openness and his will to justice forswears.

Richard's surveillance notwithstanding, the freedom he grants Bertha precludes his placing any moral constraints upon her, at least theoretically, including a claim of loyalty. "I will not blame you. You are free. I cannot blame you," he declares, as if these were one and the same proposition (*E* 70). Moreover, he is similarly restricted from providing any moral guidance, at least theoretically, including outward expressions of ethical preference. Bertha continually asks what Richard would like to her to do, and he just as adamantly refuses to tell her:

BERTHA: Am I to go to this place?
RICHARD: Do you want to go?
BERTHA: I want to find out what he means. Am I to go?
RICHARD: Why do you ask me? Decide for yourself.
BERTHA: Do you tell me to go?
RICHARD: No.
BERTHA: Do you forbid me to go?
RICHARD: No.
BERTHA: Tell me not to go and I will not.
RICHARD: (without looking at her) Decide yourself.   (*E* 69, 70)

Once again, the cross-gender pastiche of *A Doll House* is evident. Nora chafes under Torvald's moral micromanagement of her quotidian life, symbolized by his ludicrous ban on macaroons (Rank's reference to the sweets as "contraband" deliberately underscores the absurdity of the situation); Bertha suffers feelings of abandonment under Richard's equally resolute determination not to dictate or even direct conduct concerning a major episode that impacts upon them both.

In an analogous vein, while Richard claims that his intervention with Robert is intended to ensure Bertha's safety, his surveillance can engender little real sense of security if he is to avoid curtailing her liberty. Whereas the rhetoric of closure in *A Doll House* is associated with Torvald's stifling moral tutelage and material protection of Nora, the rhetoric of aperture in *Exiles* is linked with Bertha's sense of abandonment and Richard's sense of neglect. When Richard departed for Italy, he was so concerned to leave Bertha's free choice intact that he never even asked her to accompany him; but given her

lower social status and the sexual double standard in effect in
Ireland, he put her at risk simply by bringing her along. Now that
they have returned, Bertha repeatedly attributes Richard's continued
laissez-faire attitude to an indifference born of his love for Beatrice:

You have allowed me what you call complete liberty … to have complete
liberty with – that girl. (*E* 66)

That is why you give me complete liberty. (*E* 66)

I suppose it is all planned so that you may have a good opportunity to meet
her. (*E* 94)

For your own sake you urged me to it … to be free yourself … With her! …
And that is your love! (*E* 133)

Although Richard sees his present hands-off policy as potentially
more negligent than his Roman carousing, he persists anyway out of
a desire to respect Bertha's autonomy, a purpose which, as we have
already seen, does not exclude and may subserve other, less noble
desires.

   Once more, *Exiles* works a reversal of the gender positions in *A Doll
House*. Whereas Nora ultimately demands "absolute freedom" from
Torvald's willful protection, which she sees as confinement, Bertha
(Nora) demands from Richard a chivalric defense, which he sees as
tantamount to her confinement and so refuses. Arguing to the
contrary, Suzette Henke has taken Richard's rhetoric of permission
– "I have allowed you complete liberty" (*E* 65) – to mean that he
"arrogantly presumed" that Bertha's freedom "should be contingent
on spousal benevolence" and so under his control, i.e. should not be
freedom at all.[29] But it is in fact Bertha who first employs the rhetoric
of permission to justify her continued flirtation with Robert, leaving
Richard to take it up in order to sustain her in what he has some
imperfect reason to believe is her choice.

BERTHA: I think you are only pretending you don't mind. I don't mind.
RICHARD: (quietly) I know dear. But I want to find out what he means or
   feels just as you do.
BERTHA: (points at him) Remember you allowed me to go on. I told you
   the whole thing from the beginning.   (*E* 59)

Indeed, Richard's most impassioned repudiation of his own patriarchal authority comes in response to Bertha's request for the sort of
moral guidance and material guardrail that would render her
freedom entirely contingent upon spousal benevolence and control:

BERTHA: (almost passionately) Why do you not defend me against him? Why do you go away from me now without a word? Dick, my God, tell me what you wish me to do?

RICHARD: I cannot, dear. (struggling with himself) Your own heart will tell you … I have a wild delight in my soul, Bertha, as I look at you. I see you as you are yourself. That I came first in your life or before him then – that may be nothing to you. You may be his more than mine … You have drawn us near together. There is something wiser than wisdom in your heart. Who am I that I should call myself master of your heart or of any woman's? (*E* 95–6)

In this situation, Richard cannot be "[her] God" as protector without being her God as preceptor;[30] he cannot guide her without in some way governing her as well, precisely the paternalistic mode of gender relation that his anarchist–libertarian notion of justice is designed to abolish.

I do not mean to ignore other less conscious motives, expressive or supportive of male hegemony, that figure into the ethical stand whereby Richard seems to forswear that hegemony. Indeed, the last-cited passage touches upon a current of homosocial/homoerotic desire between the two male principals that Bertha is conscripted to mediate and resolve, and this aspect of the dramatic interaction is so critical, particularly as a symbolic expression of the patriarchal bias of Richard's will to justice, that I have devoted the third and concluding segment of this chapter to it. What should be at least noted at this point, however, is that this desire, being profoundly agonistic in nature, provides the dominant site for the emergence-in-denial of the intersubjective in Richard's ethos of individual autonomy.

More immediately apparent in the cited passage is yet another variant of the scopic desire I discussed earlier. In the first instance, of course, Richard's ethico-political agenda involves facilitating the emergence of some more authentic, more essential Bertha from the distorting veil of her material dependency, political subjacency, and cultural minority. Simply put, he actively purposes to cease impeding her, even by his very presence, from thinking and acting for herself. But as the above quotation makes clear, he not only wants her to *be* her core identity, so to speak, he wants to *see* her core identity as well – a possibility which has a positive erotic charge for Richard, as Joyce's careful selection of the phrase, "a wild delight" intimates. That is to say, coming to a recognition of the encumbrances his authority as *paterfamilias* has placed upon Bertha enables Richard to refashion her along typically patriarchal lines: as feminine mystery or enigma to be accessed, revealed, and beheld. Principle and desire have collaborated to produce a kind of spiritual equivalent of the striptease, reviving, in the process, a flagging sexual current in the marriage. Furthermore, the fact that Richard can conceive of himself as assisting in the unveiling of the genuine article, if only by his encouragement, is not incidental to his wild delight in gazing and tends to reinforce on a local scale the architectonics of the phallic order.

The construct of the feminine enigma constitutes the woman as a supreme value in latency, an *implicitly* transcendental signifier, the authoritative Other of the symbolic law, which cannot in principle realize itself as such but must rely on a masculine agency to bring it to manifestation, to penetrate and represent the mystery and thereby claim its imprimatur. The woman in this way must supply the phallus precisely by lacking it and can *be* the phallus that man alone *has*.[31] Women are thus culturally enjoined to be instruments of their own subordination, simultaneously empowering and disempowered. A prominent staging of this dynamic occurs during the traditional wedding ritual in which the bride occupies center stage, the site of concentrated force, but remains veiled and so symbolically *in potentia* until the moment when the groom, having loitered in the margins of the ceremonial space, lifts the veil and realizes in his gaze the mythically framed radiance and beauty of her countenance. Richard's stab at marital renewal partakes of the same dynamic. By standing on the sidelines, he brings out the supreme value, the authoritative otherness ("wiser than wisdom"), of Bertha's heart, and through the agency of the metaphorical "look," he takes possession of that value, that authority, in the same motion. The motif of the feminine enigma marks the interweaving of the phallocentric economy of desire and the masculine hegemony it advances into the very fabric of Richard's design of gender justice.

Given the interpretive history of *Exiles*, it is necessary to observe at this point that the construct of the feminine enigma is not homologous with the Pygmalion–Galatea complex and has different implications for the problem of gender justice. Perhaps the most persistent factual error in Joyce criticism is the idea that Richard esteems Bertha as his creation, the effect of his ideological labor, and in that respect an extension of himself. James Farrell, Bonnie Kime Scott, Clive Hart,

Ruth Bauerle, Suzette Henke, and Christine Froula have all made this inaccurate claim in one form or another.[32] But the play offers no textual support for this reading. It is Robert, the standardbearer of male appropriation, who expresses surprise that Richard disclaims any "rights over her – over her heart" (*E* 78) – the same heart that Richard finds "wiser than wisdom" (*E* 96). It is Robert who avers, "She is yours. Your work" (*E* 78). And it is Robert who later admonishes Richard, "Oh don't talk of guilt and innocence. You have made her all that she is. A strange and wonderful personality – in my eyes, at least" (*E* 84). The critical tradition in question has seen fit to stipulate, without corroboration, that Richard concurs in Robert's opinion, or that Robert actually speaks for Richard, an assumption untenable in its simplicity, despite the kind of intimacy they do in fact share as *doppelgänger*. What is more, Richard's reply substantially contradicts Robert in its recognition of an autonomous existence that could be marred, rather than made, by association with him:[33] "Or I have killed her ... [killed] The virginity of her soul" (*E* 84). The biographical evidence, finally, disputes the assumption that Robert speaks for Richard on this matter. In Italy, Joyce was in receipt of letters suggesting that his friends in Ireland had cast him as the Svengali-like creator of Nora's soul. Joyce responded defiantly, "Nora's disposition is much nobler than my own and in many ways in which Cosgrave and I are deficient she requires no making at all."[34] Later, urged to convince Nora of the desirability of some project, he opined, "My wife's personality ... is absolute proof against any influence of mine."[35]

Tacitly conceding that both play and life offer insufficient warrant for this interpretive line, Christine Froula has turned to Draft Fragments 1 and 2 for further support.[36] In the former, Richard declares,

You say I am like her father ... I feel as if I had carried her within my own body, in my womb ... Her books, her music, the fire of thought ... the grace with which she tends the body we desire – whose work is that? I feel that it is mine. It is my work the work of others like me now or in other times. It is we who have conceived her and brought her forth. (Fragment 1)

In the latter, Richard declares, "I have done something already. I have destroyed and recreated in my own image a woman" (Fragment 2). Since these pronouncements articulate the Pygmalion complex on a collective and personal basis respectively, they would seem to afford ample evidence for the critical chestnut Froula is preserving. But Joyce evidently made a conscious choice (a) *not* to include these statements, (b) to put miniaturized versions of them into the mouth of Robert alone, and (c) to have Richard register dissent. In other words, the history of these fragments as *discarded* and recycled testifies to Joyce's desire to dissociate his protagonist from a strictly Pygmalionesque identification, quite the opposite of the reading Froula wants to substantiate.

This decision of Joyce's consists, in turn, with his usage of Torvald as a negative analogue for Richard. During his climactic confrontation with Nora, Torvald articulates the fantasy of having (re)created or birthed his wife in a specifically ethical context: "For a man there's something indescribably sweet and satisfying in knowing he's forgiven his wife ... It's as if she belongs to him in two ways now: in a sense he's given her forth into the world again, and she's become his wife and his child as well" (*DH* 108). Enveloped in such a fantasy, the act of judgment, even in its mildest form as forgiveness, aspires to a condition of absolute tyranny; for it seeks to infantilize Nora in order to sustain her as a projection of Torvald's ego, thus eliminating her specific difference altogether. The unused fragments of *Exiles* would have discredited Richard's ethico-juridical endeavor on much the same grounds. Joyce elected instead to set in operation a far subtler interplay of high-minded principle, entrenched power, and unconscious desire. Based as it is on the construct of the female enigma, Richard's fantasy of discovery bears an undeniable structural relation to Torvald's fantasy of creation in that both tend to promote phallocentric authority by reserving effective agency to masculinity. But this relation reflects the limits of Richard's vision rather than its express focus. That is to say, Torvald's fantasy of direct, naturalized, and wholesale appropriation of the wife-woman in general – notably shared by Robert Hand – captures the very essence of the patriarchal law of desire, while Richard's sense of the female enigma, being a corrupted recognition of the autonomy of the sexual other, marks the interweaving of that law and the masculine hegemony it advances into the fabric of Richard's design of gender justice – to its vitiation, yes, but not to its complete destruction. After all, rather than looking to blot out or assimilate Bertha's distinctive otherness, Richard's fantasy involves affecting the release or recovery of her separate and inviolable quiddity, what he calls "the virginity of her soul" (*E* 84). As such, it continues the series of reversals that Richard's character works on Torvald and, in fact, culminates the sequence by approximating the heroic fantasy of liberation motivating Ibsen's play.

It is important to understand how Torvald factors into *Exiles* as Richard's foil and the kind of ethical warrant Richard enjoys as a result in order to appreciate fully the devastating irony of Bertha's one, unmistakable echo of Nora Helmer,[37] which brings Richard (and Ibsen too) into political alignment with Torvald at last. Just before Nora bids Torvald goodbye once and for all, she summarizes her reason as follows:

When your big fright was over – and it wasn't from any threat against me, only for what might damage you – when all the danger was passed, for you it was just as if nothing had happened. I was exactly the same, your little lark, your doll that you have to handle with double care now that I'd turned out so brittle and frail. (gets up) Torvald – in that instant it dawned on me that for eight years I've been living here as a stranger. (*DH* 113)

Nora has found that the smothering, fetishistic protection that Torvald has made such a show of providing, in accordance with the patriarchal division of sexual labor, belies the fantastic distance between them, wrought by his indifference to her very existence as a subject (as opposed to a doll or lark) – an indifference ultimately inscribed in the fundamental law of patriarchy itself, the Name of the Father. Hers is a response to the everyday enactment of Torvald's socially sponsored fantasy of appropriation. And yet Richard, whose gender ethos cuts, or appears to cut, in the other direction, excites an analogous desperation in Bertha at an analogously climactic moment in the drama. In their first encounter after Richard left Bertha alone with Robert, the following scene is played out:

RICHARD: ... You would like to be free now. You have only to say the word.
BERTHA: (proudly) Whenever you like I am ready.
RICHARD: So that you could meet your lover – freely?
BERTHA: Yes.
RICHARD: Night after night?
BERTHA: (gazing before her and speaking with intense passion) To meet my lover! (holding out her arms before her) My lover! Yes! My lover! [she bursts suddenly into tears] ...
RICHARD: ... Bertha, you are free.
BERTHA: ... Don't touch me. You are a stranger to me. You do not understand anything in me – not one thing in my heart or soul! A stranger! I'm living with a stranger. (*E* 134, 135)

Where Nora is disillusioned with the fair-weather form of domestic security Torvald provides, Bertha is disillusioned with the atomistic brand of license Richard proffers. She has found that his liberal–rational species of freedom, a freedom from restraints and commitments, shaped within and suited to historically masculine spheres of activity and interest, belies the concrete feeling of emotional dependency that the resulting isolation instills in her, as someone whose socially defined role has been to nurture and attend the domestic community (to make sure, for example, that Archie loved his father and expressed his love regularly) (*E* 65). Here again the marital *differend* is enacted through a synergy of verbal and gestural performance. Bertha initially embraces in both word and intonation the notion of independence that Richard tables, but her body language gradually bespeaks her interpersonal attachment, commitment, and even dependence – first, the intense gaze (135, L 2), then the upheld arms (135, L 3), finally, the tearful paroxysm (135, L 5) – only to give place in turn to a shrewd reconceptualization of this independence as a form of estrangement ("I'm living with a stranger"), literally an alienation of affection.

With this echo of Nora, Bertha recalls, revises, and advances her earlier dismissal of Richard's discourse of individual self-determination: to wit, "I know why you have allowed me what you call complete liberty ... to have complete liberty with – that girl" (*E* 56). On that occasion, the phrase reads "what you *call* complete liberty" and connotes other than genuine liberty, a counterfeit liberty foisted upon Bertha as a blind for Richard's amorous indifference toward her. Bertha's emphasis on misapprehension here, however, suggests that the phrase might be read differently in retrospect: "what *you* call complete liberty." That is, Richard's conception of liberty, though fundamentally incongruent with what Bertha calls liberty, might be a nonetheless authentic version thereof and the socially dominant or hegemonic version at that. By the same token, the indifference Bertha senses is not necessarily personal, as she suspects at first, a desire on Richard's part to be rid of her, but likely structural: a failure on Richard's part to recognize an alternative evaluation of liberty, precisely because he happens to espouse the approved or hegemonic version, that which circulates within and helps to define the male-dominated public sphere. This is particularly relevant, of course, *outside* Ireland, which is why Richard undertook his "spiritual exile" in the first place, and why, having sojourned so long abroad with

Bertha, he is able to take this conception of freedom for granted. Richard does not deploy strategic blinds, he is himself strategically blinded by a modality of gender privilege that he has had some hand in arranging.

The combined effect of Richard and Bertha's diverse investments in the prospect of marital freedom, their differing conceptions of such freedom, and the discrepant social force their respective investments and conceptions enjoy is precisely the wrecked communication of which Bertha complains. Aptly enough, her complaint reflects in both style and substance the impasse from which it issues and upon which it dwells. In responding to Richard's assurance, "Bertha, you are free," with the sentiment that he understood "not one thing in [her] heart or soul," she insists upon her affective, centripetal interpretation of liberty as the heartfelt, consensual production of a jointly anticipated happiness, as opposed to the undisturbed existential choice of the fundamentally self-interested but ethically responsible individual. But in the process she implicitly concedes the *effective* power of the latter view, Richard's view, which has imposed itself upon their marriage by misrecognizing and ignoring her own. Thus, her complaint itself testifies to both the need and the inefficacy of her complaint. At the same time, this *differend*, in which one party, one phrase regimen, prevails largely through its positive incapacity to give the other a hearing, puts asunder what liberal thought has always claimed to join together as the seal of its own legitimacy: liberty and justice. Nor can this conceptual marriage be saved on the present terms. The divergent and supposedly complementary responsibilities of men and women for the maintenance and reproduction of the family unit, the very cell of their gendered identification and interaction, generate interlocking yet contradictory sets of priorities, which can neither be independently accomplished, enabling universal liberty, nor impartially adjudicated, ensuring universal justice, because they are themselves always already prioritized according to the law of the phallus – i.e. not just a unitary male ruler or standard but the rule of the unitary as the rule of man.[38]

It is as an instantiation of this positive metalaw (no less positivistic for being meta, nor meta for being positivistic) that Richard's husbandly performance and gender politics finally cease to oppose those of Torvald and actually enlarge upon them, giving the ironic repetition of Nora's grievance in Bertha's mouth its underlying political as well as dramatic bite. Torvald sees his marriage and his wife in the mirror of his eye/I, meaning his own gendered perspective. He represents the unitary male ruler or standard. For example, when Krogstad returns Nora's note, Torvald exuberates – "Nora! Wait – better check it again – Yes, Yes, it's true. I'm saved. Nora, I'm saved" – to which Nora tautly replies, "And I," prompting him to elaborate, "You too of course" (*DH* 106). The incident is symptomatic of Torvald's tendency to treat Nora's desires, fortunes, etc., her self-interests in short, as fully and naturally incorporate in his own. His assumption in this regard suggests that Blackstone's comment on the status of wedlock in British common law might be extended to the *doxa* governing the institution in modern European culture at large: the husband and the wife become one person and that person is the husband.[39]

In his struggle to overthrow this very premise, Richard manages to replicate its appropriative force at a higher level and in a more insidious manner. He represents his marriage and his wife in the mirror of his I/eye, meaning his own gendered perspective *on* subjectivity, his agonistic, separatist vision of the I/eye. As such, Richard represents the rule of the unitary as the rule of the man. Instead of projecting the particular matter of his self-interest onto his wife, à la Torvald, he projects or at least enjoins upon Bertha his ethos of willful egoistic independence, his sense of himself as his own man, sovereign, singular, embattled. But this, of course, is the same image of selfhood and the same heroic self-image that Ibsen rather more flagrantly projects onto Nora at the end of *A Doll House*. Having had her pointedly question the law's abstract, masculinist disregard of sentimental ties and domestic exigencies, Ibsen climaxes the play by having her assume the male-identified role of a wandering, existential hero(ine), who places herself beyond the family pale altogether and even uses the law's anomalies as a rationale. He thus frames the liberation of woman as her realization of the masculine ideal (Ibsen's own) of remote self-reliance. Insofar as they build upon the extended parallel Joyce draws between Richard and Ibsen as polemically minded stage managers, the finally specularizing implications of Richard's project also serve as Joyce's backhand critique of Ibsen's solution to the woman question. Richard follows Ibsen in assimilating not Bertha's particular desires but the *structure* of her desire to his own, overlooking in his socially conditioned self-directedness the similarly conditioned intersubjectivity of her affective economy. Extending these implications a step, we might say that *Exiles* locates the obstacle to justice not in a given set of representational tendencies (racism, sexism, etc.) but in the very economy of representation itself.

Let us be clear about what is at issue in this default of representation. Richard does not, as Kershner has argued, perpetuate an "egregious exercise of patriarchal power" by offering Bertha "a relationship of equality on his own terms," which is to say a relationship of domination.[40] Rather, in offering Bertha a relationship of equality on the terms understood and accepted in their political and intellectual milieu, including the leading feminist movements of the time, Richard does in fact contribute to the local reproduction of patriarchal power and domination. In this, he succumbs to what we might call the positive law of justice, the necessity that any vision, program, or system of sociopolitical proportionality proceed from a certain arbitrary and invidious adequation of like and unlike, sameness and difference, rooted in the existing arrangement of power relations and the social contingencies produced thereby. In its interpersonal form, this entails that any attempt to respect the needs and desires of others, hence to be just, necessitates phrasing or representing those needs and desires in terms of something else – stereotypes, settled assumptions, past experience, situational norms, one's own needs and desires – and thus violating the cardinal need of those others to phrase their desires and needs for themselves as they live and understand them. The upshot of Richard's subjection to this law is actually *more* "egregious" than the personalized power play Kershner detects; for the law describes a vicious circle within which Richard's rejection of the paternalistic mode of gender relations turns around and produces effects strangely akin to those associated with paternalism itself. In keeping with this systemic inertia, the momentum of patriarchal hegemony works to divert Richard's efforts to relinquish control over Bertha into even subtler means of enthrallment.

This dynamic is perhaps clearest as regards the stakes of Bertha's participation in the *ménage à trois* with Robert. A number of Joyceans have opined that Bertha is forced to be free, ushered against her will into a situation of sexual choice and mobility. While not implausible, this analysis seems to me a little simplistic. It is not the sexual mobility that Bertha suffers from but the existential construction Richard places on her freedom. Joyce carefully and repeatedly broaches Bertha's interest in exploring the dalliance with Robert. As we have

seen, she tells Richard that she doesn't "mind" Robert's blandishments, and when she asks if he does, Richard replies, "I want to find
out what he means or feels *just as you do*" (*E* 59, my italics). Shortly
thereafter, struggling to obtain advice from Richard, she confirms his
sense of her motive:

RICHARD: Do you want to go?
BERTHA: I want to find out what he means.   (*E* 69–70)

Later, finding Richard at the cottage, she complains, "Now I can
find out nothing" (*E* 93). Finally, responding to an earlier accusation
of Richard's, she fleshes out her investment in the affair: "It is not
true that I want to drive everyone from you. I wanted to bring you
close together – you and him" (*E* 146). But in all instances, and this
is the key, her desire can be seen to crystallize in a joint project or
fantasy. Just as Richard "wants to find out what he means" (*E* 59),
so does Bertha, and she uses the exact same phraseology (*E* 69 and
70). In repeating this sentiment to Richard (*E* 93), Bertha seeks to
align herself with his position in the fantasy, to situate herself as a co-
observer rather than the object or even the instrument of observation.
What is more, her voyeurism is really a sharing of his voyeurism, with
her desire pegged more to the act of sharing than the particular
activity shared. Finally, her last and most developed motive – "I
wanted to bring you close together – you and him" (*E* 146) –
likewise cooperates in Richard's erotic fantasy: "I cannot hate him
since his arms have been around you. You have drawn us near
together" (*E* 96). As Suzette Henke notes, Richard's affective
involvement in the dalliance is marked not only by scopophilic
detachment but by vicarious participation.[41] For her part, Bertha not
only sees herself facilitating that vicarious participation, but once
again contrives to align herself with Richard's position. She will
participate vicariously in the (sexually vicarious) intimacy of Richard
and Robert that she helped to effect. Through the elaborate chains of
substitution and supplementation upon which the erotics of *Exiles*
mainly hang, Bertha contrives to share in Richard's phantasmatic
experience both metonymically and metaphorically.

Once Robert understands how Bertha has been informing her
husband of their furtive meetings, he proclaims, "I see. You were
making an experiment *for his sake*. On me" (*E* 98, my italics). In
many ways Bertha's twin, as Beatrice is to Richard,[42] Robert
immediately seizes upon the intersubjective orientation of her

investment in the sexual adventure, the object of her desire residing in the mutuality of the participation itself. Because she has embarked on this adventure largely for Richard's sake, she can ultimately reproach him, "You urged me to it ... *for your own sake* you urged me to it" (*E* 137, my italics), without contradicting in spirit her several prior protestations of active interest. As the repetition of the italicized phrase intimates, Bertha does not draw or maintain the rigid ego boundaries between herself and Richard that would make such a contradiction viable or relevant. To be sure, there has not been an explicit exhortation on Richard's part to initiate or prolong her dalliance, and this is a crucial point from his atomistic moral perspective. But Bertha is attuned to his "ignoble longing" to be cuckolded and even to his homoerotic "motive deeper still"[43] (*E* 88), much as she is attuned to the resurgent jealousy he continues to deny, and attuned in either case not just in the sense of apprehending or even sympathizing but of plugging into, identifying emotionally. Her express need for Richard's permission, defense, and moral tutelage is inseparably articulated with his repudiated yet threatened feeling of proprietorship over her. On the other side, her sexual curiosity and flirtatiousness vis-à-vis Robert, whom she seems to find physically *unattractive*, is triangulated from the start upon Richard's "ignoble longing," upon which it continually feeds. Instead of a contradictory attitude, a concept mortgaged to an identitarian affective and ethical logic, we have in Bertha an ambivalence of ambivalence, an ambivalence of affect or impulse emanating from an ambivalence of subject position or psychic locale. This is not to suggest that Bertha's desire is entirely beholden to Richard's, that she is simply divided in her overriding loyalty to him between satisfying his masochistic fantasies and satisfying his will to mastery. Such single-minded commitment to another does not square with the intersubjectivity of Bertha's desire; it is but the other side of the coin of self-interest. Bertha's is not a transparent unilateral desire to share, but a displaced or diffused desire in sharing, whose force, object and enactments are profoundly relational. That is why Bertha can neither own her involvement completely, without at some point attributing it to Richard's urging or manipulation, nor disown it completely under the rubric "I am or was only trying to please you."

To Richard, the intersubjectivity of Bertha's desire constitutes an indigestible, nearly incomprehensible phenomenon, his reaction to which indicates that Joyce is less concerned with gender difference in

itself, an ontological proposition, than the gender dominance it
excuses, an ethical and political proposition:

RICHARD: Then you have come here and led him on in this way on account
of me? Is that how it is... (continuing) If so you have indeed treated
him badly and shamefully.

BERTHA: (points at him) Yes. But it was your fault. And I will end it now.
I was simply a tool for you. You have no respect for me.   (*E* 94)

It is an index of patriarchal hegemony that the inability of the
unitary rule (gauge/law) of the phallus to sort out the intersubjective
mode of feminine desire – itself an effect of patriarchal social
arrangements – should redound to the disadvantage or discredit of
the female-identified way of being rather than bringing into disrepute
the logic of castration and transcendence, upon which all liberal–
rationalist accounts of human behavior are predicated. As an
exponent of such discourse, Richard almost automatically translates
his own coimplication in Bertha's motives as bespeaking her lack of
genuine affection for Robert and thus her deviousness in pursuing her
"real" Richard-centric objectives. Bertha's reply is still more
indicative of the structural constraints under which she labors in her
"freedom." For far from giving voice to her desire, it marks the
absence of any such enunciatory position. She is not, we have seen,
simply a tool for Richard any more than she is *simply* an autonomous
agent. These are merely the poles between which her self-explanation
continually slides in an attempt to register an affective and
experiential doubleness excluded from the available ethico-political
frame of intelligibility. The difficulty she has in phrasing her desire is
of a piece with the kind of misconstruction the other characters place
upon her actions. Richard in particular can only measure her design
on a monological or egoistical scale of valence. Bertha acts in terms of
intersubjectively induced, defined, and channeled desires, with the
aim of sustaining the intersubjective scenario of which she is a
member. This is in fact the mystery behind her marvelous geste of
going to Italy with Richard as his *invited* companion *without ever being
asked*. But her "present partner in life" reads her deeds off as elective
testimony to her own authentically inward, self-generated, and self-
directed wishes, liberated insofar as her courage and strength of
character will allow by his lifting of the conventional marital
restraints and obligations. True to the discourse of liberal individualism and the myth of the female enigma in one stroke, Richard

interrogates Bertha's desires as realities that exist at a significant remove from the social context in which they materialize. He in effect recodes the interlocking fantasy that the *ménage à trois* entails as a series of parallel, even disaffiliated, lines of desire, and in so doing he intensifies Bertha's vertiginous sense of exile and isolation and, with it, his own needfulness to her. Under the circumstances, his granting of "complete liberty" to Bertha turns out to be a double-barrel method of seduction whereby he constitutes himself as a powerful object of desire and a desirable subject of power.

There is evidence that Bertha is not entirely insensible of the emotional spiral I have sketched. Witness the blowup over whether Richard should intervene with Robert before the assignation at Ranelaugh. Richard makes it fairly clear, let us remember, that he intends to establish a condition of complete mutual enlightenment in which the distinct responsibility of each party to the affair can be assessed and free action ensue on that basis. But Bertha espies in this arguably principled gesture one of Richard's characteristic means for keeping her socially marooned and therefore dependent – "And then you try and turn everyone against me. All is to be for you. I am to appear false and cruel to everyone except you" (*E* 65). The truly insidious twist to this dynamic, however, stems from the fact that Richard winds up securing still greater dominion by renouncing his traditional male prerogatives and rights of possession and waiving all limits on Bertha's franchise. As a result, her route of escape dovetails inevitably with the road to confinement. Within the monological regime of discourse and practice she occupies, Bertha can relieve the solitude and sense of exclusion that heighten her insecurity and emotional dependency only by sliding back into a more immediately subordinate relation to Richard. Her pleas for moral guidance not only supply Richard with a dose of proprietorial reassurance to ballast his masochistic voyeuristic titillation, they supply her with a badly needed if but marginally effective ritual of affiliation. Bertha is caught in an emotional slipknot that tightens with each move she makes to extricate herself.

The most dramatic manifestation of this chiasmatic reversal of freedom into bondage occurs in the final tableau of *Exiles*, which is often celebrated for its purposive indeterminacy. At first glance, the scene does appear to sustain the contrast between the rhetoric of aperture characteristic of *Exiles* generally and the rhetoric of closure characteristic of *A Doll House*. Comparing the play with the work of

Ibsen generally, John MacNicholas comments, "Joyce works towards the invention of a possibility rather than the ratification of a result."[44] The former aim presumably finds its emblem in Richard's perennially open "wound of doubt" (*E* 146), the latter aim in Nora's peremptory slamming of the door. Jean-Michel Rabate, concurring in MacNicholas' opinion, argues "The plot leaves us with an open question mark."[45] But this conclusion, to my mind, identifies the structure of the play a little too closely with Richard's ethical project and his view of the action and so repeats the *differend* under which Bertha has suffered all along.

Rabate specifically credits an amalgamated Richard/Joyce figure with devising a method "to outflank sexual jealousy" by "doubling [doubt] upon itself," putting localized moments of doubt into doubt without ever effacing them altogether.[46] He moves from a negative uncertainty, marked by the compulsive question, "Has there, or hasn't there, been a sexual rapport?" to a positive skepticism characterized by the stipulation that "there is no rapport, relationship... There are only inequalities, excess... too much or too little."[47] Achieving this state of pure doubt evidently entails constructing Bertha as the pure object of doubt, the doubtful but nondoubting other, which is to say the nonsubject. "Bertha cannot doubt, must not doubt," Rabate states, "since she embodies truth."[48] While this strategy, which does in fact represent the other side of Richard's liberation of Bertha, may effectively contradict "all the classic approaches to jealousy," as Rabate claims, it clearly borrows from the classic enactment of patriarchal power and appropriation upon which such jealousy rests: symbolic castration, the emblem of which is of course Richard's "deep wound of doubt" (*E* 146). Elaborating the masculine position in the Symbolic order, which is at bottom a male Imaginary,[49] involves outflanking vacillation over the reality of castration by (1) assuming castration as an ever-present possibility, a unitary point of incertitude; and (2) constructing the feminine position as the ambivalent receptacle of this castration anxiety, i.e. as both/neither the idealized plentitude to which symbolic castration refers (Bertha as embodied truth) and, correlatively, the designated site of "real" castration (Bertha cannot doubt).

If we focus for a moment on the interplay of the couple, instead of on Richard alone, we can see that the final scene of *Exiles* stages the regeneration of patriarchal authority through its self-wounding. In repetitively, rhythmically verbalizing his state of wounded incertitude in the closing scene, Richard performs a symbolic ritual, a psychic circumcision, designed to incorporate a measure of sexual and epistemic anxiety as a constituent element of his personality and thereby master if not allay it:

BERTHA: Dick, dear, do you believe now that I have been true to you? Last night and always?
RICHARD: (sadly) Do not ask me, Bertha.   (*E* 144)
RICHARD: I am wounded, Bertha ... I have a deep, deep wound of doubt in my soul.
BERTHA: (motionless) Doubt of me?
RICHARD: Yes...
RICHARD: I have wounded my soul for you – a deep wound of doubt which can never be healed. I can never know, never in this world. I do not wish to know or to believe ... It is not in the darkness of belief that I desire you. But in restless living wounding doubt... My wound tires me.   (*E* 146–7)

This incantational expression, meanwhile, has the effect of transferring the anxiety mastered in this castration ritual to Bertha, who responds to her renewed fear of abandonment by putting herself physically and spiritually under Richard's wing:[50]

BERTHA: Dick, dear, do you believe now that I have been true to you?
RICHARD: (sadly) Do not ask me, Bertha.
BERTHA: (pressing him more closely) I have been, dear. Surely you believe me. I gave you myself – all. I gave up all for you. You took me – and you left me.   (*E* 145)
BERTHA: Wherever you go, I will follow you. If you wish to go away now I will go with you.   (*E* 146)
BERTHA: (motionless) Doubt of me?
RICHARD: Yes.
BERTHA: I am yours. (In a whisper) If I die this moment, I am yours.
          (*E* 147)

Richard's self-enervating wound seems to draw from Bertha that autonomous vitality he means to galvanize. That is because, true to its status as a castration analogue, this wound of doubt simultaneously gives pride of place to a subject-centered modality of desire, for which individual freedom is the supreme good, as opposed to Bertha's intersubjective modality, in which connectedness comes first. As a result, the doubt Richard sees as Bertha's passport to personal and sexual mobility Bertha construes as a notice threatening personal and sexual exile. That is to say, the means whereby Richard opens volitional space for Bertha ensures its still tighter closure and by her own hand. It is in the failure to take any account of this gender difference in the phrasing of desire that Richard most clearly merits Bertha's complaint, "You have no respect for me" (*E* 94).

The play culminates in a parodic twist on the traditional comic ending, where order and justice are usually restored. The lover-protagonists do indeed come together, but in a dissentient, even dystopic fashion, with Richard wounding his soul to give Bertha the freedom she dreads and Bertha rejecting that freedom to give Richard the allegiance he disdains. Richard finally characterizes his fetishized wound in ethico-political terms as a renunciation of traditional male authority and prerogatives of ownership and a declaration of Bertha's independence:

It is not in the darkness of belief that I desire you. But in restless living wounding doubt. To hold you by no bonds, even of love, to be united with you in body and soul in utter nakedness – for this I longed. But now I am tired for a while, Bertha. My wound tires me. (*E* 147)

But his speech comes on the heels of Bertha defining herself as, ultimately, an appropriable object – "If I died this moment, I am yours" (*E* 147) – and his speech in turn triggers her renunciation of her independent identity: "Forget me Dick. Forget me and love me again as you did the first time" (*E* 147). The intersubjective desire which fueled her participation in the triangular fantasy of free love returns briefly in the grammar of her last speech only to fade once more under a phallic injunction cunningly encoded in Richard Rowan's name, the Name of the Father: "I want my lover. To meet *him*, to go to *him*, to give myself to *him*. *You, Dick*" (*E* 147, my italics).

BETWEEN MEN: RICHARD AND ROBERT

In the working notes to *Exiles*, Joyce labels the play "three cat and mouse acts" (*E* 156). In conjuring with Joyce's meaning, scholars have generally translated the phrase as a game of cat and mouse and proceeded from there. But Joyce's epigram also repeats the slang term for The Prisoners (Temporary Discharge for Ill Health) Bill, the Cat and Mouse Act, which the British government passed in response to the successful use of the hunger strike as a political and public relations tactic by the suffragette movement. The Act allowed the government to release hunger strikers when they reached a point of serious illness or inanition only to return them to the prison once they had recovered their strength on the outside.[51] During the summer of 1913, as Joyce was working on *Exiles*, the proposal went forward to extend the provisions of the so-called Cat and Mouse Act to Ireland.[52] Among the leading exponents of the hunger-strike gambit, and one to whom the new law would likely apply, was Joyce's old college friend, Hanna Sheehy-Skeffington.[53] Another old college friend, Thomas Kettle, helped to organize a protest of the bill during which he seemed to betray the cause by affirming that he was in favor of postponing any social or franchise reform in order to achieve national autonomy.[54] Given the temporal coincidence of the composition of *Exiles* and the truly violent perturbation over the Cat and Mouse Act, given as well the direct personal involvement of a number of Joyce's acquaintances, it seems probable that the note refers specifically to that law, particularly since gender justice forms the ethico-political problematic of the play. That Thomas Kettle was one of the models for Robert Hand makes the likelihood all the stronger.[55] Indeed, given the time frame involved, Robert's statement, "We are approaching a difficult moment. And not only here" could well embrace the turmoil over suffrage as well as home rule or even the close but testy relationship between the two movements (*E* 44).

The last point of connection affords a clue as to the symbolic relevance of the Cat and Mouse Act for the play. Tom Kettle presented himself as a friend of the emancipation movement, but on this occasion he gave priority to more distinctively masculine concerns and to a predominantly masculinist movement, particularly as it was embodied in his co-organizer, Padraic Pearse. His speech relegating the suffrage movement to second-class status even while claiming to support it was shouted down by cries of "you're not a woman" and "that's not a woman's point of view."[56] Amid the swirling crosscurrents of feminism and nationalism, ethnically in-fluenced feminism and gender-specific nationalism, Kettle had encountered the structural deficiency of representation as a political mode and a juridical method, a lesson very much at the heart of *Exiles*. Robert Hand himself is an egregious example of the self-reflexive limits of representation, the feedback distortion built into the process. He advocates the sexual liberation of woman on principle: "For all. That a woman, too, has the right to try with many men until she finds love" (*E* 82). But whether earnestly or cynically made, this proposal answers to Robert's own sexual appetite, which has been framed in terms of a divine injunction only seconds before: "You are made to give yourself to many freely. I wrote that law with My finger on your heart" (*E* 81). The transparency of the fit between Robert's principles and his inclinations at once sets off the comparative nobility of Richard's ethical program and parodies its ultimately self-referential structure, exemplifying the complex relationship that generally obtains between the two male characters. Their agonistic intimacy, an overlapping of personal and intellectual opposition and alliance, figures as the dramatic site on which Joyce interrogates the impact of homosociality upon the possibility of a male feminism.

Near the center of *Exiles*, Robert Hand delivers himself of the most graphic expression of that sexual rapaciousness which I have likened to one side of the Giacomo persona: "Those are moments of sheer madness when we feel intense passion for a woman. We see nothing. We think of nothing. Only to possess her: brutal, bestial, what you will" (*E* 79). When Richard objects, "that longing to possess a woman is not love" (*E* 75), Robert appeals to the order of sexual necessity: "No man ever yet lived on this earth who did not long to possess – I mean to possess in the flesh – the woman whom he loves. It is nature's law" (*E* 79). Richard replies, "What is that to me? Did I vote it?" (*E* 79) and counterposes his own conception of love, "To wish her well" (*E* 79). In this exchange resides the imbrication-cum-confrontation of the law and justice thematized in various ways throughout this book. Robert lays down the law of nature, which is to say the law of the patriarchy in its most positivistic and thus authoritarian mode. Richard's initial retort goes to the liberal, democratic mechanism of political representation, where the law awaits legitimation without ceasing to be law. Richard's second reply plays out the strange temporality of representational justice in the realm of interpersonal ethics. As the definition of love, "to wish someone well" privileges the element of respect for the right to self-determination of the other person, recalling Stephen Dedalus' injunction to "be just before you are generous" (*U* 15.3604). But the gesture depends implicitly upon some representation of what the criteria of wellness are *for* the other person, not excluding the assumption that some particular version of self-determination, presumably conformable to the wisher's own notions on the subject, is a *sine qua non*. Whereas Robert openly espouses the possessiveness he feels for the body of the beloved or desired woman, Richard's apparently contrary ethos quietly evidences his analogous possessiveness over the terms of her spiritual well-being. What is more, the two modes of possessiveness tend to converge, because when it comes to Bertha, Richard defines the criteria of wellness largely in terms of amorous and specifically sexual options and imperatives. That is to say, Richard's culturally dictated assumptions about the romantic and fleshly epicenter of the typical woman's existence (her governing passions, her predominant activities and interests, the dimensions of her personal worth) do not disagree substantially with Robert's, and they plainly delimit the kind of rights he is prepared to acknowledge or foster. In keeping with the juridical dynamic I have outlined so far, Richard's ideal of love as sexual justice finds its limit as well as its foil in Robert's opposed theory of sexual predation as natural law.

By the same token, the Cat and Mouse Act, taken as a figurative paradigm of women under law, proves no less relevant to Richard's than to Robert's sexual attitudes. The Cat and Mouse Act offered women their independence and rights of self-determination contingent upon the approval of the pertinent administrators of patriarchal authority, the liberal democratic state, solely for the political expediency of that state and subject to revocation on demand. Translated onto a somewhat more abstract plane of construction, the Cat and Mouse Act can be seen to symbolize how women's rights, hence gender justice itself, is always already confined by the very law that defines it, the phallocentric system of (political/cognitive) representation. Joyce would have been sensitive to this dilemma if for no other reason than that an Irishman's rights were circumscribed in much the same fashion, and with the rise of cultural nationalism after the collapse of Parnell and the liberal/electoral strategy he spearheaded, the inadequacy of freedom and equality for Irishmen on British terms came to be thematized and popularly affirmed.[57] By extending to Bertha rights based simultaneously on masculinist conceptions of individuality and preconceptions of woman's nature or woman as nature, Richard activates the cat and mouse paradigm in the play. It is through his efforts, earnestly designed as they are, that the play constitutes "three cat and mouse acts" in the sense I have suggested. Gender justice is continually detoured, if not derailed, in its very emergence.

The central debate between Richard and Robert dramatically articulates the double-sided relationship of law and justice which informs the development of the marital intrigue, beginning with the

shared past of the two men. Robert points out to Richard that the law
he enunciates, the law of "passion, free, unashamed, irresistible," has
been culled from the "language of [Richard's] own youth that
[Robert] heard so often ... in this very place" (*E* 89). Robert then
asks, "Have you changed?" By reply, Richard only concedes, "It is
the language of my youth" (*E* 89). Robert's reference to Ranelaugh
as the common site of past and present philosophizing, along with
Richard's refusal to address the present in answering the past, hints
faintly at a certain structural complicity between their respective
sexual ethics based on a shared historical origin. This inference
becomes truly compelling, however, only because the sexual form of
life out of which Richard and Robert's positions have emerged is
repeating itself in certain respects before the audience's eyes.

The shared youth of Richard and Robert centered upon a
libertinism at once sexual, intellectual, and political in nature. As
Richard remarks, "It was not only a house of revelry; it was to be the
hearth of a new life. (musing) And in that name all our sins were
committed" (*E* 48). Robert shortly divines the sins Richard intends:
"You mean the women. I have no remorse of conscience. Maybe you
have. We had two keys on those occasions" (*E* 48). Their quasi-
Nietzschean break with the conventional strictures of a hyper-
repressive Irish society evidently unfolded by way of what Eve
Sedgwick has designated the homosocial exchange of women. In her
landmark book, *Between Men*, Sedgwick draws upon René Girard's
theory of triangulated desire and Gayle Rubin's famous article on the
traffic in women to demonstrate how, especially in liberal capitalist
versions of patriarchy, male–male relationships come to be
"cemented" in competitive and hierarchical forms of solidarity and
interdependence through the circulation and exchange of women, a
practice which additionally allows the deflection or misrecognition of
the homoerotic energies such relationships entail.[58] Women function
as a symbolic property that ensures the transmission of patriarchal
power and privilege, binding male society together in its recognition
of certain eroticized sign values (aesthetic, prestige, etc.) and
differentiating its members on the basis of their unequal authority to
determine and possess those values. As best friends who are at the
same time "master" and "disciple" respectively, Richard and
Robert share a relationship in which the tension between hierarchy
and solidarity was particularly intense. The new paganism that
animates their shared lifestyle and forms the ideological glue of their

alliance was also the specific code within which they occupied differently graded subject positions, Richard as leader, Robert as follower. The women they brought back to Ranelaugh were the vehicles through which they expressed both their philosophy of life and their competitive interpersonal relationship. As Robert points out, the pair "had two [phallic] keys on those occasions," and the female body formed the metaphorical lock clinching this classically homosocial transaction[59] (*E* 48). In their joint exploitation of women, none of whom is recollected by name or in *any* detail, Richard and Robert found the means to negotiate the contradiction that structured their friendship, displacing its element of domination or mastery onto the feminine other of heterosexual desire while reserving the element of solidarity to the masculine division of the spoils. This process entails a triangulation of desire in the Girardian mode, where a given sexual partner holds her erotic allure mainly by proxy, i.e. through her relation to some valued third person.

Bertha seems to have represented a contradictory break with and continuation of the troilistic habits of Richard and Robert. On the one hand, she never visited "the house of revelry" (*E* 48) before the exile. On the other, they "first ... met, [all] three together" (*E* 109), and "every night" Richard and Robert "came to that corner to meet [her]," a corner which under the circumstances seems emblematic. On the one hand, Richard takes Bertha away with him and so out of circulation on a more or less permanent basis, placing their liaison on an entirely different footing than those that had transpired previously. On the other hand, to judge from the comments of both Richard and Robert, the act of taking Bertha out of circulation was itself a move in the strategic exchange cycle, the salient difference being that it provoked a counter-move in the competitive rather than the collegial mode.

Robert informs Bertha that his first response to Richard's proposed self-exile was to counterpropose an alternative variant of the same scheme that would keep Bertha in play, so to speak, a little while longer, so that he might ultimately secure her for himself. While telling Richard that she would prove "a weight about [his] neck" (*E* 45), he apparently regarded her less along the lines of a millstone than along the lines of that stone paperweight he actually compares to a woman during his first conversation with Richard in the play. Both represent naturalized and aesthetically pleasing reifications of social value worthy of the "homage" of a kiss. For his part, Richard's

attitude reflects the contradictions attending the situation in which
he has helped to place Bertha. When Robert challenges Richard as to
Bertha's competency as a "young girl" to make a "free choice" to
abscond with him, Richard's reply confirms his sense of Bertha as a
prize to be won, a sign of social, intellectual, and aesthetic
achievement, an object of phallic exchange whose withdrawal from
homosocial circulation is part of the larger economy of that
circulation: "I played for her against all you say, or can say; and I
won" (*E* 47). At the same time, all concur at one point or another
that Richard's interest in Bertha's freedom and dignity was sincere in
its way, attesting to his vision of her as an end as well as a means, a
bearer of rights as well as value. This sense, extending to women in
general, lies behind his demurral at Robert's simultaneously objectifying and idealizing designation of a kiss as "an act of homage"
(*E* 49). "It is," Richard objects, "an act of union between man and
woman," a formulation which removes women from the traditional
pedestal, with the constraints and marginalization that position
implies.

Viewed from the perspective of the dramatic present, Richard's
position oscillates between a semireflexive adherence to the patriarchal version of "nature's law," an impulse he shares with Robert,
and an evolving commitment to gender justice that pits him against
Robert. But since these conflicting phases of his will are rooted in and
shaped by the homosocial relationship itself, his grounds for
agreement and disagreement with Robert can be mapped onto the
collegial and competitive aspects of that relationship respectively as
their ideological extensions and/or displacements. As a result, it is
structurally undecidable how far Richard's ethical agenda goes in
merely reproducing the itinerary of homosocial desire and how far it
goes toward exceeding it. In Richard and Robert's triangulated
friendship, Joyce traces an interpersonal site that is also an
interpersonal correlative of the doubly inscribed relation of gender
justice to phallic law.

Beginning with the collegial aspect, Richard demonstrates his
regard for and encouragement of Bertha's independence in a sexually
troilistic manner which, by his own admission, serves to tap into the
most eroticized element of his homosocial affiliation with Robert:

ROBERT: And that is why you wished that she ... from pride then?
RICHARD: From pride and from ignoble longing and from a motive deeper
    still.   (*E* 88)

Joyce elaborates upon this cryptic remark in a working note that clearly anticipates, even scoops, the theoretical lineage from Girard through Rubin to Sedgwick:

The bodily possession of Bertha by Robert, repeatedly often, would certainly bring into almost carnal contact the two men. Do they desire this? To be united, that is carnally through the person and body of Bertha as they cannot, without dissatisfaction and degradation – be united carnally man to man as man to woman. (*E* 156–7)

Using the interrogative mode, Joyce leaves open an ethically significant possibility, that the particular freedom Richard actively cultivates in Bertha might be fundamentally complicitous after all with the homosocial appropriation and circulation of women characteristic of his own past practice and implicit in Robert's locker-room exposition of "nature's law." Fending off his responsibility for destroying Bertha's distinctive essence, "the virginity of her soul," Richard earnestly claims "I tried to give her a new life" (*E* 84). But the latter phrase resonates ironically with his summary of life with Robert at Ranelaugh: "It was not only a house of revelry; it was to be the hearth of a new life" (*E* 48). The question is precisely whether the new life Richard offered Bertha in Italy and the still newer life he offers her in Dublin have been marked out in advance by that old "new life," owing to a persistent, unacknowledged overlap in his homo- and hetero-erotic energies, an overlap that Bertha is now called upon to negotiate once and for all.[60] In this regard the precise details of Richard's initial reaction to the sight of Robert wooing his wife are telling: "Your humility and confusion, I felt, united you to me in brotherhood. (He half turns around towards him) At that moment I felt our whole life together in the past, and I longed to put my arm around your neck" (*E* 87). Joyce's notes are even more explicit concerning both Richard's affect and its political implications: "Richard ... seems to feel the thrill of adultery vicariously and to possess a *bound woman Bertha* through the organ of his friend" (*E* 158).

On the other side, there is the competitive aspect of the homosocial relationship. Richard's attempt to divest himself of his patrimonial authority over Bertha also serves as a means of carrying forth, at another level, his master–disciple agon with Robert. In pitting his vision of love, "to wish her well," against Robert's predatory theory of natural law, Richard reasserts his majority status in the friendship, as well as his tutelary role, combining claims to moral superiority and an undiminished avant-gardism. Whereas Robert still holds with the sexual millennialism of the Old Ireland of their youth, Richard has left these ideas, *his* ideas, behind in the quest to articulate a more equitable form of sexual relationship. However, just by submitting his ideas to this sort of confrontation, to be subsequently played out on the field of sexual intrigue, Richard once again makes Bertha the medium of his traffic with Robert, this time as the object of a phallic contest: "a battle," Robert says, "of both our souls, different as they are, against all that is false in them and in the world. A battle of your soul against the spectre of fidelity, of mine against the spectre of friendship" (*E* 89). That is to say, at some point a battle of each soul against the other. "Richard," Robert continues, "you have driven me up to this point ... You yourself have roused these words in my brain. Your own words" (*E* 90).

Richard's programmatic effort to open for Bertha a room of her own, a space of autonomy beyond men, leads her once again to women's traditional confines between men. His ethical mission can thus be seen as itself doubly inscribed. By way of exceeding and undercutting the architecture of patriarchal gender disjunction and hierarchy, he participates in and helps to reproduce its basic unit or module, the homosocial triangle. If we return to where this chapter began, with what Joyce had to say about the deep-structural purchase of drama as opposed to literature, we shall be less prone to judge this dilemma as strictly contingent upon Richard's peculiar temperament and desire insofar as they represent the author's own and more ready to read the dilemma as a relatively ingenious device for mounting upon the stage the subtle yet inexorable operation of hegemonic momentum or inertia.

The last point becomes more convincing with due consideration of the symbolic value of the homosocial relationship. Driven by the contradiction between its collegial and competitive aspect, homo-sociality extends beyond the borders of the family romance the fundamental oedipal dynamic of conflict and identification with the Law of the Father. As such, it serves as an exemplary vehicle for dramatizing the intrapsychic, *doppelgänger* phenomenon on an inter-personal basis. As contrary aspects of Joyce's personality, which I have identified with the early and late Giacomo respectively, Robert and Richard represent opposed yet interlocking positions with respect to patriarchal hegemony. Robert is the spuriously revolutionary agent of its law, who rejects social conventionality while embracing phallocracy as the natural order. Richard is the already compromised agent of gender justice, who proclaims the sovereignty of individual volition over the phallic law only to turn around and excuse his neglect of Bertha by reference to the intractable positivity of the willing ego: "I did not make myself. I am what I am" (*E* 133). With the *doppelgänger* motif, this symmetrical relationship is internalized once more and the elements of conflict and identification telescoped accordingly. Just as in "A Mother" Joyce redoubles the masculine and feminine spheres of authority within a single space in order to reveal the bias upon which gender divisions are constructed, so in *Exiles* the *doppelgänger* motif allows him to suggest a redoubling of a structurally cooptative law and a structurally cooptable resistance within the space of a single subject in order to reveal the bias on which the resistance continually feeds back into the reproductive mechanism of the law. What emerges is an acutely self-critical insight on Joyce's part that goes to the heart of the play's ethical project. Patriarchal hegemony is, in a sense, *already internal* to Richard's protofeminist agenda and, by extension, to male feminism at large. By situating the wife–mother figure, Bertha, as the focus of contention or element of conflict between himself and the paternal law he challenges, Richard automatically repeats the classic oedipal gesture and affirms that law in its most axiomatic conceit, the en-gendering of subjecthood and desire as essentially masculinized preserves through the struggle over and possession of the Woman as phallus. At the level of the statement, Richard insists upon Bertha's freedom, rights, and dignity as a subject; but at the level of enunciation, where his desire insists, she continues to function as the objectification of value that mediates his confrontation with the patriarchal order. There is, in other words, a double bind in Richard's position and in male feminism that is more than just logical. In taking up an enunciatory position within a feminist discourse, the masculine subject reenacts his constitutive self-division in such a way that the conscious desire to promote women's interests, without being in the least insincere, is to some degree animated and diverted by the unconscious drive to revive the oedipal agon on a new and perhaps more promising footing, to defer castration with a new and improved version of the Woman as phallus. A man addressing the so-called woman question, in whatever form, is always also a man secretly addressing the Law of the Father; and, to that extent, male feminism inevitably entails a certain degree of self-misrepresentation, which conditions in turn the misrepresentation of the other.

Joyce's awareness of this bind helps to explain his rather cryptic handling of futurity in the play. Robert urges Richard to look to his son for "the freedom we seek" (*E* 143). "In him," Robert opines, "and not in us. Perhaps ... I said perhaps. I would say almost surely if ... If he were mine" (*E* 143). At this point in the action the grounds of such self-privileging on Robert's part have all but eroded, and the excision Joyce made from the episode at the draft stage evinces his decision to admit no late turn in the dialogue that might vindicate Robert's character or world view. But in allowing Robert his say, the excised portion itself witnesses to a division between Richard's political motives and his underlying desire, a split which can be read as inhibiting his capacity to father, in the larger sense, a generation of freedom:

It is I who have won freedom for myself ... I have never believed in the truth of man or woman. I have never been true myself. I have freed myself within and without. I care nothing for human or legal bonds or laws or moral prejudices. I do not even care to make my life fit my ideas. I live by what I disbelieve in. *I do not even feel the excitement of revolt against it. And that is my greatest freedom.* It is you, Richard, with all your talents who are still the slave. (Fragment 7, my italics)[61]

We need not endorse Robert's nihilistic brand of liberation theology, his self-canonization as a prophet of freedom, or even his naive, romanticized image of Archie, to appreciate his argument that the "excitement of revolt," while ennobling his friend, has also left him "the victim of a delusion" (Fragment 7). Richard's own belief "in [himself] – and in her" as "the type of the humanity which will come" (Fragment 7)[62] rests upon his possessing the self-conscious will to produce the conditions under which that new humanity can flourish. As Robert suggests, however, sustaining the feelings upon which Richard's project feeds, the excitement of revolt itself, requires not only engaging the existing system but renewing that engagement and the effective conditions thereof, which is to say the very system that confers upon Richard the always gendered status of authoritative subject, agent, revolutionary. It is for this reason that Robert contends that the type of the new humanity must be already "creedless, lawless, fearless," like Archie. By the same token, he who would expound an unexceptionable male feminism without duplicity must be already beyond men.

NOTE ON EXILE: JOYCE AND IRELAND

In his leading article on Richard Rowan, Robert Hand treats of him as one of Ireland's children who "left her in her hour of need" (*E* 129). Subsequently, when Bertha asks Richard, "Why then, did you leave me last night?," he retorts, "In your hour of need?" (*E* 133). Joyce's obvious anxiety to draw some connection between the abandoned Bertha and the abandoned Ireland, I want to suggest, constitutes a return of the repressed ethico-political discomfiture at work in Joyce's condition of (self-) exile.

(1) Let us remember that *Exiles* was written in the shadow of the coming event called home rule and makes a veiled reference in that direction; that certain of Joyce's friends and acquaintances had active roles in bringing Ireland to the verge of domestic self-determination, a fact to which *Exiles* alludes in its use of Kettle as a model for Robert Hand; and that whatever contempt Joyce harbored for exclusionary nationalism, whatever forebodings he harbored concerning the likely drift of an independent Ireland, he still felt somewhat anguished at his own complete noninvolvement in the liberation movement. Amid the scurrilous racist, sexist, and hyper-masculine epithets Shaun hurls at Shem in *Finnegans Wake*, there is an element of genuine Joycean self-criticism for a course of action which looked less heroic in retrospect, especially given the deaths of Skeffington and Clancy:

when the roth, vice and blause met the noyr blank and rogues and the grim white and cold bet the black fighting tans, categorically unimperatived by the maxims, a rank funk getting the better of him, the scut in a bad fit of pyjamas fled like a leveret for his bare lives, to Talviland ... without having struck one blow ... kuskykorked himself up tight in his inkbattle house, badly the worse for boosegas, there to stay in afar for the life. (*FW* 176)

slackly shirking both your bullet and your billet, you beat it backwards like Boulanger from Galway ... to sing us a song of alibi. (*FW* 190)

(2) Let us remember that Joyce's youthful quarrel with the nationalist movement and with Irish Catholic society in general turned on its suppression of individual freedom in the name of communal cohesion and solidarity, i.e. its enforcement of a more intersubjectively oriented model of justice than the anarchist–libertarian model endorsed by Joycean alter egos like Richard Rowan and Stephen Dedalus. Indeed, my reading in Chapter 1 of

the political debate between Stephen and Davin points up a certain theoretical parallel to the marital disagreement of Richard and Bertha. In either case, distinct visions of freedom and justice confront one another in mutual incomprehension, one grounded in the primacy of the individual soul and the law of its being, the other in the primacy of a certain connectedness. The notion of self-exile/ abandonment precisely marks the *differend* between these ethico-political positions. That is, no jointly acceptable phrase regimen exists within which the claims of either position, either model, can be heard and adjudicated when, for example, a Richard Rowan leaves a Bertha to her own devices or when Joyce banishes himself from Ireland. A leavetaking that is on one side a legitimate mode of self-expression, a heroic exercise of individual freedom, is on the other an irresponsible rupture, even a cruel or cowardly violation, of the interpersonal or social bond. In *A Portrait*, where the manifest subject in question is nationalism, Joyce emphasizes the "wrong" the *differend* entails for the anarchist–libertarian position, the one with which he felt the most immediate sympathy. In *Exiles*, where the manifest issue is gender politics, Joyce reverses perspectives and explores the wrong the *differend* entails for the intersubjectively oriented position. This is significant because the *differend* is not just a logical but also a pragmatic aporia. As such, it always affects the less empowered party in a given dispute: the individual facing the group, a wife facing her husband.

(3) Let us remember that underlying the allegorical personification of Catholic Ireland as womanly woman (Dark Rosaleen, Cathleen Ni Houlihan, etc.) and Protestant Britain as a manly man (John Bull) was a gendered distinction in the ethical systems to which each culture generally subscribed, at least by reputation, in rough alignment with the gendered distinction between their respective roles in the empire and their respective spheres of geopolitical activity. At this symbolic level, the other side of the young Joyce's *differend* with Irish nationalism can be felt. If the larger group is a feminized group, a colonial wife to an imperialistic husband, and if the individual being stymied or censored propounds an ethos or ideology associated with or representative of that imperialistic culture, then his apostasy and self-exile might be the subject not only of flatly irreconcilable constructions but of a double *differend*, a double "wrong." That is to say, it is not just that "the regulation of the conflict" between the young Joyce and the Irish-Irish nationalists

must be "done in the idiom of one of the parties while the wrong suffered by the other is not signified in that idiom,"[63] but that the hybridity of the contending idioms, their mutually compromised authority, prevents either one from assuming the power of arbitration or making its grievance properly heard. Dramatizing the same quandary in terms of a marital dispute allows Joyce to come at this *differend* from another angle, a less obviously partial angle; but his use of exile as the dominant metaphor of this enactment assures a displaced recognition of the colonial/nationalist problematic likewise in the play.

(4) Let us remember, finally, that while Joyce makes ironic reference to traditional feminine personifications of Ireland (the old milkwoman in "Telemachus," Gumma Granny in "Circe," the half-naked batwoman in *A Portrait*), Bertha is unusual, if not unique, in performing this allegorical function in a predominantly sympathetic light. What is more, in explicitly marking her allegorical status, Joyce implicitly marks her stormy domestic relationship with Richard as a microcosmic version of the so-called metropolitan marriage, in which his alter ego espouses certain masculinized English values. There is a precedent for this setup in Joyce's fiction. In "The Dead," Greta Conroy, with her Galway origins, her momentous secret, and her "country cute" reputation (*D* 187), embodies what Daniel Corkery later called "the hidden Ireland";[64] while the Joyce alter ego, Gabriel Conroy, merits in some degree the charge of being a "west Briton" leveled at him by the enthusiast, Molly Ivors. In *Exiles*, however, Joyce's gender allegory is more *directly* self-skeptical. Richard Rowan bears a closer ideological relationship to his prototype than Gabriel Conroy. And it is more *substantively* self-skeptical as well. The gender identification of Catholic Ireland and Protestant England in the play specifically connects with the communalistic ethics of the former and the individualistic ethics of the latter. The question of home rule, raised at both the national and the domestic level, is thus accorded an important new dimension: not just under whose authority, English or Irish, male or female, but under what principles, intersubjective or agonistic, communitarian or contractarian, not whose rules but what rule.

The conclusion to be drawn from this evidence, in my view, is that the exploration of gender justice conducted in *Exiles*, while profound in itself, also serves as a kind of screen behind which Joyce busily readjusts, makes just again, the precise tenor of his own exile, particularly his alignment toward his home country and its tortured politics. *Exiles* qualifies Joyce's rejection of Irish-Irish nationalism in much the same way that "The Dead" qualifies his rejection of everyday Irish culture. But for whatever reason, perhaps because Joyce's sense of disaffiliation from the nationalist cause had only answered, to his mind, the nationalist refusal to accept him as he was, he required the detour and disguise of allegory to reassess his settled posture.

The draft fragments for *Exiles* testify as much; for as MacNicholas has shown, a disproportionate amount of the material discarded pertains more or less directly to the topoi of colonial–nationalist politics.[65] One fragment is particularly relevant in this regard:

BERTHA: I thought I was in that room and I could see it, the little oil-lamp burning quietly near my bed and on the wall I could see the picture of Robert Emmet that used to be on the wall. You know? In a green uniform, with his hat off, with dark eyes. Then...
RICHARD: Then?
BERTHA: Then I thought of Robert. I felt you were gone away and would never come back to me. I felt you were not thinking of me but of her and perhaps he was. I felt lonely for someone.   (Fragment 10)[66]

At the moment of her desertion, Bertha is overtly linked with Robert Emmet, who is not just any Irish nationalist icon, but the apotheosis of the patriotic spirit at its most fondly self-sacrificial. A forerunner of Pearse's doctrine of blood sacrifice, which the latter was already promoting at the time of the play's composition, Robert Emmet personified the ethical *jouissance* of exceeding the instinct of self-preservation in the name of group imperatives. He incarnated, if you will, the "feminine" side of the hypermasculine ethos. In allying the forsaken Bertha with this hero-martyr of Irish communalism, for whom Joyce elsewhere reserves the heaviest satire ("Cyclops"), and in doing so without apparent irony, Joyce registers a certain misgiving about the terms of his own flight and a more nuanced appraisal of this Irish all too Irish ideology. In excising this passage, he does not completely efface the linkage between gender and colonial ethics, but he does disavow it, affirming under the color of a denial. The irony of the question Richard poses Bertha, "In your hour of need?," makes the nationalist gender allegory legible but leaves it disputable. Then again, justice, being fundamentally transferential, can only be pursued in a foreign language.

CHAPTER 5

Joyce's siren song: "Becoming-woman" in "Ulysses"

INTRODUCTION

As work on *Ulysses* has grown more self-consciously theoretical, a number of geological shifts have occurred in which one or another of the settled topoi have been displaced onto a new conceptual plane without rupturing the structure of the debate surrounding them. Perhaps the most prominent example of this phenomenon through the 1980s has been the critical reception of Joyce's treatment of women in *Ulysses*. Collectively speaking, we have passed from an ethical inquiry conducted along the lines of a descriptive literary analysis to an ethico-political inquiry conducted in the vocabulary of a deconstructive psychoanalysis. We had been wont to render gender(ed) judgments, for example, on the status of Molly Bloom's character as represented: Is she predominantly symbolic or realistic, earth or flesh, is she a Gae-Tellus or a conventional Irish housewife? More recently, we have been prone to interrogate the gender justice of Joyce's strategy of representation: Does he delineate archetypes or stereotypes of woman; does he liberate female desire through a male pen or ventriloquize a feminine and/or maternal voice through his own; does he identify with and thereby usurp the feminine function or does he represent in a woman like Molly all that he can never know or possess, femininity as the other behind the veil, perhaps even the otherness of *Ulysses*?[1] Recently, Kimberly Devlin brought the critical dialogue to yet another level of metareflection. Her important article, "Pretending in 'Penelope': Masquerade, Mimicry, and Molly Bloom," argues that "Joyce's representation of woman" plays out her femininity as a received sequence of roles, so that the question to be posed is whether Joyce casts woman as the "dupe" or the "deconstructor" of the patriarchal sex/gender system, whether she is shown to enact and reinforce the prevailing gender masquerade or to engage in a canny subversive form of mimicry that exposes gender identity as a labile, socially constructed simulacrum.[2] Whether defined in terms of literary comprehension or ideological demystification, the critical advances wrought through these topographical shifts are substantial, even spectacular. But they are no more profound than the law governing each of these readings and establishing their continuity, the law of representation itself. That is to say, amid all these advances, we continue to see Joyce's female characters like Molly Bloom as providing his more or less unitary, totalizing image of womanliness.

The widespread if tacit commitment to approaching the question of *Ulysses'* sexual politics on a strictly representational basis has less warrant than is generally acknowledged considering

(a) the equally widespread recognition that the trajectory of Joyce's fiction from *Dubliners* through *Finnegans Wake* is about challenging the value and the possibility of a truly representational aesthetic;
(b) the sense, enhanced by the prominence of Lacanian theory in Joyce studies, that the order of representation is itself irremediably phallocentric and patriarchal, resting as it does upon a ratio of hierarchical disjunction, identified with the Name of the Father and countersigned, or rather underwritten, by that which it excludes, the feminine (as) other. Taken together, these qualifications have tremendous consequences for the kind of ethico-political analysis of Joyce that has recently prevailed. With respect to the question of gender, any scheme of representational justice constitutes something of an oxymoron, sexual bias being always already implicit in the modality of representation. Correlatively, as it has been the business of this book to establish, Joyce's attempt to transform the pathos of his ambivalence into the ethos of justice put his work increasingly at odds with the law of representation in its interconnected political and semiological moments.

Thus, in the move from *Dubliners* and *A Portrait* to *Giacomo*, Joyce rejects the classic representational break separating the ideal authorial ego from the materiality of the text, a break which I have shown to be systematic with the patriarchal construction of gender hierarchy. In *Giacomo Joyce* itself, Joyce goes a step further. With his use of what I have called the sub-alter(n) ego, he greatly complicates the fundamental divide between identity and difference, upon which the possibility of representation as such resides. Joyce thematizes his developing counter-representational attitude still more explicitly and with specific reference to issues of sexual politics in *Exiles*, where the central action turns on Richard's deeply compromised attempt to speak for and in the interests of his wife, Bertha. In powerfully dramatizing the ethical and aesthetic constraints of gender emplacement and the preemptive force of patriarchal discourse, the play registers Joyce's own awareness of the impossibility of his liberating female desire through his pen and the danger of his appropriating that desire in the process. In so doing, the play encourages us to search Joyce's subsequent effort, *Ulysses*, for the irony, not to say self-criticism, it displays regarding its own powers of representation, particularly (cross-) gender representation.

This is a mandate easier recognized than carried out. Since irony is itself a representational strategy, irony directed at representation *as* a strategy cannot effectively take hold at the level of content alone; it must imbue the overall structure of the work. The structure determined by this brand of irony, moreover, will not be a structure of meaning in the strict sense, but a structure that interrogates, challenges, in some ways outstrips, meaning. Taking account of this anomalous type of structure, in turn, requires some realignment of our accustomed theoretical approach. The Lacanian psychoanalytic perspective, which has served us well in illuminating the ingrained sexual biases of the Symbolic order, remains nonetheless wedded to that order, which it regards as the "ineluctable modality" of subjective experience. Lacan's delphic proclamation, "there is no Other of the Other," affirms as much.[3] Gilles Deleuze and Félix Guattari have seriously undercut this position, however, by demonstrating that the reason psychoanalysis cannot peer beyond the confines of gender representation is that its own conceptual center, the oedipal model of desire, is systemic with the Symbolic order in its most repressive and phallocentric designs. The assumptions of psychoanalysis and the dictates of representation, they argue, must be exceeded in the same motion. To this end, they pose an alternative paradigm of psychic and textual function called "Becoming-(woman)," which is based on production rather than signification and operates through structures like the one described here. In this dual endeavor to critique gender representation, by critiquing psychoanalysis, and to escape the representational order altogether, the work of Deleuze and Guattari speaks directly to Joyce's evolving ethico-political concerns and does so in a form consistent with the double bind of justice, the need to struggle within and yet go beyond the law. As such, their theoretical program makes an exemplary resource for glossing the ironic structure of gender justice in *Ulysses*.[4]

To negotiate the double bind of justice in *Ulysses*, Joyce deploys a markedly gendered framework of aesthetic representation, whose very design exposes and then transgresses the limits of (cross-) gender representation. This framework should strike all serious Joyce scholars as familiar in certain respects; it embraces some of the most settled critical schemata of the novel, in particular the division of *Ulysses* into a comparatively representational first half and a comparatively experimental second half. I call it the framework of the double odyssey: on one side, the odyssey of character; on the other side, what Karen Lawrence has named the odyssey of style.[5]

The odyssey of character comprises the narrative aspect of the text, which is to say the story of the consubstantial inner lives of Stephen and Bloom as they proceed toward their dubious communion in "Ithaca." This odyssey takes the form of the archetypal romance of masculinity: the oedipal coming together of father and son – replete with a marriage "by *Father Maher*" (*U* 16.1887) – in a purely symbolic, as opposed to blood, tie. It thus links the representation of masculinity, the classic tale of male gender development, with the masculinity of representation, the definition of maleness as *the* symbolic estate. In this light, it is appropriate that the odyssey of character is rooted in, though not restricted to, the stylistic method which dominates the first half of the novel, stream of consciousness, which is perhaps the most profoundly representational of literary devices. More than the representation of some condition, object, or character, stream of consciousness offers a representation of the *act* of representation, a portrait of a mind portraying its world. The double-sidedness of the device, in turn, allows Joyce a certain internal distance from which to criticize the act of representation as it occurs in his protagonist's mind. The preeminent site of such criticism is, of course, the question of gender. For what makes the inner lives of Bloom and Stephen "consubstantial" is nothing other than that which makes Richard and Robert *doppelgänger* in *Exiles*: their seemingly opposed but in truth complementary attitudes toward the idea of woman and the possibility of occupying a female perspective. As in *Exiles*, the masculine romance is mediated from start to finish by a figure of feminine otherness that it excludes. Joyce thus proceeds from an oedipal model of desire and representation, of the kind Deleuze and Guattari deconstruct, to a critique of its practical correlative, the ethics/politics of identification. This will be the subject of the next section of the chapter.

The odyssey of style comprises the polyphonic segmentation of the text, its progression through a sequence of different modes of writing, each a radical disfiguration of the representational norm established, however flexibly, at the outset of the novel. This odyssey transpires over the course of the novel's second half and so can be seen as an answer to the odyssey rooted in the first. It is significant, accordingly, that this odyssey unfolds under the sign of the feminine, which counterposes it to the phallic authority reposed in the oedipal narrative. The first radical stylistic disfiguration occurs in the "Sirens" episode, whose mythic referent, not coincidentally, is the disembodied female voice. This odyssey subsequently attaches itself to such female archetypes as Nausicaa (the virgin), Circe (the witch), the great mother of "Oxen of the Sun," and Penelope (the wife), whose episode represents Joyce's ultimate engagement with "female" consciousness and the last great stylistic disfiguration of the novel.[6] Now, if the phallic authority of the oedipal narrative rests with the dynamic of representation, the positing and redressing of a certain lack or absence that woman has traditionally figured, then an effective answer to this narrative requires something more than an assault on "realism," something other than playful stylistic variation and multiplicity. It requires a writing that forswears *substitution*, the imitation or designation of its objects, for *institution*, the taking up of its objects in the unfolding of new relations and new dimensions, what Deleuze and Guattari call "Becoming-." While it is of course impossible in a chapter-length study to treat of each turn in Joyce's odyssey of style, I will plot the opening leg of Joyce's odyssey of style, the "Sirens" episode, to see how he proposes to avoid representing woman in order to Become-her and to what ethico-political ends; and in closing, I will chart the theoretical implications of the final leg, "Penelope," in light of "Sirens" in order to see how he clinches the project.

THE OEDIPUS AND GENDER REPRESENTATION

Deleuze and Guattari map their critique of representation onto their critique of oedipalized desire as a means of linking the ex-pressive and the re-pressive moments of patriarchal colonization at the micro-political level.[7] Oedipal desire and representational meaning share a tripartite framework of operation that forms the basic cell of social domination. The subject and object vertices of this triangle are constructed as molar entities, unified and stable finalities, through a process of division and exclusion culturally instituted in accordance with the third, transcendental term, the *phallogos*. As such, the subject and object(ified) positions are consolidated in their respective identities as fundamentally lacking with respect to that governing *logos*, which for its part grounds the social norms of truth and pleasure to be pursued. The constitutive divisions, however, of the subject and object terms operate at different phases with different degrees and types of force, and it is their divergence which propels the circulation of desire–meaning (*vouloire dire*) along its triangular route, while opening up the space for injustice under law. The subject splits between sovereignty and subordination: its mastery of the object-terms is at once authorized and forbidden, and so perpetually deferred and displaced, by its subordination to the transcendental law. Taken up by this split, repressed subject, the object form divides between subordination and insubordination, so to speak; its appropriability as a site of received truth and approved pleasure doubles as a resistant materiality, a taboo alterity, which comes to figure the authorizing exterior of the law itself. Under the oedipal regime, then, the subject participates in its own perennial frustration and the object contributes to its own perennial exploitation. Each is not only colonized by the law, but colonizes itself in the name of the law.

The two interpersonal modes of this oedipal dynamic, I would propose, are abjection and identification. Abjection is the crisis mode in which the divergence of force between the subject and object position has been reduced owing to some disturbance in their cultural construction. As a result, the sovereignty and the subordination of the subject position and the appropriability and alterity of the object position contest in more or less equal balance, so that their terrifying interdependence becomes available to affective experience. Identi-fication is the ethically normative mode in which the subordination of the subject position as its condition of sovereignty is at once assumed and repressed and the simultaneous appropriability and alterity of the object position are perpetually disavowed, in order to maintain some measure of regulated difference.

In *Giacomo Joyce*, Joyce takes the differently invidious impulses of abjection, which he locates in the son's relation to the mother, and identification, which he locates in the father's relation to the daughter, and brings them together in a cross-gender, cross-generational compromise formation (which I have dubbed the sub-alter(n) ego) in an effort to treat his designated racial and sexual other, Amalia Popper, with representational justice. In *Ulysses*, by contrast, Joyce sets out to expose the limitations of his earlier, still oedipalized, solution. The first step in his strategy is to split off the impulses of abjection and identification that he had so painfully married in *Giacomo*, assigning the former tendency to Stephen and the latter to Bloom. The second step is to establish a narrative correlation between these tendencies, so that they may be seen as symbiotic social growths, yielding cognate ethical fruit. In this fashion, Joyce contrives to set off his counter-representational stylistic, which unfolds, as I have suggested, under the sign of the feminine, with a narrative critique of representation which unfolds under the auspices of the crowning romance of masculinity, the at-onement of father and son.

The experience of Stephen, "the eternal son" (*U* 14.342), is in large part organized around the trauma of maternal abjection, which crystallizes in a series of confrontations with the specter of May Goulding.[8] In each of these visitations, Stephen's mother functions as both the exponent of the patriarchal law, the phallic mother, and its forbidden object, the woman as phallus, i.e. as the focus of Stephen's oedipal rebellion and the repressed other of his oedipal desire. This scrambling of the subject and object positions throws the contradictions defining each into sharp relief. The ghost of Stephen's mother represents a piece of psychic alterity that is at once invasive and appropriable. In "Telemachus," her fleshly disintegration impinges upon the embattled space of Stephen's self-identity, renewing the infantile struggle of corporeal intimacy and estrangement in the name of Dublin's dominant institution, the Catholic Church:

In a dream, silently, she had come to him, her wasted body within its loose graveclothes ...

Her glazing eyes, staring out of death, to shake and bend my soul. On me alone ... Her eyes on me to strike me down. (*U* 1.270–8)

But by "Nestor," Stephen has come to see her encroachment as part and parcel of a more positive messianic function, intended not to subordinate but to transfer mastery – "She was no more: the trembling skeleton of a twig burnt in the fire ... She had saved him from being trampled underfoot and had gone, scarcely having been" (*U* 2.144–7). It is just at this point that Stephen articulates the principle of "Amor matris: subjective and objective genitive" (*U* 2.165–6), the sunny side of maternal abjection, indicating that his mother's grisly visitations answer at some level to his desires.

Stephen's vampiric meditations in "Proteus" confirm this point. Framing his first aesthetic production of the day, he muses

Omnis caro ad te veniet. He comes, pale vampire, through storm his eyes, his bat sails bloodying the sea, mouth to her mouth's kiss ...
... Mouth to her mouth's kiss.
His lips lipped and mouthed fleshless lips of air: mouth to her moomb. Oomb, allwombing tomb. (*U* 3.396–402)

In crossing the blood feast of the fetus with the neonate's oral fixation (scarcely displaced from breast to neck), the myth of the vampire fuses oedipal eroticism with primary abjection in a blood lust–disgust appurtenant to being both apart from and a part of the mother (both infant and fetus).[9] Stephen directly invokes the double register of oedipal desire and abjection in the phrase, "mouth to her moomb," which not only confounds the engorging mouth and womb but recalls the "moocow coming down along the road" (*AP* 7), his father's figuration of the mother. At the same time, Stephen's recurrent fantasy of recouping the loss of his mother and returning to the charmed infantile dyad raises, even implies, the threat of his own extinction, the loss of his individuating difference in the "all-wombing tomb," and so provokes him to dissociate himself violently from her, a psychic movement which implicates him once more in her death, the ultimate separation.

At this point, Stephen's gynephobia grows explicable in terms of his maternal abjection: first, his representations of women are bound to be profoundly sexualized and oedipalized; second, the oedipalized desire animating or attached to those representations carries a strong whiff of thanatos, an eroticized hint of his own annihilation, triggering a defensive reflex of dread, disgust, and disdain followed by a measure of guilt or self-criticism. This holds true for his assessments of E—— C—— in *A Portrait*, his perceptions of the "old milkwoman" and the gypsy "mort," his memory of the "virgin at Hodges Figgis' window" (*U* 3.426–7), and for his historical fabrication of Anne Hathaway. Any protofeminist leanings Stephen might have, it would seem, are restricted to a persistent demurral at his equally persistent misogyny. The act of self-judgment, moreover, requires that the self become simultaneously subject and object, a dwelling-in-division homologous with the splitting/separation in which the self originally emerges; and because this particular species of self-judgment grows so directly out of Stephen's feelings of abjection, it cannot but resonate with the same originary ambivalence and occasion the same gynephobia.

Now, when a subject finds the decentering effects of self-criticism insupportable, according to Freud, when s/he cannot endure being suspended between self-identity and self-opposition, a condition of paranoia results in which the judgmental faculty of the mind is externalized as an inexorable prosecutorial agency.[10] Something of this dynamic obtains in Stephen's recurrent vision of his mother as inquisitor, especially in his ultimate confrontation with her in "Circe." On that occasion, the bodily decomposition that makes his maternal phantasm the very image of his own abjection also functions as the instrument of his persecution:

STEPHEN (*panting*): His noncorrosive sublimate! The corpsechewer! Raw head and bloody bones.
THE MOTHER (*her face drawing near and nearer, sending out an ashen breath*): Beware! (*she raises her blackened withered right arm slowly towards Stephen's breast with outstretched finger*) Beware God's hand!
(*A green crab with malignant red eyes sticks deep its grinning claws in Stephen's heart.*)
(*U* 15.4211–21)

Identified as "God's hand," the claws of the crab attach to Stephen as the judgment of a divine Father, with his mother in the role of coadjutor. But as the emblem of her cancer, the crab's claws attach Stephen's heart to her wasting body, linking them as covictims of a Terrible Father, "The corpsechewer." By way of dissevering this entanglement, Stephen can only repeat the pronouncement that has already promised and failed to deliver him from the nets of Mother Church, Mother Tongue, and Mother Ireland. "With me all or not at all," Stephen cries, reenacting the primordial struggle of individuation, "*Non serviam*" (*U* 15.4227–8). At this point, Stephen constructs The Mother as the summary embodiment of all the forces currently oppressing him. The sense of persecution and self-importance that inform his perennial messianic posturings suddenly issues forth in a virtual psychotic break – "No! No! No! Break my spirit, all of you, if you can! I'll bring you all to heel!" (*U* 15.4235–6)

This spectacular moment, it should be noted, is not merely an effect of Circean phantasmagoria. It dramatizes a link between abjection and paranoia that Stephen's earlier reveries of Paris already reveal ("Yes, used to carry punched tickets to prove an alibi if they arrested you for murder somewhere. Justice. On the night of the seventeenth of February 1904 the prisoner was seen by two witnesses. Other fellow did it: other me ... *Lui, c'est moi.* You seem to have enjoyed yourself," *U* 3.179–83). The unconscious rationale behind Stephen's otherwise unaccountable fear of arrest lurks in the alibi that fear produces: a splitting between the object and the subject of judgment, the "other" and "me," which remain nonetheless identical, "*Lui, c'est moi,*" necessitating a projection of the threat upon an external agency, the Paris police. The ensuing movements of Stephen's mind indicate, if it were not clear enough already, that the murder of which he is thinking is in a symbolic sense the "killing" of his mother. Stephen immediately envisions himself committing a murder in a post office where he had hoped to cash "mother's money order" (*U* 3.185); Stephen directly calls up the image of "fiery Columbanus," whose importance to Stephen is that he too "in holy zeal" left his mother "prostrate" (*U* 2.144), and Stephen then passes swiftly to a memory of his mother's doom:

A blue French telegram, curiosity to show:
—Nother dying come home father. (*U* 3.197–9)

This "crime," with its split subject, the "other me" who "enjoyed" himself, represents an unconscious echo of the self-originating crime, the repression of the (M)other, with *its* split subject, the "Nother" me, i.e. the me that arises through self-negation, that negates the other (says No-other), and that always returns "home" in abjection. Stephen continually brings himself to justice for the earlier crime by imagining himself unjustly persecuted for the later one.

If the ground of Stephen's paranoiac abjection lies in the way his mother's memory crosses the place of the law with that of the lost object of desire, the external circumstances bringing this ground to fruition surely include the political and cultural effects of Ireland's dispossession, which tends to complicate her symbolic position and his response still further. On the one hand, Stephen's resentment toward his mother focuses largely upon the obeisance she pays to the two-headed monster of colonization, the Roman Catholic Church and the patriarchal state, with their shared canons of middle-class duty. On the other, Stephen's frustration with his mother focuses largely on the desolating consequences of her submissiveness for her own life.

Insofar as his mother represents the law as its exponent, Stephen sees her as betraying his messianic office by refusing to recognize his aesthetic claim upon the Word.

THE MOTHER (*a green rill of bile trickling from a side of her mouth*): You sang that song to me. *Love's bitter mystery*.
STEPHEN (*eagerly*): Tell me the word, mother, if you know now. The word known to all men.
THE MOTHER: ... Prayer is allpowerful. Prayer for the suffering souls in the Ursuline manual and forty days' indulgence. Repent, Stephen.

(*U* 15.4189–99)

The point of Stephen's query here is not the acquisition of mystical knowledge, as is often assumed. He has already cognized "the word known to all men" in "Scylla" (*U* 9.429–30). Rather, he seeks to exploit his mother's enunciation of the word, "Love," in association with his musical rendition of Yeats' poetry, to obtain her imprimatur upon the literary as opposed to the liturgical instantiation of the universal word and so upon Stephen's priesthood of "the eternal imagination" (*AP* 221). Her response, "Prayer," continues their cycle of mutual bitterness.

Insofar as she represents the law as its exemplary victim, however, acceding in good faith to material and spiritual bondage, Stephen's mother actually stokes his messianic aspirations while kindling his fear of proving inadequate to them, of betraying them himself. Through the dream logic of paranomasia, this part of the puzzle is likewise encrypted in the above passage, specifically in the single phrase, "Ursuline manual."

The spectacular reappearance of Mrs. Dedalus as dream image in "Telemachus," which the "Circe" hallucination redoubles, is framed fore and aft by symbolic analogues that tease out the significance of her apparition to Stephen. The anterior analogue is Mulligan's "slavey," Ursula, from whom he "pinched" the "cracked lookingglass" in which Stephen views himself. Ursula's patron saint was a female martyr who led eleven thousand fellow virgins on a pilgrimage with the aim of expressing their abhorrence of the married state.[11] Mrs. Dedalus was a martyr *to* the married state, which consigned her to a domestic servitude roughly synonymous with that discharged by the present-day Ursula. Her notional reward is to be received into heaven by a "glorious choir of virgins" (*U* 1.276–7) who clearly recall the throng St. Ursula organized. Thus Ursula's name returns in Mrs. Dedalus' reference to the "Ursuline manual," a young girl's primer of domestic–religious service,[12] because Ursula stands for the Irishwoman as pious servant, precisely the role Stephen's mother played to the death.

But Stephen then gives Ursula's symbolic connection to his mother a further twist by using her lookingglass to reenact the moment of imaginary identification, what Lacan calls the *stade du miroir*,[13] wherein the child begins to conceive a self-image by reflection in the maternal other ("Stephen bent forward and peered at the mirror held out to him, cleft by a crooked crack … As he and others see me. Who chose this face for me? This dogsbody to rid of vermin. It asks me too," *U* 1.135–7). Stephen's image in the mirror, his social identity, is defined by the flaw on the mirror's surface, which "reflects" the precise flaw in the mirror-relationship itself: the internal splitting or ambivalence of the respective terms, the self and its double, owing to their mutual interposition. Stephen's apparition in the mirror seems to emanate both from his own person (as a part object) and from someone else (those who "see" or "chose" his face). It even constitutes, in the latter mode, a separate being who returns to interrogate him, rather like his mother's apparition, whose "*glazing eyes*" likewise bespeak a mirroring function. What makes the last point especially telling is his apparently strong facial resemblance to his mother, unadmitted by Stephen but twice remarked by Bloom: "Face reminds me of his poor mother" (*U* 15.4949), "the sideface of Stephen, image of his mother" (*U* 16.1803).[14] Stephen tries to focus a distinct identity only to discover the (M)other already ensconced in his frame, her "glazing eyes" staring out of his reflected gaze.

Stephen's immediate response is to delegitimate the (maternal) medium of his self-image – "It is a symbol of Irish art. The cracked lookingglass of a servant" (*U* 1.146) – but his words immediately implicate his claim to an aesthetic mission in the delegitimization. If his mother and her analogues adhere to Stephen in his very attempt to consolidate and valorize his self-identity, he adheres to them in his

very attempt to marginalize hers. In this case, his projected image of
the Irishwoman as pious servant reflects back upon him as the image
of his own racial subservience and feminization. That is to say,
Stephen aims to separate from his (m)other by making her the
emblem of colonial subjacency, by reading his transcendence in her
dependence, his freedom in her bondage, his separation in *her*
abjection, but the strategy necessarily collapses insofar as it foregrounds the condition of colonial subjacency itself, which is coinvolved in Stephen's identity crisis: "I am...[a] servant too. A
server of a servant" (*U* 1.311–12). Partly as an effect of the
overlapping gender allegories of nationalist and imperialist discourse
(Ireland as woman versus Irish as feminine) Stephen experiences his
Irishness, a fundamental constituent of his social identity, as a source
of maternal abjection, the residual sense of primordial nonidentity.

In *A Portrait*, Stephen sees in the Irish a feminized lack or blindness
(e.g. the batwoman [*AP* 183]) that solicits and then fails its political
and cultural saviors, from Tone to Parnell to Stephen himself. But by
Ulysses, he attaches this feminized lack to Irish political and cultural
saviors as a class and to himself as a member: "For that you are
pining, the bark of their applause? Pretenders: live their lives...
Paradise of pretenders then and now" (*U* 3.312–13, 317). Here the
symbolic exemplum is a namesake of *both* Joyce and Stephen, James
Stephens, the Head Centre of the Fenian Society, whom Dedalus
remembers having effected a cowardly escape disguised as a
woman.[15] More specifically, Stephen imagines Stephens wearing
bridal clothes later to appear on the ghost of "The Mother" in
"Circe":

How the head centre got away, authentic version. Got up as a young bride,
man, veil, orangeblossoms... (*U* 3.241–2)

(*Stephen's mother, emaciated, rises stark through the floor...with a wreath of faded
orangeblossoms and a torn bridal veil...*)(*U* 15.4157–8)

From Ursula's lookingglass to Circe's reversible mirror, a metonymic
chain strongly overdetermines Mrs. Dedalus as the embodiment of
Stephen's abjection: she is its corporeal *locus*, she personifies the
colonial heteronomy that is its social condition, and she typifies the
subservience and self-betrayal that is its political manifestation.

In the second analogue to Mrs. Dedalus, the old milkwoman,
Joyce yokes by violence the politicized feminine body and the

feminized body politic in order to elaborate the ratio he is beginning to develop between abjection and identification. At one level, Stephen sees the milkwoman as a purely allegorical representation of the Irish nation ("Silk of the kine ["moocow"] and poor old woman, names given her in old times," *U* 1.403–4) and sees her "feminine" deference as exemplary of Irish self-betrayal, which is simultaneously a betrayal of his agenda of cultural resistance:

lowly form of an immortal serving her conqueror and her gay betrayer, their common cuckquean ... (*U* 1.404–5)

She bows her old head to a voice that speaks to her loudly, her bonesetter, her medicineman: me she slights. (*U* 1.418–9)

Stephen's sense of balked identification with the woman focuses on her submission to a church that ritually dishonors her body and to an imperialist state apparatus that systematically displaces her language: "To the voice that will shrive and oil for the grave all there is of her but her woman's unclean loins, of man's flesh made not in God's likeness, the serpent's prey. And to the loud voice that now bids her be silent" (*U* 1.420–2). The tenor of Stephen's critical intervention, however, does nothing to arrest or reverse the cycle of Irish (self-) betrayal. Quite the opposite. He implicitly aligns himself with Haines' patronizing angle of vision in order to conceal his own substantial ignorance of Gaelic. The same mediated and defensive paternalism infuses Stephen's account of the sacramental depreciation of (the) woman's body. Here Stephen changes levels and represents the woman in interchangeably material and maternal terms. He dwells with "morose delectation" (*U* 3.384) upon her "unclean loins," the seat of birth, as he does previously upon her "old shrunken paps," the site of nurture. The rhetorical overtones of this meditation suggest that while Stephen's racial and political ambivalence is propped upon and inseparable from a more primordial abjection, this abjection itself is what I described, in Chapter 3, as a pre-post-erous political effect, propped upon and inseparable from the church's institutional and theological misogyny.[16] This is a classic case of secondary ambivalence shaping primary ambivalence as its precondition. By direct result, Stephen finds himself enveloped in a bitter irony. Precisely in distancing himself from the self-betraying compliance of the milkwoman, of Ireland as feminine, Stephen winds up judging her from the vantage of his "two masters"

(*U* 1.638) and hers and thereby replicates the "all too Irish" act of (self-) betrayal after all.

Judging from Stephen's experience, abjection constitutes a kind of pre-identification in which the intrusion of the object threatens to dissolve the subject altogether, impeding his capacity for identification in the ordinary sense, the capacity presupposed in the ethical imperatives of respect and reciprocity. In Deleuzean terms, the constitutive lack that triangulates the subject and object upon the law, defining them as molar entities while dividing each internally, is immediately reinscribed in their relation to one another. The result is a short-circuiting of the machinery of representation in which the object relays without properly mediating the subject's investment in it. For this reason, however, abjection can serve to reveal what the normative functioning of this machinery both entails and camouflages: that the originary subject–object split actually implicates each in the other, so that the terms can never be adequated with respect to some *tertium quid*, but remain incommensurable precisely *through* their contact or communication with one another. What this implies is that the normative ethics of identification, far from enacting the aim of reciprocity or interpersonal justice, operates in a field structured by the impossibility of such an aim.

The leading literary correspondence to Stephen's case of abjection is of course Hamlet "*reading the book of himself*" (*U* 9.115), i.e. Hamlet narcissistically engaged not with his mirror reflection but with the "writing" of his identity in the Mallarmean/Derridean sense, the traces of its decentering. It is telling, in this regard, that Bloom's first thoughts on the melancholy Dane gravitate to the question of cross-gender identification: "Mrs. Bandmann Palmer...Hamlet she played last night. Male impersonator. Perhaps he was a woman" (*U* 5.195–6). In this brief interlude, Joyce harnesses the mythic method to juxtapose the defining psychosexual tendencies of his protagonists: where Stephen suffers the paralysis of abjection, Bloom looks to the prospect of performative mobility.

Joyce works the narrative counterpoint of Stephen and Bloom's thoughts and actions to much the same end. Take the well-known establishing shot of this narrative counterpoint: "the reapparition of a matutinal cloud (perceived by both from two different points of observation, Sandycove and Dublin) at first no bigger than a woman's hand" (*U* 17.40–2). This literal or visual instance of parallax catalyzes a symbolic parallax involving abjection and identification as overlapping attitudes toward the feminine or feminized other. But more than that, Joyce uses it to suggest that the relation between these attitudes is itself parallactic, a matter of displacement rather than fundamental difference. For Stephen, the "matutinal cloud" bears visions of his wasted mother "crying in her wretched bed" (*U* 1.252), while the "lovely morning" (340) it leaves in its wake brings her racial–political correlative, the old milkwoman as motherland. For Bloom, the cloud brings visions of a wasted motherland personified by a "hag" whose "naggin bottle" clearly links her to the old milkwoman:

> It bore the oldest, the first race. A bent hag crossed from Cassidy's, clutching a naggin bottle ... It lay there now. Now it could bear no more. Dead: an old woman's: the grey sunken cunt of the world.
>   Desolation.
>   Grey horror seared his flesh ... Cold oils slid along his veins, chilling his blood: age crusting him with a salt cloak. (*U* 4.223–32)

Bloom's avowed racial group, like Stephen's, was the victim of material dispossession and cultural feminization attendant upon the twin processes of colonization and diaspora, a historical coincidence given a sharper edge by the circumstance that Palestine came under the imperial sway of Great Britain during the composition of *Ulysses*.[17] Like Stephen, Bloom tends to suffer this sense of dislocation and feminization in the form of a quasi-maternal abjection, "an old woman's ... grey sunken cunt" graphically recalling the milk-woman's "unclean loins." The isolated word, "Desolation," in fact, functions as a rhetorical umbilicus connecting the psychical distress of the Jewish motherland directly with Bloom's corporeal distress, the exhaustion and infertility of its earth with the chill and creeping debility of his flesh. But for Bloom, the cloud leaves in its wake a personal antidote to this racial–political "horror." Whereas Stephen's messenger "from a morning [mourning] world" (*U* 1.399) represents more of the same, the failing mother become enfeebled motherland, Bloom's messenger, a sunlight vision of his daughter as Mercury, represents a reversal of fortune,[18] an emblem of an idealized racial and personal future with which Bloom identifies himself – "Quick warm sunlight came running ... in slim sandals, along the brightening footpath. Runs, she runs to meet me, a girl with gold hair on the wind" (*U* 4.240–2).

Taken whole, these paired scenes demonstrate that Bloom's fantasy construction of woman partakes of the same narrative economy as Stephen's, but at a later phase – hence the usefulness of parallax as a metaphor. Across the staggered perspective of Joyce's protagonists, we can see that the valence of the feminine other undergoes a dramatic change as she passes from being a threat to symbolic control, the reign of the phallic mother, to being the object and possible instrument of symbolic control, the role of the idealized daughter. As in *Giacomo Joyce*, paternal identification in *Ulysses* seems a pathway of deliverance from the labyrinth of maternal abjection, particularly as it is mediated by racial feminization. Here again, the tale of James Stephens' flight serves as exemplum. Where Stephen remembers Stephens' escape as marred by the stigma of femininity, The Mother's bridal veil, Bloom remembers Stephens being delivered from imprisonment by the "Turnkey's daughter" (*U* 8.459), which is to say by the daughter *as* turnkey, with all of the allegorical resonance that carries in the Joycean family romance. As compared with *Giacomo Joyce*, however, *Ulysses* poses paternal identification as a deeply fissured ethico-political strategy, designed less to effect a disposition toward sexual justice than to allow men to re-dress the trauma of abjection by constructing and valorizing the feminine on phallocentric terms and then selectively associating themselves with the resulting projection. *Giacomo Joyce* might be said to explore the ethical virtue of identification – opening the self to the voice of the other – without entirely discounting its systematically related dangers, while *Ulysses* highlights those dangers, specifically the appropriation of the other to the demands of the ego ideal. If we consider the marked insubstantiality of Milly's image here, a mere shimmer of brightness, or the contingency of the "turnkey's daughter" upon a paternally defined function, it becomes apparent that as a point of identification the daughter figures a kind of blank potentiality or empty signifier of womanhood, supremely available to the appropriative force of male fantasy. She is the other side of the invasive mother.

This last, critically important symmetry finds further support in the extended parallelism of Stephen and Bloom's experience. At roughly the same time that Stephen narcissistically searches out his social identity in the maternal "lookingglass of a servant," only to find the "image of his mother" insistently in his face/place, Bloom narcissistically conceives his daughter as his "lookingglass" in the very act of expressing affection for her. Stephen seeks to master his incestuous feelings by exorcizing his mother's image once and for all, Bloom to repress his by adapting a rhyme that incorporates his daughter's image as a double of his own: "O, Milly Bloom, you are my darling. You are my lookingglass from night till morning" (*U* 4.287–8). Bloom's memory of Milly "finding herself" in the mirror of Godwin's hat confirms the lookingglass linkage between sexual desire and identification. Where Stephen struggles to make himself visible as a subject, Bloom's mind forges an important link between visualizing and objectifying.

Further on, Bloom reaffirms this mirror dynamic by describing Milly's interest in photography, itself a reflexive process, as an "Hereditary taste" (*U* 8.174). Since Milly is first introduced as a "photogirl" (*U* 1.686), someone who poses for the camera, Bloom's reference unwittingly marks the interplay between the specular process of identification and that of objectification. More pointedly, the phrase "hereditary taste" comically links onto the rhyme *Stephen* adapts in "Proteus," which is all about the "hereditary taste" of oedipal vampirism. Stephen's blood lust–disgust, remember, figures precisely the condition of abjection, the ambivalence surrounding the attachment-cum-separation with the maternal body; and Bloom's notion of "hereditary taste" figures the aim of paternal identification precisely, the sublimation of the somatic links between generations (the "strandentwining cables of all flesh" (*U* 3.37)) in strictly symbolic ones. Stephen's "hereditary taste" for blood, for the body, becomes Milly's "hereditary taste" for photographic representation, for the visual imaging of the body. It is thus no coincidence that when it comes to playing out the *ménage à trois* of the masculine romance, Bloom should solicit Stephen's interest in Molly by way of a photograph. At an allegorical level, he is summoning Stephen to full subjectivity or manhood, by showing him the patriarchal route out of abjection, the symbolic mediation of the maternal body/breast:

Stephen, obviously addressed, looked down on the photo showing a large sized lady with her fleshy charms on evidence in an open fashion as she was in the full bloom of womanhood in evening dress cut ostentatiously low for the occasion to give a liberal display of bosom, with more than vision of breasts. (*U* 16.1427–31, my italics)

The "slightly soiled" quality of this "photo" (1465), which Bloom likens to the "slight soiling" of bed linens (1468), marks the residual sense of abjection that adheres to any symbolic mediation, contaminating and eroticizing it.

The fetal taste for blood gives way to the infant's taste for mother's milk, which is likewise encoded in the incorporation myth of the vampire, and here again Bloom's paternal identification turns on trumping somatic with symbolic connections, in this case answering or filling the oral drive with the Word. Stephen, remember, focuses upon the milkwoman's "old shrunken paps," a metaphoric displacement of the maternal breast much as the vampire's preferred target of opportunity is a metonymic displacement. Later, Bloom finds himself on the same stretch of beach where Stephen composed his vampire poem. He is recovering from his voyeuristic liaison with Gerty, whose role as surrogate daughter impinges upon Bloom's consciousness in incipiently eroticized thoughts of Milly, which he tries to divert into forms of identification.[19] His specific focus is her "paps," not old and shrunken but new and undeveloped, still amenable to both masculine and feminine styles of embodiment: "Dearest Papli ... Her first stays I remember. Made me laugh to see. Little paps to begin with. Left one is more sensitive, I think. Mine too. Nearer the heart?" (*U* 13.1198–1201) Bloom's musings both indicate his own erotic "tastes" – "I begin to like them at that age. Green apples. Grab at all that offer" (*U* 13.1085–6) – and reconstruct them as an interest in filial affinity. At one level, Bloom comes to conceive Milly's breasts as corresponding with his own, gender differences notwithstanding, via a subtle but significant shift from the purely physical or material to the affective register, a spiritualizing shift crucial to gender hierarchy as such. At another level, he arrives at Milly's "paps" in the first place by way of his family name, "Papli," which is itself a variant of *papilla*, the Latin for nipple.[20] Bloom's chain of thought then suggests a pre-comprehension of the maternal part object in the paternal signifier, the Name of the Father.

In each of these examples, the sublimation of maternal abjection in paternal identification effects a dramatic reversal in the genders of authority and dependency, agency and passivity, origin and derivation respectively. The point Joyce seems to be making is that "the answer of the Symbolic"[21] to the problem of abjection implies the seniority of men and the infantilization of women. What counts as fully mature intersubjective relation, and what counts as intramural ambivalence, depends on the arbitrary cultural grounding of masculine authority in verbal affiliation and feminine authority in corporeal attachment. But isn't this also to say that the Symbolic itself helps to shape maternal abjection recursively as the myth of a primordial condition whose aversiveness necessitates the intervention of the father's law and gives that law its legitimacy? We have seen how certain elements of Stephen's abjection are recursive effects of Catholicism's theological and institutional misogyny, but we can now press further and speculate as to whether maternal abjection *as such* is but a retroactive presupposition through which disturbances and contradictions intrinsic to the phallocentric order of representation come to be already situated before and beyond its borders. This means that the *fundamental* injustice of the paternal law, its structuring of arbitrary male privilege into the grammar of representation, also forms an *essential* aspect of its justification.

The ethico-political limits posed by this sort of vicious circle cannot help but extend from Bloom's specifically paternal identification to his less role-restricted acts of cross-gender identification and transsexual performance, the relatively progressive or transgressive import of which has been variously defended by numerous Joyce critics.[22] First, Bloom's cross-gender identifications cannot but rely upon a symbolic network articulated in terms of gender divisions that these same identifications may seem to challenge. By the same token, such cross-gender identifications do touch upon the point of structural reversibility that obtains between the patriarchal law of representation and the radical ambivalence of maternal abjection, the point at which the subject stands in danger of losing not only his object but the illusion of his own consistency. As we shall see, this overlap of the positive constraints of the law and the negative constraints of its absence not only circumscribes but preempts the transgressive potential of Bloom's identificatory practice as "the new womanly man," binding his desire to received gender norms in overdetermined ways. In this respect, Bloom's paternal identifications constitute a prototype for his more generalized cross-gender identification, and Joyce denotes as much by consistently supplying the latter with a father–daughter cast.

In any act of identification there subsists a moment of objectification in which the identifying subject turns his model into a passive receptacle of his culturally channeled energies. Such objectification represents the structural necessity of a certain colonization of this model: the projection of the subject's assumptions upon it, the displacement of the subject's guilt and anxiety onto it, the construction of the model according to the subject's interests and ideals, and the aggressive insistence on holding the model to the terms imposed upon it. All of this is to say, in Deleuzean terms, that the act of identification comprises a splitting of the subject between the *position* of the object with which s/he identifies and the *position* of the law under which s/he legislates the nature of the identification. Through this double move, the subject takes the place of the other by taking *over* the place of the other. Just as, in Lacan's famous phrase, there is no sexual relation,[23] because each of the partners constitutes the other through the vanishing mediation of his or her own fantasies, so there is no such thing as identification-in-itself, since the identifying subject constitutes the target or model of identification through the vanishing mediation of his or her own self-image or self-interest. This narcissistic misrecognition may be necessary to protect the consistency of the oedipal subject, insulating him against the threat of outright abjection, a complete immersion in the other. But it also means that every act of identification necessarily fails of its designated object and so harbors a certain irremediable loss or deficit; and it is this inevitable loss that ensures the continued transcendence of the cultural *logos* under which the subject has enlisted.

Bloom himself recognizes without surmounting this slippery dynamic. In "Nausicaa," he remembers a "girl in Meath Street" with whom he tried to stage an erotic encounter, in which the identification of each with the other's simulated passion would generate authentic arousal in both. ("All the dirty things I made her say. All wrong of course. My arks she called it. It's so hard to find one who. Aho!...And kissed my hand when I gave her the extra two shillings. Parrots. Press the button and the bird will squeak. Wish she hadn't called me sir" (*U* 13.868–72). With its ingredients of compulsion, emotional and economic desperation, and outright ventriloquism, the incident exposes, even parodies, identification's brutally appropriative aspect, which Bloom seems to relish as a perverse ideal. Indeed, given her apparent youth and inexperience, and her insistence on calling Bloom "sir," the girl stands in for the daughter as a *tabula rasa* figure who "solicit[s]" the inscriptive force of male fantasy. But the incident no less forcefully dramatizes the programmed failure of such phallic appropriation. In attempting to insinuate a desire with which he can identify, Bloom elicits verbal signs that are less lewd than ludicrous, for they are manifestly inconsistent with *both* the girl's native idiolect and the conventions of erotic discourse that Bloom struggles to inculcate. Bloom's reference to "Parrots" only emphasizes the failure of the simulation.

While particularly flagrant in this case, an imperialistic strain factors into the most sympathetic and progressive of Bloom's cross-gender identifications, owing to their inscription within the phallogo-centric order. At the most basic level, the law of gender hinges upon a double scission in which masculinity is delimited through its alignment with legislative subjectivity and femininity is de-limited through its alignment with the appropriable yet elusive object. Accordingly, any cross-gender identification on Bloom's part necess-arily begins by repeating the grammar of gender division (male as subject confronting female as object) even as it mixes so-called secondary gender attributes. For example, during Bloom's encounter with the prostitute, Zoe (another daughter figure who clearly arouses Bloom's solicitude), he opines, "Colours affect women's characters, any they have," and immediately declares, "This black makes me sad" (*U* 15.2738–9). He thereby projects himself into the affective space of the feminine,[24] and the identification he strikes serves to oppugn the association of women *in particular* with the slavery of the senses, an automatic responsiveness to material impression. But the pragmatic form of Bloom's speech-act sustains the gendered subject–object dichotomy in spite of the semantic import. The statement announces by its very existence Bloom's consciousness of the influence of color on his outlook, while it leaves in doubt a similar self-awareness on women's part, suggesting their more organic susceptibility to the blandishments of sensation. This structural element of disaffiliation lodged within Bloom's identificatory gesture silently encodes a whole series of invidious gender polarities: male transcendence and female immanence, male restraint and female abandon, male science and female sensuality.

The structural aporia of Bloom's identification translates into the realm of gender relations the structural aporia at work in the contractual identification of liberal jurisprudence, where, let us recall, "The appearance of consensus … is one with … the inevi-tability of conflict." It will also be remembered, however, that an underlying structure of civil association or dissociation possesses no reality "fully distinct from" or "in advance of" the meaningful strategies whose unconscious it represents, but functions rather in the mode of a metalepsis or deferred action.[25] In this instance, Bloom's structural dissociation only becomes discernible and therefore effective insofar as it leaves a semantic trace in the statement of identification itself. The phrase, "any they have" questions the reality of women's character, i.e. their possession of both the independence and self-discipline constitutive of sovereign ("male") subjectivity and also the diversity and amplitude of being these qualities enable. This expressive sense of dissociation-in-identification represents the intentionalized aspect of the programmed or structural deficit of identification. It is the moment where one can see how the fact that the impulse of identification is inevitably compromised consists after all with the desire of the identifying subject, where identification stands revealed as a properly Bloomian endeavor, a matter of "*Voglio e non vorrei*" (*U* 4.327). The identifying subject wants to be at one with the other but wouldn't like to incur the possible jeopardy of such an accomplishment: specifically, (a) the disappearance of personal autonomy in an outright fusion with or slavish imitation of the other or (b) the loss of the manifold wholeness of personality upon being reduced to a narrow parameter of identification.

In other words, what gets simultaneously incurred and averted in cross-gender identification is *nothing other than the threat of abjection*: the twinned confusion of self and other, being a whole and being a part, out of which the subject emerges. Indeed, in this light *the whole ethics of identification can be seen as a way of repeating the pre-oedipal trauma in an impossible attempt to master fully its mutually exclusive incitements, to fuse and to separate*. The voluntary double inscription of the identifying subject revisits and reorganizes the involuntary double inscription of the abject. In the above example, Bloom reduces the threat of abjection by displacing the anticipated loss or lack of personal identity and diversity onto the object of his identification, "women's character," and staking his dissociative countermove on precisely these points. But the thrust of his gambit is to isolate women as the abject, the bearers of a menacingly unstable or underdeveloped self-identity. Bloom's identificatory practice would thus seem to mediate a somewhat less virulent strain of the gynephobic ambivalence exhibited by Stephen.

Bloom regularly projects the ambivalence underpinning his acts of identification upon their female objects through his free use of a rhetorical device known as the "invidious plural." In a method linking him to Boylan, by way of that ubiquitous ditty, "Seaside Girls," Bloom frequently identifies "not with one girl" but with "the lot," ascribing the relevant traits of his particular object of attention to women in the aggregate. He thus identifies with and de-individualizes women in the same blow, a double game whereby he can advance the patriarchal law of gender in the act of transgressing it and secure his legislative subject position in the act of compromising it. Bloom crosses, and thus infringes, the gender divide but does so in a manner that affirms the basic phallocentric terms of its construction.

Briefly stated, those terms are as follows:

(a) Considered as a group, the site of social normativity, women are constructed as distinctive, singular, eccentric. Taken on an individual basis, the site of social distinction, women are seen as fundamentally alike. Thus positioned against the grain of the Symbolic, women are interpellated as at once the wayward object of the law, in need of its governance, and the sublime other of the law, capable of providing it with external validation and responsible for summarizing its associated cultural norms and virtues in their person.

(b) Considered as a group, the site of social normativity, men are universalized as the human norm, as "man" in short. Taken on an individual basis, the site of social distinction, men are enjoined to be distinctive, autonomous, self-directing. Thus positioned *with* the grain of the Symbolic, men are instrumentalized as the voices and vehicles of the law, their very identity staked upon its validation, which they themselves cannot provide.[26]

By playing upon this chiasmatic relation, Bloom's method begins to mold the object of identification into a self-reflexive alibi: it is, after all, much easier to project one's fears and fantasies upon an anonymous mass conception or collective stereotype. By the same token, Bloom's method holds open an interval, within the synthetic moment of identification, between his (always particularized) self-image and his (usually generalized) mirror object, a flexible *cordon sanitaire* insulating the boundaries of the ego against the risks that accompany their expansion. For Bloom, identification is a biphasic motion in which the difference of the other is strategically attenuated beforehand, assimilated to the proportions of the self, only to be maximized on another footing afterwards, in order to consolidate the self once more. This progression, which is the *exact reverse* of Joyce's in *Giacomo*, indicates the author's increased awareness of the ethico-political limits of representation, insofar as it entails a continual resurrection of the basic grammar of gender hierarchy amid and despite any contextual changes in the gender affiliation of particular attributes.[27]

In "Sirens," for example, Bloom suspends his voyeuristic enjoyment of Lydia Douce to speculate: "Mirror there. Is that the best side of her face? They always know" (*U* 11.1046–7). He proceeds to associate himself with this shrewd vanity just after his closely related voyeuristic experience with Gerty: "Ought to attend to my appearance at my age. Didn't let her see me in profile" (*U* 13.835–6). Coming after an extended comparison of male and female modes of courtship, Bloom's latter comment clearly projects him into the "feminine" position of being the narcissistic object of the gaze. He identifies with Lydia/Gerty in the mirror of his desire for them. But I want to call particular attention to the internal distance mediating this specular relationship. In the encounter with Zoe, remember, Bloom's implicit claim to comparative self-awareness plays upon a series of received gender distinctions and marks his remove from his object of identification. But in this context, self-awareness is tantamount to self-regard, to vanity, a stereotypically feminine weakness, and Bloom accordingly sets himself off by an implicit claim to *self-blindness*. "They always know" the best side of their face, all women at all times. But Bloom only realizes out of time, after the fact, that he had denied Gerty a profile. His performance before the mirror of the other was unconscious and therefore supposedly innocent. Bloom's identification suggests, moreover, that women are universally consumed with the project of being seen and controlling the view, while his concern with appearance is both contingent upon and proper for his advancing "age."

The distinction Bloom draws between women's universal vanity and his own highly circumstantial vanity instances a broader tendency on his part to identify with *all* women in his *particular* vulnerabilities, to posit women as the repositories of man's deficiencies. Bloom's passing thought, "Always see a fellow's weak point in his wife" (*U* 13.972–3), epitomizes this attitude, which has important implications for his identificatory practice. Having projected himself into the imagined space of his sexual other, Bloom turns around and introjects the other, now reduced to a privative part or limit that contributes to his illusion of wholeness: woman becomes the type for certain fractional properties or failings of Bloom's character. Instead of simply expelling the threat of abjection onto the figure of woman, which could then haunt him indefinitely as she does Stephen, Bloom here subsumes the feminine as a localized receptacle in which to confine the threat.

Bloom's strategy invokes the same gender bias that proves so pivotal in "A Mother," where the doubling of masculine and feminine idioms works to ratify the centrality of the former and the marginality of the latter. One of Bloom's more eroticized moments of identification exemplifies the family resemblance I have in mind.[28] Initially, Bloom impersonates what he takes to be the constitutionally feminine state of profound but passive sexual desire: "They can't manage men's intervals. Gap in their voices too. Fill me. I'm warm, dark, open. Molly in *quis est homo*: Mercadante. My ear against the wall to hear. Want a woman who can deliver the goods" (*U* 11.973–6). Through his conflation of the oral, vaginal, and auricular, Bloom projects everywoman's wish to be genitally "filled" upon his remembered desire to be aurally filled by Molly's vocal delivery, so that the phrase, "I'm warm, dark, open," is spoken in his own voice even as it mimes the voice of womankind. The line between identification and identity here is very thin. Furthermore, Bloom's thoughts register an unconscious association of both pleasures with the cherished, Edenic tryst with Molly at Howth Head, where she took the dominant position and orally "deliver[ed] the goods," a seedcake, into a supine Bloom's "warm, dark, open," mouth.

But having indulged in the *frisson* of imaginatively occupying the stereotypical feminine position of sexual passivity, voracity, and dependence, Bloom shortly turns around and, picking up on the same metaphorical complex, reassumes with a vengeance the male fantasy position of sexual agency, plenitude, and control:

Blank face ... Write something on it: page. If not what becomes of them? Decline, despair. Keeps them young. Even admire themselves. See. Play on her. Lip blow. Body of white woman, a flute alive. Blow gentle. Loud. Three holes, all women ... They want it ... Say something. Make her hear. (*U* 11.1086–91)

Now it is Bloom's generic woman who needs an earful and her vaginal, oral and anal "holes" must themselves be played to produce the sound. As both audience and instrument, she is entirely defined by lack – by her bodily apertures, her absence of self-esteem and satisfaction, and by her utter dependency on men to fill the void of her existence. When one factors in her presumed sexual inexperience, it becomes clear that Bloom uses his present object, Lydia Douce, to construct woman once again as a daughter figure, a *tabula rasa* on which men alone can "write something." The line here between the heterosexual male gaze and the paternal gaze is very thin. For his part, Bloom repeatedly enjoins himself to inspirit or inscribe her, to breathe or write her into life, displays of pure phallic agency ordinarily reserved for God.

Read in tandem, these passages show that Bloom's erotic identification with what he construes to be women's distinctive sexual lack is part of an unconscious fantasy-formation through which he disavows the lack intrinsic to his own and indeed all sexual positions. In this composite fantasy, Bloom is in fact identifying with an impossible master position, where lining up on one side of the gender divide would not exclude lining up on the other, where having the phallus would not exclude being the phallus, where enacting one normative gender attitude would not exclude simultaneously enacting its opposite number with equal conviction. In other words, Bloom's unconscious identification would seem to be with a utopian state of perfect sexual reciprocity, an eroticized form of justice and a just form of eros. Far from describing Bloom's *character*, as many critics have claimed,[29] the androgynous ideal constitutes his *fantasy*, the primary or representative fantasy keying his entire identificatory activity. But, and this is an all-important but, in a testament to how identification can smuggle the subject's unacknowledged interests in an ethical wrapping, Bloom's "androgynous" master-position remains an implicitly *masculine* destiny or ideal and, as such, the locus not of sexual justice after all but of colonization. From the earlier to the later passage, the opposition of masculine positivity and plenitude to feminine nullity and desire is both subtly reconfigured and vigorously maintained. Whether as "gap," "blank," "open[ing]," or "whole," lack persists in defining Bloom's generic woman, and this persistence suggests that her "real castration" resides not in her possession of a lack but precisely in her *failure* to possess it, in her inability to get outside or take control of the gendered structure of her desire. Bloom is obsessed with her bodily apertures as functional emblems of this inability, manifest in her need to call upon the other for satisfaction and closure. By contrast, Bloom, as representative man, passes from an identification with feminine passivity and dependence in the first instance to the assertion of phallic initiative and aggressiveness in the second, and this mobility poses a masculine completeness that subsists not in being without lack, but precisely in incorporating lack as its own, i.e. in ranging across the gendered structures of desire without being reduced to any one. His conscious fantasy of possessing and controlling Lydia Douce as a musical instrument is part of an unconscious fantasy of possessing and controlling his desire as the feminine part of a masculine whole (much as he fantasizes "possessing" his own vanity in our earlier example). In this way, he can go beyond the merely exclusionary ideal of the citizen's anti-Semitic *machismo* and become, in his feminized Jewishness, more man than man.[30]

In form and function, Bloom's subliminal fantasy of a master position chimes nicely with Stephen's supernal construct of a sexual "economy of heaven." Early in the library symposium, Stephen characterizes the wives of Socrates and Shakespeare as "errors... volitional," i.e. wholly privative yet somehow productive forces in the life of genius. Asked to elucidate what Socrates learned from his shrewish mate, Stephen replies, "Dialectic," and taken in context, his remark defines Xanthippe as Platonic matter, a point of radical negation that provided the resistance necessary to hone the thinker's philosophical method – a function roughly analogous to the more eroticized negation Anne Hathaway performs in Stephen's Shakespeare theory.[31] The unconscious design of Stephen's overall thesis is to displace his rampant gynephobia, which has so inhibited his intellectual endeavors, into wish-fulfillment narratives wherein the menace posed by a woman, be it social (Xanthippe) or sexual (Anne), creates a lack or "wound" that spurs their husband's prodigious intellectual achievements. By the end of the symposium, Stephen proposes a utopian resolution to this sexual dialectic: "in the economy of heaven, foretold by Hamlet, there are no more marriages, glorified man, an androgynous angel, being a wife unto himself" (*U* 9.1050–2). Read in light of his preceding narratives, Stephen's conceit suggests that the great male mind incorporates the material lack or negativity embodied in woman, becoming "a wife unto himself," and by this very means overcomes that lack as "an androgynous angel," becoming "all in all" like the paternal "*dio boia*" (*U* 9.1049–50). For Stephen, androgyny remains a paradoxically masculine imperative as it does for Bloom and in precisely the same way: man attains to the status of the whole, a manifold organism able to comprehend and mediate gender division; while woman is defined strictly in relation to "glorified man" and reduced to a role, "wife," in his ontological economy.[32]

Indeed, this moment constitutes the linchpin of the counterpoint I have been tracing between Stephen's abjection and Bloom's cross-gender identification. At the meridian of Bloomsday, Stephen crafts a theoretical rendition of Bloom's identificatory strategy whereby abjection, Stephen's own defining pathology, can be circumvented. Quite simply, if the *essence* of woman is lack or negativity, as Bloom and Stephen envision, then she is undecidably part and whole as a matter of logic. Abjection is her proper domain. If this essential lack can be incorporated as a particular attribute (Bloom) or a functional complement (Stephen) of man, then his domain properly exceeds that of abjection. He becomes an absolute subject by engorging her, *through the act of identification*, as a part object "*unto* himself." The threat of absorption into the phallic mother is completely reversed, in keeping with Stephen's vampiric fantasies, and rather than simply containing a constitutive moment of disaffiliation, cross-gender identification is shown to operate *in the service* of such dissociation, "to take the place of the other who is, as it were, installed at the foundation of the self."[33] One might say of this identification, as Bloom does of the *Chad Gadya*, "Justice it means but it's everybody eating everyone else" (*U* 7.213–14).

There are both an empirical level of irony and an infrastructural aporia at work here. At the empirical level, Bloom's transsexual identifications forestall abjection only insofar as they substantially reinscribe the positive law of gender representation that they would seem to transgress: specifically, the gendered subject–object dichotomy and the inversion of the part, man, and the whole, humanity. In a further twist, it is precisely the compliance of Bloom's identifications with the law that vitiates their ethical warrant. At the infrastructural level, Bloom's identificatory practice succeeds in advancing the logic of male privilege only insofar as it consistently fails of its object, *even on its own terms*, i.e. fails to connect with the figure of woman, not just as she "really is," but even as Bloom himself has constructed her. We saw that the essential lackingness of the feminine position, in Bloom's mind, involves its immanence to itself, an inability to get outside or get a purchase on its own structure of desire. Given this premise, however, Bloom's cross-gender identifications are doomed to failure, since the very act of identifying exercises a mobile, legislative mode of subjectivity alien to the feminine as Bloom imagines it. Bloom's projection of himself into and out of "the feminine" attests to his transcendence of that space and so to his active dis-identification with the feminine in what is for him its defining characteristic, the inability to transcend itself. The gendered subject–object dichotomy that allows him to conceive cross-gender identification as a vehicle of transcendence or mastery betrays the identification on precisely these terms. To the extent that he claims any purchase on the figure of woman at all, he misses her in her supposed essence. Bloom's generic woman turns out to exemplify Deleuze and Guattari's oedipalized object form, divided between appropriability and unreachability.

   This default of identification has profound implications for Bloom's subject position. He turns out to be likewise incapable of freely ranging or subsuming the gendered structures of desire, of occupying the place of his self-styled other *as* other and thereby taking possession of his own lack. Instead, Bloom fits Deleuze and Guattari's correlative idea of the oedipalized subject form, the authority and mobility of which are grounded in its subordination to the *phallogos*. The agent of this law, what fixes Bloom in his culturally masculine position, is none other than the unconscious fantasy of the master position. Like all fantasies, this one only *seems* to be about representing what Blake called "the lineaments of gratified desire," but is in fact about fueling a circuit of unsatisfiable desire, the object of which might be anything at all, but the *aim* of which is to reproduce itself endlessly,[34] thus cementing the subject to its place in the symbolic order. The master position promises a transcendence of castration or lack, which is at the same time a transcendence of gendered part-iality; its lure, in short, is the possibility of compassing power and justice in one's own being. The *will* to transcendence that such a fantasy actually promotes, however, is not only a particular form of castration, it is a *lived experience* of castration, or rather it is castration as the lived experience of lack, a restless sense of the insufficiency that comes with being sexed. The resulting search for relief through mastery locks the subject into certain recognizably phallic attitudes and tendencies that not only militate against the achievement of equity but paradoxically attest to the subject's continuing sense of a certain impotency (e.g. acquisitiveness, aggressiveness, elitism, misogyny, racism, etc.). Moreover, because the lack embodied in the will to transcendence is radical, rather than relative to other social beings, none of these measures, Bloom's colonizing identification included, is strictly pertinent to the exigency they address. That is what it means for desire to be structurally unappeasable and thus endlessly self-reproductive.

The limit-form of this desire, adumbrated in the aporia of Bloom's identifications, would consist in the will to transcendence passing from mere self-extension to *self*-transcendence, i.e. from merely incorporating to actually entering a state of immanence, as culturally "embodied" in some feminine or feminized subaltern. But since the law of post-Enlightenment subjectivity calls for a certain measure or core of transcendence,[35] fulfilling this limit-desire would induce not just some sort of ultimate *jouissance* (which Lacan defines as pleasure linked to death[36]), but a return to outright abjection, a complete immersion of the self in otherness, which Bloom's strategy of cross-gender identification had looked to avert.

That is the lesson of Bloom's most notorious transsexual episode, the encounter with Bella Cohen, in which the message of his identificatory desire and practice come back to him in reverse order. Bella's appearance immediately sets two strictly correlative processes in motion: Bloom is transferred to the other side of the gendered subject–object dichotomy that typically hedges his identificatory wager and he is transferred to the other side of the masculine–feminine divide. That is to say, the discourse of Bloom's transsexual identification in "Circe" proceeds from the standpoint of the other party and is framed in the second-person imperative. Appropriately, the sequence begins with an actual object, Bella's fan, assuming the role of speaking subject and making Bloom the object of its speech. THE FAN begins by introducing an element of gender inversion that anticipates Bella's translation into Bello and Bloom's corresponding translation into his/her bondslave. Commenting on Bloom's marriage, THE FAN declares, "And the missus is master. Petticoat government" (*U* 15.2759–60). This proposition entails an inversion of gender status as well as authority, and once Bloom affirms its truth, THE FAN treats him as an object to be appropriated – "We have met. You are mine" (*U* 15.2775) – and proceeds to command him. All of this, THE FAN indicates, explodes out of the core fantasy animating Bloom's identification with woman in the aggregate, the fantasy of being "all in all": "THE FAN: Is me her as you dreamed before? Was then she him you us since knew? Am all them and the same now me?" (*U* 15.2768–9).

With the shift from Bella's fan to Bella herself as Bloom's

interlocutor, a similar interactive sequence unfolds, and the repetition marks a compulsive insistence in the course of Bloom's desire, the positive law of his *particular* inscription in the symbolic order. Where THE FAN becomes a subject to Bloom's object, implicating a certain sexual inversion as well, Bella becomes a man, Bello, to Bloom's woman, implicating a certain generational distinction as well. Like THE FAN, Bella/Bello dictates Bloom's identification to him and appropriates Bloom as his/her erotic object; but s/he also performs the paternal gesture of naming Bloom after him/herself and thereby turns Bloom into a daughter figure, the paradigmatic object of his own cross-gender identification. Indeed, Bella/Bello makes it clear that s/he only imposes upon Bloom the mode of being he has fantasized: "What you longed for has come to pass. Henceforth you are unmanned and mine in earnest, a thing under the yoke. Now for your punishment frock. You will shed your male garments, you understand, Ruby Cohen?" (*U* 15.2964–7). Once Bloom accedes to this edict, Bella/Bello marches him through a series of subaltern roles, each peculiarly associated in the dominant cultural imaginary with a material bodily stratum: (1) a prostitute; (2) a music hall "soubrette" (2985); (3) a "maid of all work" (3086), who must "souse and bat... smelling underclothes," "swab out latrines with dress pinned up to a dish clout tied to [her] tail," and "empty pisspots in different rooms" (3065–7, 3072–3); (4) a female farm animal ("quite easy to milk. Three newlaid gallons a day," 3105) with the "*initial C*" branded on its "*croup*" (3118); and (5) a mouldering corpse, the zero degree of embodiment.

Bloom responds with a call for "justice!" (3202), but Bella/Bello has in effect been justifying this proceeding all along. S/he repeatedly punctuates Bloom's forced descent into bodily immanence with demands that he recognize its origins in his own mimetic fantasies, in his attempts, as Bloom says, "To compare the various joys we each enjoy" (*U* 15.3019–20): rape fantasies, transsexual exhibition fantasies, promiscuous, declassing violation fantasies, panderer/cuckold fantasies. In each of these mimetic fantasies, Bloom made a self-reflexive spectacle of his own surrender to being "had," repeatedly and in various senses. He staged himself in a condition of immanence in order to take possession of it as an element of comparison. In "Circe," which is not just Bloom's fantasy but the book's fantasy of Bloom, he finally experiences something like immanence qua immanence in the only way possible – as an uncontrollable alterity prior to selfhood emanating undecidably from without (Bella's word) and within (his own fantasy), and so as both absolutely exciting and absolutely disgusting, *jouissance* as/and degradation. If, at the meridian of Bloomsday, Stephen fashions a theoretical rendition of Bloom's identificatory strategy, here, in the heart of Bloomsnight, Bloom offers a bodily enactment of Stephen's defining problem, abjection, thereby sealing the reversibility of these psychic tendencies.

This reversibility extends and complicates the specular economy of the masculine romance of *Ulysses*. Not only do the inner experiences of Stephen and Bloom reflect one another, in careful narrative counterpoint, but this mutual reflection consistently focuses on the respective strategies whereby the protagonists specularize the female presences in their lives. The homosocial triangulation that informs *Exiles* reappears at another, more abstract level in *Ulysses*. We saw how the affective energies of Richard Rowan and Robert Hand are routed through the person of Bertha, whom each misconstrues to his own ends. In this case, the consubstantiality of Bloom and Stephen's inner lives, and so the possibility of their symbolic at-onement, is routed through the relation of each to his own projection of feminine otherness. The climactic scene of this oedipal narrative precisely encapsulates the trajectory of the whole:

How did he elucidate the mystery of an invisible attractive person, his wife Marion (Molly) Bloom, denoted by a visible splendid sign, a lamp?

With indirect and direct verbal allusions or affirmations: with subdued affection and admiration: with description: with impediment: with suggestion.

Both then were silent?

Silent, each contemplating the other in both mirrors of the reciprocal flesh of theirhisnothis fellowfaces. (*U* 17.1177–84)

The oedipal romance of Stephen and Bloom culminates in a tableau of idealized intersubjectivity: the "reciprocal" gaze of the principals resolves itself first into their mirror likeness and then into their virtual interfusion, as signified by the synthetic coinage, "fellowfaces." But their reciprocal gaze proceeds directly from their convergent gaze upon the evacuated space of the feminine and from their joint elaboration of the woman who would fill that space. This suggests that their fellow-ship (their relationship but also their respective masculine identities) is staked upon the absence of the feminine and the feminine as absence, i.e. upon the exclusion of femininity as it might be and the simultaneous construction of femininity as lacking, castrated, the "sex which is not one." As with *Exiles*, we are dealing here with a dynamic that goes beyond individual personalities to the structure of representation. Stephen and Bloom interpret the figure of a woman, Molly, by the lights of the (male) Symbolic, here denoted by an overtly symbolic light, "a visible splendid sign, a lamp." By these lights, she remains "invisible," a "mystery." Hence, to "*elucida*te" her, as Bloom attempts, to bring her into this Symbolic light, is necessarily to preempt her. In effect, the oedipal narrative of Stephen and Bloom is mediated by the presence of woman's absence, the empty window space of Molly Bloom, precisely because the representational order exemplified in that narrative consolidates itself, seals itself off, by situating the feminine as its repressed other, the "invisible ... mystery" within the "visible splendid sign." But this is also to say that the feminine can always return to pose a challenge or an alternative *to* representation, of which the empty window space is itself a classic metaphor. It is this uncanny *nostos* that Joyce's odyssey of style proposes to enact.

THE ANTI-OEDIPUS AND THE STYLISTIC METHOD OF "ULYSSES"

In the counterpointed abjection and identification of Stephen and Bloom respectively, Joyce anticipates in narrative form Deleuze and Guattari's theoretical critique. He shows how the subject is made to contribute to its own frustration and the object to its own exploitation, how each must colonize itself in the name of the law as a condition of its existence. For Joyce, this was a matter of reading a particular geopolitics of Irish self-betrayal into the generalized micropolitics of the Oedipus. Just as he claimed that he could get to the heart of any city in Europe by way of Dublin,[37] so the hybridity of the colonial subject position afforded him special access to the vicious circularity at work in being a subject of representation. Deleuze and Guattari in turn theorize a way out of the loop in which Bloom and Stephen are caught, and the applicability of their scheme to Joyce's stylistic method allows us to see the writing of *Ulysses* as proposing a solution to the ethico-political difficulty that the narrative exposes, the incompatibility of representation and (gender) justice.

Deleuze and Guattari propose reconceptualizing desire *inversely*. Instead of framing desire as re-presentational, the repetitive ex-

pression of incurable, individual lack, they frame desire as productive, a collective, ongoing assemblage of breaks and flows, liaisons
and lines of flight, across a "plane of immanence," so called because
its dimensions continually rearrange themselves in concert with the
developing connections and fragmentations that unfold across its
surface. Under this model, desire is not about generating com-
pensatory fantasies, such as those grounding Bloom's cross-gender
identifications, but is about creating the unimagined in the real and,
as such, it continually exceeds the comparatively fixed and unified
systems, sexual, textual and otherwise, to which it gives rise. Desire
"establishes relations … across ages, sexes and reigns" in assemblages
whose "only unity is that of co-functioning" and whose mode of
organization, accordingly, is "never filiation but alliance, alloy …
not succession but contagion" (*D* 69) – not, in sum, the reinscription
of vertical power relations but the invention of horizontal, diagonal,
and transversal possibilities.

By the same token, Deleuze and Guattari require a reconceptualization of the subject and object. They are no longer defined in
essentially metaphorical terms as distinct yet interchangeable items
mediated by the current of an always displaced or metonymic desire.
Instead the subject and object themselves function metonymically as
the spare parts or residual formations of a machinic as opposed to
theatrical desire, taking their nature at any given point from the
economy of their involvements. The object form is not fully
dissociable from the inventive mechanism in what Deleuze calls the
"producing/product identity": "Every object presupposes the
continuity of a flow, every flow the fragmentation of an object"
(*AO* 6). Similarly, the subject becomes a molecular nexus formed
through encounter and transfiguration, rather than a molar structure
delimited by repression and identification – "The subject itself is not
on the Center … but on the periphery, with no fixed identity, forever
decentered, defined by the states through which it passes" (*AO* 20).
In this fugitive and kaleidoscopic notion of subjectivity, there is an
important shift from the recent emphasis on the self as a performance
of a broadly social script to the self as a variable performative within
a specific collective enunciation, from the self as an imitation,
whether deferential (masquerade) or critical and parodic (mimicry)
of a certain ensemble of norms, to the self as a machinic instrument
of manufactured connections, territorialities, and disengagements of
which such norms are but a possible local effect. With respect to the

subject and object forms alike, their emphasis is on countering the Lacanian lack-in-Being by replacing Being itself with in-be-tweenness: "Substitute the AND for IS, A and B. The AND is ... the path of all relations, which makes relations shoot outside their terms and outside the set of their terms, and outside everything which could be determined as Being, One, or Whole. The AND as extra-being, inter-being" (*D* 57).

Unlike the IS, the AND cannot be assumed to constitute a primary ontological condition or principle, lest it serve as just another univocal marker, the AND as IS, rather than a genuine assemblage. Now, an assemblage is by definition constructivist, and since it possesses no organic structure or purpose, limit or telos, it cannot properly be said to *be* at all, only to become incessantly and multiply with and as the productive activity it names. There is, in short, no Being without transcendence: "Becoming produces nothing other than itself" (*TP* 238).

Writing can exemplify assemblage for Deleuze and Guattari. On the one hand, language is staked from the outset on the AND: "The minimum real unit is not the word, the idea, the concept or the signifier, but the *assemblage* ... The proper name does not designate a subject but something which happens at least between two terms which are not subjects, but agents, elements" (*D* 51). On the other hand, it is the writer who "invents assemblages starting from assemblages which have invented him" (*D* 52). The method of executing this ontological somersault they call "Becoming-": Becoming-woman, man, child, animal, etc. Becoming consists in a particular use of style. It is not a mode of mimesis, assimilation, identification, or ventriloquism, nothing in fact that would implicate the writer in speaking for, as, or in place of another, as if points of view existed in the world as so many ready-mades awaiting representation. It is a way of "assembling between" already molecularized entities, making one multiplicity pass into another. Instead of a dialectical synthesis, the kind of unity to which molar entities aspire, the result of such a convergence is a double displacement, a setting of the terms of the encounter on asymmetrical paths of development. "You can only become an Eskimo," Deleuze writes, "if the Eskimo himself becomes something else" (*D* 53), and in this inventive ramification of the plane of immanence, new forces, new weapons, and new minoritarian perspectives can be discovered.

Ulysses clearly qualifies as a candidate for assemblage. This is not to say that it *is* an assemblage, a contradictory proposition for reasons already addressed, but rather that it can be constructed as such. The novel need not be read strictly as an image or creative reproduction of a world. It can be read as a deterritorialization of both the world to which it refers and the novelistic genre of reference. To wit, *Ulysses* subjects word and world to an "a-parallel evolution" (*TP* 11) by crossing heterogeneous historical, political, sexual, generational, and literary dimensions at the site of their convergence. Certainly the profusion of names without descriptions in *Ulysses*, the accumulation of undelineated points of local and topical reference within this massively defamiliarizing stylistic machine, would seem to solicit this approach. As for its notoriously manifold styles, they need not be read as so many strategies of representation, as if there remains some constant light, however notional and inaccessible, behind their multi-colored glass. They might be read in terms of their relationship to one another, at which point the distinction between representation and production utterly fails, the former being subsumed, as it were, in the latter. Given the irreducible specificity of the idiomatic, one cannot draw a line between imitating another style, whether in the manner of pastiche or parody, and producing through this encounter a *new stylistic option*. For there is no such thing as a parody in the abstract or in general, only a quite particular parody of a quite particular style, which is, accordingly, something novel in spite of itself and which, in its connection with other styles, parodied styles, and styles of parody, cannot but open up new rhetorical territories and lines of flight. *Ulysses* pegs this radical polyphony, in turn, to a marked segmentation of the novel form, defined in terms of distinct yet overlapping sets of mythical and historical correspondence. This strategy allows the reader to break with if not to disregard the linearities of conventional narrative logic, which align the story form in a quite fundamental way with the temporal construction of patriarchal authority: its obsessive privileging of the origin, its transmission of power and legitimacy along lines of filiation, etc. The reader is invited to detach and reattach segments for analysis to produce new micro-assemblages and with them new permutations of the cofunctioning collectivity. Joyce has anticipated in a fictional form Deleuze and Guattari's idea of the book of "plateaus."

As these plateaus go, the mode of stylistic "Becoming-" in "Sirens" is plainer than most. Whether or not Joyce's aim in the chapter was the imitation of music in writing, his achievement is an "assembling between" music and writing, in which the multiplicity of possible effects characterizing either practice pass into one another and produce something new: a displacement of music toward articulation and noise simultaneously and a displacement of language that foregrounds both its sensate constituents and its endless possibilities of meaningful recombination. On both scores, then, this assemblage allows for the elaboration and the destabilization of a recognizable expressive order at the same time. Joyce maps this stylistic potentiality onto the mythological topos of "Sirens," the female voice as the enigmatic and dangerous object of desire, in order to inscribe a two-tiered sexual politics. On the narrative tier, he represents the exclusion of femininity as an authorized mode of subjectivity in the patriarchal order and its reinstatement as an objectification of value. On the other, textual tier, he constructs a new minoritarian style, "Becoming-woman," to reassemble that order.

In this regard, "Sirens" can be seen as something of a microcosm of the *Ulysses* structure outlined above, where the feminine is repressed within the patriarchal narrative, the at-onement of Stephen and Bloom, only to return as a minoritarian alternative to narrative representation itself. As a matter of fact, in keeping with the endlessly self-referential cast of *Ulysses*, Stephen and Bloom are actually conducting a "*tete a tete* ... about sirens, enemies of man's reason," even as Joyce, manipulating the lyrics to "The Low-Backed Car," has them off "*to be married by Father Maher*" (*U* 16.1887–90). Just as the mock-marriage here implicates the figure of woman in the very act of excluding her, so the oedipal romance, the narrative of woman's exclusion, pauses to remark upon the significance and the specific textual location of her stylistic return.

Joyce's narrative method for communicating the generalized patriarchal exclusion of feminine subjectivity in "Sirens" itself is at first blush breathtakingly simple. The men, not the siren-barmaids, do the singing in the chapter,[38] and insofar as singing is a trope for the quintessence of voice in its larger sense, the women are symbolically denied the property most intimately associated with subjective interiority and spiritual depth. Women turn up, on the other hand, as the focus of many of the songs and are framed in some of the most prominent as an appealing visual image, precisely the role the barmaids actually serve to merit their siren status:

"M'appari": When first I saw that form endearing/Sorrow from me seem'd to depart.

"Under the Palm" (sung to Idolores): My star will be shining love / When you're in the moonlight calm / So be waiting for me by the Eastern sea / In the shade of the sheltering palm.

"The Last Farewell" (Bloomian association): Farewell A lovely girl, her veil awave upon the wind upon the headland ... (11:590–2)

In this last instance, Bloom is actually responding to an illustrated print of the song, rather than the song itself, a circumstance which underscores the consignment of women to the visual dimension. Instead of the sirens as pure voice, tempting in their invisibility, the narrative offers sirens as sheer spectacle, seductive in their silence. As we shall see, Joyce further underscores this inversion with a series of proleptic allusions to "Nausicaa" linking Lydia Douce with Gerty's visual self-display.

Jean-Michel Rabate points out, "the Sirens possess one major emblem, that of the large mirror behind the bar,"[39] and on my reading, this constitutes a kind of crystal reef behind which they hide in plain sight, the men's apprehension of them occulted by their sheer visibility, their absolute objectification in the male gaze. Indeed, given the scope of the mirror, Lydia and Mina must be framed therein on a more or less continual basis, and given its location, *only* Lydia and Mina are thus framed, so that the mirror itself comes to signify a distinct simulacral dimension, the male Imaginary, in which women are instrumentalized as "the fantasy of man" (in Lacan's words) or his "enlarging mirror" (in Virginia Woolf's), i.e. as a visible surface reflecting men's overlapping network of self- and other-directed desires.[40]

The specific references to the bar mirror bear this interpretation out. At the outset of the episode, Lydia Douce regards her own surface, her sunburnt skin, in the mirror, with an eye to the prospective gaze of some customer whose approval she hopes to win: "Am I woefully sunburnt? ... Miss Douce halfstood to see her skin askance in the barmirror gildedlettered" (*U* 11.118–19). In so doing, she anticipates Bloom's self-aggrandizing identification/disaffiliation with female vanity, scrutinized in the previous section: "Mirror there. Is that the best side of her face? They always know" (*U* 11.1046–7). As it happens, Miss Douce knows and heeds the dominant male standards of womanly appeal well enough to attract the attention of Boylan, and his valedictory look at her likewise takes place in the mirror: "Boylan, eyed, eyed ... His spellbound eyes went after, after her gliding head as it went down the bar by mirrors ... where it concerted, mirrored, bronze with sunnier bronze" (*U* 11.419–23). The curious phrase, "by mirrors," crosses "beside the mirror" with "by means of mirrors," imputing a *trompe l'œil* quality to Lydia, whose tag name, bronze, makes her a kind of mirror, "concerted, mirrored, bronze with sunnier bronze." Lydia thus seems to occupy a pure fantasy space for Boylan, especially since his eyes follow her "spellbound." As the reduplication of "eyed, eyed" underlines, this fantasy space is mutually narcissistic (to risk an oxymoronic construction), a site of illusory reciprocity where both parties read their own power and pleasure in the mesmerizing, culturally approved performances of the other. But since the pertinent cultural standards enforce the phallogocentric grammar of gender relations, the male and female "eye(d)" does not operate on the same level or to the same end. That is what is at stake in Boylan's command of the barroom, a fantasy space that *counts* as real (much as the male imaginary counts as the symbolic) and Lydia's corresponding relegation to the bar mirror, a fantasy space that counts as insubstantial.

In a very real sense, the exclusion of the female voice, with its connotations of female subjectivity, is *already* an exclusion of the female eye, as the vehicle of a distinct perspective on the world. A thought of Bloom's near the end of this episode illustrates the point. Gazing upon Lydia, he thinks, "See the real beauty of the eye when she not speaks" (*U* 11.1105). In thus reducing her eye from a visual organ to a visible surface reflecting man's desires, Bloom implicitly ties the positive impression a woman can make to the positive suppression of her subjectivity,[41] and even suggests that her authentic ("real"), properly aesthetic condition as a woman consists in this suppression.

Joyce's persistent and multilayered supersession of mythic feminine vocals with modern feminine visuals marks the (re)routing of the female voice, in its cognitive and literary dimension, through masculine *phantazein* and fabrication. But in this he does not substantively alter the myth so much as throw its real implications into relief while addressing the consequences of its underlying ideology on contemporary gender relations. The legend of the siren song is, after all, a testament to the force of male ambivalence toward the construct of the "Eternal Feminine," an ambivalence arising from the oedipal framework of desire. The institution of desire through a process of separation and exclusion that engenders (in both senses of the term) the subject–object dichotomy places women in the dual role of appropriable image or surface, a role played by the Ormond barmaids, and enigmatic alterity, a function signified by the infinitely receding voice of the sirens. As Deleuze observes, "that's the real idea of ... the constituent law ... of desire, desire constituted as lack ... each time that desire is conceived as a bridge between a subject and an object: the subject of desire cannot but be split, and the object lost in advance" (*D* 89). The power of the Woman as lost object derives para-doxically from her perpetual siren-like movement outside the reach of the phallocentric order, a space from which she can be enlisted to ratify the order itself, providing it with an "indispensable countersign."[42] If woman qua image is dehumanized, situated beneath subjectivity, woman qua alterity is supra-humanized, situated beyond subjectivity. As such, she remains supremely desirable and supremely dread-ful, capable of deifying the subject, which is to say identifying him *with* the transcendental law, but capable also of annulling his existence outright by withholding recognition of his authority as a subject *under* that law.

In Homer, the conventional male response to this ambivalence is to stop the ear and so reduce the world of experience to its imaginary daylight aspect, signified by the visual register. But this precaution simultaneously preserves the construct of an other-identity in the mythic dimension and, with it, a residual ambivalence of which Odysseus bound is the emblem. The structural equivalence of this response in the "Sirens" episode is to value women primarily if not exclusively as spectacle and so to reduce them to the proportions of the male Imaginary, in the process domesticating the (de-)-authorizing potency attached to them by way of their cultural identification with the other-identity of Woman. But in repeating the act of exclusion that created this potency in the first place, the modern strategy likewise mythologizes the feminine voice once more, beginning again the compulsive oedipal cycle.

The narrative of "Sirens" does not just expose the generalized operation of the male gaze. It also meticulously stages the progressive silencing of the siren "song" of the barmaids and the male appropriation of the vocalist function. At the same time, the text of "Sirens" assembles the song itself in such a way that it constitutes an ineradicable challenge to the very condition of reified visibility, a subversive element of the atmosphere of its own repression, not automatically resurgent but continually available for reconstruction. This syncopated development of incident and motif begins, appropriately enough, with the very threat that drives the process, the de-authorizing potency of the feminine voice, here given the intra-worldly form of sexual mockery.

Female mockery, of course, bulks large in Bloom's thoughts throughout the day. In "Hades," for example, he attributes Menton's enmity towards him to his having unwittingly exposed Menton long ago to the embarrassment of women's teasing: "Why he took such a rooted dislike to me ... Molly and Floey Dillon under the lilac tree, laughing. Fellow always like that, mortified if women are by" (6.1012–14). That Bloom universalizes men's vulnerability to this sort of wound and that Menton himself has yet to recover from the ensuing resentment together evince the exaggerated impact that female ridicule carries in this sexual economy. In "Nausicaa," Bloom's reflections suggest that *only* female derision really cuts: "Walk after him now make him awkward like those newsboys me today. Still you learn something. See ourselves as others see us ... so long as women don't mock what matter" (13.1056–9). Bloom's attitude here indicates that the scopic relationship is so profoundly gendered that for a man to become a spectacle for other men is something of a collegial experience in which he can see himself through their eyes, remaining the subject as well as the object of vision. A man does not properly forfeit the role of scopic subject unless he does so on a gendered basis, at which point, apparently, he forfeits it utterly. The absolute power Bloom ascribes to the mocking gaze of women – it is "what matter(s)" – is but the flip side of a set of cultural assumptions grounding the vindication of men's subjectivity upon the suppression of women's. Not coincidentally, the female mockery initiating the action of "Sirens" focuses precisely on men's, and by extension Bloom's, voyeuristic defense.

Continuing their discussion of Lydia's sunburn, Douce and Kennedy recall and mimic the bestial mannerisms of a "hideous old wretch" from whom she might procure a nostrum (11.138):

—O, don't remind me of him for mercy' sake!
— But wait till I tell you, miss Douce entreated. Sweet tea miss Kennedy having poured with milk plugged both two ears with little fingers ...
—I won't listen, she cried.

But Bloom?
Miss Douce grunted in snuffy fogey's tone...
Miss Kennedy unplugged her ears to hear, to speak. (11.127–36)

The plugging and unplugging of the ears, the refusal and yet the
willingness to listen, do more than allude in some vague sense to the
Homeric sirens; they signal the imminence of a siren song, the only
full-blown "song" to which the official sirens give "voice" in the
chapter: a delirious, mellifluent, derisive bout of laughter directed at
a prototypical male voyeur, whom the disporting narrative voice
insists upon confusing with Bloom:

Shrill shriek of laughter sprang from miss Kennedy's throat...
—O! shrieking, miss Kennedy cried. Will you ever forget his goggle eye?
Miss Douce chimed in in deep bronze laughter, shouting:
—And your other eye!
Bloowhose dark eye...
...In a giggling peal young goldbronze voices blended, Douce with
Kennedy your other eye. They threw young heads back, bronze gigglegold,
to let freefly their laughter, screaming, your other, signals to each other,
high piercing notes...
—O greasy eyes!...
...Douce gave full vent to a splendid yell, a full yell of full woman, delight,
joy, indignation.
—Married to the greasy nose! she yelled.
Shrill, with deep laughter, after, gold after bronze, they urged each to
peal after peal, ringing in changes, bronzegold, goldbronze, shrilldeep, to
laughter after laughter. And then laughed more. Greasy I knows...
Married to Bloom, to greaseabloom. (11.143–80)

The passage moves from a mimetic style, the narrative representing
the two women aping the voyeur, to a style of "Becoming-." The
onomatopoeia, interweaving terms like "high," "piercing," "peal,"
"chimed," "notes," "shrill," "blended," "ringing," makes the
idiom of music pass into the discourse of laughter, not as a way of
describing it as such but as a way of founding a new conceptual
assemblage. The song of the sirens is mapped onto "a full yell of full
woman," producing what Deleuze calls a "double capture" (*D* 2), a
Becoming-laughter of the mythic song, a Becoming-music of the
laughter.

The stylistic adjustment, in turn, parallels a shift on the barmaids'
part from representational mockery, their aping of the voyeur, to the
nonrepresentational mockery of flat-out laughter. Now, to the extent
that the voyeuristic reduction of women to spectacle has as its

ideological (and Homeric) substrate the reduction of the Real to a phallocentric framework of intelligibility (the Symbolic), the hilarity of the barmaids might be said to bear a value akin, in an emblematic sense, to the "sovereign" laughter described by Derrida:

Laughter, which constitutes sovereignty in its relation to death, is not a negativity, as has been said. And it laughs at itself, a "major" laughter laughs at a "minor" laughter... in order to be in relation to itself in the pleasurable consumption of itself.[43]

Derrida further characterizes this sovereign laughter as, "an irruption suddenly uncovering the limit of discourse... the ecstatic... in every discourse which can open itself up to the absolute loss of sense."[44] Such laughter does not register a critique, rejection, or denigration of the symbolic from some other-scenario, an act and a conception that could only renew once more the obsessive oedipal binarism. It emerges rather through an effective if momentary disruption of that binarism from within. The barmaids manage this feat at the affective level, where the consequence of the oedipal split is constitutional ambivalence. Far from simply rising above this emotional bind, the barmaids tacitly locate themselves within it, only to redouble and thereby exceed it. On one side, they express their derision of men for being "frightful idiots" with "sadness" as well as humor and with the resigned awareness that "It's them that has the fine times" (11.79–80, 84). On the other side, the climactic burst of sovereign laughter, the "full yell of full woman," is compact of "delight, joy, indignation," the two to one ratio of affirmative to critical impulses reflecting an ability to discover a certain satiric ecstasy in the ambivalence of their situation. As a result, they achieve a kind of interior release from that ambivalence and from their discrete molar identities in the process.[45] "Gold after bronze" becomes "bronze-gold" becomes "goldbronze" (11.174–5).

Joyce's stylistic assemblage allows him to translate the barmaids' affective eccentricity to the oedipal law of separation into conceptual terms. Being composed of articulate words and phrases instead of conventional signs of the inarticulate, the barmaids' laughter is neither something other than language nor even an other-language, but the Becoming-language of laughter and vice versa, an assemblage that strains the phallocentric order of words precisely by remaining on the inside, in perpetual risk of reappropriation.

At the level of the action, the interlude of sovereign mockery

screeches to a halt upon the entry of the first (male) customer, Simon
Dedalus, whose presence occasions an assumption of the normative
gender masquerade and a conversion of the sirens' primary effects
from sound to sight. It is at this point, tellingly, that the first major
prolepsis of the "Nausicaa" episode appears. Chatting up Dedalus
about her vacation, Lydia provocatively remarks, "Look at the holy
show I am. Lying out on the strand all day" (11.198–9). In so doing,
she presages Gerty's exhibitionistic performance outside the church
service, where the climax of her erotic revealment coincides with
Reverend Hanlon's monstration of the Eucharist. Dedalus' response
to Lydia, "Tempting poor simple males" (11.202), completes the
allusion by foreshadowing the presence of Gerty's spectator, Bloom,
whom she will see as "literally worshipping at her shrine" (13.564).
On the terms of the novel, the transfiguration of a siren into a visual
showpiece means turning her into a Gerty MacDowell.

But in another sense, the interlude of mockery continues unbe-
knownst to the characters and in spite of them. Even as Lydia is
exhibiting the "bronze whiteness" (11.200) of her body, the text is
exhibiting *for the first time* a stylistic blemish or disfiguration (as
opposed to an arabesque or filagree) attached to the main narrative
body: "Miss Douce of satin douced her arm away" (11.203). A
previous stylization "bidding ... her hands adieu" (11.123) appears
to have been subject to what Karen Lawrence calls "some deaf-eared
transcribing."[46] Now, there have been previous distortions of Bloom's
name, "Bloowho" (11.86) and "Bloowhose" (11.149), but each
follows immediately upon a burst of the barmaids' laughter and
seems an effect of the excess of textual energy generated by their
hilarity. The other previous distortions occur as a still more direct
function of the rollicking eruptions. Douce calls the nameless voyeur
"greasy nose" (11.173), which amid the riotous laughter becomes
"Greasy I knows" (11.176–7), the first such instance of a fractured
repetition. This distorted echo resounds in its turn as "greaseabloom" (11.180), as if to confirm that the earlier disfigurations of his
name are likewise aftershock of the barmaids' explosive mirth. Some
alteration or development in the writing, I would suggest, can be
traced to the interlude of sovereign laughter. That is to say, the
distinctive stylistic assemblage of this chapter, the "Becoming-
music" of language, is indeed a siren(s') song in that it issues forth
from the "Becoming-laughter" of the music and the "Becoming-
language" of the laughter of the sirens themselves. Moreover, as

Karen Lawrence has compellingly argued, the materiality of the "Becoming-music" style exposes the artifice at work in ordinary representation, the "gap" between patriarchal language and the reality it pretends to convey,[47] including the reality of integral subjectivity. As such, this style constitutes something of a grand extension of the sirens' song of sovereign mockery, prolonging and ramifying the implosion of the oedipal binary (subject–object, word–world) that their laughter initiates. So while the participation of the barmaids in the world of song grows more fragmentary and mediated, the irruptive effects of their "voice" grow slowly more pervasive.

If the first movement in the suppression of the sirens' song unfolds with the appearance of Simon Dedalus, the second is marked by the appearance of Lenehan, a purer specimen of voyeuristic misogyny. Lydia Douce trills a line from "Under the Palm," but this single, brief feint at singing actually serves to demonstrate the dispossession of her "voice," in the sense of an independent or interiorized perspective. The subject position in "Under the Palms," like every tune sung in this chapter, is masculine, and the narrative refuses to allow Lydia to take it up. By virtue of trilling the line "O, Idolores, Queen of the Eastern Seas!" (11.226), Lydia is repeatedly identified thereafter with the female *object* of the song, Idolores, whose name comprises the word "idol" or worshiped image. Under Lenehan's watchful eye, Lydia immediately ceases trilling the song, goes to humming it open-mouthed, then just humming it, then lapses into silence, thereby enacting the muting process in miniature.

The following stage in this progression develops with the appearance of Blazes Boylan, the epitome of virile and voyeuristic misogyny, and features the second major prolepsis to the "Nausicaa" episode. Lydia engages in a more or less unilateral competition with Mina for the attentions of Boylan, as Gerty does with Cissy for the attention of Bloom; and Lydia too ultimately resorts to a show of flesh, which she, like Gerty, looks to keep secret from her rival. The highly significant name of the striptease Lydia performs for Blazes is *sonnez la cloche* or sound the bell. The phrase indicates a musical routine, but the musical routine here is subordinated to and even subsumed within a visual, burlesque routine. The sound of the garter serves mainly to set off the jiggle of "a woman's warmhosed thigh" (11.414) (anticipating Bloom's memory in "Nausicaa" of a "Mutoscope" show entitled "A Dream of Wellfilled Hose" (13.793–4).

The ritual thus encapsulates the incorporation of auditory into visual seduction, which is to say the in-corporation of the sirens themselves. The name further recalls the earlier bout of siren laughter, which was replete with the sounds of the bell, chimes, and peals of bronze and gold. Lydia's loss of voice is thus transposed as her willing submission to the kind of phallic gaze she has previously scorned. Upon completion of her routine, the text supplements her reaction, "She smilesmirked supercilious" (11.416), with a fractional repetition of her previous response, "(Wept! Aren't men [frightful idiots])" (11.416), so as to mark the continuity amid discontinuity of the two moments. Her attitude of mockery somehow persists despite a cultural suppression so profound that it has been internalized. At the narrative level, Lydia can only express her ironic condescension toward Boylan in the terms of a genteel social piety consonant with and supportive of the sexual double standard: "You're the essence of vulgarity, she in gliding said" (11.418). But the force of this residual mockery diffuses through the text in a metastatic proliferation of productive stylistic disturbances.

To take one small example, the phrase *sonnez la cloche*, while continuing to point back to that originary burst of sovereign mockery, drifts forward and interrupts a reference to "Love's Old Sweet Song" (11.682), ironizing the romantic and sentimental ideals the tune expresses by insisting upon the voyeuristic and objectifying impulses they disguise. And while continuing to insist upon these voyeuristic and objectifying impulses, the phrase also migrates forward and interrupts the tag line of Boylan's triumphant approach to 7 Eccles Street ("Have you the? Horn. Have you the? Haw, haw horn" (11.526–7), countering the obscene male laughter of "Haw, haw" with an allusion to the laughter of feminine mockery. Moving forward yet again, it ultimately displaces outright Boylan's possession of the phallus or "horn": "Haw. Have you the? *Cloche. Sonnez la*" (11.1240).

Just as Simon Dedalus is the passive agency of the initial muting of the sirens, so he is the passive agency of the initial masculine takeover of the vocal function, and in this case his role as Stephen's "natural" father seems pertinent. Encouraged to perform a "ditty," Dedalus demurs with the words, "I was only vamping, man" (11.448). In this context, the term "vamping" carries a triple valence. "Vamping" imports both a musical improvisation and a menacing sexual destructiveness. Taken together, these meanings insinuate that

Dedalus has assumed the role of siren, and they further attach a repressed homoerotic significance to the musical boys' club of the Ormond bar. The latter implications surface more plainly, of course, at the climax of "M'appari" when the impoverished singer, Simon, the impersonated character, Lionel, and the sympathetic listener, Leopold, converge in an operatic nuptial – "Siopold" (11.752) – that is mediated by but exclusive of the visual "form endearing" of Martha (11.665). The final connotation of vamping involves vampires and refers us back to Stephen's bloodsucker poem, in which he seems to incorporate the voice of the woman/mother along with her body.[48] Like son, like father.

This vampiric linkage of Dedalus *père* and Dedalus *fils* is important in nudging the reader to note the multiple associations which exist between the upcoming union of Stephen's two fathers and the liaison of Stephen and Bloom: both are Dedalus–Bloom couplings, both take shape and significance from their musical accompaniment ("M'appari," "The Low-Backed Car"), both "feed" off the absent "form" of woman, who is at once invoked and excluded, and "Martha" herself represents Bloom's substitute for Molly just as Molly looks to be Stephen's substitute for his mother. Taken together, these associations tend to implicate the novel's traditional narrative center, the father–son reconciliation, directly in the phallic appropriation of (female) voicedness, suggesting that a Bloom–Stephen fellowship does as much to repeat as to renew the debilitating micropolitics of Dublin life.

When Big Ben Dollard joins in for a duet of "Love and War," the phallic appropriation of the vocal register becomes manifest:

—*When love absorbs my ardent soul*...
—War! War! cried Father Cowley. You're the warrior.
—So I am, Ben Warrior laughed...
—Sure, you'd burst the tympanum of her ear, man, Mr. Dedalus said through smoke aroma, with an organ like yours.
—Not to mention another membrane, Father Cowley added. (11.536–40)

Through Father Cowley's conflation of the auricular and the vaginal, the voice is here equated directly with the phallic member, a phallus admired chiefly for dimensions which enable it to serve as an instrument of violence and intimidation. Playing out the logic of this equation, the most remarkable thing about the phallic word or voice is its arbitrariness, the violence of its imposition as norm, and in this regard it is appropriate that the equation itself is drawn by an ersatz

"Father." Just as Ben the Warrior, a bass, annexes the higher register of Love in the duet, so the male-identified activity of domination supplants the female-identified activity of love in the sexual thinking of the culture and in the economy of its language.

As we are shortly reminded, however, the visible all too visible sign of phallic mastery can itself make a spectacle of its bearer, depriving him of the subject position it might have been expected to assure. Witness Molly's recorded reaction to Ben Dollard in his tight trousers:

Ben Dollard base barreltone... didn't he look a balmy ballocks sure enough that must have been a spectacle on the stage. (18.1285, 88–9)

Night he ran round to us to borrow a dress suit for that concert. Trousers tight as a drum on him. Musical porkers. Molly did laugh when he went out. Threw herself back across the bed, screaming, kicking. With all his belongings on show. O saints above, I'm drenched! O, the women in the front row! O, I never laughed so many! Well, of course that's what gives him the base barreltone. (11.554–9)

The record of Molly's hilarity in "Sirens" effects something of a temporary arrest or reversal in the normative momentum of gender positioning. Recalling the very same concert, Simon Dedalus groups Molly with the other exponents of feminine display in the novel: "Mrs. Marion Bloom has left off clothes of all description" (11.496–7). Bloom likewise recalls a musical performance he and Molly attended in terms of the visual impact she made, even borrowing a phrase she had applied to Dollard: "She looked fine. Her crocus dress she wore lowcut, belongings on show. Clove her breath was always in theatre when she bent to ask a question... Hypnotised, listening. Eyes like that. She bent. Chap in dresscircle staring down into her with his operaglass for all he was worth" (11.1056–60). This reminiscence in turn prompts Bloom to a universalizing reflection that might stand as the patriarchal motto for the narrative of this chapter: "God made the country, man the tune" (11.1061–2), i.e. woman as space/nature, man as time/culture. But in resuming the barmaid's mockery of the phallic gaze as a mockery of the phallus "itself," Molly appropriates the empowered subject position on a specifically gendered basis, specularizing Dollard as man, not as individual, and so appropriates it definitively. If Bloom's comments in "Nausicaa" tying "what matter(s)" to women's mockery can be seen as representative, then Molly's laughter at Dollard's expense bares a double bind at the heart of the phallocentric order: virile display is still (visual) display and therefore objectifying, feminizing and so all the more ridiculous in a man. Conspicuous possession of the phallus or its substitutes is itself a variant of castration. Molly's laughter renews the sovereignty of the barmaids' mockery as well, transgressing the oedipal binary (male/female, subject/object, castrated/phallus) on its own terms.

Molly's recorded laughter also *reiterates* the repressed sovereignty of the barmaids' laughter. They "threw young heads back," Molly "threw herself back," they were "screaming," Molly was "screaming," they repeatedly say "O," Molly repeatedly says "O," Miss Douce says "saints above," Molly says "saints above," Miss Douce says "I never laughed so much," Molly says "I never laughed so many," Miss Douce says "I feel all wet," and Molly says "I'm drenched."[49] By putting these moments of textual delirium in such close verbal contact with one another, Joyce invites the reader to draw the connection between the chorus of productive stylistic disturbances unleashed from the barmaids' laughter and the disturbance in Molly's epithet for Dollard, "base barreltone," or even in her "met-him-pike-hoses," the novel's primal scene of productive verbal rupture (8.1148/4.336).[50] In the stylistic assemblage of "Sirens," the "Becoming-music" of language passes through other "Becomings," other assemblages involving the laughter, mockingly ironic yet joyfully excessive, of women. The result is *a* "Becoming-woman" of writing.

At the risk of repeating myself, "Becoming-woman" should not be confused with *écriture féminine*.[51] It should not be conceived as imitating, expressing, or representing certain essential gender properties, or enacting a gender performance, whether masquerade or mimicry, or counterposing some (m)other tongue to the patriarchal symbolic. Becoming-woman rather comprises a continuing production of a new "minor" style, a shift from performance to performativity, which "speaks with, writes with" women (*D* 52), subjecting the operation of language to the impact of their social and political habitus, but which displaces women in the interim, and so it can hardly be said to speak *for* them. As we have seen, sovereign mockery is characterized by the exceeding of any particular identity for which to speak. Most importantly, unlike *écriture féminine*, "Becoming-woman" has no determinate or determinable political effects precisely because it has no Being. Its effects, staked upon the

AND, always remain to be constructed. That is the importance, in the "Sirens" episode, of the divergence, however provisional and precarious, between the representational narrative line and the counter-representational textual whirl. Not only does this divergence enable Joyce to portray women as socially oppressed and sexually exploited without reducing them to the status of pure victims or striving after artificial heroics, it creates an indefinitely permeable space of resistance across which actively political construction can occur.

Take the high point of the chapter itself. Does the momentary fusion of Simon, Lionel, and Leopold repeat the dominant narrative motif of excluding the possibility of female (inter)subjectivity by reducing women to endearing forms? The content of the aria might well indicate as much. Or does this fusion enact the molecularization of identities begun with the sovereign laughter of the barmaids and critical to the Becoming-woman of style? And are gender differences, hence gender exclusions, "consumed" (11.753) with personal identities? The enunciation of the aria might well indicate as much; indeed, the special *jouissance* of the tenor's high note may derive from the listener's experience of the normative gender determinations of the human voice being shattered, a possibility Bloom's mental "marriage" of the participants would seem to thematize. Thus "Sirens" once again encapsulates the defining oscillation or vacillation of *Ulysses*' gender politics: is this fusion a homosocial exchange of women (narrative/content) or is it the Becoming-woman, in the properly Deleuzean sense, of the men (style/enunciation)? A general economy of justice would need to respect both of these elements in their interconnection, the one as the positive law of gender representation, the other as an attempt to realize *in* that law the law's excess.

At a still deeper level, there remains a question as to whether moments such as these carry any decisive political weight at all. After all, Bloom's participation in the Ormond scenario concludes not with the musical obliteration of his personal/gender identity, but with the third major prolepsis of his voyeuristic exercise in "Nausicaa": a still more coercive imposition of the phallic I/eye, in which he absorbs the unwitting and unconsenting Lydia into his masturbatory fantasy world (11.1112–17).

These are all matters very much "to be constructed," not just in the interpretive sense but in the ethico-political sense as well. As an assemblage, Becoming-woman, unlike *écriture féminine*, necessarily crosses over into the next stage of productive activity and only exists in the crossing over. It authorizes Joyce's readers in a particular way, not only to decipher possible meanings or analyze structures, but to submit the book to an inventive displacement and ourselves to the very species of gender(ed) judgments that we have been rendering on Joyce's strategy of representation.

WRITING THE BODY (WITHOUT ORGANS)

Judgment as creative responsibility, that is the kind of authority that the sister episode of "Sirens," "Penelope," imposes upon the reader. In "Sirens," Joyce's immersion of the mythic female voice in the spectacle of modern womanly flesh opens a constructive space of resistance between narrativity and textuality. In "Penelope," Joyce inverts these coordinates. He immerses in a modern, nominally female voice purely *mythical* womanly flesh, flesh never to be *seen*, precisely what Deleuze and Guattari call "the body without organs": "a body without an image," without "totality," without teleology (*AO* 8). Joyce's purpose is to situate the episode entirely *within* that space of resistance, hence to situate the figure of woman neither within nor beyond the representational field but in the crossing over of dimensions, a strategy designed to unsituate gender itself. Staked not on the IS of essentialism, but on the "AND as extra-being, as interbeing" (*D*57), this episode takes the form of what Deleuze and Guattari call a "rhizome":

It is not a multiple derived from the One, or to which One is added ($N+1$) ... It has neither beginning nor end, but always a middle (milieu) from which it grows and which it overspills. It constitutes linear multiplicities with n dimensions having neither subject nor object which can be laid out on a plane of consistency and from which the One is always subtracted ($n-1$).(*TP*, 21)

The One which is always subtracted not from but *in* a rhizomatic format is the supplementary dimension of ontological consistency and fixity upon which the notion of lack and the possibility of re-presentation depend. Joyce's formal method of forgoing this supplementary ontological dimension is to dispense with the spatial and temporal framing devices that would ordinarily guarantee the abstract unity of the episode. In so doing, he effects a transfer of authority whereby the reader becomes implicitly but radically accountable for whatever representation, gender or otherwise, s/he discovers. I want to suggest, in this regard, that the most basic assumptions we generally make as readers of "Penelope," while not necessarily "wrong," are without sufficient warrant and tend to implicate us in the kind of gender injustice with which Joyce is sometimes charged.

"Penelope" has typically been construed as a species of interior speech, a representation of Molly's inner life or of a specific performance of that life. But in the process of assimilating the episode to what we readers have come to know, the "*monologue intérieur*" characteristic of the male protagonists, we have failed to respect discursive differences in accordance with which gender is being (re)constructed. For all the talk of otherness, our method of reading "Penelope" has turned it into a specular image of the Bloomiad.

Throughout the earlier stream of consciousness chapters, the visual or spatial register constitutes the prevailing site of narrative intrusion, the place where the presence of an author is felt securing ontological consistency and remarking the representational transaction. It is precisely this intrusion, apparently neutral, even banal, and yet carrying overtones of authorial omniscience and transcendence, that broaches the distinction between the private experiences of the characters and the object world, that constitutes the interior monologue *as* interior by setting over against it the furniture of an exterior domain. At the same time, throughout most of *Ulysses*, and especially in "Sirens," Joyce thematizes the visual–spatial register as the prevailing site for the social reification and materialization of women. By contrast, he gives "Penelope" its distinctive quality precisely by eliminating the visual–spatial register altogether. Now on the terms the novel establishes, for Joyce to eliminate this frame at just this point, and in specific connection to the question of female consciousness, signals something like a refusal of representation itself in its various aspects: a refusal of the subject–object, internal–external scission, which he has already earmarked as *both* invidiously gendered and fundamental to the very construction of gender hierarchy, *and* a refusal to identify himself with the position of the Law by inscribing these dichotomies. Without such a supplementary ontological dimension, in turn, Molly's "indispensable countersign" constitutes writing in the Derridean sense, not an *internal* speech or monologue, split off from the exterior milieu that delimits it, but a simultaneous comprehension and disruption of these polarities, "a middle (milieu)" unto itself, coterminous with its field of operation $(n-1)$, "from which it grows and overspills itself."

That is the lesson of the extraordinary outburst, "O Jamesy let me up out of this pooh" (*U* 18.1128), which refers Molly's countersign outward to Joyce, using a name he apparently used in addressing himself: "Easy now Jamesy" (*GJ* 17). With this remark, the "Penelope" episode "overspills" the bounds of the fictive universe in which Molly can be represented as a psychological ego communing with itself and "grows" into an assemblage with the existential space of the author, enfolding him in turn into the fiction. Instead of depicting, mimicking, or capturing (a) woman's voice, Joyce succeeds in author-izing it, in engineering a reversal of the authorial function whereby he is called, in the most personal terms, out of his own text, or rather out of a text that is no longer his "own." Having disappeared as a subjective narratorial presence, he reinstates himself in the "feminine" position, as an objectification of (dis)pleasure or negative value, installing a woman's voice in his place as creative agency. But since he does so through a productive assemblage across dimensions, thus breaking the magic circle of representation, exactly *what* gets authorized under the name of woman's voice is always in-construction, i.e. always already in place as a cultural construct and always still to be constructed from that place, much as Molly Bloom already occupies a determined locale in the novel's social world and yet is only to be "found" in "Penelope" crossing over into other dimensions. The woman whose voice Joyce authorizes is not woman in general, a specific woman, (a) man's idea of woman, woman as type, woman as a figure or metaphor or alterity, or even woman exclusive of man, including Joyce himself. But neither is she simply some other thing, outside of the ongoing inventive displacement of these and like categories.

Joyce's refusal of representation in "Penelope" makes such inventive displacement the exclusive responsibility of the reader, and the simultaneous indispensability and insufficiency of the materials at hand make the responsibility an ethical and political rather than merely epistemological one. Indeed, it does not seem too much to say that the sexual politics of "Penelope" exist entirely as a reflection of our own sexual politics, whatever they may be, including our construction of the limits and biases endemic to the male construction of women.

The layers of contradiction in "Penelope," systematically interpolated throughout the revision process, subserve precisely this function. On the one hand, they not only enable variable constructions of Molly, depending upon the evidence selected, they *compel* partial and so unwarrantable constructions of her as a condition of reading the chapter. On the other, the law of contradiction is predicated on a given *punctum* or a decidable *period* of time (A cannot equal and not equal A at the *same time*), and "Penelope" officially stands outside the temporal spectrum altogether, which is why it has no periods or punctuation. Contradictions in "Penelope" are thus entirely an effect of our interpretive modality, which imposes a continuous, extended present, roughly consonant with the time of the reading experience, upon events that properly have no linear progression, coherent periodization, or chronological order whatever. That is, these contradictions are not already "there" in "Penelope," but emerge with our reduction of its textual whirl to a representational narrative line or "flow," characterized by, of all things, the three dramatic unities (action, time, place). Derek Attridge has objected to the recent fixation on "flow" as a metaphor for the language of "Penelope" because, he says, the reader automatically supplies the missing punctuation, bringing the prose into articulate sequence.[52] But it is in fact this same interpretive automatism that preselects the image of flow out of the myriad possibilities for arranging this atemporal discourse.[53] Accordingly, the most widely accepted premise concerning the episode, that Joyce represents Molly as the very embodiment of contradiction – whether because he fell in with the conventional stereotype of women as illogical or anticipated the fashionable stereotype of women as other-logical – rests upon stereotyping procedures foundational to the act of reading and so to every strain of ethnic and gender injustice.

This too is sovereign mockery "uncovering the limit of discourse." It is not staged in the text, as in "Sirens," but instilled in its audience; and it is not produced as a vertiginous exceeding of the *phallogos*, but induced as a vertiginous sense of responsibility for the limits the *phallogos* imposes on our judgment. It is also therefore a call to ad-just them.

CODA

The provisional space of resistance between representational narrativity and counter-representational textuality, which "Sirens" stages and "Penelope" inhabits, may be taken as an exemplary case of the ambivalent relationship that defines Joyce's writing generally and keys the running debate we have seen on the nature of his gender politics: the always undecidable relationship between the transgressive and reinscriptive operations he performs on the phallogocentric economy of discourse. How does this relationship unfold? What is the substantive character of this relationship, its ethico-political dimensions?

Regarding the first, methodological question, one might begin with the compatibility of Joyce's High Modernist aesthetic – with its conflation of tradition and experiment, the archetype and the innovation, cliché and neologism – and his double-ended sexual politics. By subjecting decidedly conventional gender roles and relations to defamiliarizing modes of formal and stylistic composition, Joyce perpetuates certain stereotyped images even as he contests the gender system that produces them, as we have seen in the case of the Kearneys and the Rowans alike, and he likewise dispels certain individual stereotypes even as he underwrites that larger system, as we saw with regard to Amalia Popper in *Giacomo Joyce*. Insofar as it registers the play of difference and repetition informing our experience, Joyce's so-called mythic method works to denaturalize and unsettle received gender associations by exploring the heterogeneity of their construction, but in the process of doing so, it submits them to an "endless vicus of recirculation," thereby reinforcing their hold on the political unconscious. The relationship of narrative line and textual whirl in "Sirens" neatly encapsulates this process of iteration (other/repetition), the former addressing and thus recycling what the latter destabilizes.

The second, substantive question is more difficult to answer. Indeed, because the inquiry necessarily embraces the biunivocal logic of phallocentrism while putting the authority of that logic at stake, it cannot in principle yield an ultimate solution. Any determinate relation between transgression and reinscription of the economy governing such relations is always already in the position of repeating one of the related alternatives and thus of reproducing and extending the oppositional framework at large. This abyssal structure is analogous to and interconnected with the double bind immanent in the liberal conceit of justice: its indissolubly yet incommensurably positivistic and utopian make-up.

On one side, striking a balance or staging a contest between the de- and restabilization of gender hierarchies entails the arrogation of a (re)centered perspective whence these gestures could be construed as distinct, opposable, gendered in their own right, and needful of adjudication. The masterful erection of such an abstract, universal vantage, a site of identification and judgment beyond the variables of gender, is of course a classic patriarchal ploy for installing an elect part, man, as representative of the whole, human, and then teasing out scrupulous gender symmetries from that fundamentally skewed frame of reference. In symbolic shorthand, to represent the purport of Joyce's work in this manner would be to restore him to the role of O'Madden Burke, reducing the ambivalence of his sexual politics to an androcentric positivism. On the other side, attempting to instance or articulate the mutual contaminations of the de- and restabilizing gestures is to sustain at a further discursive regress the destabilizing endeavor, subverting not just specific forms of gender opposition and stratification but any possible fulcral point from which such gendered distinctions might be secured. This sovereign decentering of the logic of gender, which is to say the logic of (male) privilege, points the way to a truly plural sexuality, a reciprocity of sexually inflected modes of being without a corresponding reduction of their difference. To portray the significance of Joyce's work along these lines would be to enshrine him once more in the role of ALP, remaking his ambivalent sexual politics in the image of a feminist utopianism.

Like the aspects of justice they represent, these alternative formulations are *supplements* of one another; each compensates for the other, makes good its deficiencies as an account, but supplants it in the same motion. Both are essential to a satisfactory comprehension of Joyce's treatment of gender, but as they clash on whether or not that treatment issues in an ethico-juridical synthesis, they cannot themselves be reconciled in a more global perspective. They are jointly imperative and mutually exclusive. What their impossible relationship indicates is that Joyce reproduces the sexual *differend* in the act of representing it. The gender ethics posed in his text at once insist upon and resist being "phrased." The law of genre passes into the law of gender.

As a result, the performative dimension of reading Joyce on gender is brought to the fore. This turns out to be a double-edged sword. Because the reader is called upon to frame an ethico-political position out of symbiotic but contradictory alternatives, s/he enjoys extra-ordinary interpretive latitude: after all, this is not a problem that can be solved, inductively or deductively, but a crux, an impasse, that must be negotiated imaginatively. By the same token, however, the interpretive option that the reader exercises and the principles of selection s/he employs cannot be justified on strictly epistemic grounds, either inductive or deductive, and so must be understood as already carrying a certain ethico-political charge, a solution of interests, desires and attitudes that have crystallized in and are open to morally effective judgments or evaluations. In inscribing his own ethical double bind, Joyce deputizes the reader as a creative agent; in deputizing the reader as a creative agent on this score, Joyce simultaneously interpellates the reader as an ethical being. He thus prompts the reader to confront the creative opportunity ethical consideration affords and the ethical responsibility creative labor incurs. At the same time, he underlines the mutual dependence of ethics and aesthetics upon the condition of undecidability. Paradoxically, in setting a structural limit to being and knowledge, in requiring of interpretation something other than programmed response or purely logical deduction, the element of undecidability makes genuine decisions at once possible and necessary.

In this strategy, we can discern Joyce's mature rebuttal of the aesthetic pietism that permeated late-Victorian culture and aroused in him an antipathy which helped to mold and energize his literary apprenticeship. In his collegiate essays and polemics, Joyce discounts the "special ethical claims" traditionally made for literature as at best incidental to the properly aesthetic project of contemplating intensely "the truth of the imagination and the world" (*CW* 43, 45). He thereby participates in the Modernist drift from a pragmatic to an objective aesthetic orientation, from an emphasis on social effect to an emphasis on internal design. As we have seen, however, Joyce's major work treats aesthetics and ethics as correlative forms of imaginative activity, discovering in undecidability an integral nexus between them which beggars by comparison the merely instrumental connection espoused in the demand that art serve to inculcate moral lessons or political credos. Joyce comes to rely on the radical coimplication of these two registers, rather than their autonomous jurisdiction, to confute "the antique school ... that the end of art is to elevate, instruct and amuse" (*CW* 43). In keeping with this theoretical shift, Joyce's novels anticipate the postmodernist attempt to rehabilitate the pragmatic mode by exploring and embracing those principles previously taken to undermine it: the plurality of perspective, the polyvalence of language, and the performativity of the law. Instead of elaborating, for the reader's edification, a particular model of sexual justice, the Joycean text enacts, with the reader's collaboration, something akin to the ethico-juridical condition itself.

Epilogue: trial and mock trial in Joyce

The trial is a dominant motif in Joyce's work, the court a recurrent site for the exploration and enactment of gender, racial, and generational politics. Joyce regularly represents juridical or quasi-juridical proceedings to this end throughout his career. At the conclusion of Chapter 1, I catalogue the most salient of these trial scenarios – the impromptu trial of Father Dolan in *A Portrait*, the double trial of Bloom in "Circe," the Festy King trial and the Anita–Honophurious trial in *Finnegans Wake* – and I should like to close with an analysis of their rhetorical form and political implications.

Each of these trials represents a strongly parodistic moment in the text, and is represented as a site of comic excess and carnivalesque exaggeration. The boys at Clongowes mimic the address of Roman law in order to mount a mock inversion of the institutional hierarchy of the College, and they punctuate their effort with riotous cheers and gestures that answer to Bakhtin's conception of carnival misrule: a merging into a collective body, a gay parody of authority figures, "festive laughter ... gay, triumphant but at the same time mocking and deriding," the nondistinction of participants and spectators, etc.[1] It is, further, in terms of such holiday misrule, with its reversal of social values, that we can understand the momentary promotion of Stephen Dedalus from locker-room misfit to big man on campus.

Bloom's trials in "Circe" take the notorious trials of Oscar Wilde as a background context for parodying the evidentiary procedures and declamatory rhetoric of the British courtroom,[2] showing them to be little more than a legitimating mask of ideological violence, the vehicles whereby the received stereotypes of patriarchal and imperialistic discourse become the stuff of apparently rational judgment. Holding a "fullblown waterlily," a Wildean touch, Bloom likewise undergoes feminization, infantilization, and bestialization, all couched in the lexicon of a newly dominant medical–forensic science,[3] which constructs him as an object of ridicule to be "howled down" by the "laughing hyenas" in attendance. In Bakhtin's terms, Bloom emerges as a debased modern form of the grotesque Rabelaisian body.

The Festy King trial, while drawing upon Wilde's ordeal, retails the Maamtrasna murder trial of Myles Joyce,[4] the gross inequity of which Joyce had already detailed in "Ireland at the Bar" (*CW* 197–200). It specifically parodies the processes of judicial interrogation and cross-examination, casting them as what Susan Schwartzlander has called a "structured misunderstanding."[5] Designated "a child of Maam" (*FW* 85), short for Maamtrasna, Festy King/Beggar Festy makes explicit the *festi*val or carnivalesque aspect of the inquisition. He is "wearing, besides stains, rents and patches ... a policeman's corkscrew trowswers all out of true" (*FW* 85) and a carnival mask of "any luvial peatsmoor" (86) on his face. The "policeman's corkscrew trowswers all out of true" theatricalize what Bakhtin calls the "gay parody" of the symbols of "official reason" and "official truth,"[6] while the mask, which Bakhtin takes "to contain the playful element of life,"[7] marks the intimate alienation of the face from itself, the inability of the face to behold itself except as other. Since the face functions as the sign and focus of social identity, the appearance of the mask in this legal context tends to subvert the notion of in-dividuality, hence in-dividual responsibility, upon which modern liberal jurisprudence is founded. This is all the more relevant in the case of Festy's mask, which, being made of mud, foregrounds the imbrication of the juridical concept of the abstract individual, centered on the face, with the carnivalesque experience of the primacy of the material–bodily stratum. Not coincidentally, among the charges against Festy is "making fesses immodst of his forces on the field" (*FW* 85), i.e. making faces and making feces, or makes faces that are feces, or making feces of his face, in any case of instituting a profound confusion between the image of ideal subjectivity and the image of material abjectivity. In other words, he is hauled into court not for lawlessness alone but for disturbing the basic distinctions necessary for the law as we know it to function.

With the trial of Anita and Honophurious, Joyce returns to the Roman origins of British law to parody its fundamentally materialistic nature, exemplified in the bourgeois marriage contract.

Here the mutually alienated spheres of public and domestic life are yoked together under the double value of property/propriety, a value comically shown in this episode to institute and aggravate the sexual degradation and depredation it is supposed to contain.

Taken together, these examples indicate that the trial in Joyce is always a mock trial. My aim is to determine why this is so or, more specifically, what is at stake in Joyce's frequent and quite consistent linkage between humor and the law, justice and the joke – a linkage, incidentally, which includes not only parody but paronomasia, especially in *Finnegans Wake*, of course, where the Norwegian captain's suit of clothes is also a suit of matrimony and a lawsuit, where to court is also to go to court, and where the bar always refers simultaneously to the space of legal judgment and the space of drunken excess. (The Festy King, for example, "appeared in dry dock" "soaked in methylated" (*FW* 85).)

Let me propose, first of all, that the juridical, in its liberal mode, and the comical, particularly those forms that Joyce affected, partake of a structural symmetry, a symmetry he may well have divined. As I argued in the opening chapter, the import of the democratic revolution lay in its evacuation of the ultimate site of social and political authority;[8] and because any given body of law is thereby deprived of any ultimate or ultimately secure grounds of legitimacy, it can only come into being as law rather than mere contingency or violence by constituting such grounds retroactively through the performative gesture of its own inauguration. Both the retroactive and the performative elements of this gesture, it will be remembered, are crucial. No legal agency can *simply* rely on a final ground of authority, for none exists outside of the ongoing performative institution thereof; but no such performative institution of such grounds is possible unless it assumes those grounds to be already in existence. As Derrida has noted, the law possesses a metaleptic temporality, positing as a juridically pertinent or decisive entity that which legitimates its own positing capacity.[9] His exemplar of this dynamic is the Declaration of Independence, in which Jefferson must assume the independent status of the colonies/states in order to authorize their claim to independence.[10] In the established nation-state, in turn, the continuance of popular sovereignty depends upon a body of law that takes popular sovereignty as its own constituting authority.

This enabling misprision of the law, its necessary movement

through error to achieve its truth, relates every enactment of the law in its very inception to the rhetorical modes of parody and paranomasia. Of course, this is assuming what I will now state outright: that the countersong of parody and the countername of the pun likewise unfold under the aegis and in the form of originals, precedents if you will, which themselves exist as such only in the various attempts to invoke, cite, repeat, and deform them. In a remarkable paper on Joyce and film, Nicholas Miller has paraphrased Lacan to suggest that "There is no textual relation,"[11] and this would be my way of interpreting his words: that each text establishes relationships with other texts, critical, reverential, or otherwise, only by assimilating them to itself, embedding them in its own marrow, so that they are not "other" texts any more; and yet, paradoxically, it is only under such conditions that these other texts come to be in the first place. In this textual ambivalence that precludes textual relation reside the *formal* conditions of the humor attaching to parody and paronomasia alike, what Koestler called bisociation, Bakhtin double-directed discourse, and Freud duplicity,[12] the vertiginous sense of a doubleness that is both proper and improper at the same time, a part of and apart from the word or text in question.

At this stage of analysis, then, we might say that Joyce does not link the juridical and the comical so much as juxtapose them as a way of demystifying the principle of humor already at work as a structural possibility of the solemnity of the law. He all but remarks as much in the "Circe" trial. With Bloom being pilloried mercilessly, his defense lawyer, J. J. O'Molloy, rises to deliver a "pained protest": "This is no place for indecent levity at the expense of an erring mortal disguised in liquor. [Note the bar/bar pun here.] We are not in a bear garden nor at an Oxford rag nor is this a travesty of justice" (*U* 15.939–42). Every time I have read the last line cited, I have felt a twinge of anxious confusion. Why is O'Molloy saying, this is not a travesty of justice, while complaining of "indecent levity" more suitable to a bear garden or an Oxford rag? Why doesn't he declare "This is a travesty of justice"? Unless in the textual unconscious of "Circe," where the repressive reign of logical binarism collapses, O'Molloy inevitably speaks both the conventional sacredness of the law and its underlying impropriety to itself. If judicial procedures are never supposed to fall into mere parodies of themselves, travesties, and yet the law is parodistic at its core, in the manner I have outlined, then travesty, improper self-parody, is strangely interior to these procedures, an improper constituent of their being. O'Molloy's ensuing words confirm the point. They continue his defense of Bloom, which triggered his complaint about the travesty, precisely by continuing the travesty he complained of:

My client is an infant, a poor foreign immigrant... The trumped up misdemeanor was due to a momentary aberration of heredity, brought on by hallucination, such familiarities as the alleged guilty occurrence being quite permitted in my client's native place, the land of the Pharaoh... I would deal in especial with atavism... His submission is that he is of Mongolian extraction and irresponsible for his actions. Not all there, in fact. (*U* 15.943–55)

This convergence and cohabitation of the proper with the improper serves to expose all values, indeed the category of value itself, to what Bakhtin calls a "gay relativity," the generic hallmark of the carnivalesque.[13] Joyce's representation of a trial like Bloom's, which is to say his parody of a trial like Wilde's, would seem to suggest that liberal jurisprudence rests not on a fixed set of oppressive values but on the repressive dissimulation of the relativity of all values. Such an ideological formation, being inherently defensive, is tremendously vulnerable to comic parody at one level. But because the truth of parody is also the hidden truth of jurisprudence, because the repressive dissimulation of relativity is itself based on that relativity and so can take any and all forms, can undergo the most protean self-revision, this ideological formation is at another level quite immune to comic parody. Liberal jurisprudence can always be parodied, but the parody must be done incessantly and on an always different footing.

In her well-known work on postmodern parody, Linda Hutcheon tries to develop an account of the estranged intimacy of a parody and its precedents which I have characterized as textual ambivalence without textual relation.[14] She effectively refutes the supposition that parody as a genre entails a critical attitude toward its source materials and the correlative proposition associated with Bakhtin that parody bears a necessarily liberatory valence. In their stead, she articulates the pragmatics of parody as one of "authorized transgression," a formulation which takes the radical enfolding of primary and parodistic texts into one another, their mutual shimmering between figure and ground, to entail a political bidirectionality as well, a shimmering between reaffirmation and resistance. On the one hand, this formulation both poses and begs the question: What is being transgressed, given the imaginary status of any law or norm wholly anterior to the parody itself? But at the same time, it serves as a useful reminder that both parody/paronomasia and juridical enactment/decision not only institute performatively their own precedents qua precedents, but also institute their own disjunction from these precedents qua precedents. That is to say, both rhetorical species operate through an internal splitting or dehiscence that establishes the norm in the act of diverging from it. They are not just an authorized transgression, they are also a transgressive authorizing, or rather they each figure a relation between authorized transgression and transgressive authorizing.

This is the symmetry between humor and law raised to another plane. But it is also a plane upon which they can be teased apart once more. For humor and the law institute this relation between distance from and identification with the origin in contrary ways. As I suggested earlier, in what gets called the pursuit of justice under law, the distance between the law and its instantiation is open *only* to be closed, *only* to allow the identification of model and instance to be recognized. The authority of an always imaginary law depends equally upon its apparent purchase on individual enactments and decisions, hence its difference from them, and upon the effectiveness of this purchase, hence their external identification with it. The "para" forms of humor, on the other hand, identify with their precedents precisely to enforce some sense of their *internal* difference, not to say dissidence from them. As Derek Attridge has written of paronomasia, "it is ambiguity *unashamed of itself*... the pun is a product of a context deliberately constructed to *enforce* an ambiguity, to render impossible the choice between meanings."[15] The law splits against itself in order to facilitate and authorize decision, even as this split inflicts each decision with a liability to interpretive self-revision; but comic parody or paronomasia splits against itself in order to impede decision, to trigger the possibility of oscillating self-revision at the *moment* of decision. Logically symmetrical, the juridical and the comical have a different temporality. It is this temporal difference, on one side, that allows comic parody–paronomasia to expose what the juridical veils through narrative metalepsis and extension: the sublimity of judgment, the fact that judgment has no ultimate grounds of operation and needs none.

At the local level, accordingly, comic parody can serve to puncture the hegemonic illusion of the legitimacy of any particular grounds of authority and so can be harnessed on this basis as an instrument of political resistance. It can induce a shift from the pursuit of justice under law to an interrogation of the justice of the law. In the case of Anita and Honophurious (alias Pepigi), for example, the insurgent son, Shem, as Judge Jeremy Doyler, turns the "estreat[ing]" (*FW* 575) of his father's "cogniscences" into the cheating of them and turns his own treason into "treuson" (German for loyal son) through a careful parody of legal language that opens several key terms to an ambiguity that cannot be resolved. The "judaces" (Latin for factfinders)[16] are also Judases, perpetrators of a treason that Shem's apparent treason neatly redresses by "reversing the findings of the lower correctional" (575). Moreover, he holds that "mammy's *mancipium* act" (576) does not apply by reading it neither as a slavery or mancipium (Roman law)[17] act nor as a manumission (emancipation) act, either one of which would, in context, have upheld Pepigi's claim, but as indistinguishably one and the other. Doyler is thus left "reserving judgment" (575) with the words "[w]ill you, won't you, pango with Pepigi? Not for Nancy, how dare you do!" (576). This moment of judicial oscillation in effect frees Anita after all, while indicating, in accordance with Shem's revolutionary oedipal designs (his "derring-do"), that she "dare not" use her freedom to "pango with Pepigi."[18]

At the broader metalevel, however, para-humor can puncture the illusion of legitimate authority itself and as such, it resists political resistance no less than hegemonic authority, insofar as the former is staked upon its comparative legitimacy vis-à-vis the latter. Accordingly, while Joyce's humor is always political, it is also generally ambivalent, a vehicle for enforcing his recognition that the political as the pursuit of justice is inevitably doubly inscribed, complicit through conflict, authorizing the law it transgresses. Thus, if we look at the examples I have provided, their humor for the reader depends on his or her temporary identification with forces s/he would likely prefer to disown. The humor of the Clongowes "trial" for the reader derives from the boys' absurd overestimation of the efficacy of Stephen's complaint to Conmee, and our laughter, I suspect, is a laughter of recognition which only occurs once Simon Dedalus relates the tale of the Jesuits' amusement over Dolan's "sentence":

Mr. Dedalus imitated the mincing nasal tone of the provincial.

—Father Dolan and I, when I told them all at dinner about it, Father Dolan and I had a great laugh over it. *You better mind yourself, Father Dolan*, said I, *or young Dedalus will send you up for twice nine*. We had a famous laugh together over it. Ha! Ha! Ha! (*AP* 72)

Our laughter, in other words, is inseparable from that of the church/state complex embodied in the school fathers.

More disturbingly, our laughter at Bloom's plight in "Circe" is at some level a matter of finding humor in the politically vicious stereotypes into which he is projected: deviant "black sheep" (*U* 15.901), "plebeian Don Juan" (1064), "Barefoot, pigeon-breasted" "Mongolian" (954–7), "Ikey Mo" (1040–1), "the new womanly man" (1778–9), and a "female impersonator" (3010), not to mention a prostitute pandering to "Gomorrahan vices" (3122) and of course a transvestite showing off "in various poses of surrender" (2992). In particular, I would like to call attention to the way Joyce capitalizes upon the *ontological underdetermination* of the "Circe" episode in order to solicit our compromised laughter, our willing suspension of value(s), which is also our willingness to go, like Lanty McHale's goat, down the road a piece with any of them. Bloom at once *suffers* and merely *fantasizes* that he suffers racial, gender, sexual, class, and cultural degradation; and in the space between the reality and the fantasy, between his suffering and his self-pity, is lodged the reader's license to laugh, but to laugh uncomfortably.

The Festy King or "child of Maam" trial, finally, complicates still further the overlap of (dis)identification endemic to the para-forms of humor. Taken specifically as a parody of the "sensational trial" at Maamtrasna (*CW* 197), this episode not only dialogizes and confuses the politico-symbolic value of its various textual motifs, it also and more disturbingly confounds the possibility of attaching a determinant political value to any given enunciative position.

Like most matters of import in Joyce, this disturbance unfolds at the level of the name, here the name of Joyce itself. He first wrote of the Maamtrasna trial in an Italian-language newspaper article translated as "Ireland at the Bar." In that essay, he recounts the strange and pathetic plight of a member of "the ancient tribe of the Joyces" (*CW* 197), Myles Joyce, who in the year of James Joyce's birth was convicted of murder and condemned to death in a court whose English laws and customs he did not share and whose English language he could not understand. His long histrionic protestations and explanations on the witness stand were converted into dry English monosyllables by the court translator. As Jeanne Flood has proposed, the nub of this travesty for Joyce lay "in the interplay of law and language," the preemption of a properly Irish subjectivity through the nullification of the Gaelic tongue and the culture it bespoke.[19] In other words, Joyce's essay recognizes the Maamtrasna proceedings to be an instance of the *differend* writ large and in blood. But this same insight paradoxically served to interrupt Joyce's sense of identification with the victim that ethnic and tribal brotherhood (not to mention the sort of natal coincidence Joyce fetishized) might have been expected to produce. Thus, it is wrong to suppose, as Flood goes on to do, that in writing this article, Joyce was affirming in a straightforward way "the very kinship to dead generations" of indigenous Irish folk "that Stephen Dedalus renounced."[20] To the contrary, the vital trait enabling Joyce to portray the tragifarcical proceedings against his namesake so eloquently – his mastery not only of the language in which they were held but a whole spectrum of European languages, such as Italian – insists upon his dramatic sociocultural distance from the figure memorialized. Joyce acknowledges as much in what may well be the defining moment of the essay:

The figure of this dumbfounded old man, a remnant of a civilization not ours, deaf and dumb before his judge, is a symbol of the Irish nation at the bar of public opinion. Like him, she is unable to appeal to the modern conscience of England and other countries. (*CW* 198)

Even as Joyce renders Joyce a personification of the Irish nation, he associates himself, as one of the "twenty million Irishmen scattered all over the world" (*CW* 199), with the "civilization," the modernity, of his Italian audience ("not ours"). In so doing, Joyce discloses a division in the Irishness for which Myles Joyce seems to function as the unifying symbol, and he even discloses a dehiscence in the name or symbol, Joyce. When Joyce takes up the Maamtrasna trial in the *Wake*, the internal fissure of the Irish estate, as reflected in the symbolic mandate of being a Joyce, comes to the fore.

As John Garvin has demonstrated, the Festy King trial refers insistently to Maamtrasna.[21] Not only is Festy explicitly designated "a child of Maam," he is presented "deposing for his exution with all the fluors of sparse in the royal Irish vocabulary," a phrase which brings together the Irish tongue of Myles Joyce, his role as tribal patriarch, the sparseness of his vocabulary in the "royal" language,

English, the reduction of his flowers of speech to sparseness in the translation process, the excesses of the Royal Irish Constabulary, and the idea that his death was a foregone conclusion given his method of self-expression ("deposing for his exution" (*FW* 85–6)).

As for the trial itself, it is a critical commonplace that the Festy King trial features a certain oedipal confusion of the principals. The Festy King figure, a variant of HCE, is said to comprise "the whole padderjagmartin tripiezite suet" (*FW* 86), which is to say HCE himself *and* his filial plaintiffs Shem and Shaun. What is pertinent for us in this oedipal entanglement is its symbolic fidelity to the "supreme confusion of persons, motives, and meaning" that "clusters around this crime, most particularly around the name of Joyce."[22] Not only were the defendants, Myles and others, predominantly Joyces, but the murder victims were Joyces and certain of the Irish informers to the British constabulary were also Joyces. Whether conceived in terms of ethnic, sept, or national allegiances, to be a Joyce qua Joyce in this case was to be divided against oneself and complicit with one's most intimate adversaries; it was to find the hybridity native to the colonial estate inscribed along and across bloodlines and grotesquely exaggerated. Via the complexities of tribal consanguinity and incestuous rivalry, the ultimate victim of the piece, Myles Joyce, was in some sense implicated in his own victimization, much as the Earwickers are all implicated in one another's "sins," and much as the Irish people at large (whom Myles Joyce personifies in "Ireland at the Bar") were always to some degree responsible for their own colonization – a point Joyce stresses throughout his career.

Of course, the issues of language disability and identity instability are by no means unrelated. From a psychoanalytic standpoint, the individual enters upon the universalizing dimension of subjectivity, which is to say social identity, by acceding to the relevant cultural language, a rite of passage which unfolds concurrently with the solution of that incestuous entanglement known as the oedipus complex. And as Flood correctly argues, Myles Joyce "could not distinguish himself from the incestuous tangle of Joyces involved in the crime, victims...murderers...[and] accusers," primarily because he lacked the relevant cultural language, the language of the law, and was consequently denied a place in that symbolic network.[23] It is precisely on these grounds, in turn, that another of the tribe of Joyces, James, does manage to distinguish himself from this incestuous tangle, which he consigns to a pre-modern "civilization not ours" (*CW* 198). His parody of Maamtrasna in the *Wake*'s "child of Maam" (*FW* 86) trial would seem to reiterate and extend this self-distinguishing gesture. For if "Ireland at the Bar" centers upon Myles Joyce "having no English" and being provided with no proper translator, the Wakean parody of Maamtrasna showcases Joyce's comparative mastery of languages precisely as an exercise in *simultaneous translation*. For its part, simultaneous translation has always represented the *ne plus ultra* in the negotiation of disparate idioms and cultural perspectives, i.e. of the kind of *differend* that Maamtrasna typifies. Thus, even as the cross-examination of W. P. (*FW* 88–9) deteriorates into a series of virtual nonsequiturs indicating the mutual incomprehension of the interlocutors, the event is coded in such a way as to account, however undecidably, for every possible meaning they might be taken to intend.

But if the "child of Maam" trial marks an irreducible distance between Joyce and Joyce, Myles and James, as subjects of language, it also poses an irreducible connection between them on precisely the same grounds. Where Myles knew no English and so was murdered, James "murdered all the English he knew" in response (*FW* 93). After all, the mode of translation Joyce essays in the *Wake* is so fully simultaneous as to dissolve his benchmark tongue, English, into the other languages it encounters. The result is a kind of transverbal parody which is also, in Joyce's own terms, "nat language at any sinse of the world" (*FW* 83). Extremes meet, as it were, at both ends. James and Myles share a last name, the signifier of legal identity, which in the event proves to be a site of difference and division rather than unanimity. But they also have in common a certain legal difference or difference with the law, a predicament of marginalization from the official circuit of the signifier. Whereas the marginalization of Myles Joyce was absolute, complete exile from the legally constituted network of meaning, the marginalization of James Joyce was what I have been calling *radical*, a subject position between the margin and the mainstream: between colony and metropole, Dublin and western Ireland, continental residence and island home, masculine hegemony and feminized abjection, and in between the often incommensurable sociolects informing each circumstance. In this sort of cultural position, all translations are in some sense simultaneous.

At once a counter-song and a beside-song, parody expresses both the advantages and the drawbacks inherent in such a border zone.

Just as parody necessarily depends upon the law that it nevertheless transgresses, so Joyce can only stand outside the individual, politically charged enunciative positions that his text unfolds by remaining within and determined by the economy of their interplay. To all of the bitterly opposed Joyces of Maamtrasna, he remains at once a counter-Joyce and a beside-Joyce, politically allied and disaffiliated with each in the irruptive moment of his humor. That is to say, the infinite translatability of James Joyce's text, no less than the untranslatability of Myles Joyce's testimony, entails a breakdown of political agency, wresting from every utterance its ironizing alterity. Whereas Myles' deficiency of language made his trial a virtual model of the problems that heteroglossia and incommensurability pose for the administration of justice, James' proficiency shows this heteroglossia and incommensurability to be already at work producing a certain inevitable indeterminacy in the law itself. His para-humor uncovers a signifying excess *in* the law that spells a deficit *of* the law, its structural inconsistency with its own ideal of legitimacy, just as Myles' deficit in law, his ignorance of the duly authorized language, is the site of certain excesses of the law, the manifestation of this inconsistency in its grossest form.

What Joyce's Wakean parody serves to reveal, then, is that in appealing for justice in a foreign language, the language of otherness, Myles Joyce not only symbolized the Irish nation at the bar, he exemplified the appeal for justice as such, insofar as this appeal can only be answered by that *in* language which is most foreign *to* language, by the otherness of language to itself. All of this is to say that the appeal for justice can never really be answered at all, which is why it must be repeated endlessly and in endlessly variable forms. We cannot go to the heart of justice, making things "square" once and for all; we can only orbit the notion of justice, "circling the square" forever (*FW* 186), a necessity structured into the narrative and stylistic method of the *Wake* as a whole.

Notes

1 JUSTICE UNBOUND

1 J. Derrida, "The Law of Genre," in *On Narrative*, ed. W. J. T. Mitchell, University of Chicago Press, 1981, 61.

2 *Ibid*.

3 S. Fish, "The Law Wishes to Have a Formal Existence," Address given at the Deconstruction and the Possibility of Justice Conference, New York, 1989. Theories of autopoesis derive from the discipline of biology, where the classic generalist text is H. Maturana and F. Varela, *The Tree of Knowledge*, Boston, MA: New Science, 1988. For its most notable legal application see N. Luhman, "Closure and Openness: On Reality in the World of Law," in *Autopoetic Law: A New Approach to Law and Society*, ed. G. Teubner, Berlin: de Gruyter, 1981, 337ff. and "Operational and Strategic Coupling," *Cardozo Law Review* 13.1 (1991), 1–38.

4 Quoted in C. Norris, *Paul De Man: Deconstruction and the Critique of Aesthetic Ideology*, New York: Routledge & Kegan Paul, 1988, 133–4.

5 It is not that the law is necessarily general while justice is always and radically singular, as Jacques Derrida has recently argued in J. Derrida, "Force of Law," *Deconstruction and the Possibility of Justice, Cardozo Law Review* 11.5–6 (1990), 949. No such Maginot line can be erected between justice and the law without destroying them both: radical generality and radical singularity are but alternate versions of the utterly inconceivable. It is rather that the notion of justice both demands and promises a resolution of the contesting levels of generality, with their "divergent interior norms," which are at work in any singular circumstance of legal application and judgment. See B. H. Smith, "The Complex Agony of Injustice," *Cardozo Law Review* 13.4 (1991), 1274.

6 The irreducibly rhetorical and partisan nature of the law has been at the center of the controversy surrounding the Critical Legal Studies movement, in which deconstructive insights and methodologies have been applied to every aspect of the discipline of jurisprudence. See R. Unger, *The Critical Legal Studies Movement*, Cambridge, MA: Harvard University Press, 1983; S. Fish, *Doing What Comes Naturally*, Durham, NC: Duke University Press, 1989. For a more strictly philosophical

approach, see J. Derrida, "The Politics of Friendship," *Journal of Philosophy* 88 (1988), 632–48, where he asserts that an "assymmetrical and heteronomical curvature of a sort of originary sociality is ... perhaps the very essence of the law" (633). For a more politically oriented approach, see B. H. Smith, "The Unquiet Judge: Activism without Objectivism in Law and Politics," *Annals of Scholarship* 9 (1992), 111–33.

7 C. Lefort, *Democracy and Political Theory*, Minneapolis: University of Minnesota Press, 1988, 39.

8 See J. Derrida, "Declarations of Independence," *New Political Science* 15 (1986), 7–20; P. De Man, *Allegories of Reading*, New Haven: Yale University Press, 1979, 246–77.

9 M. Sandel, *Liberalism and the Limits of Justice*, Cambridge University Press, 1982, 17.

10 See S. Weber, "In the Name of the Law," *Deconstruction and the Possibility of Justice, Cardozo Law Review* 11.5–6 (1990), 1523.

11 C. Mouffe, "Radical Democracy," in *Universal Abandon*, ed. A. Ross, Minneapolis: University of Minnesota Press, 1988, 33.

12 As paraphrased by J.-F. Lyotard in *The Lyotard Reader*, ed. A. Benjamin, Oxford: Basil Blackwell, 1989, 286.

13 Derrida, "Force of Law," 935–41.

14 For Kant's regulative or transcendental Idea, see I. Kant, *The Critique of Pure Reason*, New York: St. Martin's, 1929, 308–483.

15 L. Krieger, "Through a Glass Darkly," *Hypatia* 2.1 (1987), 45–61; E. Wolgast, *Equality and the Rights of Woman*, Ithaca, NY: Cornell University Press, 55–76.

16 E. Levinas, *Otherwise than Being or Beyond Essence*, The Hague: Martinus Nijhoff, 1981, 160–1.

17 Derrida, "The Law of Genre," 61.

18 J.-F. Lyotard, *The Differend*, Minneapolis: University of Minnesota Press, 1988, 1–31.

19 *Ibid.*, 13.

20 *Ibid.*, 136.

21 *Ibid.*, 9–10.

22 For justice as a virtual reality, see J. Rawls, "Justice as Fairness: Political Not Metaphysical," *Philosophy and Public Affairs* 14.3 (1988), 235–6. For justice as a contextually limited good, see A. MacIntyre, *After Virtue*, University of Notre Dame Press, 1981, 367–98. For justice as an eternally revisable ideal, see D. Cornell, "From the Lighthouse," *Deconstruction and the Possibility of Justice, Cardozo Law Review* 11.5–6 (1990), 1687–1715. For the "permanently unresolved question," see C. Mouffe, "Rawls: Political Philosophy without Politics," in *Universalism and Communitarianism*, ed. D. Rasmussen, Cambridge, MA: MIT Press, 1990, 229.

23 The standard for contractarian models of jurisprudence is John Rawls, *A Theory of Justice*, Cambridge, MA: Harvard University Press, 1971. For

a feminist jurisprudence sympathetic to Rawlsian contractarianism, but nonetheless acute in its reservations, see S. M. Okin, "Reason and Feeling in Thinking About Justice," *Ethics* 99 (1988), 229–48, and *Justice, Gender and the Family*, New York: Basic Books, 1989. For communitarian challenges to the contractarian paradigm, see Sandel, *Liberalism and the Limits of Justice*; MacIntyre, *After Virtue*; S. Benhabib, "The Generalized and the Concrete Other," in *Feminism as Critique*, ed. S. Benhabib and D. Cornell, Minneapolis: University of Minnesota Press, 1988; C. Taylor, *Philosophy and the Human Sciences*, Cambridge, MA: Harvard University Press, 1985.

24 Rawls, *A Theory of Justice*, 54–65.

25 S. Benhabib, "The Generalized and the Concrete Other," 89.

26 Sandel, *Liberalism and the Limits of Justice*, 62.

27 Taylor, *Philosophy and the Human Sciences*, 200.

28 MacIntyre, *After Virtue*, 367–98.

29 It is not surprising, therefore, that Sandel's eminent critique of liberalism proceeds by way of prioritizing benevolence over justice.

30 This problem is evident in Rawls' recent attempt to strike a compromise between his former contractarian position and that of his communitarian critics. See "The Idea of an Overlapping Consensus," *Oxford Journal of Legal Studies* 1 (1987), 1–27.

31 See J. Derrida, "Signature-Event-Context," in *Margins of Philosophy*, University of Chicago Press, 1982, 309–30. See my article "Against Robust Relativism," *The Philosophical Forum* 17 (1986), 296–321.

32 Lyotard, *The Differend*, 70.

33 Sir Henry Maine, *Ancient Law*, London: Dent, 1972.

34 MacIntyre, *After Virtue*, 367–98. MacIntyre sees justice and all virtues as *entirely* contextually determined. Hence he marks the point at which positivism, even a highly intersubjective, communalistic, "touchy-feely" positivism, can easily pass into authoritarianism.

35 Valente, "Against Robust Relativism," 315–16.

36 Rawls, *A Theory of Justice*, 17–22; J. Habermas, *Theory of Communicative Action*, Boston, MA: Beacon, 1984.

37 E. Laclau and C. Mouffe, *Hegemony and Socialist Strategy*, London: Verso, 1985, 154.

38 J. Derrida, *Dissemination*, University of Chicago Press, 1981, 193.

39 E. Fox-Genovese, *Feminism without Illusions*, Chapel Hill: University of North Carolina Press, 1991, 225.

40 Wolgast, *Equality and the Rights of Woman*, 30–2.

41 Quoted in T. Moi, *Sexual/Textual Politics*, London: Routledge, 1985, 103.

42 Several of the major works in this field include R. West, "Jurisprudence and Gender," in *Feminist Legal Theory*, ed. K. Bartlett and R. Kennedy, Boulder: Westview, 1991, 201–34; C. A. MacKinnon, "Difference and Domination: On Sex Discrimination," in *Feminist Legal Theory*, 81–94;

C. A. MacKinnon, *Feminism Unmodified*, Cambridge, MA: Harvard University Press, 1987; C. A. MacKinnon, *Toward a Feminist Theory of the State*, Cambridge, MA: Harvard University Press, 1989; Wolgast, *Equality and the Rights of Woman*; Krieger, "Through a Glass Darkly"; S. Sherry, "Civic Virtue and the Feminine Voice in Constitutional Adjudication," *Virginia Law Review* 72 (1986), 493–617; D. Cornell, *Beyond Accommodation*, New York: Routledge, 1991.

43 A. R. Jones, "Writing the Body: Toward an Understanding of *Ecriture Féminine*," in *Feminist Criticism*, ed. E. Showalter, New York: Pantheon, 1985, 368–9.

44 R. Milkman, "Women's History and the *Sears* Case," *Feminist Studies* 12.2 (1986), 394–5.

45 Fox-Genovese, *Feminism without Illusions*, 225–6.

46 MacKinnon, *Feminism Unmodified*, 9.

47 MacKinnon, *Toward a Feminist Theory of the State*, 219–20.

48 *Ibid.*, 220–1.

49 *Ibid.*, 224–5.

50 *Ibid.*, 218.

51 MacKinnon, *Feminism Unmodified*, 22; *Toward a Feminist Theory of the State*, 249.

52 For the relation of the development of philosophical relativism to the colonial adventure, see S. P. Mohanty, "Us and Them," *Yale Journal of Criticism* 2.2 (1989), 1–31. For an articulation of philosophical relativism to the sort of dialogical model of justice I am trying to elaborate here, see B. H. Smith, *Contingencies of Value*, Cambridge, MA: Harvard University Press, 1988 in tandem with her article "The Unquiet Judge: Activism without Objectivism in Law and Politics," *Annals of Scholarship* 9 (1992), 111–33.

53 H. Bhaba, "DissemiNation," in *Nation and Narration*, New York: Routledge, 1991, 300.

54 R. Coward, *Patriarchal Precedents*, London: Routledge & Kegan Paul, 1983, 21–5.

55 *Ibid.*, 26–7.

56 Quoted in Coward, *Patriarchal Precedents*, 32.

57 O. Banks, *Faces of Feminism*, New York: St. Martin's, 1981, 85–103.

58 Coward, *Patriarchal Precedents*, 48.

59 *Ibid.*, 73.

60 E. Cullingford, *Gender and History in Yeats's Love Poetry*, Cambridge University Press, 1993, 82.

61 E. Said, *Orientalism*, New York: Vintage, 1978, esp. 113–97. For the Irish as an "essentially feminine race," see, among others, D. Cairns and S. Richards, *Writing Ireland*, Manchester University Press, 1988, 42–57.

62 A. Nandy, *The Intimate Enemy*, Oxford University Press, 1983, 9–10.

63 *Ibid.*, 3.

64 *Ibid.*, 48–63 (Gandhi) and 43–5 (Wilde).

65 G. Deleuze and F. Guattari, *Kafka: Toward a Minor Literature*, Minneapolis: University of Minnesota Press, 1986, 16–27.

66 R. F. Foster, *Modern Ireland: 1600–1972*, New York: Penguin, 1988, 175. The social historian P. W. Joyce speaks directly to this rift and to its location in time: "the whole tenor of Irish Literature … shows the great respect the Irish entertained for justice pure and simple according to law, and their horror of unjust decisions … But later on the Penal Laws changed all that, and turned the Irish natural love of justice into hatred and distrust of law." P. W. Joyce, *A Social History of Ireland*, vol. I, Dublin: M. H. Gill & Son Ltd., 1920, 170–1.

67 *Ibid.*, 175–6.

68 *Ibid.*, 223–4.

69 O. MacDonagh, *States of Mind*, London: George Allen & Unwin, 1983, 41.

70 See M. M. Bakhtin, *The Dialogic Imagination*, Austin: University of Texas Press, 1981, 270–3.

71 R. Ellmann, *James Joyce*, New York: Oxford University Press, 1982, 12.

72 MacDonagh, *States of Mind*, 44.

73 *Ibid.*, 57.

74 Foster, *Modern Ireland*, 343.

75 I. Kant, *Critique of Practical Reason*, New York: Macmillan, 1956, 17–70.

76 Lyotard, *The Differend*, 27.

77 *Ibid.*, 151.

78 For Joyce's interest in Tucker and other anarchist philosophers, see D. Manganiello, *Joyce's Politics*, London: Routledge & Kegan Paul, 1980, 74ff.

79 Not coincidentally, if one transposes *A Portrait* into the real time of Joyce's life, the conversation with Davin takes place in the same year, 1902, that *Cathleen Ni Houlihan* had its debut.

80 On Celtic sow goddesses, see P. Keane, *Terrible Beauty: Yeats, Joyce, Ireland, and the Myth of the Devouring Female*, Columbia: University of Missouri Press, 1988, 51.

81 Contemporary feminism has been attuned to the homology between sexual and colonial oppression. S. Rowbotham writes, "certain similarities exist between the colonization of the underdeveloped country and female oppression within capitalism. There is the economic dependence, the cultural take-over, the identification of dignity with resemblance to the oppressor." Marilyn French goes further, "if we transpose the descriptions of colonized and colonizer onto women and men, they fit at almost every point." Cited in L. Donaldson, *Decolonizing Feminisms*, Chapel Hill: University of North Carolina Press, 1992, 6–7.

82 H. Bhaba, "Of Mimicry and Man," *October* 28 (1984), 126–30.

83 MacDonagh, *States of Mind*, 54.

84 L. Curtis, *Nothing But the Same Old Story*, London: Information on Ireland, 1984, 56. For an expanded version of the argument made in the

next few pages, see my article "Gender in the Literature of Irish Nationalism," *ELH* 61 (1994), 189–210.

85 Curtis, *Nothing But the Same Old Story*, 53.

86 *Ibid.*, 57.

87 L. P. Curtis, *Anglo-Saxons and Celts*, Bridgeport, CT: University of Bridgeport Press, 1968, 61.

88 *Ibid.*, 61–2.

89 E. Cullingford, "Thinking of Her as Ireland," *Textual Practice* 4 (1990), 149.

90 MacDonagh, *States of Mind*, 55.

91 Manganiello, *Joyce's Politics*, 56–7; Ellmann, *James Joyce*, 237–9.

92 Ellmann, *James Joyce*, 11.

93 M. Norris, *Joyce's Web*, Austin: University of Texas Press, 1992, 203–7.

94 P. W. Joyce, *A Social History of Ireland*, 171.

2 JOYCE'S SEXUAL *DIFFEREND*: AN EXAMPLE FROM *DUBLINERS*

1 See Luce Irigaray in *Speculum of the Other Woman* and *This Sex which is not One*, Ithaca, NY: Cornell University Press, 1985.

2 S. Grace, "Rediscovering Mrs. Kearney," in B. Benstock, ed., *James Joyce: The Augmented Ninth*, Syracuse, NY: Syracuse University Press, 1988, 273–81. 3. For a ground-breaking treatment of the reproduction of authority in "The Sisters," see V. Mahaffey, *Reauthorizing Joyce*, Cambridge University Press, 1988, 26–32.

4 Without developing this opposition in any detail, Shari Benstock points out that women in Joyce's Dublin are "strictly confined to the domestic spaces reserved for them, where they wield a limited measure of power and influence." See "City Spaces and Women's Places in Joyce's Dublin," in *James Joyce: The Augmented Ninth*, 303–7.

5 Most saliently, the identification of women with the personal, the local, and the domestic has worked in modern societies to justify their political exclusion by seeming to establish their inherent inability to fulfill the liberal ideal of universal citizenship, i.e. the assumption of an abstract, disinterested perspective geared to the common good. See I. M. Young, "Polity and Group Difference: A Critique of the Ideal of Universal Citizenship," *Ethics* 99.2 (1989), 250–74.

6 D. Gifford, *Joyce Annotated*, Berkeley: University of California Press, 1976, 98.

7 A shift into the philosophical regime of discourse makes the stakes here even plainer. The male space comprises sites of occupation, of Being, and thus conforms with the Aristotelian identification of masculinity with essence, that which is proper to itself. The female space comprises sites of transition or Becoming and thus conforms with the Aristotelian identification of femininity with matter, that which has its center outside

of itself. See D. Fuss, "Essentially Speaking," in *Hypatia* 3.3 (1989), 62–81.

8 J.-F. Lyotard, *The Differend*, Minneapolis: University of Minnesota Press, 1988, 9.

9 G. Bennington, *Writing the Event*, New York: Routledge, 1988, 176.

10 Lyotard, *The Differend*, 151.

11 For the phallic significance of Burke's umbrella, see Jean-Paul Rabate, "Silence in *Dubliners*," in C. MacCabe, ed., *James Joyce: New Perspectives*, Bloomington: Indiana University Press, 1982, 54.

12 Lyotard, *The Differend*, 143.

13 J. Marlowe, *The Uncrowned Queen of Ireland*, New York: Dutton, 1975, 255.

14 F. S. L. Lyons, *Charles Stewart Parnell*, New York: Oxford University Press, 1982, 513.

15 Marlowe, *The Uncrowned Queen*, 270.

16 *Ibid.*, 259.

17 Benstock, "City Spaces and Women's Places," 304. Sherrill Grace also remarks, in a concession to Joyce's irony, that "he at least allowed us to see that in trouncing a mother the men have not improved their own state." "Rediscovering Mrs. Kearney," 279.

18 J. Derrida, "The Politics of Friendship," *Journal of Philosophy*, 88 (1988), 642.

19 J. Valente, "The Politics of Joyce's Polyphony," in B. K. Scott, ed., *New Alliances in Joyce Studies*, Newark: University of Delaware Press, 1988, 56–72.

3 DREAD DESIRE: IMPERIALIST ABJECTION IN *GIACOMO JOYCE*

1 James Joyce, *Giacomo Joyce*, ed. R. Ellmann, New York: Viking, 1968. All citations are by frame, not page number.

2 V. Mahaffey, "Giacomo Joyce," in *Companion to Joyce Studies*, ed. Z. Bowen and J. F. Carens, Westport, CT: Greenwood, 1984, 391.

3 V. Mahaffey, "The Case against Art," *Critical Inquiry* 17 (1991), 672–4.

4 R. Barthes, "From Work to Text," in *Image, Music, Text*, New York: Hill and Wang, 1977, 155–64.

5 S. Freud, *The Interpretation of Dreams*, New York: Hearst, 1953, 564.

6 Peter Costello disputes the claim that Amalia Popper was the model for *Giacomo Joyce*, noting that "the dates" connecting the notebook to Joyce's familiarity with Amalia "don't fit." But no one has said that *Giacomo* constitutes a *simultaneous translation* of Joyce's experience, the only claim to which Costello's contention is relevant. Costello's other tack is to cite Helen Barolini as effectively confuting Ellmann's identification of Amalia as the *Giacomo* girl. But in "Fascism and Silence: The Coded History of Amalia Popper," forthcoming in *James Joyce*

Quarterly, Vicki Mahaffey effectively confutes Barolini on both factual and motivational grounds, restoring Amalia as the only viable candidate. Finally, Costello ignores the envoy to *Giacomo Joyce*, which clearly ascribes the initials, A. P., to his paramour. P. Costello, *James Joyce: The Years of Growth*, New York: Pantheon, 1992, 308.

7 Mahaffey, "The Case against Art," 672.

8 Mahaffey, "Giacomo Joyce," 417. As evidence of this passage's belated inclusion, Mahaffey adduces not only the immediate historical reference to *Ulysses* but the character of the handwriting, cramped so as to be squeezed into the only available space in the notebook.

9 H. Bhaba, "Signs Taken for Wonders," *Critical Inquiry* 12 (1985), 153–4.

10 Mahaffey, "The Case against Art," 671. Mahaffey argues that Joyce's understanding of sexism and racism grew out of his inadvertent complicity in both. I would say that Joyce's understanding of racism and sexism inadvertently grew out of his complicity in both.

11 *Ibid.*, 673. Mahaffey makes a good case for the rather more direct effects of Joyce's economic weakness.

12 J. Kristeva, *Powers of Horror*, New York: Columbia University Press, 1982, 10.

13 The capitalized terms "Imaginary" and "Symbolic" have their origins in Lacanian psychoanalysis but have since achieved much wider critical application. The Imaginary refers to a series of psychic relations to the infantile, presocial fantasy-experience of gratifying plenitude and to the forms of awareness accompanying that experience. This mythic plenitude is located in the maternal body, re-membered in the mother–child dyad, re-placed, albeit conflictually, in the totalized body image of the developing child (during the "mirrorstage" of consciousness), and then re-covered in fractional and embattled forms once one submits to the differentiation of the Symbolic. At the same time, however, such Symbolic forms of "re-covery" constitute deferred actions which bring the mythic maternal plenitude into existence in the first place as lost or repressed, i.e. as their own *retrospective condition* of existence.

The Symbolic is the patriarchal law instituted at the level of verbal and conceptual as well as social organization. It infuses the emerging subject with the anxiety of difference or lack, enjoining his/her separation from the maternal body and the assumption of a gender position. But it also provides, even constitutes, a system of substitutes for lost/repressed infantile satisfactions: the hierarchically arranged and socially approved network of signifiers that makes up the representational order. Here again, the dynamic of recursion is important. If the Symbolic succeeds and dissolves the Imaginary, introducing the subject to his/her finitude of being, it also engenders the Imaginary within its domain. For its own hierarchies of meaning and value fuel the fantasy of transcending the limits that they themselves demarcate. And because gender is constructed as the site of primary difference or loss, the hierarchies erected there feed the most powerful and insistent of these fantasies of plenitude.

14 The term "phallic mother" refers to the maternal body as it exists for the infant before his/her perception of lack or desire in the mother, hence the maternal body as a boundless power and an inexhaustible resource, capable of answering or refusing the child's every need.

15 E. Gross, "The Body of Signification," in *Abjection, Melancholia and Love*, ed. J. Fletcher and A. Benjamin, London: Routledge, 1990, 86.

16 *Ibid.*, 88.

17 V. Bergen, "Geometry and Abjection," in *Abjection, Melancholia and Love*, 118.

18 Kristeva, *Powers of Horror*, 7.

19 *Ibid.*, 13.

20 *Ibid.*, 47.

21 *Ibid.*, 10.

22 For the political operation of the norm of respectability, see G. Mosse, *Nationalism and Sexuality*, New York: Howard Fertig, 1978, 1–21. For an account of political abjection which unfortunately degenerates into yet another theory of false consciousness, see I. M. Young, *Justice and the Politics of Difference*, Princeton University Press, 1990.

23 J. Butler, *Gender Trouble*, New York: Routledge, 1989, 128–49.

24 I use "normative subject" to speak to the privilege certain subjects enjoy of seeing the social norms created more or less in their image, i.e. of participating directly or indirectly in the construction of norms which they themselves happen to embody.

25 I have elected to map gender difference onto the elite–subaltern split in my pronominal usage in recognition of the genderizing of colonial/racial hierarchies and owing to the immediate subjects of analysis, Joyce and Amalia Popper.

26 A. JanMohamed, "The Economy of Manichean Allegory," *Critical Inquiry* 12 (1985), 62–5.

27 For the significance of the Medusa myth, see H. Cixous, "The Laugh of the Medusa," *Signs* 1 (1976), 875–99.

28 Throughout the chapter, *without exception*, I use the word "disavowal" in the Freudian sense, meaning to deny something with "one current of the mental processes" while remaining "fully aware" of that reality with another current. S. Freud, *Sexuality and the Psychology of Love*, New York: Macmillan, 1963, 208.

29 For Joyce's conversance with Weininger's theories, see R. Brown, *James Joyce and Sexuality*, Cambridge University Press, 1985, 101. For Joyce's teasing of Weiss, see R. Ellmann, *James Joyce*, New York: Oxford University Press, 1982, 464. For the feminization of the Irish race, see Chapter 1, nn. 83–90 above; Chapter 2, nn. 17 above; and nn. 69–71 of this chapter.

30 Joyce had been unable to get *Dubliners* published through nearly the

entire period covered in *Giacomo Joyce*. In terms of public recognition, he was as yet more of a language teacher and amateur journalist than a literary artist.

31 H. Bhaba, "Of Mimicry and Man," *October* 28 (1984), 131.

32 Ellmann, Introduction to *Giacomo Joyce*, xi.

33 JanMohamed, "The Economy of Manichean Allegory," 65–8.

34 G. Spivak, "Can the Subaltern Speak?," in *Marxism and the Interpretation of Culture*, ed. C. Nelson and L. Grossberg, Urbana: University of Illinois Press, 1988, 297.

35 Another Lacanian coinage that has passed into wider circulation, the "subject who knows" is a fantasy-subject held to be in full control of the Symbolic field: e.g. God, the master, the psychoanalyst, etc. The ordinary subject erects the "subject who knows" as a point of transference or even identification, so that some sense of stable meaning can be assured. It would seem that the figure of the artist performed this function for Joyce in *Giacomo* and elsewhere. Certainly, Stephen's assertion – "A man of genius makes no mistakes. His errors are volitional and are the portals of discovery" (*U* 9.228–9) – is a classic elaboration of the "subject who knows."

36 James McMichael makes Joyce's idea of sentimentalism the center of his study of justice. *Ulysses and Justice*, Princeton University Press, 1991.

37 Mahaffey, "Giacomo Joyce," 398–9. Mahaffey explains that the news of Joyce's mother's illness, "coming as it did on Good Friday [1903] seems to have prompted Joyce to identify his own suffering... with Christ's crucifixion... In 1914, Good Friday again fell on April 10th, as it had eleven years earlier, and Joyce seems to be glossing the memory of that excruciating Good Friday with the pain that his lovely student was currently causing him."

38 Ellmann, *James Joyce*, 129.

39 Ewa Ziarek has noted maternal abjection at work in Stephen's hallucinations. "'Circe': Joyce's *Argumentum ad Feminam*," *James Joyce Quarterly* 30 (1992), 61–2.

40 Ellmann, *James Joyce*, 129–30. The maternal visitation in "Circe" refers to a dream Joyce had, during his first Parisian separation, in which his mother actually said, "Who has pity for you when you are among strangers? Years and years I loved you when you lay in my womb." See P. McGee, *Paperspace*, Lincoln, NB: University of Nebraska Press, 1988, 139.

41 Ellmann, *James Joyce*, 132.

42 Joyce's fantasies of being the literary messiah of the Irish people were likewise tied up with the fantasy of burial in the womb, confirming the connection in Joyce's own subconscious between crucifixion and abjection. In 1909, he had written to Nora: "O take me into your soul of souls and then I will become indeed the poet of my race. I feel this,

Nora, as I write it. My body soon will penetrate yours, o that my soul could too! O that I could nestle in your womb like a child born of your flesh and blood, be fed by your blood, sleep in the warm secret gloom of your body," *LII*, 248.

43 Different acquaintances of Joyce on the continent found him inhibited in the expression of emotion. August Suter wrote that "Joyce was ashamed of showing that he was capable of love; he hid his feelings." Nino Frank commented on "his coolness, his reserve." A. Suter, "Some Reminiscences of James Joyce," N. Frank, "The Shadow that had Lost its Man," in *Portraits of the Artist in Exile*, ed. W. Potts, Seattle: University of Washington Press, 1979, 63, 86.

44 N. Chodorow, *The Reproduction of Mothering*, Berkeley: University of California Press, 1978, 92–130.

45 C. Kahn, *Man's Estate*, Berkeley: University of California Press, 1981, 9–10.

46 S. Benhabib, "The Generalized and the Concrete Other," in *Feminism as Critique*, ed. S. Benhabib and D. Cornell, Minneapolis: University of Minnesota Press, 1988, 86.

47 Stephen himself makes this connection in a number of ways. For example, he outfits Shakespeare "in the cast-off mail of a court buck" (*U* 9.164–5) even as he himself wears the cast-off boots of stately Buck Mulligan.

48 See in particular Ellmann's account of their relationship in *James Joyce*, 645–739.

49 *Ibid.*, 682.

50 *Ibid.*, 679.

51 *Ibid.*, 650.

52 *Ibid.*, 676.

53 This will be taken up further in the last chapter.

54 For the most exhaustive meditation on this topos, see P. Kuberski, "The Joycean Gaze: Lucia in the I / Eye of the Father," *Substance* 46 (1985), 49–66.

55 Ellmann, *James Joyce*, 262; Brenda Maddox, *Nora*, Boston, MA: Houghton Mifflin, 1988, 82.

56 Kuberski, "The Joycean Gaze," 50.

57 Maddox, *Nora*, 82.

58 The mother in Joyce has often been conceived along the lines of the Real in Lacan's early writings, the irrepressible, unrepresentable origin/ exterior of the Symbolic. Karen Lawrence calls the maternal a "fiction before identity or law"; Patrick McGee suggests that the name of the mother in *Ulysses* is foreclosed in the institution of the paternal *logos*; Maud Ellmann declares "[her] namelessness engraves itself upon the flesh before the father ever carved his signature." But by placing abjection in an ethico-political register, we can see that the mother in

Joyce operates more like the Real in Lacan's later writings, the impossible coimplication of interior and exterior, before and after, self and other, at once posed and denied in the Symbolic, "inscribing," in Shari Benstock's words, "an undecidable limit of textuality." See K. Lawrence, "Joyce and Feminism," in *The Cambridge Companion to James Joyce*, ed. D. Attridge, Cambridge University Press, 1990, 248; M. Ellmann, "Polytropic Man," in *James Joyce: New Perspectives*, ed. C. McCabe, Brighton: Harvester, 1987, 96; McGee, *Paperspace*, 50; S. Benstock, *Textualizing the Feminine*, Norman: University of Oklahoma Press, 1992, 186. For modernity's tendency to equate the feminine with unrepresentability, see A. Jardine, *Gynesis*, Ithaca, NY: Cornell University Press, 1985, 31–49.

59 Ellmann, *James Joyce*, 296–7.
60 J. Gallop, "Reading the Mother Tongue: Psychoanalytic Feminist Criticism," *Critical Inquiry* 13.2 (1987), 320.
61 My argument is consistent on this score with Spivak's well-known conclusion that the subaltern can in fact speak but not, strictly speaking, as a subaltern. See "Can the Subaltern Speak?," in *Marxism and the Interpretation of Culture*.
62 M. Whitford, "Rereading Irigaray," in *Feminism and Psychoanalysis*, ed. T. Brennan, New York: Routledge, 1989, 117–20.
63 I borrow the phrase from W. Connolly, *Identity/Difference*, Ithaca, NY: Cornell University Press, 1991.
64 S. Tifft, "The Playboy Riots," in *Nationalisms and Sexualities*, ed. A. Parker et al., New York: Routledge, 1992, 321.
65 Jacqueline Rose defines the Lacanian concept of The Woman as follows: "the place onto which lack is projected and through which it is simultaneously disavowed – woman is a symptom for the man." *Feminine Sexuality*, ed. J. Mitchell and J. Rose, New York: Norton, 1985, 48.
66 Mahaffey, "Giacomo Joyce," 407.
67 Cixous, "The Laugh of the Medusa," 875–99.
68 Brown, *James Joyce and Sexuality*, 101.
69 D. Cairns and S. Richards, *Writing Ireland*, Manchester University Press, 1988, 46.
70 L. Curtis, *Nothing But the Same Old Story*, London: Information on Ireland, 1984, 57.
71 M. Arnold, *Lectures and Essays in Criticism*, Ann Arbor: University of Michigan Press, 1962, 347. On this basis, Arnold held the Irish incapable of self-government, calling them "ineffectual in politics" (346).
72 L. P. Curtis, *Apes and Angels*, Washington, DC: Smithsonian, 1971.
73 Ellmann, *James Joyce*, 230.
74 D. Manganiello, *Joyce's Politics*, London: Routledge & Kegan Paul, 1980, 52.
75 For identification with the aggressor, see A. Nandy, *The Intimate Enemy*, Oxford University Press, 1983.

76 Mahaffey, "Giacomo Joyce," 397. Mahaffey notes, "After the operation...she exchanges her role as passive victim for the role of aggressor, and Giacomo, who has imagined himself the aggressor, becomes her victim."

77 *Ibid.*

78 B. Johnson, *The Critical Difference*, Baltimore: Johns Hopkins University Press, 1980, 146. "If we could be sure of the difference between the determinable and the indeterminable, the indeterminable would be subsumed within the determinable."

79 Ellmann, *James Joyce*, 641.

80 *Ibid.*, 658–9.

81 *Ibid.* Only once did Joyce propose using Lucia's *lettrines* to illustrate a work not his own, Chaucer's *ABC*, and even this incident betrays the paternal identification motivating his efforts. He wrote to Sylvia Beach, "I spent a wobbly half hour on the top of your ladder today looking for the *father of English literature* but could not find him. Can you lend me a complete Chaucer for a few days. *Mine is locked up*" (my italics).

82 For an analysis of bibliographical codes and their importance, particularly in Modernist literature, see J. McGann, *The Textual Condition*, Princeton University Press, 1991.

83 Ellmann, *James Joyce*, 659.

84 Bhabha, "Of Mimicry and Man," 125–33; and "Signs Taken for Wonders," 162.

85 L. Irigaray, *This Sex which is Not One*, Ithaca, NY: Cornell University Press, 1985, 84.

86 G. Harpham, *On the Grotesque*, Princeton University Press, 1982.

87 F. Restuccia, *James Joyce and the Law of the Father*, New Haven: Yale University Press, 1989, 131.

88 *Ibid.*, 139.

89 *Ibid.*, 153.

90 Mahaffey, "Giacomo Joyce," 398.

91 J. Gallop, *The Daughter's Seduction*, Ithaca, NY: Cornell University Press, 1985, 20. Gallop notes that "pro-portion" signifies "for the side of" etymologically and so carries the idea of disproportion already within it.

4 BETWEEN/BEYOND MEN: MALE FEMINISM AND HOMOSOCIALITY IN *EXILES*

1 B. K. Scott has noted the comparability of Amalia and Beatrice. *James Joyce*, Atlantic Highlands: Humanities, 1987, 69. So too has V. Mahaffey, "Giacomo Joyce," in *Companion to Joyce Studies*, ed. Z. Bowen and J. F. Carens, Westport, CT: Greenwood, 1984, 392.

2 Quoted in R. Brown, *James Joyce and Sexuality*, Cambridge University Press, 1985, 34.

3 T. Dumerowski, "Joyce's *Exiles*: The Problem of Love," *James Joyce*

Quarterly 15 (1978), 118–27; Brown, *James Joyce and Sexuality*, 112; R. B. Kershner, *Joyce, Bakhtin and Popular Literature*, Chapel Hill: University of North Carolina Press, 1989, 262–7, 286–96; S. Henke, *James Joyce and the Politics of Desire*, New York: Routledge, 1990, 85–105.

4 Brown, *James Joyce and Sexuality*, 112; R. A. Maher, "James Joyce's *Exiles*: The Comedy of Discontinuity," *James Joyce Quarterly* 9 (1972), 471; Henke, *James Joyce and the Politics of Desire*, 87; Kershner, *Joyce, Bakhtin and Popular Literature*, 292.

5 Henke, *James Joyce and the Politics of Desire*, 91.

6 S. Brivic, "Structure and Meaning in James Joyce's *Exiles*," *James Joyce Quarterly* 5 (1968), 51. Brivic suggests that Richard and Bertha conclude the play as exiles from one another, though for other reasons.

7 The most heralded and exhaustive systematization of this ascetic model of interpersonal ethics is E. Levinas, *Beyond Essence or Otherwise Than Being*, The Hague: Martinus Nijhoff, 1981. J. McMichael's *Ulysses and Justice*, Princeton University Press, is primarily informed by Levinasian ethics.

8 The phrase belongs to P. Gabel, "The Phenomenology of Rights-Consciousness and the Pact of Withdrawn Selves," *Texas Law Review* 62 (1984), 1563–99.

9 N. Chodorow, *The Reproduction of Mothering*, Berkeley: University of California Press, 1978, 57–130; C. Gilligan, *In Another Voice*, Cambridge, MA: Harvard University Press, 1982. R. West, "Jurisprudence and Gender," in *Feminist Legal Theory*, ed. K. Bartlett and R. Kennedy, Boulder: Westview, 1991, 201–34; S. Sherry, "Civic Virtue and the Feminine Voice in Constitutional Adjudication," *Virginia Law Review* 72 (1986), 493–617. See also E. Wolgast, *Equality and the Rights of Woman*, Ithaca, NY: Cornell University Press, 1980.

10 V. Mahaffey, "Joyce's Shorter Works," in *The Cambridge Companion to Joyce Studies*, ed. D. Attridge, Cambridge University Press, 1990, 201.

11 Quoted in G. B. Shaw, *The Quintessence of Ibsenism*, New York: Hill and Wang, 1913, 48. For Joyce's exposure to this book see Brown, *James Joyce and Sexuality*, 136.

12 *CW*, 44.

13 For Joyce's friends in the Irish women's movement, see B. K. Scott, *Joyce and Feminism*, Bloomington: Indiana University Press, 1984, 29–39. For Joyce's familiarity with the new sexual dimorphism, see Brown, *James Joyce and Sexuality*, 96–102.

14 Brown, *James Joyce and Sexuality*, 114.

15 J. Templeton, "The *Doll House* Backlash: Criticism, Feminism, and Ibsen," *PMLA* 104 (1989), 34.

16 A. Power, *Conversations with James Joyce*, New York: Barnes and Noble, 1974, 35.

17 Kershner, *Joyce, Bakhtin, and Popular Literature*, 288.

18 Brown, *James Joyce and Sexuality*, 95–6.

19 Quoted in Templeton, "The *Doll House* Backlash," 36.
20 The personalization of the ethical represents a well-defined pattern for Nora. When Torvald asks her how his prospective creditors could be paid in the event of his death, she responds, "Them, who cares about them, they're strangers" (*DH* 44).
21 Gilligan, *In Another Voice, passim.*
22 Quoted in Templeton, "The *Doll House* Backlash," 28.
23 *Ibid.*, 28–31.
24 *Ibid.*, 32, 36.
25 R. Ellmann, *James Joyce*, New York: Oxford University Press, 1982, 266.
26 Templeton, "The *Doll House* Backlash," 34.
27 Kershner makes much of this failure: *Joyce, Bakhtin and Popular Literature*, 296.
28 Henke, *James Joyce and the Politics of Desire*, 92; Kershner, *Joyce, Bakhtin and Popular Literature*, 265; B. Benstock, "Paradox Lust and Lost Paladays," *ELH* 36.4 (1969), 741. Benstock holds that Richard binds Bertha by the gift of freedom itself.
29 Henke, *James Joyce and the Politics of Desire*, 91.
30 Benstock, "Paradox Lust and Lost Paladays," notes the "my God" pun on 751.
31 J. Butler, *Gender Trouble*, New York: Routledge, 1989, 43–57.
32 To name a few, Scott, *James Joyce*, 69; C. Hart, "The Language of *Exiles*," in *Coping with Joyce*, ed. M. Beja and S. Benstock, Columbia: Ohio State University Press, 1989, 137; Henke, *James Joyce and the Politics of Desire*, 95–6; C. Froula, "History's Nightmare, Fiction's Dream: Joyce and the Psychohistory of *Ulysses*," *James Joyce Quarterly* 28 (1991), 862–3; R. Bauerle, "Bertha's Role in *Exiles*," in *Women in Joyce*, ed. S. Henke and E. Unkeless, Urbana: Illinois University Press, 1982, 116.
33 Jean-Michel Rabate treats Richard's killing of Bertha's soul as consequent upon his creation of her, but the text presents the two as distinct implications of his conduct, the one proposed by Richard and the other by Robert. *Joyce upon the Void*, New York: St. Martin's, 1991, 40.
34 B. Maddox, *Nora*, Boston, MA: Houghton Mifflin, 1988, 58.
35 *Ibid.*, 131.
36 Froula, "History's Nightmare, Fiction's Dream," 862–3. The draft fragments are published in J. MacNicholas, *James Joyce's Exiles: A Textual Companion*, New York: Garland, 1979.
37 This echo was first noted by Dumerowski, "Joyce's *Exiles*: The Problem of Love," 123.
38 For this definition of the law of the phallus, see J. Gallop, *The Daughter's Seduction*, Ithaca, NY: Cornell University Press, 1985, 70.
39 R. Porter, *English Society in the Eighteenth Century*, New York: Penguin, 1982, 38.
40 Kershner, *Joyce, Bakhtin and Popular Literature*, 288.

41 Henke, *James Joyce and the Politics of Desire*, 91.
42 V. Mahaffey, *Reauthorizing Joyce*, Cambridge University Press, 1988, 149–50.
43 Kershner mentions her possible awareness of this longing, but insists that she does *not* want to participate. *Joyce, Bakhtin and Popular Literature*, 292.
44 J. MacNicholas, "The Argument from Doubt," *James Joyce Quarterly* 11 (1973), 37.
45 Rabate, *Joyce upon the Void*, 24.
46 *Ibid.*, 32, 35.
47 *Ibid.*, 34.
48 *Ibid.*, 41.
49 See Chapter 3, n. 56 above.
50 Brivic, "Structure and Meaning in Joyce's *Exiles*," 51.
51 R. C. Owens, *Smashing Times*, Dublin: Attic, 1984, 64–6. Hannah Sheehy-Skeffington later wrote, "Hunger-strike was then a new weapon – we were the first to try it out in Ireland – had we but known, we were the first in a long line," Owens, *Smashing Times*, 63.
52 *Ibid.*, 65.
53 *Ibid.*, 45–6.
54 *Ibid.*, 66.
55 MacNicholas, *James Joyce's Exiles: A Textual Companion*, 7–8.
56 Owens, *Smashing Times*, 66.
57 D. Cairns and S. Richards, *Writing Ireland*, Manchester University Press, 1988, 89–113.
58 E. Sedgwick, *Between Men*, New York: Columbia University Press, 1985, 1–27.
59 Christine Froula picks up on this metaphorical usage to suggest that Bertha is Richard's vehicle for accessing and providing Robert access to his female self or himself as female. "History's Nightmare, Fiction's Dream," 863.
60 In the article, "Giacomo Joyce," Mahaffey points out that the phrase *vita nuova* in Dante's Italian could mean either "new life" or "young life." Joyce is likely then working a bilingual pun on this occasion. Much depends upon whether Richard is offering Bertha a new life or a version of his young life, but through the translation to another tongue, the alternatives themselves have become obscured and so nonnegotiable – *differend* with a vengeance. See "Giacomo Joyce," 408–9.
61 MacNicholas, *James Joyce's Exiles: A Textual Companion*, 175.
62 *Ibid.*
63 J.-F. Lyotard, *The Differend*, Minneapolis: University of Minnesota Press, 1988, 9.
64 Cairns and Richards, *Writing Ireland*, 125.
65 MacNicholas, *James Joyce's Exiles: A Textual Companion*, 151–92.
66 *Ibid.*, 179–81.

5 SIREN SONG: "BECOMING-WOMAN" IN *ULYSSES*

1 The idea that he liberates female desire through a male pen belongs to Colin McCabe, *James Joyce and the Revolution of the Word*, London: Macmillan, 1978, 131. The argument concerning ventriloquism belongs to Christine Froula, "History's Nightmare, Fiction's Dream: Joyce and the Psychohistory of *Ulysses*," *James Joyce Quarterly* 28 (1991), 857–72. The notion that Molly represents what Joyce can never know or possess belongs to Patrick McGee, *Paperspace*, Lincoln, NB: University of Nebraska Press, 1988, 188. The identification of woman's other-identity with the otherness of *Ulysses* belongs to Christine Van-Boheemen, *The Novel as Family Romance*, Ithaca, NY: Cornell University Press, 1987, 177. So does the sense of Joyce's "usurpation of the feminine function." See "Joyce, Derrida and the Discourse of the Other," in B. Benstock, *The Augmented Ninth*, Syracuse University Press, 1988, 99–100.

2 K. Devlin, "Pretending in 'Penelope': Masquerade, Mimicry and Molly Bloom," *Novel* 25 (1991), 71–89.

3 J. Lacan, *Ornicar?* 24 (1981), 30–3.

4 I would note that the value of Deleuze and Guattari to politically minded interpretations of Joyce, scarcely recognized and openly doubted when I began this project, has in the last year received increasingly widespread acknowledgment: the *James Joyce Quarterly* ran a Deleuze and Guattari cluster, including a portion of this chapter; in a major address at the 1993 "California Joyce," Cheryl Herr, referring specifically to essays by Vicki Mahaffey and myself, declared Deleuze and Guattari to have displaced Lacan as the leading theoretical perspective on Joyce; and Deleuze was invited to be the keynote speaker at the 1994 International James Joyce Symposium.

5 K. Lawrence, *The Odyssey of Style*, Princeton University Press, 1981.

6 For the relation of expression and repression in Deleuze and Guattari, see V. Mahaffey, "Minxing Marrage and Making Loof," *James Joyce Quarterly* 30 (1993), 219–37.

7 Restuccia likewise connects Joyce's representational style(s) with phallic authority and his nonrepresentational style(s) with feminine subversion, beginning with "Sirens." But she identifies representation with realism and nonrepresentation with all word play, implicit definitions substantially different than mine. She thus continues to see Molly as Joyce's representation of woman, actually treating her as if she "really" exists. F. Restuccia, *James Joyce and the Law of the Father*, New Haven: Yale University Press, 1989, 156.

8 For different versions of Stephen's abjection, see McGee, *Paperspace*, 211 and E. Ziarek, "'Circe': Joyce's *Argumentum ad Feminam*," *James Joyce Quarterly* 30 (1992), 61–2.

9 For the oedipal eroticism aspect, see Froula, "History's Nightmare, Fiction's Dream," 866.

10 S. Freud, *General Psychological Theory*, New York: Collier, 1963, 29–48. I thank Christy Burns for calling my attention to this text.

11 D. Gifford, *Ulysses Annotated*, Berkeley: University of California Press, 1988, 16.

12 *Ibid.*, 517–18.

13 J. Lacan, *Ecrits*, New York: Norton, 1977, 1–7.

14 Ziarek, "'Circe': Joyce's *Argumentum ad Feminam*," 61.

15 Joyce revealed the seriousness with which he regarded just this coincidence by opining that another James Stephens, the poet, might be the man to finish *Finnegans Wake* on account of his name. R. Ellmann, *James Joyce*, New York: Oxford University Press, 1982, 591–2.

16 See Chapter 3, p. 75.

17 J. Bormanis, "*Ulysses* and the Motherland," talk at "California Joyce," 1993.

18 R. Newman, "Narrative Transgression and Restoration: Hermetic Messengers in *Ulysses*," *James Joyce Quarterly* 29 (1992), 320–3.

19 Tilly Eggars notes Bloom's identification with Milly in "Darling Milly," *James Joyce Quarterly* 12 (1975), 392.

20 J. Bormanis, "in the first bloom of her new motherhood," *James Joyce Quarterly* 29 (1992), 599.

21 The phrase is modeled after Lacan's "answer of the real," *passim*.

22 Most comprehensively by J. A. Boone, "A New Approach to Bloom as Womanly Man," *James Joyce Quarterly* 20 (1982), 67–85.

23 J. Lacan, *Encore*, Paris: Seuil, 1975, 46.

24 Boone, "A New Approach to Bloom," 71.

25 See Chapter 1, pp. 15–17 above.

26 This is a substantial amendment of Lacan's gender logics as retailed in S. Melville, "Psychoanalysis and the Place of *Jouissance*," *Critical Inquiry* 13 (1987), 351–8.

27 Thus, Joyce anticipates Van-Boheemen's critique of Joyce's "usurpation" through identification (see n. 1 above).

28 Boone, "A New Approach to Bloom," 71.

29 See M. Beja, "The Joyce of Sex," in *The Seventh of Joyce*, ed. B. Benstock, Bloomington: Indiana University Press, 1982, 263; S. Henke, *James Joyce and the Politics of Desire*, New York: Routledge, 1990, 114, 160, 162; Boone, "A New Approach to Bloom," 81.

30 Bloom simultaneously appears more woman than woman, combining in his aggregate identification mutually exclusive feminine attributes. He exemplifies "the identification of the masculine subject with his own idealization of the feminine" (McGee, *Paperspace*, 123). For example, as he progresses from specific empathy with Mrs. Purefoy to a generalized identification with "woman's woe" to the famous accouchement scene in "Circe," Bloom compasses the contradictory ideals of being a "*virgo intacta*" (15.1785) and a proliferant life source.

31 Christine Froula adeptly treats of Stephen's gender dialectics, which

she naively conflates with Joyce's. See "History's Nightmare, Fiction's Dream," 862–4.

32 Jeri Johnson, "Beyond the Veil: *Ulysses*, Feminism and the Figure of Woman," *Joyce, Modernity and its Mediation*, ed. C. Van-Boheemen, Amsterdam: Rodopi, 1989, 225.

33 R. Leys quoted in *Inside/Out*, ed. D. Fuss, New York: Routledge, 1992, 26.

34 J. Lacan, *The Four Fundamental Concepts of Psychoanalysis*, New York: Norton, 1978, 177–81.

35 See Chapter 3, p. 78.

36 M. David-Menard, *Hysteria from Freud to Lacan*, Ithaca, NY: Cornell University Press, 1989, 4.

37 Ellmann, *James Joyce*, 505.

38 Jean-Michel Rabate observes, "Indeed, the Sirens rarely sing in the episode," without tying this oddity to questions of gender. Jean-Michel Rabate, "The Silence of the Sirens," in *James Joyce: The Centennial Symposium*, Urbana: University of Illinois Press, 1986, 85.

39 *Ibid.*, 86.

40 For woman as the fantasy of man, see J. Mitchell and J. Rose, eds., *Feminine Sexuality*, New York: Norton, 1985, 49–50.

41 K. Devlin, "Castration and its Discontents: A Lacanian Approach to *Ulysses*," *James Joyce Quarterly* 29 (1991), 136–7.

42 Joyce wrote, "The last word (human, all too human) is left to Penelope. This is the indispensable countersign to Bloom's eternity" (*SL* 278).

43 J. Derrida, *Writing and Difference*, University of Chicago Press, 1978, 256.

44 *Ibid.*, 261.

45 Attridge notes that the barmaids' orgasmic laughter works a "displacement, decentering and exchange" of bodily and verbal identities "going well beyond (and indeed undermining) any notion of mimesis or iconicity." D. Attridge, "Joyce's Lipspeech: Syntax and the Subject in 'Sirens'" in *James Joyce: The Centennial Symposium*, 64.

46 Lawrence, *The Odyssey of Style*, 95.

47 *Ibid.*, 91.

48 Froula, "History's Nightmare, Fiction's Dream," 864–7.

49 The correspondences may be catalogued as follows:

Miss Douce and Miss Kennedy	Molly Bloom
They "threw young heads back"	Molly "threw herself back"
They were "screaming"	Molly was "screaming"
They repeatedly say "O"	Molly repeatedly says "O"
Miss Douce says "saints above"	Molly says "saints above"
Miss Douce says "I never laughed so much"	Molly says "I never laughed so many"
Miss Douce says "I feel all wet"	Molly says "I'm drenched"

50 See V. Mahaffey, *Reauthorizing Joyce*, Cambridge University Press, 1988, 141–2.

51 For the essentialistic quality of *écriture féminine*, see A. R. Jones, "Writing the Body: Toward an Understanding of *Ecriture Féminine*," in *Feminist Criticism*, ed. E. Showalter, New York: Pantheon, 1985, 361–77.

52 D. Attridge, "Molly's Flow," *Modern Fiction Studies* 35 (1989), 543–65.

53 The same holds for those critically privileged forms of Penelopean contradiction, like the varied and conflicting gender performances which Kim Devlin has recently attributed to Molly ("Pretending in 'Penelope'"). Without the assumption of temporal unity, these changes in gender position become just that, not mimetic or parodic performances but wholesale alterations, radical innovations, in gender and subject position. Just as Becoming-Eskimo, for Deleuze, means that "the Eskimo himself becomes something else" (*D* 53), so the Becoming-woman of "Penelope's" style entails that Molly Bloom becomes something else, that she engages an assemblage beyond the representational limits of *écriture féminine*.

EPILOGUE: TRIAL AND MOCK TRIAL IN JOYCE

1 M. Bakhtin, *Rabelais and his World*, Cambridge, MA: MIT Press, 1968, 11–12.

2 P. McGee, *Paperspace*, Lincoln, NB: University of Nebraska Press, 1988, 120.

3 For the effects of medical–forensic discourse in Wilde's trial, see E. Cohen, *Talk on the Wilde Side*, New York: Routledge, 1993, 91–3.

4 D. Rose, *Understanding "Finnegans Wake"*, New York: Garland, 1982, 66.

5 S. Schwartzlander, "Multiple Meaning and Misunderstanding: The Mistrial of Festy King," *James Joyce Quarterly* 23 (1986), 473.

6 Bakhtin, *Rabelais and his World*, 39.

7 *Ibid.*, 40.

8 C. Lefort, *Democracy and Political Theory*, Minneapolis: University of Minnesota Press, 1988, 17.

9 J. Derrida, "Force of Law," *Deconstruction and the Possibility of Justice*, *Cardozo Law Review* 11.5–6 (1990), 942–3.

10 J. Derrida, "Declarations of Independence," *New Political Science* 15 (1986), 7–15.

11 N. Miller, "A Reservation Under the Name of Joyce," at "California Joyce," June 1993. For Lacan's famous phrase, "There is no sexual relation," see *Feminine Sexuality*, ed. J. Mitchell and J. Rose, New York: Norton, 1982, 46–7.

12 A. Koestler, *The Act of Creation*, New York: Macmillan, 1964, 51; M. Bakhtin, *Problems in Dostoevsky's Poetics*, Minneapolis: University of Minnesota Press, 1973, 153; S. Freud, *Jokes and their Relation to the Unconscious*, New York: Norton, 1960, 172.

13 Bakhtin, *Rabelais and his World*, 11.

14 L. Hutcheon, *A Theory of Parody*, New York: Methuen, 1985, 30–84; and "The Politics of Postmodernism: Parody and History," *Cultural Critique* 5 (1986), 179–207.

15 D. Attridge, "Unpacking the Portmanteau, or Who's Afraid of *Finnegans Wake*," in *On Puns*, ed. J. Culler, Oxford: Basil Blackwell, 1985, 141.

16 R. McHugh, *Annotations to Finnegans Wake*, London: Routledge, 1980, 575.

17 *Ibid.*, 576.

18 The pango is a parody of the "lobster quadrille" from *Alice in Wonderland*, an episode which is prelude to the most celebrated Victorian parody of the judicial process, the case of the stolen tarts. Anxious to get to the point of the trial, the Red King repeatedly instructs the jury to "consider your verdict" (94) before the testimony has been heard. For her part, the Red Queen seizes prematurely upon the absence of evidence, the knave's signature, as proof of his guilt. She then disputes the King's "twentieth" injunction that the jury "consider their verdict" with the still more precipitate exclamation, "Sentence first, verdict after" (96). Her words, like the entire trial, emphasize the rush to judgment in law, the imperative to decision-making that parody is specifically designed to inhibit. "Decision" comes from the Latin *decidere* (to cut off), and her sentence is precisely to cut off their heads. L. Carroll, *Alice in Wonderland*, New York: Norton, 1971.

19 J. Flood, "Joyce and the Maamtrasna Murders," *James Joyce Quarterly* 28 (1991), 883, 885.

20 *Ibid.*, 880–1. Cheryl Herr recently declared "Ireland at the Bar" a rare, unambiguous statement of political sentiment on Joyce's part. I want to suggest, however, that the ambiguity returns in what the article does *not* say, an ambiguity more fully unpacked in the *Wake*. C. Herr, "The Silence of the Hares," major address at "California Joyce," 1993.

21 J. Garvin, *James Joyce's Disunited Kingdom and the Irish Dimension*, Dublin: Gill & Macmillan, 1976, 159–69.

22 Flood, "Joyce and the Maamtrasna Murders," 881.

Index